ENCYCLOPEDIA OF
THE UNITED STATES
IN THE TWENTIETH CENTURY

Encyclopedia of
The United States
in the Twentieth Century

Stanley I. Kutler
Editor in Chief

Robert Dallek
David A. Hollinger
Thomas K. McCraw
Associate Editors

Judith Kirkwood
Assistant Editor

Index

CHARLES SCRIBNER'S SONS
Macmillan Library Reference USA
Simon & Schuster Macmillan
New York

SIMON & SCHUSTER AND PRENTICE HALL INTERNATIONAL
London   Mexico City   New Delhi   Singapore   Sydney   Toronto

Charles Scribner's Sons
An Imprint of Simon & Schuster Macmillan
1633 Broadway
New York, NY 10019-6785

Library of Congress Cataloging-in-Publication Data

Encyclopedia of the United States in the twentieth century
  / Stanley I. Kutler, editor in chief; Robert Dallek,
  David A. Hollinger, Thomas K. McCraw, associate
  editors; Judith Kirkwood, assistant editor.

    p.   cm.

  Includes bibliographical references and index.

    ISBN 0-13-210535-7 (set: hc: alk. paper). —
0-13-307190-1 (vol. 1: hc: alk. paper). — 0-13-307208-8
(vol. 2: hc: alk. paper). — 0-13-307216-9 (vol. 3: hc:
alk. paper). — 0-13-307224-X (vol. 4: hc: alk. paper).
— 0-684-80481-6 (vol. 5: pb: alk. paper).

    1. United States—Encyclopedias.   I. Kutler, Stanley
I. E740.7.E53 1996
973'.003–dc20
95-22696   CIP

    3 5 7 9 11 13 15 17 19   20 18 16 14 12 10 8 6 4
PRINTED IN THE UNITED STATES OF AMERICA

The paper in this publication meets the requirements of
ANSI/NISO Z39.48-1992 (Permanence of Paper)

Contents

Contents of the Encyclopedia

VOLUME I

Part 1

THE AMERICAN PEOPLE

Introduction   3
Stanley I. Kutler

Regionalism   7
John L. Thomas

The East   25
David C. Hammack

The Midwest   41
James H. Madison

The South   61
David R. Goldfield

The West   81
Patricia Nelson Limerick and Jon Coleman

Gender Issues   101
Lizabeth Cohen and Mark Tebeau

Race   129
Earl Lewis

Ethnicity and Immigration   161
Rudolph J. Vecoli

Class   195
Olivier Zunz

Family   221
Steven Mintz

Part 2

POLITICS

Introduction   247
Robert Dallek

Nationalism   251
Stuart McConnell

Political Ideas and Movements   273
James T. Kloppenberg

Parties and Interest Groups   295
Graham K. Wilson

The Presidency   321
Bert A. Rockman

Congress   355
Joel D. Aberbach

The Courts   377
Mary L. Dudziak

The Constitution   401
Michal R. Belknap

Federalism and the States   427
Harry N. Scheiber

City and Suburb   451
Jon C. Teaford

Social Welfare   471
Edward D. Berkowitz

Foundations and Public Policy   491
Barry D. Karl

Bureaucracy   513
Herman Belz

CONTENTS

VOLUME II

Part 3

GLOBAL AMERICA

Introduction 539
Robert Dallek

Pacifism and Arms Limitation 541
David S. Patterson

Foreign Policy 569
Melvin Small

The National-Security State 593
Mark M. Lowenthal

The World Wars 621
David M. Kennedy

Limited Wars 651
George C. Herring

World Regions 675
Akira Iriye

Cultural Interactions 695
Emily S. Rosenberg

America and the World Economy 719
Jeffry A. Frieden

Part 4

SCIENCE, TECHNOLOGY, AND
MEDICINE

Introduction 737
David A. Hollinger

Large-Scale Scientific Enterprise 739
Robert W. Smith

Aerospace Technology 767
Roger E. Bilstein

Computer and Communications
Technology 799
Steven W. Usselman

Industrial Research and Manufacturing
Technology 831
David A. Hounshell

Evolutionary Theory 859
Gregg A. Mitman and Ronald L. Numbers

The Human Mind and Personality 877
Jon H. Roberts

Gender Theories 899
Jill G. Morawski

Society 917
Howard Brick

Medical Science and Technology 941
Susan E. Lederer

Health and Disease 957
Richard A. Meckel

Health Care Delivery 987
Vanessa Northington Gamble

VOLUME III

Part 5

THE ECONOMY

Introduction 1011
Thomas K. McCraw

Consumption 1017
Susan Strasser

Marketing 1037
Richard S. Tedlow

Wealth and Poverty 1067
James T. Patterson

Work 1091
Shoshana Zuboff

Industrial Production 1127
Alfred D. Chandler, Jr.

Economic Performance 1155
Richard H. K. Vietor

Depressions and Recessions: The Business
Cycle 1183
Michael A. Bernstein

Capital Markets 1209
George David Smith and Richard Sylla

Foreign Trade and Foreign
Investment 1243
Mira Wilkins

CONTENTS

Economic Policies   1267
  Ellis W. Hawley

Economic Thought   1289
  Jack High

Taxation   1309
  W. Elliot Brownlee

The Infrastructure   1331
  William R. Childs

Conservation and the Environment   1357
  Arthur F. McEvoy

Natural Resources   1383
  Gavin Wright

The Professions   1407
  Kenneth J. Lipartito and Paul J. Miranti, Jr.

VOLUME IV

Part 6

CULTURE

Introduction   1433
  David A. Hollinger

Literary Culture   1435
  David A. Hollinger

The Mass Media and Popular
Culture   1461
  Ronald G. Walters

Protestantism   1491
  Richard Wightman Fox

Catholicism   1511
  Patrick W. Carey

Nontraditional Religions   1539
  Catherine L. Albanese

Judaism and Jewish Culture   1565
  Deborah Dash Moore

African American Cultural
Movements   1593
  Kenneth W. Warren

Music   1609
  Richard Crawford

Philosophy   1635
  David J. Depew

Architecture   1665
  Robert Twombly

The Visual Arts   1693
  George H. Roeder, Jr.

Patronage of the Arts   1725
  Kathleen D. McCarthy

Leisure and Recreation   1743
  Randy Roberts

Sports   1761
  Peter Levine

Clothing and Appearance   1785
  Nancy E. Rexford

Elementary and Secondary Education   1803
  Carl F. Kaestle

The University   1819
  Hugh Hawkins

Contributors   1841

Index   1853

Alphabetical Table of Contents

Aerospace Technology   II   767

African American Cultural
  Movements   IV   1593

America and the World Economy   II   719

Architecture   IV   1665

Bureaucracy   I   513

Capital Markets   III   1209

Catholicism   IV   1511

City and Suburb   I   451

Class   I   195

Clothing and Appearance   IV   1785

Computer and Communications
  Technology   II   799

Congress   I   355

Conservation and the Environment   III   1357

The Constitution   I   401

Consumption   III   1017

The Courts   I   377

Cultural Interactions   II   695

Depressions and Recessions: The Business
  Cycle   III   1183

The East   I   25

Economic Performance   III   1155

Economic Policies   III   1267

Economic Thought   III   1289

Elementary and Secondary Education   IV   1803

Ethnicity and Immigration   I   161

Evolutionary Theory   II   859

The Family   I   221

Federalism and the States   I   427

Foreign Policy   II   569

Foreign Trade and Foreign Investment   III   1243

Foundations and Public Policy   I   491

Gender Issues   I   101

Gender Theories   II   899

Health and Disease   II   957

Health Care Delivery   II   987

The Human Mind and Personality   II   877

Industrial Production   III   1127

Industrial Research and Manufacturing
  Technology   III   831

The Infrastructure   III   1331

Judaism and Jewish Culture   IV   1565

Large-Scale Scientific Enterprise   II   739

Leisure and Recreation   IV   1743

Limited Wars   II   651

Literary Culture   IV   1435

Marketing   III   1037

Mass Media and Popular Culture   IV   1461

Medical Science and Technology   II   941

The Midwest   I   41

Music   IV   1609

The National-Security State   II   593

Nationalism   I   251

Natural Resources   III   1383

Nontraditional Religions   IV   1539

Pacifism and Arms Limitation   II   541

Parties and Interest Groups   I   295

Patronage of the Arts   IV   1725

Philosophy   IV   1635

Political Ideas and Movements   I   273

The Presidency   I   321

The Professions   III   1407

Protestantism   IV   1491

Race   I   129

Regionalism   I   7

List of Maps

1   The East   26
2   The Midwest   42
3   The South   62
4   The West   83
5   Europe before World War I   622
6   World War I: The Western Front   629
7   World War II: Pacific Theaters of War   640
8   World War II: Internal Migration   644
9   World War II: European Theaters of War   645
10   Limited Wars   653
11   The Korean War   655
12   The Vietnam War   665
13   The Caribbean   677
14   Europe after World War I   680
15   The Middle East after World War II   681
16   Cold War Alliances   689

Common Abbreviations Used in This Work

Ala.	Alabama		Me.	Maine
Ariz.	Arizona		Mich.	Michigan
Ark.	Arkansas		Minn.	Minnesota
Art.	Article		Miss.	Mississippi
b.	born		Mo.	Missouri
c.	*circa*, about, approximately		Mont.	Montana
Calif.	California		n.	note
cf.	*confer*, compare		N.C.	North Carolina
chap.	chapter (plural, chaps.)		n.d.	no date
Colo.	Colorado		N.D.	North Dakota
Cong.	Congress		Neb.	Nebraska
Conn.	Connecticut		Nev.	Nevada
d.	died		N.H.	New Hampshire
D	Democrat, Democratic		N.J.	New Jersey
D.C.	District of Columbia		N.Mex.	New Mexico
Del.	Delaware		no.	number (plural, nos.)
diss.	dissertation		n.p.	no place
ed.	editor (plural, eds); edition		n.s.	new series
e.g.	*exempli gratia*, for example		N.Y.	New York
enl.	enlarged		Okla.	Oklahoma
esp.	especially		Oreg.	Oregon
et al.	*et alii*, and others		p.	page (plural, pp.)
etc.	*et cetera*, and so forth		Pa.	Pennsylvania
exp.	expanded		P.L.	Public Law
f.	and following (plural, ff.)		pt.	part (plural, pts.)
Fla.	Florida		R	Republican
Ga.	Georgia		Rep.	Representative
ibid.	*ibidem*, in the same place (as the one immediately preceding)		rev.	revised
			R.I.	Rhode Island
Ida.	Idaho		S.C.	South Carolina
i.e.	*id est*, that is		S.D.	South Dakota
Ill.	Illinois		sec.	section (plural, secs.)
Ind.	Indiana		Sen.	Senator
Kan.	Kansas		ser.	series
Ky.	Kentucky		ses.	session
La.	Louisiana		supp.	supplement
M.A.	Master of Arts		Tenn.	Tennessee
Mass.	Massachusetts		Tex.	Texas
Md.	Maryland		UN	United Nations

COMMON ABBREVIATIONS USED IN THIS WORK

U.S.	United States	Wash.	Washington
U.S.S.R.	Union of Soviet Socialist Republics	Wis.	Wisconsin
v.	versus	W. Va.	West Virginia
Va.	Virginia	Wyo.	Wyoming
vol.	volume (plural, vols.)		
Vt.	Vermont		

CHRONOLOGY

CHRONOLOGY

Year	The American People	Politics	Global America
1898			Spanish-American War; Spain cedes Puerto Rico and Guam, and surrenders the Philippines, to the United States
1899	W. E. B. Du Bois, *The Philadelphia Negro*		Beginning of Philippine insurrection; first Hague Peace Conference on arms limitations
1900	Census counts 75,994,575 Americans	William McKinley reelected president	
1901		Assassination of McKinley; Theodore Roosevelt becomes president	
1902			End of Philippine insurrection
1903	Bureau of the Census established	Joseph Cannon becomes Speaker of the House of Representatives	United States recognizes independence of Panama; Canal Zone established; first Dick (Militia) Act
1904	Chinese Exclusion Act	Theodore Roosevelt elected president; Lincoln Steffens, *The Shame of the Cities*	Construction of Panama Canal begins
1905			Treaty of Portsmouth (N.H.) ends Russo-Japanese War
1906	Naturalization Act; San Francisco earthquake		The Navy's "White Fleet" sails around the world; Theodore Roosevelt receives Nobel Prize for peace
1907	Oklahoma admitted to the Union		Second Hague Peace Conference on arms limitations
1908		William Howard Taft elected president; Bureau of Investigation created	Second Dick (Militia) Act

CHRONOLOGY

Science, Technology, and Medicine	The Economy	Culture	Year
	U.S. Industrial Commission established	Charlotte Perkins Gilman, *Women and Economics*	1898
Guglielmo Marconi makes first wireless broadcast	Thorstein Veblen, *The Theory of the Leisure Class*	Kate Chopin, *The Awakening* (novel); John Dewey *School and Society*; Scott Joplin, "Maple Leaf Rag"	1899
	Negro Business League founded; Gold Standard Act	Ellis Island reception center (Boring & Tilton) completed; Charles W. Chesnutt, *The House behind the Cedars;* Theodore Dreiser, *Sister Carrie* (novel)	1900
	First Oldsmobile; U.S. Steel founded	American Philosophical Association founded; Jewish Theological Seminary (New York City) founded; Frank Norris, *The Octopus* (novel); American League (baseball) established	1901
	Reclamation Act; anthracite coal strike	John Dewey, *The Child and the Curriculum*; Carson Pirie Scott department store (Chicago; Louis Sullivan) and New York Public Library (Carrère and Hastings) completed; first Rose Bowl football game	1902
Wright brothers' first flight	Department of Commerce and Labor established	Enrico Caruso debuts at the Metropolitan Opera; W. E. B. Du Bois, *The Souls of Black Folk;* Henry James, *The Ambassadors* (novel); Edwin S. Porter, *The Great Train Robbery* (movie); first World Series	1903
Mount Wilson Solar Observatory established; first New York City subway opens	*Northern Securities* v. *U.S.*; Robert Hunter, *Poverty*	George M. Cohan, *Little Johnny Jones* (musical); Lincoln Steffens, *The Shame of the Cities;* Wisconsin state capitol (George B. Post) completed	1904
	Industrial Workers of the World founded; U.S. Forest Service established; *Swift* v. *U.S.*	Thomas Dixon, *The Clansman* (novel); Edith Wharton, *The House of Mirth* (novel)	1905
	Meat Inspection Act; Pure Food and Drugs Act	Beginnings of Pentecostalism; American Jewish Committee founded; Charles Ives, *The Unanswered Question* (orchestral piece); Upton Sinclair, *The Jungle* (novel)	1906
	Panic of 1907	Russell Sage Foundation established; William James, *Pragmatism*; Walter Rauschenbusch, *Christianity and the Social Crisis*	1907
	General Motors founded; Ford introduces the Model T		1908

CHRONOLOGY

Year	The American People	Politics	Global America
1909	National Association for the Advancement of Colored People (NAACP) founded	Herbert Croly, *The Promise of American Life*	Payne-Aldrich Tariff
1910	Census counts 91,972,266 Americans; *The Crisis* (NAACP magazine) founded	Edwin D. White becomes chief justice; House of Representatives revolts against Speaker Cannon	
1911			
1912	Arizona and New Mexico admitted to the Union	Woodrow Wilson elected president	
1913		Seventeenth Amendment (direct election of senators); Walter Lippmann, *A Preface to Politics*	Underwood Tariff reduces rates
1914	Marcus Garvey founds Universal Negro Improvement Association		World War I begins; Panama Canal opens; Mexican border conflict
1915			
1916		Woodrow Wilson reelected president	National Defense Act; second Mexican border conflict; Reserve Officers Training Corps (ROTC) established

CHRONOLOGY

Science, Technology, and Medicine	The Economy	Culture	Year
Sigmund Freud's trip to the United States		Beginning of "The Fundamentals" tracts; Scofield Reference Bible; Israel Zangwill, *The Melting Pot* (play; premiere, 1908)	1909
	Mann-Elkins Act	Jane Addams, *Twenty Years at Hull House;* Victor Herbert, *Naughty Marietta* (operetta); Horatio Parker, *Mona* (opera); Edward E. Slosson, *Great American Universities*; Jack Johnson wins heavyweight boxing championship; Grand Central Terminal (New York; Warren and Wetmore) and Pennsylvania Station (New York; McKim, Mead and White) completed	1910
American Psychoanalytic Association founded	Triangle Shirtwaist Company fire; *Standard Oil Company of New Jersey v. United States;* Supreme Court announces "rule of reason" for antitrust suits	Irving Berlin, "Alexander's Ragtime Band"; Scott Joplin, *Treemonisha* (opera); Carnegie Corporation founded	1911
	Pujo Committee investigates securities industry	Hadassah (Jewish women's service organization) founded; *Titanic* sinks; James Weldon Johnson, *Autobiography of an Ex-Colored Man*; L. L. Bean begins its mail-order clothing business	1912
	Recession (to 1914); Sixteenth Amendment (income tax); Federal Reserve System established; Department of Commerce and Labor split into Department of Commerce and Department of Labor; Ford establishes moving assembly line	Anti-Defamation League of B'nai B'rith founded; Rockefeller Foundation established; Woolworth Building (New York; Cass Gilbert) completed; Charles Beard, *An Economic Interpretation of the Constitution;* Eleanor Hodgman Porter, *Pollyanna* (novel); Edward L. Thorndike, *Educational Psychology*	1913
First long-distance telephone connection	Agricultural Extension (Smith-Lever) Act; Clayton Antitrust Act; Federal Trade Commission Act; Hetch Hetchy water project	First issue of the *New Republic;* W. C. Handy, "St. Louis Blues"; Charles Ives, *Three Places in New England* (orchestral piece); Walter Lippmann, *Drift and Mastery;* Walter Rauschenbusch, *Christianizing the Social Order*	1914
		Palace of the Fine Arts (San Francisco; Bernard Maybeck) completed; John Dewey and Evelyn Dewey, *Schools for Tomorrow;* D. W. Griffith, *Birth of a Nation* (movie)	1915
	American Institute of Accountants founded; National Park Service established; Federal Aid Road Act	Roy Wood Sellars, *Critical Realism*	1916

CHRONOLOGY

Year	The American People	Politics	Global America
1917			United States enters World War I (April); Selective Service Act; Espionage Act; Soviet Union established
1918			Sedition Act (May); armistice ends World War I (11 November)
1919	Eighteenth Amendment (prohibition); Chicago race riot	Red Scare; Boston police strike	Paris Peace Conference; Senate rejects Versailles Treaty
1920	Census counts 105,710,620 Americans; 51 percent live in urban areas; Nineteenth Amendment (women's suffrage)	Warren G. Harding elected president	Senate again rejects Versailles Treaty; National Defense Act creates modern U.S. Army and National Guard; *Missouri* v. *Holland*
1921		Budget and Accounting Act; William Howard Taft becomes chief justice	Beginning of Washington Naval Conference
1922			Fordney-McCumber Tariff; Treaty of Washington
1923		Harding dies; Calvin Coolidge becomes president; Teapot Dome scandal	
1924	National Origins Act	Calvin Coolidge elected president	Dawes Plan for reparations and war debt payments
1925		First national convention of Ku Klux Klan	Geneva Protocol bans chemical weapons
1926			
1927	Sacco and Vanzetti executed		Beginning of Sandinista war in Nicaragua
1928		Herbert Hoover elected president	Kellogg-Briand Pact

CHRONOLOGY

Science, Technology, and Medicine	The Economy	Culture	Year
		National Catholic War Council founded	1917
Influenza pandemic (to 1919); William I. Thomas and Florian Znaniecki, *The Polish Peasant in Europe and America*		Willa Cather, *My Ántonia* (novel)	1918
	Steelworkers' strike; first commercial radio station, KDKA (Pittsburgh) established; Radio Corporation of America (RCA) formed	National Catholic Welfare Conference established; first major mosque opens at Highland Park, Mich.; United Artists formed; Sherwood Anderson, *Winesburg, Ohio* (novel)	1919
	First commercial radio broadcast (KDKA, Pittsburgh)	John Dewey, *Reconstruction in Philosophy;* Sinclair Lewis, *Main Street* (novel); Edith Wharton, *The Age of Innocence* (novel); Babe Ruth joins New York Yankees; American Professional Football Association (later National Football League) formed	1920
	Recession (to 1922)	Sheppard-Towner Maternity and Infancy Protection Act	1921
Insulin introduced		First issue of *Reader's Digest;* Sinclair Lewis, *Babbitt*	1922
		Henry Luce founds *Time*	1923
John B. Watson, *Behaviorism*		George Gershwin, *Rhapsody in Blue;* first issue of *Commonweal* magazine	1924
Bell Laboratories established	Kelly (Air Mail) Act	Scopes trial; Theodore Dreiser, *An American Tragedy;* F. Scott Fitzgerald, *The Great Gatsby* (novel); Sinclair Lewis *Arrowsmith* (novel); first issue of *The New Yorker;* Chicago Tribune Tower (John Mead Howells and Raymond Hood) completed	1925
Robert Goddard launches first liquid-propellant rocket	National Broadcasting Company (NBC) formed	Book-of-the-Month Club founded; Dale Carnegie, *How to Win Friends and Influence People;* Ernest Hemingway, *The Sun Also Rises* (novel); Lewis Mumford, *The Golden Day*	1926
Charles Lindbergh makes first solo flight across the Atlantic	Columbia Broadcasting System (CBS) formed	Willa Cather, *Death Comes for the Archbishop* (novel); Sinclair Lewis, *Elmer Gantry* (novel); *The Jazz Singer* (first sound movie)	1927
			1928

CHRONOLOGY

Year	The American People	Politics	Global America
1929	League of United Latin American Citizens founded		Young Plan for war debt payment
1930	Census counts 122,775,046 Americans; "Star-spangled Banner" becomes national anthem	Charles Evans Hughes becomes chief justice	Smoot-Hawley Tariff
1931		Scottsboro case	Japan seizes Manchuria from China
1932		Bonus Army march on Washington; Franklin D. Roosevelt elected president	End of Sandinista war in Nicaragua
1933	Twenty-first Amendment (repeal of prohibition)	Twentieth Amendment (presidential and congressional terms; presidential election and vacancy); New Deal begins; Tennessee Valley Authority established	Adolf Hitler becomes chancellor of Germany; U.S. recognizes USSR
1934	Wheeler-Howard Indian Reorganization Act	Dr. Francis Townsend proposes Old Age Revolving Pensions plan; Huey Long establishes Share Our Wealth Society; Rev. Charles Coughlin establishes National Union for Social Justice	

CHRONOLOGY

Science, Technology, and Medicine	The Economy	Culture	Year
E. O. Lawrence develops first cyclotron	Stock market crash	William Faulkner, *The Sound and the Fury* (novel); Ernest Hemingway, *A Farewell to Arms* (novel); Walter Lippmann, *A Preface to Morals;* Robert Lynd and Helen Merrell Lynd, *Middletown;* Museum of Modern Art (New York) opens	1929
	First King Kullen supermarket opens	John Dewey, *Individualism Old and New;* William Faulkner, *As I Lay Dying* (novel); Twelve Southerners, *I'll Take My Stand;* Sinclair Lewis, first American to win Nobel Prize for literature; McGraw-Hill Building (New York; Raymond Hood) completed; movie-industry Production Code established	1930
		Nevada legalizes gambling; Duke Ellington, *Creole Rhapsody;* Edmund Wilson, *Axel's Castle;* Empire State Building (New York; Shreve, Lamb and Harmon) completed	1931
Beginning of Tuskegee syphilis study	Reconstruction Finance Corporation and Home Loan Bank System established	James T. Farrell, *Young Lonigan* (novel); William Faulkner, *Light in August* (novel); Reinhold Niebuhr, *Moral Man and Immoral Society;* Philadelphia Savings Fund Society building (William Lescaze and George Howe) completed	1932
	National Industrial Recovery Act; Agricultural Adjustment Act; Farm Credit Act; Glass-Steagall Act; Public Works Administration and Civil Works Administration established	Civilian Conservation Corps created	1933
Invention of nylon	National Labor Relations Board, Securities and Exchange Commission, Federal Communications Commission established	Malcolm Cowley, *Exile's Return;* T. S. Eliot, *After Strange Gods;* Zora Neale Hurston, *Mules and Men;* Henry Roth, *Call It Sleep* (novel); first issue of *Partisan Review;* first comic book, *Famous Funnies;* Legion of Decency established; motion-picture Production Code Administration established	1934

CHRONOLOGY

Year	The American People	Politics	Global America
1935		Bureau of Investigation renamed Federal Bureau of Investigation; assassination of Huey Long	Italy invades Ethiopia; Neutrality Act
1936	John Dollard, *Class and Caste in a Southern Town*	Franklin D. Roosevelt reelected president; *U.S.* v. *Curtiss Wright*	German troops occupy the Rhineland
1937		Court-packing controversy; Brownlow Committee report on government organization	Beginning of war between Japan and China; Roosevelt's "Quarantine Speech"
1938		House Un-American Activities Committee formed	Germany annexes Austria and Czech Sudentenland; Munich Conference
1939	E. Franklin Frazier, *The Negro Family*		Pact between Germany and Soviet Union; alliance of Italy and Germany; World War II begins
1940	Census counts 131,669,275 Americans; Alien Registration Act	Franklin D. Roosevelt reelected president (third term)	Selective Service and Training Act; destroyers-for-bases agreement with Britain
1941	A. Philip Randolph leads March on Washington Movement; Fair Employment Practice Committee established; Allison Davis et al., *Deep South*	Harlan F. Stone becomes chief justice	Lend-Lease Act; Pearl Harbor (7 December); United States enters World War II
1942	Internment of Japanese Americans		Formation of Joint Chiefs of Staff

Science, Technology, and Medicine	The Economy	Culture	Year
	Committee for Industrial Organization (CIO) splits from American Federation of Labor (AFL); Wagner National Labor Relations Act; Connally Hot Oil Act; *Schechter* v. *U.S.*; Resettlement Administration, Rural Electrification Administration, Works Progress Administration, National Youth Administration established	Social Security Act; National Housing Act; Kirsten Flagstad debuts at Metropolitan Opera	1935
Radiation Laboratory (Berkeley, Calif.) established; Ralph Linton, *The Study of Man*	First sit-down strike	Ford Foundation established; William Faulkner, *Absalom, Absalom!* (novel); Jesse Owens wins four gold medals at Berlin Olympics; Fallingwater and Johnson Wax Administrative Building (Frank Lloyd Wright) completed	1936
Talcott Parsons, *The Structure of Social Action;* first television broadcasts	Farm Security Administration established; Supreme Court reverses itself on minimum-wage and labor legislation cases	Zora Neale Hurston, *Their Eyes Were Watching God;* Robert Lynd and Helen Merrell Lynd, *Middletown Revisited*	1937
	CIO renamed Congress of Industrial Organizations; Fair Labor Standards Act; second Farm Security Act; Civil Aeronautics Authority established	Louis Mumford, *The Culture of Cities;* Benny Goodman plays jazz in Carnegie Hall	1938
Albert Einstein's letter to President Roosevelt		Marian Anderson's Washington, D.C., recital; John Steinbeck, *The Grapes of Wrath* (novel); first scheduled television broadcast; *Gone with the Wind* (movie); Museum of Modern Art building (New York; Philip L. Goodwin and Edward Durell Stone) completed	1939
National Defense Research Committee established		Richard Wright, *Native Son* (novel)	1940
	3.8 million passenger cars produced	James Agee and Walker Evans, *Let Us Now Praise Famous Men;* F. O. Matthiessen, *American Renaissance*	1941
Beginning of Manhattan Project; Enrico Fermi produces first controlled chain reaction; Kaiser Permanente health-care plan established	War Production Board, War Manpower Commission established	National Association of Evangelicals founded; Alfred Kazin, *On Native Grounds*	1942

CHRONOLOGY

Year	The American People	Politics	Global America
1943			Teheran Conference (Roosevelt, Churchill, Stalin)
1944	Gunnar Myrdal, *An American Dilemma*	Franklin D. Roosevelt reelected president (fourth term)	D-Day invasion of Normandy (6 June); Bretton Woods accords
1945	Horace Cayton and St. Clair Drake, *Black Metropolis*	Roosevelt dies; Harry S. Truman becomes president	End of World War II; Yalta Conference; Potsdam Conference; United Nations, World Bank, International Monetary Fund founded
1946	Benjamin Spock, *Baby and Child Care*	Administrative Procedure Act; Fred F. Vinson becomes chief justice	NSC-68 (national security policy statement); Philippine independence; first portrayals of kisses in Japanese movies (*A Certain Night Kiss* and *Twenty-year-old Youth*)
1947		Americans for Democratic Action formed	Truman Doctrine pledges aid to countries threatened by communism; George Kennan's "X" article; Central Intelligence Agency, National Security Council, and National Military Establishment (by merger of War and Navy departments) created
1948	Displaced Persons Act	Harry S. Truman elected president	Rio Pact; Marshall Plan established; Berlin airlift begins
1949		First Hoover Commission report on government organization	North Atlantic Treaty Organization (NATO) established; National Military Establishment renamed Department of Defense; Berlin airlift ends; first Soviet atomic test; communist victory in China
1950	Census counts 150,697,361 Americans	Joseph McCarthy charges communist influence in State Department	Korean War begins; General Agreement on Tariffs and Trade (GATT) founded; Alger Hiss convicted of perjury
1951		Twenty-second Amendment (president limited to two terms); Kefauver Committee investigates organized crime	Truman dismisses MacArthur

CHRONOLOGY

Science, Technology, and Medicine	The Economy	Culture	Year
	Smith-Connally Labor Relations Act	T. S. Eliot, *Four Quartets* (poetry); Duke Ellington, *Black, Brown, and Beige* (jazz suite); Rogers and Hammerstein, *Oklahoma!* (musical); All-American Girls Professional Baseball League formed; zoot-suit riots in California	1943
	610 passenger cars produced	Serviceman's Readjustment Act (GI Bill of Rights); Aaron Copland, "Appalachian Spring" (dance suite); Reinhold Niebuhr, *The Children of Light and the Children of Darkness*	1944
First atomic bomb detonated at Alamagordo, N.M.		First issue of *Commentary* magazine	1945
Brookhaven National Laboratory established; atomic bombs tested at Bikini Atoll	Employment Act	Robert Penn Warren, *All the King's Men* (novel)	1946
Atomic Energy Commission established	Taft-Hartley Labor-Management Relations Act	Levittown, Long Island, established; House Un-American Activities Committee investigation in Hollywood; Christian Dior's "New Look" in women's clothing; Jackie Robinson joins Brooklyn Dodgers	1947
	4 million passenger cars produced	James Gould Cozzens, *Guard of Honor* (novel); Norman Mailer, *The Naked and the Dead* (novel); Thomas Merton, *The Seven Storey Mountain* (autobiography); B. F. Skinner, *Walden Two*; Paramount decision	1948
	First Diners Club credit cards	Housing Act; Ezra Pound, *Pisan Cantos* (poetry); Aldo Leopold, *Sand County Almanac*	1949
National Science Foundation established		First broadcast of Billy Graham's *Hour of Decision*; David Riesman, *The Lonely Crowd*	1950
Talcott Parsons, *The Social System;* UNIVAC computer	Du Pont begins manufacturing Dacron polyester	Hannah Arendt, *The Origins of Totalitarianism;* W. V. O. Quine, "Two Dogmas of Empiricism"; J. D. Salinger, *The Catcher in the Rye* (novel)	1951

CHRONOLOGY

Year	The American People	Politics	Global America
1952	Puerto Rico becomes a U.S. commonwealth; McCarran-Walter Immigration and Nationality Act	Dwight D. Eisenhower elected president; *Youngstown* v. *Sawyer*	Construction of first atom-powered submarine, *Nautilus*
1953	Termination policy for Native Americans	Department of Health, Education, and Welfare established; Earl Warren becomes chief justice	Korean War ends; establishment of U.S. Information Agency; Julius and Ethel Rosenberg executed
1954	*Brown* v. *Board of Education*	Army-McCarthy hearings; Senate censures McCarthy	Southeast Asia Treaty Organization (SEATO) established; Vietnamese defeat French at Dien Bien Phu
1955	Rosa Parks begins Montgomery, Ala., bus boycott	Second Hoover Commission report on government organization	
1956	Little Rock desegregation crisis	Dwight D. Eisenhower reelected president	Suez Crisis; USSR invades Hungary
1957	Southern Christian Leadership Conference established		European Economic Community (Common Market) founded
1958			
1959	Alaska and Hawaii admitted to the Union		Nixon-Khrushchev kitchen debate; Castro comes to power in Cuba; Central Treaty Organization (CENTO) established
1960	Census counts 178,464,236 Americans	John F. Kennedy elected president	
1961		Twenty-third Amendment (District of Columbia residents vote in presidential elections)	Bay of Pigs invasion of Cuba fails; Soviets build Berlin Wall; Peace Corps established

CHRONOLOGY

Science, Technology, and Medicine	The Economy	Culture	Year
Livermore Laboratory established; United States explodes first hydrogen bomb	Truman seizes steel mills; J. K. Galbraith, *American Capitalism*	Federation of Islamic Associations founded; first issue of *Mad* magazine; John Cage, *4'33"*; Ralph Ellison, *Invisible Man* (novel); Ernest Hemingway, *The Old Man and the Sea* (novel); Reinhold Niebuhr, *The Irony of American History;* Norman Vincent Peale, *The Power of Positive Thinking*; 860–880 North Lake Shore Drive (Chicago; Ludwig Mies van der Rohe) completed	1952
B. F. Skinner, *Science and Human Behavior*	Submerged Lands Act	James Baldwin, *Go Tell It on the Mountain* (novel); Saul Bellow, *The Adventures of Augie March* (novel); United Nations headquarters (New York) completed	1953
Bell Telephone Co. develops solar battery	Agricultural Trade Development and Assistance Act	Wallace Stevens, *Collected Poems; On the Waterfront* (movie)	1954
Distribution of Salk polio vaccine; first atomic-generated electric power in United States; Herbert Marcuse, *Eros and Civilization*	Ray Kroc franchises McDonald's; AFL and CIO reunite	Daniel Bell, "The End of Ideology" (article); Will Herberg, *Protestant, Catholic, Jew*; first issue of *National Review*; Disneyland opens	1955
	Interstate Highway Act; William H. Whyte, *The Organization Man*	C. Wright Mills, *The Power Elite*; Elvis Presley records "Heartbreak Hotel"; *Invasion of the Body Snatchers* (movie)	1956
Beginning of International Geophysical Year; Soviet Union launches *Sputnik*	McClellan Committee investigates labor unions	Leonard Bernstein, *West Side Story* (musical); Vladimir Nabokov, *Pnin* (novel); Vance Packard, *The Hidden Persuaders*; Brooklyn Dodgers move to Los Angeles, New York Giants move to San Francisco	1957
First U.S. satellite launched; National Aeronautics and Space Administration (NASA) established	J. K. Galbraith, *The Affluent Society*	National Defense Education Act; John Barth, *The End of the Road* (novel); Seagram Building (New York, Ludwig Mies van der Rohe and Philip Johnson) completed	1958
C. Wright Mills, *The Sociological Imagination*	Landrum-Griffin Labor-Management Reporting and Disclosure Act	William Burroughs, *Naked Lunch* (novel); Lorraine Hansberry, *A Raisin in the Sun* (play); José Antonio Villarreal, *Pocho* (novel)	1959
FDA approves birth control pill			1960
Erving Goffman, *Asylums*		Joseph Heller, *Catch-22* (novel); Jane Jacobs, *The Death and Life of Great American Cities*	1961

CHRONOLOGY

Year	The American People	Politics	Global America
1962		Students for a Democratic Society issue Port Huron Statement	Cuban missile crisis
1963	Civil rights march on Washington; Betty Friedan, *The Feminine Mystique*	Assassination of Kennedy; Lyndon Johnson becomes president; *Gideon* v. *Wainwright*	Nuclear test ban treaty
1964		Lyndon B. Johnson elected president; Warren Commission report; Twenty-fourth Amendment (prohibition of poll tax); Civil Rights Act; *New York Times* v. *Sullivan*	Gulf of Tonkin Resolution
1965	Immigration Act; *Griswold* v. *Connecticut*; Daniel P. Moynihan, *The Negro Family*	Voting Rights Act; assassination of Malcolm X; Watts riot in Los Angeles	American combat troops first sent to Vietnam; United States invades Dominican Republic
1966	National Organization for Women founded	*Miranda* v. *Arizona*	
1967	*Loving* v. *Virginia*	Twenty-fifth Amendment (presidential disability); Thurgood Marshall appointed to Supreme Court (first African American)	Six-day War in Middle East
1968	Bilingual Education Act; widespread urban riots; Kerner Commission report on violence	Assassinations of Robert F. Kennedy and Martin Luther King, Jr.; Richard M. Nixon elected president	Tet Offensive in Vietnam; USSR invades Czechoslovakia; Outer Space Treaty; *Pueblo* incident
1969	Stonewall riot	Warren E. Burger becomes chief justice	
1970	Census counts 203,302,031 Americans; suburbanites outnumber city dwellers	Ash Council report on government organization	United States invades Cambodia; Kent State and Jackson State shootings
1971		Twenty-sixth Amendment (voting age lowered to eighteen); U.S. Postal Service established	Nixon ends convertibility of dollars to gold; Pentagon Papers published
1972	Equal Rights Amendment approved by Congress and sent to the states	Richard M. Nixon reelected president; Watergate break-in; Revenue Sharing Act	Antiballistic Missile (ABM) Treaty (SALT I treaty) with Soviet Union; Nixon visits People's Republic of China

CHRONOLOGY

Science, Technology, and Medicine	The Economy	Culture	Year
Rachel Carson, *Silent Spring*; Du Pont begins manufacturing Lycra spandex fiber	Kennedy forces rollback of steel prices; Michael Harrington, *The Other America*	Daniel Bell, *The End of Ideology* (book); Clark Kerr, *The Uses of the University*; Thomas Kuhn, *The Structure of Scientific Revolutions*	1962
			1963
Herbert Marcuse, *One-dimensional Man*	Wilderness Act	Model Cities program established; Saul Bellow, *Herzog* (novel); Ken Kesey, *Sometimes a Great Notion* (novel); *The Autobiography of Malcolm X*; Beatles' American tour	1964
Medicare established	Department of Housing and Urban Development established; Ralph Nader, *Unsafe at Any Speed*	Higher Education Act; Elementary and Secondary Education Act; National Endowment for the Arts established; Pope Paul VI visits United States	1965
Barrington Moore, Jr., *Social Origins of Dictatorship and Democracy*	Department of Transportation established; first BankAmericards (later VISA) issued	Super Bowl I	1966
	First microwave oven introduced	Corporation for Public Broadcasting established; first issue of *Rolling Stone;* Donald Barthelme, *Snow White* (novel); William Styron, *The Confessions of Nat Turner* (novel)	1967
Garrett Hardin, "The Tragedy of the Commons"; first heart transplant (South Africa)		Marshall McLuhan, *The Gutenburg Galaxy;* motion-picture rating system established	1968
Neil Armstrong walks on the moon	National Environmental Policy Act	Philip Roth, *Portnoy's Complaint* (novel); Jonas Salk Institute buildings (La Jolla, Cal.; Louis I. Kahn) completed; Woodstock music festival	1969
			1970
	Nixon imposes wage and price controls	Disney World opens near Orlando, Fla.; John Rawls, *A Theory of Justice*	1971
Fermilab opens; Endangered Species Act		Supplemental Security Income (SSI) established; Indian Education Act; first woman Reform Jewish rabbi ordained; Richard Rorty, "A World Well Lost"; Transamerica Pyramid (San Francisco; William Pereria) completed; Pruitt-Igoe Houses (Saint Louis) dynamited	1972

CHRONOLOGY

Year	The American People	Politics	Global America
1973	*Roe* v. *Wade*; Rehabilitation Act ("Civil Rights Act for the Handicapped"); standoff at Wounded Knee		End of fixed currency-exchange rates; Paris Peace Accords between United States, North Vietnam, and South Vietnam; end of draft; War Powers Act; Organization of Petroleum Exporting Countries (OPEC) quadruples oil prices
1974	Education for All Handicapped Act	Nixon resigns; Gerald Ford becomes president; Congressional Budget and Impoundment Control Act	
1975			Saigon falls to North Vietnamese Offensive; *Mayaguez* incident
1976	Bicentennial of the Declaration of Independence; Hyde Amendment	Jimmy Carter elected president; *National League of Cities* v. *Usery*	
1977			
1978	*Bakke* v. *University of California*		
1979			SALT II treaty with Soviet Union; Soviet Union invades Afghanistan; Tehran embassy crisis
1980	Census counts 226,542,199 Americans; Refugee Act; Mariel boatlift	Ronald Reagan elected president; Paperwork Reduction Act	
1981		Sandra Day O'Connor appointed to Supreme Court (first woman)	
1982	Equal Rights Amendment defeated		
1983		*INS* v. *Chadha*	United States invades Grenada
1984		Ronald Reagan reelected president	
1985			Mikhail Gorbachev becomes general secretary of Soviet Communist party
1986	Immigration Reform and Control Act	William H. Rehnquist becomes chief justice	Iran-Contra controversy
1987			Intermediate-range Nuclear Forces (INF) Treaty with Soviet Union
1988		George Bush elected president	Department of Veterans Affairs established
1989			United States invades Panama; communist regimes collapse in central and eastern Europe
1990	Census counts 248,709,873 Americans		

CHRONOLOGY

Science, Technology, and Medicine	The Economy	Culture	Year
Clifford Geertz, *The Interpretation of Cultures*			1973
		Sears Tower (Chicago; Skidmore, Owens and Merrill) completed	1974
E. O. Wilson, *Sociobiology*	First videocassette recorder (VCR) introduced	Maxine Hong Kingston, *The Woman Warrior* (novel)	1975
Viking II lands space probe on Mars; Apple II computer introduced			1976
Clean Air Act	Department of Energy established		1977
	Airline Deregulation Act; Humphrey-Hawkins Full-Employment Act	*Roots* television series	1978
Three Mile Island nuclear reactor accident		Department of Education established	1979
Department of Health, Education, and Welfare renamed Health and Human Services	Beginning of deregulation of savings-and-loan industry	Cable News Network (CNN) established; Maxine Hong Kingston, *China Men* (novel)	1980
First space shuttle flight; IBM personal computer introduced; acquired immune deficiency syndrome (AIDS) identified	Economic Recovery Tax Act	Richard Rodriquez, *Hunger of Memory* (autobiography)	1981
		First issue of *USA Today*	1982
		"A Nation at Risk" report on education	1983
	Breakup of Bell System		1984
	Gramm-Rudman-Hollings balanced budget act		1985
Space shuttle *Challenger* explodes	Tax Reform Act		1986
	Stock market crash	Allan Bloom, *The Closing of the American Mind*	1987
DNA fingerprinting introduced			1988
First human gene therapy experiment; cold fusion scandal	Savings-and-loan bailout enacted; Time-Warner communications corporation formed; *Exxon Valdez* oil spill	David Harvey, *The Condition of Postmodernity*	1989
Hubble Space Telescope launched	Clean Air Act	Ramon Saldívar, *Chicano Narratives*	1990

CHRONOLOGY

Year	The American People	Politics	Global America
1991	Tailhook scandal		Persian Gulf War; START I treaty with Soviet Union; Soviet Union dissolved; end of Cold War
1992	Los Angeles riots	Bill Clinton elected president; Twenty-seventh Amendment (congressional pay raises)	Euro Disneyland opens
1993			START II treaty with Russia
1994	Proposition 187 approved in California		
1995	Oklahoma City bombing		

Science, Technology, and Medicine	The Economy	Culture	Year
IBM–Apple cooperation agreement	Pan American Airways goes out of business		1991
Food and Drug Administration restricts breast implants			1992
		Martin Scorsese, *The Age of Innocence* (movie)	1993
		Baseball players strike	1994
			1995

INDEX

Numbers in boldface refer to the main entry on the subject. Numbers in italic refer to photographs, illustrations, and maps. Numbers followed by tab refer to tables. Titles of films appear under "Films"; museums are listed under "Museums"; titles of musicals appear under "Musicals"; orchestras are listed under "Orchestras"; titles of radio programs appear under "Radio programs"; Supreme Court cases under "Legal cases"; and titles of television programs and series under "Television programs."

A

AAA. *See* Agricultural Adjustment Act
Aaron, Daniel, 1443a
AARP. *See* American Association of Retired Persons (AARP)
AAUP. *See* American Association of University Professors (AAUP)
Abbey, Edward, 1378b
Abbott, Berenice, 1709b
Abbott, Edith, 121b, 922a
Abbott, Grace, 121b
Abbott, Shirley, 63a
ABC. *See* American Broadcasting Company (ABC)
ABC (American-British Conversation) Talks, 602a
ABC-1 agreement, 635b
Abelson, Philip, 754a
Aberbach, Joel D., *as contributor,* 355a–376b
Aberdeen Proving Ground, 810b
ABMA. *See* Army Ballistic Missile Agency
ABM Treaty. *See* Antiballistic Missile Systems (ABM) Treaty
Abortion
　Catholics, 1512a, 1528a, 1531a, 1532a–b
　feminists, 120b, 121a
　interest groups, 317a,b
　legislation, 448a
　Protestants, 1506a
　state laws, 240b
　Supreme Court appointments, 392a–b
　Supreme Court decisions, 421b
Abramovitz, Moses, 1184a
Abrams, Creighton, 662b
Absalom, Absalom! (Faulkner), 10a, 1445b
Absolutists, 556a
Abstract Expressionism, 1712a 1714a, 1715b
　Jews and, 1587a
Abundance
　divorce and, 215b
　middle class and, 199a,b
Abyssinia, 1596a
Academic and Industrial Efficiency (Cooke), 1409a
Academic community
　during Cold War, 687b
　and federal government, 605b
　foundations and, 498a

internationalization, 498a
scholarly writing peer review, 1831a
Acadia Institute, 948b
Accommodationism, 1534a
Acconci, Vito, 1720a
According to What (Johns), 1718b
Accountancy
　accreditation, 1412a,b
　corporate auditors, 1219b, 1226b, 1411a–b
　evolution of profession, 1410a
　Great Depression, 1419a
　New Deal, 1420a
　restricted access to, 1416b
　standardization of practice, 1231a, 1420b
　stratification, 1413a
Accumulatorem Fabrik (Germany), 1138b
Acheson, Dean, 610b, 656b, 659b, 662b, 725b
Ackerman, Bruce, 388b
ACLU. *See* American Civil Liberties Union (ACLU)
Acquired Immunodeficiency Syndrome. *See* AIDS
Act Further to Promote the Defense of the United States. *See* Lend–Lease Act
Action intellectuals, 1832a
Act of 29 April 1943, 165a–b tab
Act of 14 June 1940, 165a–b tab
Act of 3 March 1875, 154a–b tab
Acton, Lord, 427b, 1506b
Adamic, Louis, 174a, 176a, 178b
Adams, Ansel, 1373a,b, 1709b, 1714b
Adams, Frederick Upham, 382a
Adams, Henry, 1669b, 1744a,b
Adams, Henry Carter, 919a, 1291b
Adams, John, 260a
Adams, John Taylor, *574b*
Adams, Roger, 837a
Adams, Thomas, 13a, 16b, 18a
Adams, Thomas S., 1315a, 1317b, 1321a, 1329a–b
Adamson Act (1916), 519b
Adam's Rib (Herschberger), 910a
Addams, Jane, 49b, 51b, 121b, 256b, 275a–b, 453b, *547a,* 697a, 1068b, 1495a, 1804b
　Dewey, John, and, 277b, 1641a
　on *The Melting Pot,* 1568b
　neutral mediation of World War I, 546b

on women's role, 102a
Address Unknown (Wright), 123a
Adelman, Morris A., 1050a, 1399b
ADL. *See* Anti–Defamation League (ADL)
Adler, Alfred, 234b
Adler, Celia, 1570b
Adler, Cyrus, 1574b
Adler, Felix, 1567b
Adler, Jacob, 1570a
Adler, Mortimer, 1648b
Adler, Samuel, 1567b
Adler and Sullivan, 1675b, 1676a,b
Administrative law, 521b
Administrative Procedure Act (1946), 333b, 525b, 526a, 528b–529a, 534b
Administrative state, 513a,b
　economic regulation, 1269b–1270a
　expansion under Johnson, 485b
　reasons for the creation, 517b–518a
　See also Bureaucracy
Admirals, Generals, and American Foreign Policy, 1898–1914 (Challener), 594b
Admirals Lobby, The (Davis), 599a
Adolescence
　consumption, 1793b
　as defined stage of life, 226a
　teenage subculture, 230b
Adorno, Theodor W., 1485a–b, 1486a, 1584b, 1826a
ADP. *See* Automatic Data Processing (ADP)
Adrian, Gilbert, 1790a
Adventures in Art (Hartley), 1703a
Adventures of Augie March, The (Bellow), 1450a,b, 1450b, 1457a, 1587b
Adventures of Huckleberry Finn, The (Twain), 1438a, 1456a
Advertisements for Myself (Mailer), 34a
Advertising, 28a–b, 31a, 1017a–b, 1019b, 1022b–1023b, 1025b
　American cultural references, 714b
　cable television, 1032b
　consumption, 1021a, 1024b
　incorporated in paintings, 1702b
　industrial production, 1129b, 1131b
　liquor industry, 1132a
　movies stars, 1466b
　in politics, 116b
　radio, 807a,b–808b, 1059b, 1467a, 1474b
　specialists, 1411a
　suffragists, 117a

Advertising (*cont.*)
   television, 817a, 818a–b, 1029b–1030a,
      1059b, 1476b, 1477b
   See also Marketing
Advertising Age, 31a
Advertising Club of America, 1055a
Advisory Commission on Intergovernmental
   Relations, 439a–b, 441b
Advisory Committee on Industrial
   Research, 842a
AEC. *See* Atomic Energy Commission
   (AEC)
AEG (Germany), 1137b, 1138b, 1142b
Aerial Experiment Association, 769b
Aerial shows, 769b–770a
Aerodynamics, 841b
Aerospace technology, **767a–797b,**
   786b–787a, 1145a, 1150a
   computers, 812a
   research, 772a
   in Southern California, 462a
   trade performance, 1200b
AFBF. *See* American Farm Bureau
   Federation (AFBF)
AFDC. *See* Aid to Families with Dependent
   Children (AFDC)
Affirmative action, 180b, 181a, 529a
   effect on higher education, 1833a
   feminist agenda, 120b, 121a
   focus on race, 214a
   as reverse discrimination, 181a
Affluent Society, The (Galbraith), 199a, 285a,
   1031a, 1301a
Afghanistan, 617a, 692b
AFL. *See* American Federation of Labor
   (AFL)
AFL–CIO. *See* American Federation of
   Labor–Congress of Industrial
   Organizations (AFL–CIO)
African American artists, 1703b, 1710b,
   1714a, 1732a, 1738a,b
   black group unity, 1593b
   Harmon Foundation, 1703b
   in WPA programs, 1731a
African American churches, 74a
   African American Catholic Church,
      1530a
   civil rights movement, 66a
   and politics, 1600a
   urban storefront churches, 1600a
African American cultural movements,
   1593a–1607b
African American family, 235b–236a,
   1086b–1087a
   deindustrialization, 112b
   effect of job discrimination against men,
      108a–b
   single-parent families, 105b
African American music, 73b, 149b–150a,
   1618b, 1623b
   black Pentecostal churches, 1624b
   blues, 48a, 1595b
   Gospel music, 67b, 1624b
   influence on American music, 1614b
   integration of jazz bands, 1601b–1602a
   street music, 1488b
African Americans, 55b, 95a
   Academy Awards, first, 1466b
   on AFDC, 1087a
   artisans, 66b
   black identity, 180a, 1603b, 1606a

black nationalism, 180a
business, 66a
Catholics, 1514a–b, 1517b, 1524a,
   1529b–1530a, 1534b
civil rights, 71a–b, 95b, 96a, 1505a
clothing, 1792a
color consciousness, 147b–148a
Congress, 365a, 366a–b tab
consumption patterns, 116a
crisis among men, 123b
cultural movements, 1462a, 1593a–607b
deindustrialization, 112b, 210a
Democratic party, 331b, 342b
disfranchisement, 64b, 65b, 73a, 74a,
   141b
Eastern region, 37b
and ecology, 1378a
elites in the 1920s, 212b, 1598b
empowerment strategies, 145a
films, 151a, 1466b
ghettoization, 1598b
GIs during World War II, 263b
government employees, 1082a
Great Depression, 229b
Great Migration, 50b, 67a, 108b–109a
health care access, 992a, 1005b
in higher education, 1819b, 1825b,
   1828a–b, 1832a
and identity politics, 155b
and Islam, 1548a–b
Jews and, 1584a
job discrimination against men, 108a–b
job segmentation by sex, 108a
and Korean Americans, 98a
and the Left, 1600b–1601b
leisure patterns, 116a
literature, 34a, 150b, 1455b–1456a
in medical science, 947b–948a
Midwest, 43a, 50a, 58b
migrations, 57a, 146a–b, 153a,
   458b–459a, 464b
militancy among, 343a–b
missionaries to Africa, 696b
mortality decline, 963a–b
nationalism, 259a–b
and new immigrants, 188b, 212a–b, 217b
Nixon and, 345a
playwrights, 1725a
in politics, 141b–142a
population, 29a, 1739b
poverty, 76b, 210a, 1071a, 1086a–b
Protestantism, 1492b, 1505a
public education, 1803b, 1809b, 1813b
radio broadcasts, 818a
records, 1470b–1471a
Roots, 1477b
social classes, 76b, *213a–b*, 214b
sociology and, 925a–b
Southern politics, 65b
space programs, 790b
sports, 1769b–1773a, 1777a–1779a, 1782a
Supreme Court and, 419b–420a
television programming, 824b–825a
urbanization, 1597a
in vaudeville, 1464a
veterans, 73a
voting power, 141b
voting rights, 65b, 71a–b, 74b
welfare impact, 122b
West, 95b
during World War II, 71a, 177b

African American women
   boycotts, 115a
   civil rights movement, 118b–119a
   South, 65b
   in suffrage movement, 118a–b
   working after marriage, 102b
   writers, 1604b–1605a
Afrocentrism, 1605a–1606a
Afro-Cuban immigrants, 138a
AFSC. *See* American Friends Service
   Committee (AFSC)
After Auschwitz (Rubenstein), 1589a
After Strange Gods (Eliot), 1444b, 1445a
Aged. *See* Senior citizens
Age Discrimination in Employment Act
   (1967), 527b
Agee, James, 10a
   Let Us Now Praise Famous Men, 1709b
Agent Orange, 784a
"Age of Criticism, An" (Jarrell), 1449b
Age of Reform, The (Hofstadter), 286a–b
Ager, Waldemar, 171a
Agnew, Spiro T., *344b*, 346a, 587a
   presidential elections, 336a–b tab
Agricultural Adjustment Act (1933), 53a,
   68b, 69b, 1277a
   invalidated by Supreme Court, 381a,
      409b, 1320b
Agricultural Adjustment Act (1938), 1278a
Agricultural Adjustment Administration,
   524b, 1277a
Agricultural conservation, 53b
Agricultural Extension Service, 1160b
Agricultural Marketing Act (1929), 1275b
Agriculture, 90b, 1107a, 1146b, 1155a,
   1384b–1387a
   airplanes, 775a–b, 792b–793a, 794b
   cropland harvested and labor hours in
      U.S. agriculture, 1910–1990, *1385a–b*
   Eastern region, 25b, 27a, 38b
   economic performance, 1159b, 1160b
   energy intensification, 1371b
   equipment, 1136b
   exhibitions, 48b
   foreign trade, 1243a–b
   golden age, 45a
   government intervention, 311a
   Great Depression, 1162b
   intensive, 1367a–1368a
   internal combustion engine, 1141b
   labor unions, 86b
   mechanization, 1192b
   Midwest, 59a
   mixed, 44a
   New Deal, 300b, 432b
   overproduction after World War I,
      1191a–b
   as percentage of economy, *1157a–b*
   politics, 309a–b
   productivity, 1165b–1166a
   products, 45b
   1920s, 1192b
   schools, 49a
   scientific, 50b
   soil erosion, 1192b, 1368a
   South, 63b–64a, 68b, 71b–72a, 452b
   subsidy programs, 312a
   sustainable, 1386b
   technological developments, 1367a–b
   water, 1367b, 1386b
   West, 84b, 87b–88b, 97a

wheat, corn, and cotton, yields per acre, 1900–1990, *1385a–b*
and World War I, 1190b, 1191a
Agriculture, Department of, 84b, 309a, 311b, 1025a, 1272a,b, 1281a, 1321b
Consumers' Council, 1026b
Agudath HaRabbonim, 1575b
Agudath Israel of America, 1585a
Ahmad, Mirza Ghulam, 1548a
AIA Guide, 1686b
AIDS, 947a, 954a–b, 960b, 969b, 979a
Catholics, 1531b–1532a
political art, 1719b
See also HIV infection
Aid to Dependent Children (ADC), 1075a
Aid to Families with Dependent Children (AFDC), 122b, 239a, 471b, 484a, 1075b, 1082a–b, 1085a, 1088a
cost of, 1088a
cuts, 489a, 1204a
racial dimension, 485a, 486b–487a
Aid to Families with Dependent Children-Unemployed Parents (AFDC-UP), 1082b
Aid to the Permanently and Totally Disabled, 1076b
Aiken, Howard, 810b–811a
AIM. *See* American Indian Movement (AIM)
Ain, Gregory, 1682b
AIPAC. *See* American Israel Public Affairs Committee (AIPAC)
Air Commerce Act (1926), 1275b
Air conditioning
Southern development, 72b, 462b
Western development, 462b
Air Corps Act (1926), 777a
Aircraft carriers, 778a–b, 780b–781a, 782b
Aircraft industry, 72a, 841b, 849a–850a, 1128b, 1141a, 1144a,b–1145a, 1150a, 1160b, 1164a
aerospace, 786b
Los Angeles, 462a
South, 70b, 457a
trade performance, 1200b
West, 85a
women, 779b
World War I, 770b–771a
World War II, 777b–779b
Air Force, 333b, 608a, 779b, 782b, 849b
aircraft, 795b–796a
computers, 811b, 827b
intercontinental ballistic missile system, 849b
missiles, 786b
Airline Deregulation Act (1978), 531b, 1352b
Airlines, 1349b
commuter, 1352b
deregulation, 794a–795a, 1283b
government subsidiation, 1342a
hubs and spokes, 1353a
small packages transport, 1351a
travel, 1344b–1345a
Air mail, 773a
Air Mail Act, 773a
Airplanes
airbuses, 796b
fighter planes, 1144a
jet aircraft, 781a–782a, 792a–b
jet fighters, 782a–b

swept wings, 781a–b, 792a
types, 773a–b, 778a–779a, 780a, 783a, 793a–794b
warfare, 770b, 778a–779a, 782a–784b, 796a
Air pollution, 458a–b, 462b
Airport Act (1946), 72a
Airports
development, 438a
funding, 1927-1970, 1352b tab
governmental aid, 1342a
Airships, *777a–b*, 777b
Air transportation, 1341b, 1352a–b
democratization, 1751b–1752a
Alabama Dry Dock and Shipping Company, 71a
Alaskan Salmon Act (1924), 1275b
Alba, Richard, 190a
Albanese, Catherine L., *as contributor*, 1539a–1564b
Albania, 350b
Albee, Edward F., 1464a,b
Albers, Annie, 1827a
Albers, Josef, 1710a, 1827a
at Black Mountain College, 1715b
Albert Einstein College of Medicine (Yeshiva U.), 1585b
Albin, Peter, 1117b
Albright, Ivan, 1714b
Albright-Knox Gallery, 33a
Alchian, Armen, 1303b
Alcoa, 457a
research, 849a
Alcohol taxation, 1314a
Alcott, Louisa May, 1438a
Aldrich, Nelson, 1295b
Aldrich Plan of 1910, 1295b
Aldrich–Vreeland Act (1908), 1188b, 1295b
Aldridge, George, 1807a
Aldrin, Edwin E., Jr., 788a–b, *789a–b*
Aleichem, Sholom, 1569b
Aleutian Islands, 551b
Alexander, Adele, 133a
Alexander, Jeffrey, 933b
Alexander, John, 1695b–1696a
Alexander, Will, 65a
Alexanderson, Ernst, 815a
"Alexander's Ragtime Band" (Berlin), 1615b
Alger, Horatio, 206b, 255a, 1787a
Algonquin, 625a
Ali, Muhammad, 143b, 267b, 1778b–1779a
Alianza Federal de Mercedes, La (Federal Alliance of Land Grants), 95a
Alien Property Custodian, 840a, 1245a, 1248a
Alien Registration Act (1940), 178a
Aliens
illegal. *See* Immigration: illegal
Supreme Court, 421a
Alinsky, Saul D., 442a, 1524a
All–American Girls Professional Baseball League, 1779b
Allee, Warder Clyde, 870a
Allen, Fred, 1025a, 1473a, 1476a, 1755a
Allen, Frederick Lewis, 179b
Only Yesterday, 1699a
Allen, Gracie, 1025a, 1473a, 1755a
Allen, Ida Bailey, 1025a
Allen, Robert, 1390b
Allen, Steve, 1477a

Allen, Woody, 1578b
Alliance for Labor Action, 1110b
Alliance for Labor and Democracy in Europe, 697a
Alliance for Progress, 690a, 728a, 1253b
Allied Chemical, 1139a, 1143b
Allied Signal, 1145a
Allies, 1252a
loans, 1247b, 1248a,b
Allis-Chalmers, 1141b
Allport, Gordon, 888b
All the King's Men (Warren), 1445b, 1446a–b
All Volunteer Force (AVF), 616a
Alsberg, Henry, 1730b
Alter, Karl, 1530b
Altmann, Alexander, 1585b
Altmeyer, Arthur, 479b, 482a, 484b, 485a
Aluminum, 1164a
Aluminum Company of America, 1136a
Alvarez, Luis, 750b
Alystyne, William Van, 391b
AMA. *See* American Medical Association (AMA)
Amahl and the Night Visitors (Menotti), 1737a
Amalgamated Association of Iron, Steel, and Tin Workers, 1096b
Amalgamated Clothing Workers, 167a, 1108b, 1574a, 1749b
Amalgamated Meat Cutters and Butcher Workmen of North America, 167a
Amateur Athletic Union, 1764b
Amateur radio, 800b, 803a–b
Amateur Rowing Association, 1744a
Amateur sports, 1776a
Amateur Sports Act, 1781b
Ambassadors, The (H. James), 1439b
Amendments, Constitutional. *See* Constitution, Amendments
"America: Still a Melting Pot?," 191a
America and the World Economy, **719a–734b**
America (Benet), 706a
"America" (Bloch), 1581a
America Comes of Age (Siegfried), 1072b
America First movement, 55b, 176b, 555b, 635a, 1251a
America Houses, 704a
American Abstract Artists, 1710b
American Adam, The (R. W. B. Lewis), 1451b
American Airlines, 795a
SABRE computer system, 814a
American Amateur Photographer, 1697b
American Anthology 1787–1900, An (Stedman), 1436b
American Apartheid (Massey and Denton), 214b
American Art Annual (1913), 1693b
American Artists' Congress, 1706b, 1707a,b–1708a
American Artists' Union, 1706b
American Art-Union, 1693b
American Association for Applied Psychology, 896a
American Association for Labor Legislation, 990a
American Association for the Advancement of Science, 832a, 861b, 873b
forests, 1402a
misconduct in research, 948b

INDEX

American Association of Fund-Raising
    Counsel, 1736b
American Association of Museums, 1729a
American Association of Public
    Accountants, 1412a
American Association of Retired Persons
    (AARP), 308b, 1483a
American Association of University
    Professors (AAUP), 1644a, 1823b,
    1835b
American Association of University
    Women, 120b
American Ballet Theater (ABT), 1727b,
    1733a
American Bar Association, 396b, 413b,
    1411b, 1420b
American Bell Company, 1138b
American Bible League, 861a
American Breeders' Association, 864a
American Broadcasting Company (ABC),
    816a, 1030a, 1472b, 1475b
    American Football League, 1774a
    college sports, 1776b
    television, 1476a, 1478b
    television series with Disney, 1476b
American Buddhist Congress, 1556b
American Cancer Society, 946b
American Capitalism (Galbraith), 285a,
    1301a
American Catholic, The (Greeley), 1527b
American Catholic Historical Association,
    1515a
American Catholic Philosophical Society,
    1517a
American Chemical Society, 839b
American Citizens for Justice, 156a
American City, 257b
American Civic Association, 1359a
American Civil Liberties Union (ACLU),
    31b, 413b, 550a, 597a, 1497b
    campus regulations, 1834a
    Scopes trial, 866a
American College of Surgeons, 992a
American Commonwealth, The (Bryce), 675b
American Cotton Oil, 1132a
American Council for Judaism, 1582b,
    1584a
American Council of Christian Churches,
    1503b
American Council of Learned Societies,
    1824a
American Council on Education, 1822a
American Cyanamid, 1139a, 1143b
    research, 835b
American Dilemma, An (Myrdal), 177b, 214a,
    263a, 927a
American Dream, 173a
American Economic Association, 1289a,
    1291b, 1329a
    membership, 1305b
American Economic Review, 850b, 1292a,
    1298b, 1299a–b
American Evasion of Philosophy (West), 291b
American Expeditionary Force (AEF), 627a
American Express, 1028b, 1032a, 1746a
    ouster of chief executive, 1239a
American Family Association, 1740b
American Farm Bureau Federation (AFBF),
    51a, 309b, 310b, 318b, 1369b, 1370a
American Federation of Catholic Societies,
    1515a

American Federation of Labor (AFL),
    167a, 204b, 309b, 697a, 705a, 1071b,
    1096a
    desegregation of, 155a
    foreign policy, 575a
    merger with CIO, 1110a
    opposition to AALL medical insurance
        plan, 990b
    women in work force, 107a
American Federation of Labor-Congress of
    Industrial Organizations (AFL-CIO),
    310b, 314a, 1110a
    Medicare, 312b
    support of Democrats, 300a
    trade protectionism, 727b
    See also Congress of Industrial
        Organizations (CIO)
American Federation of Teachers, 1835b
American Federation of the Arts, 1729a
American Flag Association, 254a
American Foreign and National Security Policies
    (Buckley), 599b
American Freedom and Catholic Power
    (Blanshard), 1521b
American Friends Service Committee
    (AFSC), 549a
    nuclear pacifism, 558b
American Fur Company, 1048b–1049a
American Geography, The (Morse), 7b
American Gothic (Wood), 1706a
American Guide Series, 54b
American Heart Assocation, 946b
American Hebrew, 1566b
American High School Today (Conant), 1812a
American Home Economics Association,
    1021a
American Hospital Association, 998b
    hospital service plans, 994a
American Indian Movement (AIM), 93a,
    156a, 267a
American individualism, 279b, 281a
American Individualism (Hoover), 197b, 279b,
    280b
American Institute of Accountants, 1412a,
    1416a, 1417a
American Institute of Architects, 1666b,
    1678b
    Guide to New York City, 1684b
American Institute of Banking, 1102a
American Institute of Electrical Engineers,
    1414a
American Institute of Mining Engineers,
    1414a
American in the Making, An (Ravage), 1578a
American Invasion, The (Williams), 709b
Americanism, 1518b
    African Americans, 261a
    Catholicism, 1514b–1515a
    heresy, 1514b
    laborers, 261b
    as not-communism, 265a
    pluralist conceptions, 261a
    unitary conceptions, 264a
Americanism: A World Menace (Colyer), 702a
"Americanism and Localism" (Dewey),
    257b
American Israelite, 1566b
American Israel Public Affairs Committee
    (AIPAC), 1590a
Americanization
    as antibolshevism, 257a–b

    Fourth of July as Americanization Day,
        257a
Americanization of Edward Bok, 33b
American Jewish Committee, 182a, 1567b,
    1568a, 1576b–1577a, 1584a,b, 1586b
American Jewish Conference, 1583b
American Jewish Congress, 1576b–1577a,
    1583a, 1584a, 1586b
    Women's Committee, 1587b
American Jewish Joint Distribution
    Committee, 1583a
American Journal of Sociology, 212b,
    920b–921a, 1102b
American Judicature Society, 396b
    on state courts, 395b
American Kaleidoscope, The (Fuchs),
    213b–214a
American Legion, 380b, 995b
    foreign policy, 575a
American Magazine of Arts, 1703a–b
American Marconi Company, 804a–b,
    1471b
American Marketing Association, 1052b
American Medical Association (AMA),
    988b, 1411b, 1419b, 1425b
    against socialized medicine, 998a
    birth control, 229a
    Council on Medical Education, 991b,
        1408b
    health insurance, 1076b
    Medicaid, 486a
    Medicare, 312b
    research grants, 943b
American Mining and Smelting, 1135b
American Motors, 1030a
American Muslim Mission, 1548a
American Mythologies (Blonsky), 714a
American National Exhibition (Moscow),
    1031a
American Nationalism (Kohn), 264b
American Negro Academy, 1595a
American Neutral Conference Committee,
    548b
American Notes (Dickens), 1067a
American Nurses Association, 1001b
American Peace Society, 542a, 546a
    legalist approach to war prevention, 553a
American Philanthropy (Bremner), 503a
American Philosophical Association, 1636a
American Physical Society, 841a
American Presidency, The (Milkis and Nelson),
    326b
American Prose Masters (Norton), 1439a
American Protective Association, 254b
American Protective League, 171a
American Psychoanalytic Association, 882b,
    895b
American Psychological Association, 880a,
    896a, 1639a
American Public Health Association, 957a,
    998b
American Regionalism (Odum and Moore),
    10a, 13b
American Renaissance (Matthiessen), 1446a,
    1449a
American Revolution
    ideology and taxation, 1311a
    taxation, 1310a, 1313b
American Rolling Mill, 1142b
Americans, The (Boorstin), 651b
Americans, The (Frank), 1715a

"American Scene, The" (Davis), 1706b
American Scene, The (H. James), 1439b
"American Scene" painters, 1704b, 1705b
American Scientific Affiliation, 868a
Americans for Democratic Action (1947), 284b
American Sheet Steel, 1135a
American Socialists, 549b
American Social Science Association, 1408a
American Society for Pharmacology, 840a
American Society for Testing Materials, 833a
American Society of Certified Public Accountants, 1417b
American Society of Composers, Authors, and Publishers (ASCAP), 1472a
American Society of International Law, 553a
American Society of Mechanical Engineers, 1414a
American Sociological Society, 1823b
American Steel and Wire, 1135a
American Steel Hoop, 1135a
American Stock Exchange, 1211b
American Strategy in World War II (Greenfield), 604a
American Studies, 1831a
  in European universities, 701a
American Studies Association, 1449a
American Sugar, 1132a
American system, 1273a
American Telephone & Telegraph (AT&T), 801b–802b, 826a–b, 1138b, 1148b, 1150b, 1284a, 1336a, 1411a, 1471b, 1475a,b
  communications technology, 800a
  deregulation, 819b, 820b–821a
  facsimile service, 815a
  Long Lines Division, 819a–820a
  radio broadcasting, 805b–807a
  regulated telecommunications monopoly, 1348b–1349a
  research, 835b, 837a–b, 841b, 848b
  telex services, 819a
  transistors, 812a
  vacuum tubes, 803b–804a
American Telephone & Telegraph Building (New York), 1687b, 1688a
American Testament, An (Freeman), 1444a
American Tin Plate, 1135a
American Tobacco Company, 1052a, 1131a, 1132b, 1219b
  penetration pricing, 1052a
  vertical integration, 1042b–1043a
American Trade Association Executives, 1280a
American Tragedy, An (Dreiser), 1359a
American Union Against Militarism, 547b, 548b, 549b
American Window Glass, 1142b
American Woman, The (Chafe), 215b
American Zionism, 1573b, 1577b, 1581b
America's Music (Chase), 1610a
America's National Game (Spalding), 1762b
America Today (Benton), 1705b
Amerika und der Amerikanismus (Halfeld), 702a
Ames, Jessie Daniel, 1495a
Amherst College, 32a
  new core curriculum, 1831a
Ammerman, Nancy, 1499a

Amoros, Sandy, 1777b
Amos 'n' Andy show, 151b–152a, 1025a, 1473a, 1476a, 1620b
  race and, 151b–152a
  racial humor, 1473a
Ampex Corporation, 816b
Amputations (White), 1712a
AM radio, 1474a,b, 1475a
  See also FM radio; Radio
Amtrak, 1350a
Amusement parks, 1030a, 1463a, 1465a
  Coney Island, 1021a, 1462a, 1463a, 1748b, *1749a–b*
  Disneyland, 59b, 91b, 1030a, 1034a, 1476b
  Disney World, 463a
  EuroDisney, *709a–b*
  Freedomland USA, 1030a
  Knott's Berry Farm (Calif.), 1034a
  Midwest, 48a
  Six Flags over Georgia, 1030a
  Six Flags over Texas, 1030a
  West, 91b
Anaconda, 1135b
Anaheim-Santa Anna, 212a
Analytic philosophy, 1645b–1646b
Anarchism
  and conscientious objectors, 549b
  Jews, 1568a
Ancient Law (Maine), 918b
Ancient Society (Morgan), 918b
Anderson, Benedict, 131a–b, 161a, 252b, 268b
Anderson, Benjamin, 1293a–b
Anderson, Clinton, 1001b
Anderson, Elizabeth Milbank, 493a
Anderson, Jack, 393b
Anderson, John B., 336a–b tab
Anderson, Marian, 1601b
Anderson, Sherwood, 10a, 52a, 279a, 1440a
  Winesburg, Ohio, 1702a
Andover, 1808a
Andrews, Elisha B., 1068b, 1291a
Andrews, William, 129a
Andrews Sisters, 1571b
Angell, James Rowland, 494b, 495a, 878b, 879b
Angelou, Maya, 1772b
"Angle Worm Wiggle," 1464a
Anglo-American Agreement (1946), 1253a
Anglo-Americans, 162b–163a
Anglo-Japanese alliance abrogation, 682a
Angoff, Charles, 1580b
Angola, 616b, 692b
Anheuser Busch distillery, 1132a
Animal psychology, 879a
Ankeny, John S., 1708a
Annals of the American Academy of Political and Social Science, 18a
Anna T. Jeanes Fund, 1803b
Anorexia nervosa, 1798a
Another Country (Baldwin), 34a
Anscombe, G. E. M., 1655a
Anshutz, Thomas, 1694a
Ansky, S., 1570b
Antarctica exploration, 740a
Antarctic Treaty (1959), 560a
Anthropology
  gender theories, 904a
  and society, 922a
Antibacterial drugs, 977a

Antiballistic Missile Systems (ABM) Treaty (1972), 563b, 566a–b tab, 615a, 616b
Antibiotics, 977a, 1146b, 1147b, 1372a
Anticommunism, 178b, 334a
  Americans for Democratic Action (1947), 284b
  Catholics, 1518b, 1519a
  informational policy, 704b
Anti-Defamation League (ADL), 1577a, 1584a
  See also B'nai B'rith
Antievolution laws, 866a
Antifeminists, 121a
Anti-imperialist movement
  after Spanish-American War, 542b
  peace movement and, 543a
Anti-Merger Act (1950), 1280b
Antimony, 1387b
Antin, Mary, 33b, 1578a
Antinuclear movement
  education campaign against nuclear testing, 559a
  SANE, 1505b
Anti-Preparedness Committee, 547b
Antiquities Act (1906), 1360a
Anti-Semitism, 138b–139a, 1565a, 1567b, 1578a–b
  American Jewish Congress, 1576b
  Catholics, 1519b
  Europe, 1582a
  film industry, 1467b
  foreign policy, 576a–b
  Holocaust, 1589b
  literature, 1581b
  movies, 1580a
  in professions, 1426a
  quotas, 1578b
  during World War II, 177b
Antitrust Division (Justice Department), 520a, 532a, 847a–b, 852b
Antitrust Improvements Act (1976), 520a, 1283b
Antitrust legislation, 1249b, 1251b, 1253b–1254a, 1263b, 1271a, 1275a, 1279a, 1280b
  and administrative state, 520a
  and baseball, 1769a–b
  effect on R&D programs, 839a, 849a
  See also Clayton Antitrust Act; Sherman Antitrust Act
Anti Vietnam War movement, 562a–563a, 616a, 668a–b, 670a
  Catholics and, 1529b
  Chicago Democratic convention, 301a–b
  Moratorium, 586b
  political satire on television, 1477b
AP. *See* Associated Press (AP)
A&P, 700b, 1022a, 1025b, 1064a
APEC. *See* Asia Pacific Economic Cooperation group
A&P Gypsies, 1024b
Apollo-Soyuz Test Project, 790b
Apollo space program, 763a, 788a–b, *789a–b*
Appalachia, 63b–64a
Appalachian Spring (Copland), 1581a, 1617b
Apparel industry, 28b, 452a, 1020b, 1130b, 1146a, 1150b
  See also Clothing; Fashion industry
Appeal to Reason, 257a

"Appeal to the Nations of the World for Peace and for the End of Economic Chaos" (F. Roosevelt), 633a
Appel, Toby, 758b
Appelbaum, Eileen, 1117b
Apple Computers, 823a–b, 826b, 1031b, 1149a
Applied psychology, 885a
Appropriations Act (1981), 532a
Aqueducts, 89a
Aquifers, 56b, 59a, 88a, 98b, 1164b, 1368a
    Ogallala aquifer, 1386b
    See also Water supply
Arabic (ship), 624a
Arafat, Yasir, 693a
Arbitration
    international, 543b
    treaties, 544b
Arbuckle Brothers, 1023a
Arbus, Diane, 1714b
Architects
    professionalization, 1666b
    stratification, 1666b
Architectural Forum, 1685a
Architectural League of America, 1667b
Architectural Record, 453b
Architecture, **1665a–1692b**
    Eastern region, 35b–38a
    Main Street, 59b
    Midwest, 47a–b
    Prairie School, 47b, 59b
Arendt, Hannah, 284b, 1584b, 1657a
Arensberg, Louise, 1699a
Arensberg, Walter, 1699a
Argentia Conference, 602a, 636a
Argonne National Laboratory, 754a
Arkansas, 872b
Arledge, Roone, 1774b
Armat, Thomas, 1752b
Armco Steel, 1135b
Armed Forces Network, 704a
Armed Forces Radio Service, 1473b
Armed services
    American army in 1917, 627a
    desegregation, 1777b
    expansion under Reagan administration, 1201b
    intelligence testing, 171b
    organized reserves, 598b
    Regular Army, 598b, 599a
    research sponsorship, 1828b
    scientific investigations in, 942a,b
    training for World War II in South, 70b
    See also Air Force; Army; Navy
Armed Ship Bill, 624b
Armenian Apostolic Church, 1547b
Armory Show (1913), 1698a,b, 1700a, 1728b
    site, 1698a
Armour company, 1132a–b
Arms control, 559b–562a, 613b
    nuclear weapons, 613a
Arms Control and Disarmament Agency (ACDA), 560b, 613b
Armstrong, Edwin, 815b
Armstrong, Louis, 1615b, 1623b, 1630b
Armstrong, Neil, 788a, 789a–b
Armstrong committee (NY legislature), 1224b
Army
    Air Corps, 599a, 777a

aircraft, 771a–b, 778a–b
Air Service, 775a–b
chief of staff, 594a
Corps of Engineers, 85a, 1369b
General Staff Corps, 594b
intelligence testing, 881a
Ordnance Department production system, 1112a
role overseas after Spanish-American War, 593b
Signal Corps, 809a
Army Appropriations Act (1916), 523a
Army Ballistic Missile Agency (ABMA), 786b, 787a
Army Defense Act (1916), 1820a–b tab
Army-Navy Munitions Board, 602a
Army of Topographical Engineers, 741a
Army War College, 594b
Arnaz, Desi, 154b
Arneson, Robert, 1720a
Arnold, H. L., 1098b
Arnold, Harold D., 841b
Arnold, Henry H. "Hap," 603b, 770a, 781a
Arnold, Thurman, 437b, 1278a, 1419b
Arnold, Thurmond, 281b
Arnott, Trevor, 1409b
Aronson, Boris, 1570b
Arrington, Leonard, 85a
Arrow, Kenneth, 1299a,b, 1300a, 1305b
Arrowsmith (Lewis), 1440b
Art and Architecture Building (Yale), 1689b
"Art and Government" (Goodrich), 1735a
Art Deco, 1681a
Artef, 1574a
Arteriosclerosis, 970a
"Art for Taxpayers," 1713a
Artforum, 1720a
Art Front, 1706b
Art institutions
    discriminatory policies, 1703b
    Eastern region, 33a
Artist in America, An (Benton), 1705b
Artists, 1732b
    activists, 1707a
    and Communist International, 1707b
    minorities, 1738a
    modernists and African art, 1703a
    modernists and Native American art, 1703a
    salaries, 1735b
    West, 83b
    See also African American artists; Women artists
Artists and Writers Union, 1708b
Art News, 1703a
Art of This Century Gallery, 1712b, 1728b
Arts, 1703a
Arts
    black group unity, 1593b
    censorship, 1740a
    democratization, 1725a
    funding coalitions, 1734a, 1741b
    Judaism, 1567b, 1581a, 1586a, 1590a
    in liberal curriculum, 1827a
    Midwest, 55a
    national policy making, 1728b–1735a
    private donors, 1725b–1728b
    public funding, 1725b, 1730b, 1740a
Arts and crafts movement, 37b
"Arts and the National Government, The" (Heckscher), 1735b

Artzt, Edwin L., 1063b
Aryan Nations, 97b
ASCAP. See American Society of Composers, Authors, and Publishers (ASCAP)
Asch, Sholem, 1569b, 1570b
Ash, Roy, 529a
Ashcan School, 35a, 1696b
Ash Commission, 529b
Ashe, Arthur, 157b, 1778a
Asia
    aggressive trade expansion, 693b
    industrial research, 853b
    mutual defense agreements, 688b–689a
    Wilson and, 679b
Asian Americans, 83b, 95a–b, 96a–97a, 571b–572a
    Congress, 365a
    education, 1803b, 1811a, 1832a
    ethnicization, 181a
    literature, 1456a–b
    poverty and, 1086a
Asian immigrants, 134b–135a, 140a–b
    East Asian population, 29b
    labor unions, 309b
Asian Indian immigrants, 97a, 140b–141a, 152b–153a, 186a
    interracial relations, 152b–153a
    religion and, 1552b–1553a
Asian religions
    ethnic manifestation, 1541a,b
    export manifestation, 1541a
    introduction by Theosophical Society, 1543b
Asia Pacific Economic Cooperation group (APEC), 1263a
As I Lay Dying (Faulkner), 1445a
As Seen by Both Sides, 1721b
Assemblies of God, 1493a
Assembly lines, 46b, 47a, 1140a, 1141b, 1142b, 1144b
Assembly of Captive European Nations, 179a
Assimilation
    and class, 195b, 211a
    ethnicity, 211a
Assimilation in American Life (Gordon), 184a
Assistant, The (Malamud), 34a
Associated Medical Care Plans, 994b
Associated Press (AP), 31a–b, 698b
Association for Evolutionary Economics, 1303b
Association of American Colleges, 1826a
Association of American Law Schools, 1408b
Association of American Universities, 1409a, 1821b, 1824b
Association of Universities for Research in Astronomy, 753a
Astor, Brooke, 508a
Astor, John Jacob, 1048b
Astor, Vincent, 508a
Astrology, 1558b
Astronauts, 788a–b, 789a–b, 790b
Astronomy, 753a–b
Astrophysics, 741b, 743b
Asylums (Goffman), 928a
"At a Georgia Camp Meeting" (Mills), 1614b
Ateleta Beneficial Association, 148b
Athanagoras I, 1528a

Atherton, Lewis, 43a, 1050a
Athletic clubs, 1743b
Atlanta
    Los Angeles Times on, 468b
    revitalization, 1346a
    suburbs, 468b
Atlanta Constitution, 69b
    regional heritage, 77a
Atlantic Charter, 602a, 636a, 724b, 1252a
Atlantic Monthly, 8a, 31b, 862a
    on science, 741b
Atmospheric Test Ban Treaty (1963), 1374b
Atomic bomb. *See* Nuclear weapons
Atomic Energy, Joint Committee on, 759a
Atomic Energy Commission (AEC), 748b,
    749a–750b, 751b, 754a, 759a–760b,
    811b, 1374b
    research funding, 850a, 1828b
Atoms for peace, 559b
Atom smashers, 746a–b
AT&T. *See* American Telephone &
    Telegraph (AT&T)
Attack on Leviathan, The (Davidson), 10a
Atterbury, Grosvenor, 1679b
At the Deathbed of Darwinism, 859b
Auchincloss, Louis, 34a
Auden, W. H., 1449a
Audiences
    immigrants, 1462a
    popular culture meaning, 1488b
    study of, 1487a
Audio tapes, 1471a, 1488b
    eight-track, 1471a
Audubon Society, 1370b
    Echo Park, 1373a
Auerbach, Erich, 1593b
Auletta, Ken, 210a
Ault, George, 1702a
    Construction Night, 1701b
"Aunt Sammy," 1025a
Austin, John, 1653b–1654a
Australia, 960b
    bauxite, 1395a
    foreign policy, 589b
    mutual defense agreement with, 689a
Austria, 679a
    Lincoln Center, 1734b
Authoritarian Personality, The (Adorno),
    1584b
Autobiography of an Ex-Colored Man, The
    (Johnson), 1596a
Autobiography of Lincoln Steffens, 33b
Autobiography of Malcolm X, The, 287b, 288a
Automatic Data Processing (ADP), 1150b
Automation in the Office (Hoos), 1115a
Automobile industry, 30a, 55a, 457a,
    1155a–b, 1392a
    consumer movement, 1031a
    eroded market share, 1235b
    foreign policy, 589b
    Great Depression, 1024a–b, 1161b
    impact on associated sectors in the 1920s,
        1192a
    imports, 1244a, 1258a, 1259a
    industrial growth, 1160b
    internal combustion engine,
        1139b–1142b
    international investments, 1262a–b
    international trade, 57b, 313a, 731b–732a,
        1200a, 1254a
    labor turnover, 1098a, 1099b

market segmentation, 1061a
    Midwest, 46a–47a, 51b, 57a, 59a
    prices, 1257a
    production, 1128b
    safety, 1031a
    steel, 1134b
    World War II, 55b
Automobiles, 91a, 1751b
    consumer credit, 1022a, 1028b
    consumer culture, 1021b–1022a
    Eastern region, 27b
    effect on cities, 458b, 1337a
    natural gas, 1348a
    and petroleum, 1397a
    suburbs, 455b, 459a
    tourism, 91b
Autry, Gene, 84a, 1792b
Avery, Sewell, 1233b
Awake and Sing (Odets), 1581b
Awakening, The (Chopin), 1438b,
    1458a
Axelrod, Robert, 1305a
Axel's Castle (Wilson), 1442a, 1446a, 1448b
Aycock, Alice, 1720b
Aydelotte, Frank, 1826b
Ayer, Alfred J., 1648b, 1655a
    Language, Truth, and Logic, 1646b
Ayres, Clarence, 924a

B

Babbitt, Irving, 1823a
Babbitt, Milton, 1622a, 1629b
Babbitt (Lewis), 52a, 115b, 702a, 1027a,
    1440a
Babcock & Wilcox, 1136b
Baby and Child Care (Spock), 976a
Baby boom, 1028b, 1345a
    and consumption, 1198b
    effect on entertainment, 1474a
Baca, Judy, 1719b
"Back of the Yards" movement, 1524a
Bacon, Peggy, 1704b
Bacteriological weapons, ban on, 552a
Badanes, Jerome, 1589b
Baez, Joan, 1627a
Bagdikian, Ben H., 1482b, 1487b
Baghdad Pact, 610a
Baha'i, 1550a
Baier, Kurt, 1655a
Bain, Joe S., 1297b
Baird, John Logie, 815a
Baker, George. *See* Divine, Father
Baker, George F., 1216b, 1217a, 1229b
    and Pujo committee, 1221a–b
Baker, George Pierce, 1827a
Baker, Houston A., Jr., 1456a, 1596b
Baker, Josephine, 701b, *701b*
Bakke, Alan, 1833a
Bakker, Jim, 824b, 1506a
Bakker, Tammy, 824b
Balaban and Katz, 1469a
Balance Agriculture with Industry, 72a
Balance of payments, 1155b, 1166b, 1169b,
    1255b–1256a,b
Balance of trade, 1254a, 1256b
Balanchine, George, 1710b, 1727b, 1733a–b
Balch, Emily Greene, 546b, 697a
Baldwin, James, 34a, 1456a, 1601b, 1602b

    "Everybody's Protest Novel," 1601b
    Go Tell It on the Mountain, 1601b
Baldwin, Roger, 549b
Baldwin locomotive works, 1095a
Balenciaga, 1790b
Bales, Robert Freed, 929a
Balfour Declaration (1917), 1576b
Ball, Lucille, 1476a
Ball, Robert, 486a,b, 488b
Ballet companies
    and government funding, 1727b
    nonprofit, 1727b
    patronage, 1727b, 1738a
Ballinger, Richard A., 1364b
Balloon-frame house, *43a–b*
Balsham, Leah, 1712a
Baltimore, David, 1834a
Baltimore, revitalization, 1346a
Baltzell, E. Digby, 33b
Banana wars, 652b
Bane, Mary Jo, 239a
Banjo (McKaye), 1600b
Banker's Trust, 1216b
Banking, 27b–28b, 31a, 38a, 402b, 1160a,
    1281a
    central bank, 1295b
    debate about structure, 1220a
    deregulation, 1283b, 1284a
    early banks, 1211b
    Eastern region, 38b
    Export-Import Banks, 1250b
    and financial disruption, 1185a
    foreign banks, 1249a, 1255b, 1257a,
        1258b, 1259a
    foreign investments, 1245a,b, 1248b,
        1249a, 1255a, 1258a–b
    foreign loans, 1247a,b–1248a
    foreign policy, 575b
    foreign trade, 1259a
    fragmented system, 1211b–1212a
    Great Depression, 1161b–1162b, 1194a–b,
        1251a
    growth in post-World War II era, 1234a
    and high tariffs, 1312b
    international banks' dollar reserves, 1167a
    investigation by TNEC, 1229a
    Jewish bankers, 1214a–b
    market restoration, 1285a
    national banks, 1212b
    reform, 1295b
    regulation, 429a, 433a, 1168a–b, 1261a
    restructuring, 1890–1914, 1188a–1190a
    role in world economy, 723a
    state-chartered banks, 1212b
    war bonds, 1252b
    world economy, 727a, 733b
    Yankee bankers, 1214a–b
    See also Commercial banks; Investment
        banks
Banking Act (1935), 1227b
Banking (Glass-Steagall) Act (1933). *See*
    Glass–Steagall Act (1933)
Bank of America, 1028b
Bank of North America, 1212b
Bank of the United States, 1211b, 1212b
    See also Second Bank of the United States
Bankruptcy, 1161b–1162a
Bank Street College of Education, 276a
Bannister, Robert, 920b, 923a
    Sociology and Scientism, 920b, 923a
Bannister, Roger, 1782b

Banting, F. G., 944b
Baptism in Kansas (Curry), 55a, 1706b, 1707a–b
Baptists
  liberalism, 1494a, 1500b
  population percentages, 1492b
Bara, Theda, 173a
Baraka, Amiri, 1456a, 1602a, 1603a,b
  Black Community Development, 1604a
  Dutchman, 1604a
  Slave, The, 1604a
Baran, Paul, 1304a
Barbarians at the Gate, 1238a
Bardeen, John, 812a
Baring Brothers, 1215a
Barkley, Alben W., 606a, *611a–b*
  presidential elections, 335a–b tab
Bar mitzvah, 1572b, 1577b, 1588b
Barnard, Chester, 1102b
  Functions of the Executive, The, 1101a
Barnard, Christian, 953a
Barnard College, 32a, 102a
Barnes, Djuna, 1458a
Barnes Collection, 33a
Barnett, Harold J., 1383b
Barnstormers, 774b–775a
Barnum, Phineas T., 1049b, 1462b, 1746a–b, 1748b
Baron, Salo, 1579a–b
Barondess, Joseph, 1567a
Barone, Enrico, 1299b
Barr, Stringfellow, 10b
Barrie, Dennis, 1721a
Barrios, The (Moore and Pinderhughes), 210b
Barron's, 1053b
Barth, John, 1452b, 1453b
Barth, Karl, 282b, 1502a–b
Barthelme, Donald, 1453b
  Snow White, 1452b
Bartholdt, Richard, 544a–b
Bartók, Béla, 1621a, 1728b
Barton, Bruce, 115b
Barton, Clara, 1414a
Baruch, Bernard, 557b, 597a
Baruch Plan, 557b–558a, 613a
Baseball, 38a,b, 173a
  African American involvement, 1770b
  American Association, 1775b
  Americanization of immigrants, 1766a
  American League, 1769a
  "Black Sox" scandal, 1768a
  Federal League, 1769a,b
  increasing number of teams, 1773b–1774a
  middle class, 1745a–b
  National League, 1762b, 1769a, 1775b
  National Negro League, 1771a
  Player's League, 1775b
  players salaries, 1774a
  rise of professional, 1762b
  segregation, 173b
  teams in Southern cities, 462a
  teams in Western cities, 462a
  World Series, 1745b, 1768a
Basel international standards, 1263b
BASF, 835b
Basie, Count (William), 58b, 1623b, 1630b
Basketball, 38b
  all-black professional teams, 1771b
  American Basketball League, 1768b, 1773b

increasing teams, 1773b
Jewish fans, 1579b
National Basketball Association, 1769b, 1773b
Baskin, Leonard, 1579a
Bateman, Alan M., 1392b, 1393a
Bateson, William, 866b, 874a
Bathing suits, 1797b
Bat mitzvah, 1588b
Batt, William L., 1392b
Batteries, 1138a–b, 1143b
Battle of the Overpass, 1108b
Baudrillard, Jean, 936b
Bauer, Louis Agricola, 742b–743a
Bauer, Raymond, 310b
Baumol, William J., 1735b
Bauxite, 1392b, 1394b–1395a
  world bauxite production, 1890–1976, *1395a–b*
Bavli, Hillel, 1573b
Baxter, James P., 846b
Baxter, William, 821a
Bayer, Freidrich, A.G., 835b, 838a
  research, 835a
Baym, Nina, 1457b
Bay of Pigs incident, 788a
BBC, 709a
BCA. *See* Business Committee for the Arts (BCA)
Bear, Stearns, 1236a
Beard, Charles A., 380a, 696b, 1657a
  Economic Interpretation of the Constitution, An, 920a
Bearden, Romare, 1710b
Beat aesthetic, 1603b
Beatles, 1628a
Beatrice, leveraged-buyout, 1237b
Beat style, 1793a
Beaux, Cecilia, 1704a
Beaux-Arts classical style, 1671a–b
Bebop, 1623b
Becker, Gary S., 934b, 935a
Becker, Howard P., 927a
Beckett, Samuel, 1451b
Beechcraft airplanes, 776a
Beecher, Catharine, 226b
Beecher, Henry Knowles, 950a–b
Beers, Clifford, 884a
Behavioral Approach to Historical Analysis, A (Berkhofer), 925b
Behaviorism, 279a, 879a, 887a–888a
  behavior modification techniques, 892a
  education and, 1806a
  radical, 891b
Behaviorism (Watson), 889a
Behrman, S. N., 1581b
Being and Time (Heidegger), 1657a
Being There (Kosinski), 1756a
Beis Yaakov schools, 1585a
Belkin, Samuel, 1585b
Belknap, Michal R., *as contributor,* 401a–425b
Bell, Alexander Graham, 769b, 1475a
Bell, Daniel, 169b, 197b, 286a,b, 287a, 1486a, 1582a, 1586a
  Coming of Post-industrial Society, The, 208b
  Cultural Contradictions of Capitalism, The, 290a–b
  End of Ideology, The, 199a, 287a, 1831b
Bell, James "Cool Papa," 1771a, *1771a–b*
Bell, Thomas, 176a

Bellah, Robert, 290b, 1507a–b, 1558a
  Habits of the Heart, 197a
Bell Aircraft, 70b
Bellamy, Edward, 274a, 921a, 1068a
Bell Companies, 801b–802a, 819b
Bell Laboratories, 28a, 837b, 844b–845a, 1138b, 1143a
  computers, 812a
  transistor, 848b
Bellow, Saul, 1450a–b, 1457a, 1587b, 1588a
  Adventures of Augie March, The, 1450a,b, 1450b, 1457a
  Herzog, 1450a
Bellows, George, 1704b
Bell System, 819a–820a, 827b
Bell Telephone, 1336a
Belmont, Auguste, 769a, 1214a
Belsky, Jay, 238b
Belz, Herman, *as contributor,* 513a–535b
Bem, Sandra, 912b
Bemen, Solon S., 1675b
Ben Ami, Jacob, 1570b
Bender, Thomas, 33b
Benderly, Samson, 1567a, 1576a
Bendix, 1141a, 1145a
Bendix, Reinhard, 926b, 930a
Benedict, Ruth, 263a, 922b
  influence on Abstract Expressionism, 1713a
Benet, Stephen Vincent, 706a
Benglis, Lynda, 1720a
Ben Gurion, David, 1584a
Benjamin, Walter, 1485b
Bennett, Hugh Hammond, 1369b, 1370a
Bennett, William J., 189b, 1833a
Bennington College, 1824b
Benny, Jack, 1025a, 1473a, 1755a
  television, 1476a
Benson, Allan L., 335a–b tab
Bentley, Arthur, 279a
Benton, Thomas Hart, 10a,b, 41b, 42b, 55a, 261b, 1705b, 1710b
  America Today, 1705b
  Artist in America, An, 1705b
  Social History of the State of Indiana, The, 1705b
Bentsen, Lloyd, 336a–b tab
Bercovici, Konrad, 949b
Berenson, Senda, 1763a
Bergdorf Goodman, 1789b
Berge, Wendell, 1279a
Bergen, Edgar, 1473a
Berger, Raoul, 388a, 422a
Berger, Victor L., 167a
Bergheim, Louise, 1758a
Bergmann, Gustav, 1645b–1646a
  Metaphysics of Logical Positivism, The, 1652b
Berk, Fred, 1579a
Berkhofer, Robert, 925b–929a
Berkner, Lloyd V., 752a–b
Berkowitz, Edward D., *as contributor,* 471a–490b
Berkson, Isaac, 1576a, 1577b
Berkson, Libbie, 1576a
Berlage, H. P., 1667a
Berle, Adolf, 1296a,b
  Modern Corporation and Private Property, The, 1233a
Berle, Milton, 1476a, 1756b
Berlin, 849b

airlift, 782a
blockade, 608b
Kennedy and, 341b
wall, 341b, 693a, 853a
Berlin, Irving, 1323b, 1581a, 1615a–b, 1619a, 1625b
Berman, Marshall, 1455a
Bernard, Luther L., 886b, 923a,b
Bernbach, William, 1064a
Bernstein, Leonard, 1586b, 1621a, 1625b
Bernstein, Richard J., 189a, 291b, 292a, 1658a
Berrigan, Daniel, 1529a
Berrigan, Philip, 1529a
Berry, Brian J. L., 18b
Berry, Chuck, 58b, 1625a
Berstein, Michael A., as contributor, 1183a–1207b
Berube, Allan, 104a
Bessemer steel process, 1134b–1135a
Best, Charles H., 944b
Bestor, Arthur, 1811b
Bether, Hans, 558b
Bethlehem Steel, 1135b
Betsy Ross House, 37a
Bettelheim, Bruno, 1584b
Bettercare, 1002a
Betts, Richard, 610b, 612a
Bevatron. See Particle accelerators
Beveridge, Albert, 255a
Beyond Ethnicity (Sollors), 190b
Beyond Freedom and Dignity (Skinner), 891b
Beyond Separate Spheres (Rosenberg), 904b, 922a
Beyond the Melting Pot (Glazer and Moynihan), 184a
B-52 Stratofortress, 783a–b
Bhagwan Rajneesh, 1552b
Bhaktivedanta, A. C., Swami Prabhupada, 1552a
Bias, Len, 1776b
Bible
Catholics, 1511a, 1533a–b
fundamentalists, 1499a–b
Judaism, 1566b
liberal Protestants, 1495b
Presbyterians, 1500a
Bible institutes, 1499a, 1503a–b
Bicentennial, 267b, 268a
Bickel, Alexander, 388b
Bidault, Georges, 582a–b
Biddle, Francis, 176b, 1705a
Biddle, George, 1705a
World War I, 1701b
Biddle, Livingston J., Jr., 1736b, 1738b
Biden, Joseph, 393a
"Bie Mir Bist Du Sheyn," 1571b
Biennial Census of Manufacturers, 1057b
Bierce, Ambrose, 1437b
Big bands, 1620b
Big Brother and the Holding Company, 1628b
Big Daddy Paper Doll (Stevens), 1720a
Bigelow, Maurice, 861b
Big Science, 739b, 763a–b, 846a, 849b, 852a
critics, 751b–754a
as term, 745a, 753b
See also Large-scale science
Big Sea, The (Hughes), 1597b, 1601a

Big Sleep, The (Chandler), 1363a
Biker style, 1793a
Bilbo, Theodore, 66b
Bilingual Education Act (1968), 1812a–b tab, 1814a
Bilingualism, movement against, 187b
Billboards, 1023a
Billiards, 1747b
Bill of Rights, 435b–436a, 440a
applicability to states, 414a–415b
Billy the Kid (Copland), 1581a, 1617b
Bilstein, Roger E., as contributor, 767a–797b
Biltmore, 1669a
Binet, Alfred, 881a
Bintel brief column, 1569a
Biograph, 1469a
Biological Sciences Curriculum Study, 871b
Biological weapons, 850a
tests on American civilians, 950a
Biological Weapons Convention (1972), 563a
Biologics Control Act (1902), 996a–b tab
Biomedical research, 1836a
Biotechnology, 854a
research, 852b
Birth control, 30a, 103b, 227b
Catholics, 1512a, 1528b, 1531a–b
funding of research, 228a, 946b
growing public acceptance, 229a
pill, 235a
restricted access, 227b
restricted information, 227a,b
Sanger, Margaret, 226b
United States v. One Package of Japanese Pessaries, 228a
Birth rate, 222b
Bishop, Isabel, 1704b, 1710b
Bishops, Roman Catholic, 1515b–1516a, 1522b
"Discrimination and Christian Conscience" (1958), 1524b
politics, 1532a–b
on secularism, 1521a
Bismarck, Otto von, 990a
Bitter Cry of the Children, The (Spargo), 1804b
Bituminous Coal Conservation Act (1935), 380b
Black, Brown, and Beige (Ellington), 1602a, 1620b
Black, Charles, 388a
Black, Hugo L., 382b, 390a–b tab, 415a, 417a, 436a, 444a,b
Black, Joe, 1777b
Black Aesthetic, 1602b
Black Aesthetic, The (Gayle), 1603a,b
Black Arts movement, 1602a–1604a
Black Arts Repertory Theater and School, 1604a
"Black Boys and Native Sons" (Howe), 1601b
Black Catholic Clergy Caucus, 1529b
Black Community Development, 1604a
Black Culture and Black Consciousness (Levine), 1595b
Black Fire (Baraka and Neal), 1603a
Black Hair (Soto), 1456b
"Black Man Brings His Gifts, The" (Du Bois), 259b
Black Metropolis (Cayton and Drake), 213a–b, 925b

Black Mountain College, 1715b, 1827a
Blackmun, Harry A., 390a–b tab, 392a
Blackmur, R. P., 1447a, 1448a
Black Muslims, 266b, 287b
Black nationalism, 259b, 260a
Black Panthers, 180a, 266a, 288b
Black Political Convention, 1604a
Black Power, 180a, 266b, 1602b
Black pride style, 1793a
Blacks. See African Americans
Black separatism, 259b
Black Skin, White Masks (Fanon), 1603b
Black societies, 1514b, 1515a
Black Star Line, 259b, 1599a–b
Black studies, 1604a–1605a, 1831b
Black Worker, The (Harris and Spero), 929b
Blades, Rubén, 1632b
Blake, Peter, 1665a
Blakelock, Ralph, 1693b
Blakey, Art, 1624a
Blanshard, Paul, 1521b
Blatch, Harriot Stanton, 117b
Blatz distillery, 1132a
Blauner, Robert, 155b, 1113b, 1114a
Blaut, James, 252b
Blavatsky, Helena, 1540b, 1543b, 1554b
Blease, Cole, 66b
Bleier, Ruth, 913b
Bleriot, Louis, 770a
Blewett, John P., 750a
Blimps. See Airships
Bliss, Lillie P., 1684b, 1699a, 1705a
Bliss, Lizzie, 1728b
Bliss, William Dwight Porter, 275a
Blitzkrieg, 601a, 634b, 778a
Bloch, Erich, 852a
Bloch, Ernest, 1581a
Blonsky, Marshall, 714a
Bloom, Allan, 189a
Closing of the American Mind, The, 1836a
Bloom, Hyman, 1714a, 1721a
Bloomgarden, Solomon, 1569b
Blue Army of Mary, 1518b
Blue-Collar Marriage (Komarovsky), 929a
Blue Cross, 486a, 993b, 994b, 1078a
Blue laws, 1749a
"Blueprint for Negro Writing" (Wright), 1600b
Blue Shield, 994b, 1078a
Blue-sky laws, 1224a–b
Blues music, 48a, 149b, 150a, 1597b
African Americans, 1595b
female singers, 1597b
Southern origin, 67b
Bluestone industry, 27b
Bluford, Guion, 790b
Blumberg, 1648b
Blume, Peter, 1721b
Eternal City, 1708b
Blumer, Herbert, 1484b
Bly, Carol, 59b
B'nai B'rith, 1566b, 1577a, 1583b
Klutznick Museum, 1590a
women, 1587b–1588a
Board for International Broadcasting, 614a
Boards of equalization, 1315a
Boas, Franz, 161a, 173b, 261a, 869b, 886b, 922a, 925a, 1567b, 1599a
Bobbitt, Franklin, 1806a
Bob Jones University, 1833a

Bodnar, John, 259a, 260a–b, 268a, 269a
Body fashions, 1797a–1800b
Boeing, 773b, 796a,b, 1144b
    707 Stratoliner, 793a–b
Boesky, Ivan, 1238b
Bohan, Ruth L., 1700a
Bok, Edward, 33b
Boland Amendment (1984), 589a
Bolcom, William, 1630a
Boldt, George, 92b
Boldt decision (1974), 92b
Bole, S. James, 866b
Bolling Committee, 362b–363a
Bolshevism, 171b, 597b
Boltzmann, Ludwig, 1637b
Bombers, 778b–779a, 780a–b, 782a,
    784a
Bonald, L. G. A. de, 918a
Bonaparte, Charles, 141a
Bonds
    convertible, 1216a
    corporate, 1209a
    government, 1209a, 1211b
    market, 1209a
    and railroads capitalization, 1215b
    sales to middle classe during World War
        I, 1316b–1317a
    tariffs, 1312b
Bonds, Bobby, 1774b
Bonfire of the Vanities (Wolfe), 34a, 1238b
Bonhoeffer, Dietrich, 1504b
Bonneville Dam, 1026a
Bonneville Power Administration, 1339a
Bonsack, James, 1042b, 1131a,b
Booking agencies, 1463b–1464a,b
Book-of-the-Month Club, 1482b
Book publishers, 1482b, 1483a
Books
    paperbacks, 1757b
    popular culture, 1481a–1482b
Books in Print, 1482b
Bookstores, 1482b
Boomtowns, 86b, 87b
Boone, Pat, 232a
Boorstin, Daniel J., 264a, 265b, 285b, 700b,
    1023b, 1746a,b, 1751b–1752a
    Americans: The Colonial Experience, The,
        651b
Borah, William E., 380b, 551b, 553b, 554a,
    599a, 631a
Borden, Gail, 1131b
Borg, Bjorn, 1775a
Borg-Warner, 1140b–1141a, 1145a
Boring & Tilton, 1670b, 1671a, 1671a–b
Bork, Robert H., 315b, 391a–b tab, 392b,
    422b–423a
Born-again Christians, 1491b, 1493a, 1498b
Borofsky, Jonathan, 1717b
Borowitz, Eugene, 1587a
Borscht circuit, 1579a
Boston
    financial crisis, 464b
    during Great Depression, 457b
    subway, 453a
Boston City Hall, 1691a–b
Boston College, 32a
Boston Museum of Fine Arts, 33a, 1693b,
    1726a,b
    Great Depression, 1731b
Boston Public Library, 32b
Boston University, 32b

divestment of stock in corporations doing
    business in South Africa, 1835a
Botkin, Benjamin, 10a,b
Boulding, Kenneth, 1271b
"Bound for the Promised Land," 146b
Bourdieu, Pierre, 932a
Bourke-White, Margaret, 1710a
Bourne, Randolph, 170a, 171a, 257b,
    258a,b, 269b, 549b, 1439b, 1440a,
    1444a, 1496b, 1497a, 1651b
    "Transnational America," 1444a
Bowdoin College, 32a
Bowen, William G., 1735b
Bowlby, John, 238a
Bowling, 1747b
Bowman brothers, 1684a
Boxing, 1745b, 1747b
    immigrants in, 1766a
Boy Scouts, 697a
Bozell, L. Brent, 1525a
Braceros, 94b
Bradbury, Malcolm, 1452b
Braddock, W., 1236a
Braden, Thomas, 706b
Bradley, Bill, 30a, 1328a
Brady, David, 323b
Bragdon, Claude, 1681a
Brand, 1049a
    definition, 1052b
    leading brands, 1925 and 1985, 1053a tab
    marketing, 1065b
    national brands in nineteenth century,
        1050a
    recognition, 1022b
    value, 1053a
Brandeis, Louis D., 258a,b, 259b, 278a,
    378b, 389a, 390a–b tab, 407b, 448a,
    838b, 1568a, 1574a, 1576b, 1577b,
    1581b
    Abrams v. United States (1919), dissent in,
        416a
    Black and White Taxicab Co. v. Brown and
        Yellow Taxicab Co. (1928), dissent in,
        383b
    "Other People's Money," 1221b
Brandeis University, 32a
    divestment of stock in corporations doing
        business in South Africa, 1835a
    modern Jewish scholarship, 1585a–b
Brando, Marlon, 1060a
Brandt, Richard, 1655a
Brandwein, Naftule, 1571a
Braniff International, 795a
Branson, William, 1166b
Brass industry, 27b
Brattain, Walter, 812a
Braun, Wernher von, 786a–b
Braverman, Harry, 200b, 215a,
    1112b–1113a
Brazil
    film industry, 707b
    television, 709a
Bread Givers (Yezierska), 397a, 1578a
Breast cancer, 947a
Breckinridge, Sophonisba, 922a
Breech, Ernest, 847a
Breen, Joseph, 1467b
Breen, T. H., 132b
Bremner, Robert, 503a
Brennan, William J., Jr., 390a–b tab, 420b,
    444b

Brentano, Franz, 1642b
Bretton Woods conference (1944), 687a,
    724b–731a, 1166a,b, 1198b, 1252b,
    1256b
    international monetary system, 726b,
        1167a
    system collapse, 730a, 1199b, 1235a
Breuer, Marcel, 1682b
    Whitney Museum of American Art (New
        York), 1690b
Breuilly, John, 252b
Breyer, Stephen G., 391a–b tab
Briand, Aristide, 553b
"Briar Patch, The" (Warren), 1444b
Brice, Fanny, 1579b
Brick, Howard, as contributor, 917a–939b
Bricker, John W., 335a–b tab
Brigham Young University, 1833b
Bright, James, 1112b–1113a
Bright, John, 542b
Brill, A. A., 883a–b
Britain, 960b
    aircraft, 792a
    arbitration treaty with, 545a
    banks, 1220b
    disability insurance, 485a
    exports, 1166b
    film agreement with, 707a
    foreign policy, 573a–b
    labor productivity, 1156a–b
    manufacturing productivity, 1202a
    radio and television, 712b
    real GDP per person, 1156a–b
    unemployment insurance, 1071a
    World War I, 623a, 624a, 631b
Britain, Battle of, 634b
British Journal of Political Sociology, 209a
Broadway musical theater, 1613b, 1614a,
    1619a–b
    mass market, 1631a
    See also Musicals
Brodie, Bernard, 613a
Brodie, Maurice, 946a
Brodkin, Herb, 1589b
Bromfield, Louis, 55a
Bronx Primitive (Simon), 1586b
Bronze industry, 27b
Brooke, Ed, 30a
Brookhaven National Laboratory (N.Y.),
    749–750b, 759b, 849b
Brookings Institution, 228b–229a, 374b,
    497a, 499b
    social sciences application, 496a
Brooklyn Bridge, 35a–b
    artists celebrating the, 1701b
Brooklyn Dodgers, 1777b
Brooklyn Historical Society, 37b
Brooklyn Jewish Center, 1578b
Brooklyn Museum, 33a
    Great Depression, 1731b
Brooklyn Polytechnic Institute, 32b
Brooklyn Tablet, 1519a
Brooks, Cleanth, 1448a
Brooks, Gwendolyn, 1602b, 1603b, 1604a
Brooks, Harvey, 851a
Brooks, Mona L., 1545b
Brooks, Phillips, 1669b
Brooks, Van Wyck, 33b
Brooks, William Keith, 860a
Brotherhood of Sleeping Car Porters,
    214a

Brotherhood War, 1762b
Brothers Ashkenazi, The (Singer), 1569b
Broun, Heywood, 1777b
Brower, David, 1373a, 1380a
Brown, Arthur I., 866b
Brown, Edmund G., Jr., 1369a
Brown, Fred, 1720b
Brown, George, 758a
Brown, James, 1631a
Brown, Jerry, 445a
Brown, Josephine, 1072b
Brown, Milton W., 1693b, 1695a
Brown, Robert McAfee, 1505b
Brown, Rosellen, 34b
Brown and Root, 758a
Brownell, Herbert, 1280b
Brownell, William Crary, 1439a,b
    Standards, 1439b
Brown Girl, Brownstones (Marshall), 1602b
Brownlee, W. Elliot, *as contributor,*
    1309a–1330b
Brownlow, Louis, 524b
    Public Administration Clearing House,
    496a
Brownlow Committee, 524b–525a
Brown University, 1833a
    coeducation, 1824b
Brown v. *Board of Education* (1954), 73a,
    153b, 180a, 266a, 386b–387a, 420a,
    1524b, 1602b, 1777b, 1809b, 1812b
    Eisenhower and, 339b–340a
    influence on higher education, 1828b
    legal scholars on, 388a
Bruce, Blanche, 141b
Bruce, Edward, 1705b
Bruce, Patrick Henry, 1703a
Bruce, Robert, 740b
Brumbaugh, Martin, 1810a
Brundage, Avery, 1773a
Bruner, Frank C., 255b
Bruner, Jerome, 892b, 1812a
Brutalism (architecture), 1689b
Bryan, Charles W., 335a–b tab
Bryan, William Jennings, 25a, 297b, 308b,
    543a, 545b, 548b, 571a, 572b, 624a,
    720a, 721b, 722a, 801a, 805b, 865a–b,
    1291a, 1497a
    conciliation treaties, 545b
    peace treaty with Spain, 542b
    presidential elections, 335a–b tab
Bryant, William Cullen, 1436b, 1437a
Bryce, James, 355b, 675b
Bryn Mawr College, 32a, 102a, 1826a
Brzezinski, Zbigniew, 561a
Buber, Martin, 1713a
Buchanan, James, 1299a, 1302a
Buchanan, Patrick J., 188b, 1740b
Bucholz, Roxanne, 1118b–1119a
Buck, Lossing, 697a
Buckley, Oliver B., 841b
Buckley, Thomas, 599a,b
Buckley, William F., Jr., 289b, 1525a
Budapest Quartet, 1579a
Buddhism, 1541b, 1553a–1556b
    Americanization, 1554b
    ethnic manifestation, 1553a, 1556a–b
    export manifestation, 1553b
Budget and Accounting Act (1921), 328a,
    358a, 359b, 360b, 361a, 372b, 523a,
    1318a
Budget balancing, 1319b

Budget deficits, 1155b, 1173b, 1174a–b,
    1175a–b, 1177a–b, 1285a,b, 1345a
    financing of, 731a–b
    and military spending, 1202b
    1970–1988, 1202a–b
    under Reagan, 349a, 1327a–b
Budget Enforcement Act (1990), 1174b
Buenos Aires (1936), 685a
Bugbee, George, 999b
Buggy-whip industry, 27b
Buick, 1058b
Building America, 261b
Bulgaria, 350b
Bulge, Battle of the, 646b
Bulimia, 1798a
Bull, Ole, 1612a
Bulletin of the Atomic Scientists, 559a
Bullitt, William, 634b
Bully pulpit, 274a, 327b–328a, 406b
Bulosan, Carlos, 153a
Bundy, McGeorge, 503b, 584a, 615a
Burchfield, Charles, 1701b–1702a
"Burden for Critics, A" (Blackmur), 1447a
Bureaucracy, **513a–535b**
    effect on individual rights, 413b
Bureau of Animal Industry, 942a
Bureau of Corporations, 1271a, 1402b
Bureau of Education, 1821b
Bureau of Fine Arts, 1735a
Bureau of Foreign and Domestic
    Commerce, 700a
Bureau of Indian Affairs, 92a, 140a
    education, 1810b
Bureau of Internal Revenue, 1316a, 1317a,
    1323b
    See also Internal Revenue Service (IRS)
Bureau of Investigation, 171b
Bureau of Labor Statistics, 215a, 475a
Bureau of Land Management, 84b
Bureau of Mines, 1416a
Bureau of Reclamation, 84b–85a, 90b–91a,
    1358b, 1362b, 1373a
Bureau of Social Hygiene, 228a
Bureau of the Budget, 358a–b, 1318a,
    1322a
    See also Office of Management and
    Budget (OMB)
Bureau of the Budget (Treasury
    Department), 523a, 527a
Bureau of the Census, 135b
BuRec. *See* Bureau of Reclamation
Burgee, John, 1688a
    American Telegraph and Telephone
    Building (New York), 1687b, *1688a*
Burger, Warren E., 388b, 389b, 390a–b tab,
    416b
    and docket congestion, 394b
Burgess, Ernest W., 17b, 103a, 222b, 922b
Burhoe, Ralph Wendell, 871a
Burke, James E., 1052b
Burlesque, 1461b, 1463a
    Jews, 1579b
Burnett, Carol, 1578b
Burnham, Daniel H., 47a, 1672b
    Chicago Plan, 1673b
Burnham, D.H., and Co., 1675b
Burnham, Walter Dean, 330b
Burnham and Root, 1675b
Burns, George, 1025a, 1473a
    Allen, Gracie, 1755a
    Third Time Around, The, 1766a

Burns, James MacGregor, 332b
Burns, Tommy, 143a
Burns and Allen, 1755a
Burroughs, Bryson, 1699a
Burroughs, Floyd, *70a–b*
Burroughs, William, 1452b
Burroughs Adding Machine, 1148b, 1149a
Burroughs Corporation, 809a
Burroughs Wellcome, 947a
Burton, Harold H., 390a–b tab
Bus boycotts, 266a,b, 1602b
Busemann, Hans, 781b
Bush, George, 155b, 302a, 322b,
    350a–351b, 617b, 1285a–b
    abortion, on, 392a
    arts patronage, 1740a–b
    budget deficit, 1174b
    court appointments, 392a–b
    economy, 30b
    elections of 1992, 303b–304a, 307a
    federalism, 447a,b
    foreign policy, 589a–590b
    foreign trade, 1263a
    Gulf War, 672a–b, 693a
    moral majority, 184b
    new world order, 618a
    Operation Desert Storm, 364b, 413a
    presidential elections, 185a, 336a–b tab
    Supreme Court appointments, 418b–419a
    taxation, 1328b
    Thousand Points of Light, 510b
    trade barriers, 733a
    vetoes, 347a tab
    Willie Horton advertisements, 77a
    world economy, 731b
Bush, Vannevar, 811a, 846b–847b, 849a,
    945a
    Science, 1828b
Business
    demand for governmental regulation,
    405a
    interest groups, 309b, 313b
    political involvement, 313a
    psychological testing, 885b
    regulation, 312b, 315b
    South, 66a, 76a
    See also Corporations
Business administration
    Education of American Businessmen, The,
    1423b
    Harvard, 1409a
    Taylorism in shools, 1103b
    Wharton School, 1409a
Business and Professional Women, 120b
Business Committee for the Arts (BCA),
    1736b–1737b
Business cycles
    analysis, 1292a, 1293b, 1298a
    countercyclical policy formation,
    1202b–1204b
    depressions and recessions, 1183a–1207b
    mathematical theories, 1184a–b
    See also Trade cycles
Business Cycles (Mitchell), 1294a, 1298a
Business-Cycle Theory (Hansen), 1298a
Business equipment, 1136b, 1148b–1149a,
    1149a,b
Business-government cooperation, 1280a
Business institutions
    communications, 800a–801a
    computers, 810a, 812b, 813b

Business Roundtable, 313b, 1284a
Business Week, 75a, 1115b
Butler, Nicholas M., 335a–b tab
Butler, Pierce, 382b, 390a–b tab
Butler, Richard, 97b
Butler, Smedley, 654a
Butterfield, Deborah, 1720a
Byington, Margaret, 215a
Byrd, Harry F., 336a–b tab
Byrds, 1628a
Byrne, Barry, 1678b
Byrne, John W., 1002a
Byrnes, James F., 382b, 390a–b tab, 603b
Byrnes, John, 486b
By the Waters of Manhattan (Reznikoff),
    1580b

C

CAB. *See* Civil Aeronautics Board (CAB)
Cabell, James Branch, 1439a
Cable, George Washington, 1593a
Cable News Network (CNN), 824a,
    1478a,b
Cable television, 38a, 799a, 800a, 823b,
    824a–825a, 1032b, 1476a, 1479b–1480a
    increased viewer participation, 1480a
    New York City, 31b
Cable Television Act (1992), 1488a
CAD. *See* Computer Aided Design
Cadeau (Man Ray), 1704b
Cadillac, 1058b, 1061a
Caesar, Sid, 1477b
Cage, John, 1453b, *1622b,* 1622b–1623a,
    1629b
    at Black Mountain College, 1715b
Cagney, James, 151a, 1466a
Cahan, Abraham, 33b, 1569a, 1570b, 1578a,
    1765b
Cahill, Holger, 15b, 1730b
Cain, Louis P., 1388a
Cairo conference, 654b
Calculus of Consent, The (Buchanan and
    Tullock), 1302a
Calder, Alexander, 1714a, 1729b
Calderón, Mauricio, 150a
Caldicott, Helen, 564a
California
    aircraft industry, 457a
    Proposition 13, 1326a
    taxpayers' revolt, 1326a
California Institute of Technology (Caltech),
    745a, 840b, 843a
Calkins, Mary Whiton, 878b, 1636a
Callahan, Harry, 1714b
Call It Sleep (H. Roth), 34a, 1443b, 1580b
Calutrons, 748a
    See also Cyclotrons
Cambodia, 586b, 587b
Cambodians, 97a, 186a
Camera Notes, 1697b
Camera Work, 1697b
Camp, Walter, 1767b
Campaign contributions, 296a, 318a
    corporate, 313b
    See also Political action committees (PAC)
Campaign management, 308a–b, 319a
Campanella, Roy, 1777b
Campbell, Bebe Moore, 155a

Campbell, J. E., 1672b
Campbell Soup Company, 1020b, 1131b
Camp Cejwin, 1576b
Camp David Accords (1977), 692a
Campeau, Robert, 1238a
Cana Conference, 1521a
Canada
    five industrial countries compared, 1990,
        1332a–b tab
    foreign policy, 572b
    free trade with, 733a, 1205b
*Canadian Journal of Economics and Political
    Science,* 1300a
Cancer, 968a,b, 969a, 970a
    nuclear weapons, 85b
    research, 746b–747a
"Cancer Alley," 76b
Cane (Toomer), 1597a
Canning industry, 1191a
Cannon, Joseph, 297b, 303a, 324b,
    355b–356a, 368b
Canseco, José, 1774b
Cantor, Eddie, 1025a, 1464b, 1755a
Cantors, 1571a
    School of Sacred Music, 1585b
    women, 1589a
Cantwell, Daniel, 1524a
Cape Hatteras National Seashore, 1373a
Cape Kennedy, 756a
Capital accumulation, 1155b
Capital gains taxes, 1317b, 1324b, 1328a
Capital intensive industries, 1150a–1154b
Capitalism
    advanced, 1487b
    and sports development, 1762a–b
    unavoidability of cycles, 1184b
    world economy, 726a
Capitalism, Socialism, and Democracy
    (Schumpeter), 1300b–1301a
Capital markets, **1209a–1241b**
Capital (Marx), 202b
Capital punishment. *See* Death penalty
Capital to labor ratio, 1127a–1128a,
    1130a,b, 1131a, 1134b, 1136a–b,
    1139a–b, 1145b, 1151b
Capone, Al, 51b, 172b
Capper, Arthur, 51a
Capra, Frank, 703b, 1467b, 1754a
Captive, The, 104a
Caraley, Demetrios, 609a
Carby, Hazel, 1597b
Cardinal Principles, 1805b, 1807b
Cardiovascular disease, 978b
Cardozo, Benjamin N., 382b, 390a–b tab,
    414a
Cardozo School of Law (Yeshiva U.), 1585b
Card punch machines, 809a–810a, *809b,*
    810b
Care and Feeding of Children, The (Holt),
    976a
Carey, E. Raymond, 1065a
Carey, Patrick W., *as contributor,*
    1511a–1537b
Caribbean
    American sphere of influence, 594b,
        720a–721b
    interventionism in, 676a, *677a–b*
Carleton College, 1821a
Carlos, John, 1782a
Carlson, Chester, 822a
Carmichael, Stokely, 1602b

Carnap, Rudolf, 1645b, 1649a–b
    Logical Structure [Aufbau] of the World, The,
        1648b
Carnegie, Andrew, 195a, 206b, 742b, 744b,
    862b, 1135a–b, 1215b, 1268b, 1727b
    Bellevue Hospital Medical College, 943b
    Midwest libraries, 48b
    peace movement, 542b, 543b
    U.S. Steel creation, 1218b–1219a
Carnegie, Dale, 234b, 1496a
    How to Win Friends and Influence People,
        1102a
    *Public Speaking and Influencing Men in
        Business,* 1102a
Carnegie, Hattie, 1790a
Carnegie Commission report on
    intercollegiate athletics (1929), 1768a
Carnegie Corporation, 31b, 173b, 493b,
    498a
    arts support, 1729a, 1732b
    Graduate Library School (University of
        Chicago), 496b
    grants, 32b
    industrial research, 842b–843a
Carnegie Endowment for International
    Peace, 493a, 545a, 546a, 575b
    legalist approach to war prevention, 553a
Carnegie Foundation, 491b, 943b, 1729b
    arts patronage, 1737b
    Public Broadcasting System, 1479b
Carnegie Foundation for the Advancement
    of Teaching, 991a, 1408b, 1409a,
    1821b, 1822a
Carnegie Hall (New York), 33a, 1611b,
    1621a
Carnegie Institute at Pittsburgh, 493a
Carnegie Institution in Washington, 33a,
    493a,b, 742a–743a, 943b
    Advisory Committee on Astronomy, 744a
    Eugenics Records Office funding, 864a
Carnegie (ship), 743a
Carnegie South Works, 1095b–1096a
Carosso, Vincent, 1229b
Carothers, Wallace H., 845a–b
Carpenter, Edward, 226b
Carrel, Alexis, 953a
Carrère and Hastings, 1671a–b
Carriers of the Dream Wheel (Niatum), 1456a
Carson, Gerald, 1049b
Carson, Johnny, 1477a
Carson, Rachel, 1371b, 1374a, 1375a–b,
    1380a,b
    Silent Spring, 1375a, 1378a
Carswell, G. Harrold, 391a–b tab, 391b
Carter, Betty, 1623b
Carter, Dan, 155b
Carter, Elliott, 1630a
Carter, Jimmy, 268a, 322b, 331b, 334b,
    346b–348a, *347b,* 445a, 820b, 1203b,
    1284a
    American Dream, 1170a
    blanket amnesty to draft evaders, 563a
    deregulation, 531b, 1259b
    energy conservation, 1171b–1172a, 1260a
    federalism, 443a–b
    foreign policy, 583a, 588a–b, 589b
    hostages release, 412a
    labor unions, 314a
    Middle East, 692a
    nuclear disarmament, 563b
    presidential elections, 336a–b tab

Program for Better Jobs and Incomes, 488a
  regulation, 527b, 1174a
  tax reform, 1326a–b
  vetoes, 347a tab
  welfare reform, 488a
  white majority, 74b
  world economy, 730b
Carter bonds, 1258b, 1262a
Cartoons, 1484a
  racially coded scripts in, 151a–b
  See also Comic books
Carty, J. J., 837b, 841b, 843a
Caruso, Enrico, 1470b, 1611b, *1612a*
Case Western Reserve University, 506b
Casey, William, 617a
Cash, Johnny, 73b
Cashin, Bonnie, 1790b
Cassatt, Alexander Johnston, 1673a
Cassatt, Mary, 1694b, 1704a
Cassell, Gustav, 1299b
Cassini, Oleg, 1790b
Casson, Herbert N., 256b
Castelli, Jim, 1492b, 1533a,b
Castle, W. E., 869a
Castle Clinton, 36b
Castro, Fidel, 583a, 788a
Catcher in the Rye (Salinger), 1451a
Catch-22 (Heller), 1452a
Caterpillar Tractor, 1141b
Cathell, D. W., 941a
Cather, Willa, 10a,b, 52a, 1441b, 1457b, 1458a
  Death Comes for the Archbishop, 1441b
  My Antonia, 1441b
Catholic Action, 1521a
Catholic colleges and universities, 1517a, 1520b, 1522b, 1528a, 1529a, 1832b
  enrollment, 1528b
Catholic Education Association, 1515a
Catholic Hospital Association, 1515a
Catholic Left, 1529a
Catholic Press Association, 1515a
Catholic Relief Services, 1520b
Catholics and Catholicism, **1511a–1537b,** 1562b
  arts, 1726a
  Catholic Third Plenary Council, 1808a
  Congress, 365b
  Eastern rite, 1514a, 1528a
  evolution, 859b
  film industry, 1467b
  foreign policy, 575a, 576b
  geographical distribution, 1511b, 1512a–b tab
  immigration, 254b
  institutions, 32a–b
  journals, 1517a, 1519b, 1523b, 1524a, 1525a,b
  Neuhaus, Richard, 1507b
  piety, 1523a–b
  population, 1492a–b, 1498b, 1511b–1512a, 1520b, 1527b
  post-Vatican II, 1527a–1535b
  press, 1533b
  Progressive Era, 1514b–1516a
  radicalism, 1517b
  schools, 1807b, 1815a
  traditionalists, 1533b
Catholics United for the Faith, 1533b

Catholic University of America, 1522a,b, 1528b, 1531b
Catholic War Council, 1515a
Catholic Worker, The, 1519a, 1520a
Catholic Worker (Day), 282b
Catholic Worker movement, 282b, 1517b, 1519a
Catholic World, 1519b
Catonsville trial (1968), 1529b
Catskill mountains, 1578b–1579a
Catt, Carrie Chapman, 118a, 546b
Cattell, James McKeen, 880b, 881a, 1823b
Cattle, 87b–88a
  open-range system, 1362a
  ranching industry, 81a, 87b–88a, 312a, 433b
CATV (Community Antenna Television). *See* Cable television
Causes of Evolution, The (Haldane), 868b
Cavell, Stanley, 1654b, 1656a
Cayley, George, 767a
Cayton, Horace, 213a, 925b, 929b
CBN, 824b
CBO. *See* Congressional Budget Office (CBO)
CBS. *See* Columbia Broadcasting System (CBS)
CCC. *See* Civilian Conservation Corps (CCC)
CDC. *See* Centers for Disease Control (CDC)
CEA. *See* Council of Economic Advisers (CEA)
Celestial Seasonings tea, 1031b
Celibacy, 1512a, 1527a, 1531a, 1534a
Celler, Emmanuel, 1281a
Censorship
  arts, 1708a–b, 1740a
  entertainment, 1467a–1468b
  movies, 1580a
  print media, 1483a
  religion, 1521a
  television, 1478b
Census
  and gender, 136a–b tab
  Midwest, 41a
  and race, 135b, 136a–b tab
  regional definitions, 25a, 27a
  suburban classifications, 468b
Census of 1870, 7b
Census of 1880, 7b
Census of 1900, 162a
Census of 1910, 454b
Census of 1990, 191a
Census of Manufactures, 1137a
Center for Advanced Study in Theology, 871a
Center for the Study of Responsive Law, 1031a
Centers for Disease Control (CDC), 38a
CENTO. *See* Central Treaty Organization (CENTO)
Central America, interventionism in, 676a, *677a–b*
Central Conference of American Rabbis, 1566a
Central Intelligence Agency (CIA), 580a, 581a, 587b, 608b, 609a,b, 614a, 687b
  Nixon, 442a
  sponsorship of cultural activities, 710b–711a

use of foundations, 504a
Central Park (New York), 1744b, *1745a–b*
Central place theory, 16b–17a
Central Railroad of New Jersey, 1217b
Central Treaty Organization (CENTO), 610a, 689b
Central Valley Project, 90b
Century, 1359b, 1481b
Cerebrovascular disease, 968a, 970a
Cermak, Anton, 172b, 300b
Cervantes, Lorna Dee, 1456b
Cervantes, Miguel de, 1436b
Cessna Airmaster, 776a
CETA. *See* Comprehensive Employment and Training Administration
Cézanne, Paul, 1697b, 1698a, 1705a
Chadwick, George Whitefield, 1612b
Chafe, William, 215b
Chafee, Zechariah, Jr., 416a
Chagall, Marc, 1710a
Challener, Richard, 594b
Challenge of Peace, The (1983), 1529b
Challenge of Waste, The (Chase), 1027a
Challenger shuttle, 790b–791a, *791a–b*
Challenge to Liberty, The (Hoover), 282a
Chamberlain, John, 1715b
Chamberlain, Owen, 750a
Chamberlin, Edward, 1297a,b
Chamber music, 1728b, 1730a
Chamber of Commerce, 310b, 313b, 318b, 1280a
  creation, 309b
  and social security, 483b
Chan, Charlie, 1466a
Chandler, Albert "Happy," 1777b
Chandler, Alfred D., Jr., 208b, 833a, 838b, 1042a–b, 1052b, 1092b, 1101b, 1384a
  as contributor, 1127a–1154b
  Visible Hand, The, 197b, 1042a, 1158b, 1302b
Chandler, Raymond, 1363a
Chaney, James, 153b
Changing Face of Inequality, The (Zunz), 206a
Chang-Lin Tien, 1835b
Chanute, Octave, 767b
CHAOS, 616b
Chapin, Stuart, 923a,b, 924a
Chapin (school), 1808b
Chaplin, Charlie, 1465b, 1754a
Chapman, Harriet Alice, 1641a, 1805a
Chapters on the Theory and History of Banking (Dunbar), 1291a
Charismatics
  Catholics, 1533a
  Protestants, 1491b, 1493a, 1499a
Charity regulation (1972), 1000a
Charles, Ray, 1631a
Charleston, Oscar, *1771a–b*
Charlotte Observer, 64a
Chase, Gilbert, 1610a
Chase, Jeanne, 1670b
Chase, Lucia, 1727b
Chase, Stuart, 458a, 1026a, 1027a, 1298b
Chase, William Merritt, 1694b, 1698b
Chase Manhattan Bank, 1028b
Châteauesque style, 1669a
Chautauqua, 48b
Chávez, César, 95a, 149a
Chavez, Joe, 149a
Checks and balances, 358a, 359b, 361a–b
Cheever, John, 34b

Chemical Foundation, 840a
Chemical industry, 28a, 840a–b, 847b, 850b,
        1127a–b, 1137b, 1138b–1139a, 1142b,
        1143a–b, 1144a, 1145b–1148a, 1160b,
        1164a
    computer controls, 1150b–1151b
    Germany, 835a, 840a
    Midwest, 59a
    processes, 1130b, 1132b, 1134b, 1141b
    tariffs, 1248a
    technology transfer, 1249b
    World War I, 1191a
Chemical warfare, 850a
    ban on, 552a
    weapon testing, 950a
Chemical Warfare Service, 840a
Chemical Weapons Convention (1993),
        564b, 565b
Chemotherapies, 977a, 978b
Cheney, Lynne, 189b
Cheney, Sheldon, 1702b
Chernobyl accident, 565a
Cherokee, 134b
    schools, 1810b
Chesler, Phyllis, 912a
Chesnutt, Charles, 129a, 1594b
    writing in dialect, 1596a
Chetverikov, Sergei, 869a
Chevalier, Maurice, 1620b
Chevrolet, 1058b, 1061a
Chevron, 1737a
Chicago, 451b, 452a, 456b
    electric power system, 1335a
    immigrants, 212a
    railroad and development, 1051a
    school segregation, 1810a
    skyscrapers, 1674a–b, *1674b*
    suburbs, 460a, 467a
    working class evolution in, 205b
Chicago, Judy, 1719b
Chicago Board of Trade, 1681a
Chicago Civic Federation, 1640b
Chicago Daily News, 55b
Chicago Defender, 67a
Chicago Herald, 621b
Chicago Imagists, 1719a
Chicago philosophers, 1641a
Chicago Pneumatic Tool, 1136b
Chicago school of architecture, 1675a–b,
        1676a, 1680a
Chicago school of sociology, 173b, 222b,
        922b
    films study, 1484b
Chicago Tribune, 55b, 466b
Chicago White Stockings, 1762b
Chicano movement, 95a
Chicano Narratives (Saldívar), 1456b
Chicanos
    La Raza Unida, 266b
    literature, 1456b
Chickasaw schools, 1810b
Child and the Curriculum, The (Dewey), 1805a
Child care, 225a
    on feminist agenda, 120b, 121a
    hygiene, 976a
    on national policy agenda, 1205a
    products, 1033b
    services, 1033b
Child-centered pedagogy, 1805a
Child-Centered School, The (Rugg and
        Shumaker), 1808a

Child labor
    Hammer v. Dagenhart (1918), 379b, 408a,
        432a
    laws, 49a, 65a, 122a
    Progressive reform, 224b
    Supreme Court and, 406b, 408a
Child Labor Amendment, 408b
Children
    cartoons, 1477a
    child study movement, 226a
    clothing, 1795a
    impact of divorce on, 236b–237a
    poverty, 237a–b
    rights in family law, 240a
*Children of Light and the Children of Darkness,
        The* (Niebuhr), 284a
Children's Bureau, 122a, 237b, 477b, 975b,
        976a, 1804b
Children's Division of the American
        Humane Association, 237b
Childs, William R., *as contributor,*
        1331a–1355b
Chin, Vincent, 156a
China
    Americanization and youthful protests,
        712a
    five industrial countries compared, 1990,
        1332a–b tab
    foreign policy, 581a
    intervention in Korea, 658b
    Open Door policy, 571a–b, 572a, 599b,
        678a, 679b, 720b
    United States and, 616b, 686a
    See also People's Republic of China
China Medical Board, 697b
China Men (Kingston), 1456b
Chinese Americans, 96a–b
Chinese Exclusion Act (1882), 96a, 135a,
        163b, 165a–b tab
Chinese immigrants, 186a
    in nineteenth century, 134b
    religion, 1541b
Chinese Must Go!, The, 135a
Ch'ing (Qing) dynasty, 679b
Chipkin, Israel, 1577b
Chippewa, 50b
Chiropractic, 1417b
Chisholm, Roderick, 1657a
Choate (school), 1808b
Choctaw schools, 1810b
Chodorow, Nancy, 913a, 929a
Chogyam Trungpa, 1556a
Cholera, 959b
Chomsky, Noam, 892b
Chopin, Kate, 1438b
    Awakening, The, 1438b, 1458a
Chotzinoff, Samuel, 1586b
Christ, Carol, 1506a
Christian Americanization, 170a
Christian Broadcasting Network (CBN),
        824b
Christian Century, 287b, 1501b
Christian Coalition, 1492a, 1507a,
        1740a
Christian Family Movement, 1521a
"Christianity and Democracy" (Dewey),
        277b
Christianity and Liberalism (Machen), 1500a,
        1501a
Christianity and the Social Crisis
        (Rauschenbusch), 275a

Christianizing the Social Order
        (Rauschenbusch), 275a, 478a
Christian Left, 1497a
Christian Right, 188b, 1492a
Christian Science, 881b, 1540a, 1542b,
        1544a–1545a
Christian Science Monitor, 1545a
Christian Spiritual Church, 1543a
Christian View of Science and Scripture, The
        (Ramm), 871b
Christ in Concrete (Di Donato), 34a
Christman, Elisabeth, 118a
Christman, Margaret, 1788b
Christopher movement, 1523b
Chronic diseases
    as causes of death, 967b
    liver disease, 970a
Chrysler Building (New York), 1681a,
        1682a
Chrysler Corporation, 46b, 57b, 1140a–b,
        1284a
    tank sales, 313a
Church
    Catholic attendance, 1523a, 1527b, 1533b
    link with colleges, 1819a, 1820a
    membership in Midwest, 41a
    membership in South, 66a
Church, Frank, 588b
Churchill, Winston, 577b, 635b, 636a,
        648b, 1252a
    at Argentia Bay, 602a
    Iron Curtain speech, 579a
    postwar organization, 556b
    radio broadcasts, 808b
    at Yalta, *606a–b,* 687a
Church of Divine Science, 1540a
Church of Jesus Christ of Latter-day Saints.
        See Mormons
Church of Religious Science, 1540a
Church of the Higher Life, 1546a
CIA. *See* Central Intelligence Agency (CIA)
Ciba-Geigy, 1249b
CIO. *See* Congress of Industrial
        Organizations (CIO)
Circulation crises. *See* financial panics
Circuses, 1461b, 1463a
Cirrhosis, 970a
Citibank, 1255a
Cities
    administration, 64a
    African American migrations, 146b
    African American women, 108a–b
    artists, 1701a–1702a
    beautification, 65a
    black employment, 66b
    black mayors, 74b–75a
    crime, 51b
    decay, 51b, 457b–458a, 463b
    decentralization, 451a, 467b–469b
    Eastern region, 34b, 35a, *35a–b*
    versus farming, 51a–b
    foundations, 504b
    growth at turn of the century, 1334a
    improvement, 47a
    industry, 27b–28a
    infrastructure, 1334a, 1337a
    managers, 49b, 64a, 299b
    Midwest, 43b, 47a–48a, 49b
    migrations to, 1070b
    municipal ownership of services, 1334a
    planning, 47a, 454a, 496a

population by race, 147a–b tab
population in ten largest metropolitan
    areas in the U.S., 1950 and 1980,
    462a–b tab
population of ten largest in the U.S.,
    1950 and 1980, 461a–b tab
population percentages, 89a–b
poverty, 504b
revitalization, 467b
riots, 1478b
road development, 1337b
segregated housing patterns, 168a
slums, 168a
and suburbs, 451a–470b
twenty largest in the U.S., 1900, 452a–b
    tab
underclasses, 1087b
West, 81a, 95b
See also Urban renewal
Citizens' councils, 73a
City, The (Park), 17b
City and Country School (Greenwich
    Village), 1808a
City and suburb, **451a–470b**
See also Cities
City Center (New York), 1734b
City College of New York, 1827a
    basketball team, 1776a
City Homes Association (Chicago), 453b
City of Memphis, 625a
City Trenches (Katznelson), 203b–204a
City University of New York, 32b, 506b
Civic humanism and taxation, 1311a
Civic Repertory Theater, 1727b
Civic values, 1310a
Civil Aeronautics Authority. *See* Civil
    Aeronautics Board (CAB)
Civil Aeronautics Board (CAB), 820b,
    1168b, 1342a
Civilian Conservation Corps (CCC), 1073b,
    1369a
    education programs, 1808b
    traditional family and, 122b
Civilian Public Service, 555b
Civilization in the United States (Stearns),
    279a
Civil Liberties Bureau. *See* American Civil
    Liberties Union (ACLU)
Civil liberties lobby, 413b
Civil Liberties Unit (Justice Department),
    413b
Civil religion, 1507a–1508b
    Protestants, 1492b
Civil rights, 436b–437b, 440b, 442a, 444b,
    447b
    foundations and, 508b
    state constitutional law, 392a
Civil Rights Act (1964), 74a–b, 180b, 266b,
    288b, 527b, 529a, 1602b, 1813a
    hospital desegregation, 1003a
    litigation under, 394b
    sex discrimination, 120a
Civil Rights Act (1968), 394b
Civil Rights Act for the Handicapped. *See*
    Rehabilitation Act (1973)
Civil rights legislation, 342a
Civil rights movement, 76a, 266a,b, 267a,
    339b, 365a, 516b, 1498a
    African American women in, 118b–119a
    arts, 1738a
    Brown and, 388a

Catholics, 1524b
    civil disobedience, 74a
    education, 1812b
    health care delivery, 1002b
    influence on sports, 1777b
    Jews, 1584a, 1590b
    Kennedy and, 342a
    Midwest, 50a, 58b, 59a
    nonviolence, 74a
    political art, 1719b
    political ideas, 287b
    religion, 1504b, 1505a–b
    sit-in demonstrations, 74a
    sources, 287a
    South, 71b, 73a–75a
    Southern identity, 77a–b
    television, 1478b, 1479a
    unions' contributions to, 155a
    West, 95a–b
Civil service, 49a, 295b, 299a, 326b, 361a,
    437b
    lack of, and welfare, 1071b
    reform, 309a
Civil War, 652a
    emergency taxation, 1311b–1312a
    foreign policy, 570a–b
    interpretation by Turner, 8b–9a
    pensions, 476b–477a
Civil Works Administration (CWA), 1073b,
    1729b
Claiborne, Liz, 1791a
Clancy, Tom, 1482b
Clancy, William, 1525b
Clan na Gael, 1748a
Clansman, The (Dixon), 1593a
Clark, Austin H., 874a
Clark, Champ, 356a
Clark, David, 69a–b
Clark, Edward, 1044b
Clark, Grenville, 558b
Clark, John Bates, 919a, 1290a–b, 1295a,
    1296a, 1297a
Clark, John Maurice, 1298b
Clark, Mark, 662b
Clark, Reuben, 682b
Clark, Tom C., 390a–b tab
Clark, William, 1048a
Clark, William Andrews, Jr., 1726a
Clark Amendment (1976), 585a
Clarke, Caspar Purdon, 1696a
Clarke, Edward, 902a
Clarke, Herbert L., 1613b
Clarke, John H., 390a–b tab
Clarke, Kenny, 1623b
Clark University, 32b
Class, 25a, **195a–220**
    biological basis for differences, 868b
    clothing, 1785a–1788b
    consciousness, 195b, 308b
    consumption patterns, 115b
    ethnicity, 164b
    gender, 106b
    income levels, *216a–b*
    legislation, 516b, 524a
    leisure, 115b
    race, 139a, 930b
    reform organizations, 299a
    Southern education, 64a
    voting behavior, 300a
Class and Caste in a Southern Town (Dollard),
    927a

Class (Fussell), 1785b
Classic Comics, 1483b
Classic Point of View, The (Cox), 1696a
Classics Illustrated, 1483b
Class Structure of the Advanced Societies, The
    (Giddens), 207a
Clay, Cassius. *See* Ali, Muhammad
Clayton Antitrust Act (1914), 520a, 521a,
    1271a, 1272b, 1314a
    economists and, 1295a
    as result of the Pujo hearings, 1223b
Clayton & Dubilier, 1236a
Clean Air Act (1970), 528a
Clean Air Amendments (1970), 1377a
Clean Water Act, 1377a,b
Clemenceau, Georges, *598a–b*
Clement, Frank, 72b
Clerical work, 1103b–1106a, 1107a, 1118a,
    1123a
    change in sex composition, 1106a
    growth of, 1105a
    internal contradictions, 1116a
    skyscrapers and, 1674a
    women, 198a
Cleveland, 451b
    financial crisis, 464b
    during Great Depression, 457b
    race riots, 180b
    Shaker Heights, 454b, 459a, 466b
    suburbs, 458a
Cleveland Foundation, 495a
Cleveland Trust Company, 495a
Clifford, Clark, 579b, 580a
Clifford, James, 291a
Clinical psychology, 895b
Clinical research ethics, 950a–b
Clinical trials, 948b
Clinton, Bill, 188b, 273a, 331b, *351b,*
    351b–352b, 1285b
    communications technology, 799a, 801a
    Eastern region, 30b
    foreign trade, 1263a
    Graham, Billy, 1504a
    health care reform, 987a–b
    industrial research, 854a
    presidential elections, 303a–306b, 336a–b
        tab
    religion, 1492a
    taxation, 1328b
    vetoes, 347a tab
    White House telephones, 800b
    white majority, 74b
Clinton, Hillary Rodham, 121a, 510a, 987a
Close, Chuck, 1718a
Closing of the American Mind, The (Bloom),
    1836a
Clothing and appearance, 1020b,
    1785a–1801b
    See also Apparel industry; Fashion
    industry
Cloward, Richard, 1080a, 1082b
Clower, Robert, 1303a
Club Med, 1033a
Club of Rome, 1376a
CNN. *See* Cable News Network (CNN)
Coady, Robert, 1703a
Coal industry, 27b, 1024a, 1135a, 1164b
    coal production in the U.S., U.K., and
        Germany,1870-1930, *1387a–b*
    coal towns, 29b
    comeback in energy mix, 1347b

Coal industry (*cont.*)
  Gillette syndrome, 87b
  Great Depression, 1161b
  South, 63b
Coal Question, The (Jevons), 1387a–b
Coase, Ronald, 1301b
Coast and Geodetic Survey, 742b
Coast Survey, 741a
Coats, A. W., 1299a
Coca, Imogene, 1578b
Coca-Cola, 700b, 1059a
  advertising material distributed in 1913,
    1056a–b tab
  distribution system, *1038a–b,* 1039a
  market power, 1054a
  mass marketing, 1045b, 1053a–b
  penetration pricing, 1052a
  product line in 1993, 1038a tab
  product variety, 1040a
  railroad and sales, 1051b–1052a
Code-breaking. See Cryptanalysis
Cody, Buffalo Bill, 83b, 697b
Coffin, Charles, 1137b
Coffin, James, 741a
Coffin, William Sloane, Jr., 1505b
Cogley, John, 1524a, 1525b
Cognitive psychologists, 892b–893a
Cohan, George M., 1614a
Cohen, Andy, 173a, 1766b
Cohen, Arthur A., 1589a,b
Cohen, Elliot, 1581b, 1586b
Cohen, Gerson, 1588b–1589a
Cohen, Lizabeth, 175a, 260b, 261b
  as contributor, 101a–127b
  Making a New Deal, 206a
Cohen, Morris R., 1579b, 1644b–1645a,
    1652b
Cohen, "Nudie," 1792b
Cohen, Wesley, 852b
Cohen, Wilbur, 485a, 486a,b
Cohen, William, 397b
Cohn, Harry, 1580a, 1752b
COINTELPRO, 616b
Colander, David, 1306b
Cold War, 284a, 687a–688b
  aircraft industry, 462b, 779b–784b, 796b
  and American intellectual life, 501a
  and the arts, 1713b, 1735b
  Catholics, 1520a–1526b
  civil liberties, 614b
  consensus, 615b
  corporatism, 687b
  displacement of Fair Deal, 334b
  dissolution of Jewish Left, 1586a
  domestic policy, 687b
  Eastern region economy, 28b
  end of, 349b
  foreign policy, 578b–584a, 589a
  higher education, 1829a
  immigrants and immigration, 178a,b
  Korea, 654b
  militarization, 612a, 688b–691a
  National Defense Education Act
    (NDEA), 615a
  national highway system, 615a
  national security state, 333a–b
  research funding, 849a–851b, 850a–b,
    1424b, 1425a
  responsibility for, 607b
  space program, 615a
  strains on civil-military relations, 610b

  traditional gender roles, 104b
  United World Federalists' decline, 558b
  and Vietnam War, 615b–616a
Cole, Leon J., 861b
Coleman, James S., 933b, 934b, 935a–b
Coleman, Jon, *as contributor,* 81a–99b
Coleman, Ornette, 1624a
Collapse of Evolution (Townsend), 861a
Collected Poems (Stevens), 1449b
Collective security, 679b
College and University Finance (Arnott),
    1409b
College Equal Suffrage League, 1823a
College football, 1767a–b, 1768a
  1929 Carnegie Report, 1768a, 1776a
  games as entertainment, 1745b
  1920s, *1767a–b*
Colleges
  buildings, 36b
  community colleges, 1827b, 1836b
  Eastern region, 32a–b, 32b, 36b
  land-grant. See Morrill land-grant
    colleges
  Negro colleges, 1824b
  women, 1764b, 1824b, 1831b
  See also Catholic colleges and universities;
    Liberal arts colleges; Universities
"College Sport and Motherhood," 1765a
College sports
  integrated teams, 1771b
  unequal financial support for women,
    1780b
  at women's colleges, 1764b
  See also College football
Collier, Jane, 933a
Collier, John, 92a, 1810b
Collier's, 703b, 1482b
Collins, Michael, 788b
Collins, Randall, 932a
Collyer, Joseph, 7a
Colonialism, 726a
Colonial musical culture, 1611a–b
Colorado Fuel and Iron Company, 86b
Colorado River, 91b
  hydroelectric power, 85a
Colored American, 1594a, 1595a
Color of a Great City, The (Dreiser), 33b
COLOR plans, 595a
Coltrane, John, 1630b
Columbia, S.C., 118b
Columbia Basin Project, 1026a
  hydroelectric power, 85a,b
Columbia Broadcasting System (CBS), 18a,
    262a, 807a, 1472b, 1473a, 1475b,
    1755a
  cable television, 1480a
  news, 1478a
  radio shows, 1025a
  revenues, 1474a
  sports, 1774a, 1776b
  television, 1476a
  world news format, 1473b
Columbia Pictures, 1469a, 1754a
  foreign ownership, 715a
  Japanese investment, 1263a
  television, 1476b
Columbia Records, 1471a
Columbia School of Mines, 1389b
Columbia University, 1821a
  coeducation, 1824b–1825a
  Dewey, John, move to, 1641a

  general education courses, 1831a
  law school, 31a
  Office of Radio Research, 1485a
  student violence, 1830a
  Teachers College, 1574b
Columbus Platform, 1582b
Colwin, Laurie, 34a
Colyer, W. T., 702a
Comedies
  radio, 1473a
  situation (sitcoms), 1477a
  slapstick, 1462a
Comic books, 1481a, 1482a
  censorship, 1468a, 1483b
  publishing, 1483a
  violence, 1483b
Comics Code Authority, 1483b
Comic strips, 708a
Cominform, 687b
Coming Crisis of Western Sociology, The
    (Gouldner), 931a
Coming of Age in Samoa (Mead), 908b
Coming of Post-industrial Society, The (Bell),
    208b
Comintern, 682a
Commander in Chief
  Lincoln, 402b
  president as, 326a
Commentary, 1586b
Commerce, Department of, 1250a, 1254a,
    1280a, 1281a,b
  under Hoover, 1275a
  Industrial Economics Division, 1322a
Commerce Clause
  congressional power under, 382a, 384b
  and economic regulation, 379a
  Supreme Court interpretation, 379a,
    402a, 405b, 408b, 409b
Commercial banks
  foreign branches, 1249a
  and investment banking, 1222a, 1226a
  and long-term securities, 1213b
Commercial broadcasting, 1478a
Commercial entertainment, 1461b 1463a
  home, 1470b
Commercial insurance companies
  group hospitalization insurance, 994b
  health insurance, 999b
Commercial nationalism, 266a, 268a
Commercial power, 516a
Commission on Country Life, 51a
Commission on Immigration Reform, 189a
Commission on Industrial Relations,
    1272b
Commission on Intergovernmental
    Relations, 438b–439a
Commission on Law and Social Action,
    1584a
Commission on Private Philanthropy and
    Public Needs, 505b
Commission on the Humanities, 1736a
Commission on the Reorganization of the
    Executive Branch. See Hoover
    Commission
Commission to Study the Bases of a Just
    and Durable Peace, 556b
Commission to Study the Organization of
    Peace, 556b
Committee against the Extension of Race
    Prejudice in the Church, 1517b
Committee for Cultural Freedom, 282b

Committee for Economic Development, 499b, 1279a, 1324a
Committee for Industrial Organization, 1108a
Committee for Medical Research, 945a
Committee for Non-Violent Action, 559a
Committee of One Hundred Thousand, 281b
Committee of Ten, 1805b
Committee on Business and Government Relations, 1280a,b
Committee on Classification of Personnel, 881a
Committee on Economic Security, 997a, 479a–480b, 481a
Committee on Foreign Investment in the United States, 1259a
Committee on Immigration and Naturalization, 864b
Committee on Interracial Cooperation, 65a
Committee on Maternal Health, 228a
Committee on Medical Research, 1000b
Committee on Public Information (CPI), 171a, 173b, 257a, 407a, 597a, 626a, 698a
    Division of Films, 698b
Committee on Social Trends, 496b
Committee on the Bill of Rights, 413b
Committee on the Costs of Medical Care, 992b–993a
Committee on the Federal Constitution, 380a
Committee on the Present Danger, 588a
Committee on the Reorganization of Secondary Education, 1805b, 1807b
Committee to Defend America by Aiding the Allies, 55b, 176b, 635a
Committee to Re-Elect the President (CREEP), 312b–313a
Common Cause, 120b
Common Council for American Unity, 176a
Commoner, Barry, 1374b, 1375a, 1376a, 1380a
    Losing Ground, 1375a
Common Faith, A (Dewey), 277b
Common Ground, 176a
Common Market, 692a, 725b, 726a,b, 727a, 732b, 1253b, 1254b–1255a, 1256b, 1257b, 1262b
    American research laboratories in Europe, 853b
    foreign policy, 589b
    value-added tax, 1326a
Commons, John R., 137a,b, 274b, 1095b, 1296a–b, 1303b, 1305b
    History of Labor in the U.S., 204b
Common Sense (Paine), 918a
Commonweal, 1517a, 1519a, 1525b
Commonwealth Fund, 495a–b, 498a, 509b
    American law, 495b
    health programs, 974b
    medical research, 943b
Commonwealth government, 49a
Commonwealth of Independent States, 1205a
Communications, 837b, 1281a
    deregulation, 1283b
    early mergers, 1218a
    international investments, 1262a
    regulation, 433a

standardization, 799b
studies, 818a
systems, 1128a,b, 1130a, 1148a, 1155a
technology, 799a–829B
Communism
    after World War II, 1253a
    Catholics, 1520b, 1523b, 1525a–1526a
    foreign policy, 575a, 576a, 578a,b–581a
    Jews, 1568b, 1584b
    world economy, 725b
Communist Information Bureau. See Cominform
Communist Party, 175a, 176a
    black writers in, 1600b–1601a
    racism within, 1601a
Communitarians, 290b
Community action programs, 466a, 1081a
Community and Society (Toennies), 918b
Community Antenna Television (CATV). See Cable television
Community Arts Project, 1738b
Community Chests, 509a
Community foundations, 495a
Compact disks (CD), 1031b, 1034a, 1470b, 1471a
"Comparison of the Sexes'" (Hollingworth), 903a
Competition and Entrepreneurship (Kirzner), 1304a
Composers, American, 1629b
    music teaching and, 1621b–1622a
Comprehensive Child Development Bill, 123b
Comprehensive Employment and Training Act (1972), 1736b
    under Reagan, 1740a
Comprehensive Employment and Training Administration (CETA), 1085a
Comprehensive Environmental Response, Compensation, and Liability Act (1980), 1377b
Comprehensive General Plan for the Development of the Northeastern Illinois Counties Area, 20a
Compton, Arthur H., 842a, 848a
Computer Aided Design (CAD), 1151b–1152b
Computer and communications technology, 799a–829b, 1120a
    industrial automation, 1114a–b
Computers, 28a–b, 1031b–1032a, 1148a–1152a
    electronic, 809a, 810a,b–814b
    hackers, 800b, 819b, 823a
    home, 823a
    languages, 814b, 1150a
    mainframe, 823b
    memory, 812a–b
    microcomputers. See Personal computers
    minicomputers, 821b
    networks, 814a, 821b, 822b–823a, 827a–b
    operating systems, 826b
    programmers, 821b
Computer Sciences Corporation, 1150b
COMSAT, 1349a
Comte, Auguste, 918a, 1647b
Conant, James B., 751a, 837a, 846b, 1655b–1656a, 1811b, 1832a
    American High School Today, 1812a
Concerto for Cootie (Ellington), 1620b
Concerts, 1461b

training, 1738a
Concorde SST, 792b
Condit, Carl, 1685b
Condition of Postmodernity, The (Harvey), 1454b, 1455a
Cone Mills, 1065a
Confederation of British Industry (Britain), 311a
Conference of Chief Justices, 440b
Conference of the Presidents of Major Jewish Organizations (1955), 1584a
Conference on Jewish Relations, 1579b
Conference on Science, Philosophy and Religion in their Relation to the Democratic Way of Life, 1583b
Conference on Security and Cooperation in Europe (CSCE), 692b
Confessions of Nat Turner, The (Styron), 1603a
Confucianism, 1541b
Congregationalists
    liberalism, 1494a, 1500b
    population percentages, 1492b, 1493a
Congregation for Doctrine (Roman Catholic), 1528b
Congregation Kehillath Jeshurun, 1575b
Congress, 355a–376b
    budget deficit, 1174b
    budget process, 358a–360b, 371a–b
    civil rights, 440b
    committees, 314b–315a, 359a, 360a, 361a–b, 364a, 367b–370b, 372b, 374b, 771b See also House of Representatives: committees; Senate: committees
    decentralization of power, 357a–b, 360b, 370a–b, 372a, 373a
    energy conservation, 1260a
    expanded role, 529b
    Export-Import Banks, 1250b
    federal authority, 431a
    foreign investments, 1259a
    foreign policy, 580a–b, 585a, 587a, 588a
    foreign trade, 1248b
    income taxes, 1323a
    legislative powers delegated to executive, 528b
    party unity, 307b–308a
    political careers, 356a, 357a
    professionalization of, 323b
    public housing, 458b
    relative dominance in 19th century, 324b
    seniority system, 298a, 300b, 303a, 306a, 313a, 314b–315a, 356a, 365a, 368a
    tariffs, 1250a
    television investigation, 1479a
    voice votes, 312b
    Watergate. See Watergate affair
    Watergate babies, 313a, 314b
Congress against Itself (Davidson and Oleszek), 361b
"Congress and the Quest for Power" (Dodd), 356b
Congress for Cultural Freedom, 286b, 705a, 711a
Congress Hall, 37a
Congressional Black Caucus, 1378a
Congressional Budget and Impoundment Control Act (1974), 315a, 359b, 360a, 530a, 1326a
Congressional Budget Office (CBO), 315a–b, 359b, 530a, 1087a, 1326a

Congressional Government (Wilson), 322a, 355b, 361a
Congressional oversight, 360b–363b, 373a
Congressional power
  political limitations, 411b
  restricted by President, 413a
  restricted by Supreme Court, 404b
  spending restricted by Supreme Court, 409b
Congressional Reorganization Act (1946), 333b
Congress of Industrial Organizations (CIO), 69a–b, 310b
  desegregation, 155a
  ethnic workers, 175a
  merger with AFL, 1110a
  women in, 109b
Congress of Mothers, 226b
Congress of Racial Equality, 178a
Congress Weekly, 1576b
Conklin, Edwin Grant, 861b, 863a,b, 864b
Connally, Tom, 556b
Connally Hot Oil Act (1935), 1398a
Connaught, Duke of, *627a–b*
Connecticut Yankee in King Arthur's Court, A (Twain), 1438a
Connell, Francis J., 1522a
Connors, Jimmy, 1775a
Conover, Willis, 706b
Conrad, Frank, 1755a
Conrad, Joseph, 1446a
Conscientious objectors
  exemption rates, 556a tab
  historical peace churches, 541b, 549a
  sources, 549a–b
  World War I, 597a
  World War II, 555b
Consciousness-raising, 120b
Conservation and the environment, 58b–59a, **1357a–1382b**
  See also Environment and environmentalism
"Conservation of Races, The" (Du Bois), 1595a
Conservative Christians, 1491b, 1498a–1501b, 1503a–1504b
Conservative ideas, 289b
  pro-family movement in 1970s, 239b
  resurgence, 290a
Conservative Judaism, 1574b–1575a, 1585b, 1590b
  translation of prayerbook, 1588a
  women, 1588b–1589a
Conservative Judaism, 1587a
Conservative party (Britain), 295a, 303b
Conservatories of music, 1612b
Consolidated Vultee Aircraft Corporation, 70b, 457a
Constitution, Amendments, 429a, 434b
  Eighteenth, 172a, 309a
  Fifteenth, 403a, 404a, 429a
  First, 417a, 447a, 1521b, 1522a
  Fourteenth, 214b, 403a, 404a, 415a, 429a, 435b–436a, 441b, 444a
  Nineteenth, 295a, 309a
  Seventeenth, 356a
  Sixteenth, 1313a, 1314b
  Tenth, 432a, 434a, 435a, 443b–444a, 448a
  Thirteenth, 403a, 404a, 414a, 429a
Constitution, United States, **401a–425b,** 448a

budget process, 360b
  and limited government, 515a–b
  New Deal, 434b
  Progressive amendments, 256a
  and public administration, 515a
  and role of the courts, 380a
  taxation, 1311a–b
Constitutional Government in the United States (Wilson), 428a
Constitutional Reform and Effective Government (Sundquist), 363b
Constitutional Union, 117a
Construction industry
  house, *43a–b*
  internal combustion engine, 1141b
Construction Night (Ault), 1701b
Consultants on Hospitalization, 995b–996a
Consumer Advisory Board, 1026b
  See also National Recovery Administration
Consumer credit, 1028b–1029a, 1031a, 1032a–b
  See also Credit cards
Consumer Credit Protection Act (1968), 1031a
Consumerism, 1338b
Consumer movement, 1026b–1027a
  World War II, 1031a
Consumer products, 1020b, 1031b
  cultural influence, 708a
  expensive, 1022a
  safety, 1377b
Consumer Products Safety Commission, 1283a
Consumer Reports, 1027b, 1031a, 1032b
Consumers' Research, Inc., 1027a
Consumers' Research Bulletin, 1027a–b
Consumers Union, 1024b, 1027b
Consumers Union Reports. See Consumer Reports
Consumer taxes, 1321b
Consumption, **1017a–1035b,** 1170a
  fluctuations and trade cycle, 1184b
  gender, 113a–116a, 124a–b
  leisure, 1757b
  new attitudes in 1920s, 1768a
  post–World War II, 1198a,b
  women and, 115a
  World War II, 1164a
Container Corporation of America, 1714a
Containment, 608a, 610a, 666a, 688a
  application to Korea, 688b
  expansion of U.S. areas of interest overseas, 614b
Contemporary American Philosophy, 1636a
  Lovejoy, Arthur O., in, 1644a
  Sellars, Roy Wood, in, 1643b
  Singer, Edward, in, 1636a
  Tufts, James Hayden, in, 1641a
  Woodbridge, Frederick J. E., in, 1644b
Contingency, Irony, and Solidarity (Rorty), 291a
Continuous asssembly line production, 1098a
Continuous-process technology, 1133a,b, 1136a
Contraception. *See* Birth control
Control Data Corporation, 813b, 1148b
Control of Trusts, The (Clark), 1295a
Convention centers, 467b
Conzen, Kathleen, 162b

Cook, Thomas, 1746a
Cooke, Alistair, 187b
Cooke, Jay, 1213b–1214a
Cooke, Morris L., 1409a, 1414a
Cooley, Charles Horton, 274b, 920a
Coolidge, Calvin, 328a, *329a,* 632a
  disarmament and, 552a
  foreign policy, 575a
  presidential elections, 335a–b tab
  vetoes, 347a tab
Coolidge, Elizabeth Sprague, 1728b
Coolidge Foundation, 1728b
Coon song, 1594a, 1596a
Coontz, Stephanie, 232b
Cooper, Frank, 1807b
Cooper, James Fenimore, 150a, 1436b
Cooper, Peter, 836a
Cooperative Clinical Group, 948b
Cooper Union, 32b
Cope, Edward Drinker, 860a
Copland, Aaron, 175b, 1581a, 1617a, *1617b,* 1617b–1618a, 1621a, 1728b
Copper, 1135b, 1387b, 1388b, 1392b
  imports, 1164b
  production in the United States and Chile, 1840-1950, *1389a–b*
Coptic Church, 1547b
Copyrights (music), 1472a
Coral Gables, Fla., 459a
Corbett, James J., 143b, 1745b
Corcoran, Thomas, 1518a
Corcoran Art Gallery, 1708b
Corn Belt, 41b, 44a–b, 45a, 56b
Cornell, Joseph, 1714a
Cornell University, 102a
  College of Engineering, 32b
Coronary arteriography, 953a
Corporate architecture (1950s), 1687a
Corporate Bond Quality and Investor Experience (Braddock), 1236a
Corporate commonwealth, 1279b–1282b
Corporate equity
  increase of institutional share of, 1231b–1232a
  share held by major types of financial institutions, 1232a–b tab
Corporate Ideal in the Liberal State, 1900-1918, The (Weinstein), 207b
Corporate liberalism, 1313b–1314a, 1318a, 1319a–b, 1324a
Corporate mergers
  first wave, 1217a–1218b
  fourth wave: 1980s, 1235b–1236a
  second wave: utility holding companies, 1223a
  third wave: conglomerate movement (1960s), 1234a
  use of debt in 1980s, 1235b–1236a
Corporate physics, 747a
Corporate raiders, 1236b
Corporate Reconstruction of American Capitalism, 1890-1916, The (Sklar), 208b
Corporate Sole (Kantowicz), 1515b
Corporate welfare state, 1078a
Corporation for Public Broadcasting, 1479b
Corporations
  airplanes, 775b–776a, 793a–794b
  diversified corporate combines, 1234b
  and environmental regulations, 315b

INDEX

financial disclosure. *See* Financial
  disclosure
foreign investments, 1244b, 1245a
high-tech, 30b
hostile takeovers, 1236b–1237a
labor unions, 312a
large-scale operations, 1158b
management freedom, 1222a
and mass society, 197b–198a
multinational. *See* Multinational
  corporations
opposition to New Deal tax reform,
  1321a
PACs, 313a–314a
pension plans, 1078a
philanthropy, 500b–501b, 1737a, 1738a
politics, 299a
regulation, 431b
scientific research, 1411a
separation of ownership and control,
  1233a
specialized knowledge, 1410b
standard accounting procedures, 1231a
support of universities, 1825a
taxes, 1167b, 1315b–1316a, 1320a–b,
  1320b–1321a, 1324b
Tax Reform Act (1986), 1327b–1328a
undistributed profit tax, 1320b
and unions in the 1970s, 316b
vertical integration, 1312b
world economy, 727a, 733b
Correll, Charles, 152a, 1473a
Cortisone, 945a
Cortissoz, Royal, 1729a
  "Ellis Island Art," 1703b
Cosby, Bill, 156b, 1833b
Cosell, Howard, 1774b, 1778b
Coser, Lewis, 930a
Coser, Rose Laub, 929a
Cosmonauts, 787b, 790b
Cosmopolitanism, 1444a–b
  as alternative to pluralism, 190a
Cosmotron. *See* Particle accelerators
Cotton Club, 1620b
Cotton industry, 301a
  effect of AAA, 68b
  exports, 1243a–b, 1246b
  mechanical cotton picker, 1386a
  vertical integration, 1040b–1041a
  See also Crops: cotton
Couch, William T., 10b, 13b
Coughlin, Charles E., 55b, 175b, 199a,
  282a, 554a, 605b, 1517b, 1519a,b,
  1578b
  Radio Priest, 807b
Council of Economic Advisers (CEA),
  333b, 526b, 527a, 1080a, 1167b,
  1279a, 1280a, 1300b, 1324a,b, 1421a
Council of Jewish Federations and Welfare
  Funds, 32a, 1582b
Council of National Defense, 257a, 596a,b
Council on Environmental Quality, 345a
Council on Foreign Relations, 208a, 575a
Council on Foundations, 502b
Council on Policy Studies, 1829b
Council on Wage and Price Stability, 1172b
Counterculture, 31a, 1031b
  clothing, 9a, 76, 1791b, 1792a–b
  music, 1793a
Country-and-western music, 67b, 1626a–b,
  1631a

Country clubs, 1743b, 1744a, 1763a–b
  Del Monte, California, Country Club,
    1764a–b
  women in sports, 1763b
Counts, George, 1808b
Courage to Be, The (Tillich), 1505a
Court Act (1922), 393b–394a
Courtaulds, 1249b, 1252a
Court-packing plan, 381a–b, 410a
Courts, The, **377a–399b**
  intervention in ongoing marriage,
    240b
  policy making, 315b
  reform, 393b–394a
  rules governing standing to sue, 315a–b
Cousins, Norman, 558b, 559a
Cover, Robert, 419b
Cowan, Paul, 1586b
Cowell, Henry, 1617a, 1622b
Cowley, Malcolm, 1442b
  Exile's Return, 1442b
  Portable Faulkner, The, 1445b
Cox, Henry, 1504b
Cox, James M., 1519b
  presidential elections, 335a–b tab
Cox, Kenyon, *1694a–b,* 1705a
  Classic Point of View, The, 1696a
Cox, Oliver Cromwell, 930b
Cox Committee, 502a
Cozzens, James Gould, 34a, 1445b, 1446b
  Guard of Honor, 1445b, 1446b
  Just and the Unjust, The, 1446b
  Men and Brethren, 1446b
Cramer, Malinda E., 1545b
Crane, Philip, 1740b
Crane, Stephen, 1437b, 1438b
  Red Badge of Courage, The, 1438a
Cravath, Paul D., 1410a
Craven, Thomas, 1703a
Crawford, George, 844a
Crawford, Joan, 1790a
Crawford, Ralston, 1702a, 1713a, 1721b
Crawford, Richard, *as contributor,*
  1609a–1634b
Crawford, Ruth, 1617a
Cray, Seymour, 813b
Creation/Evolution, 873b
Creationism
  day-age theory, 861a–b, 865b
  Gallup poll (1991), 874b
  gap theory, 861a–b
  revival, 871a–874b
  scientific, 872b
  teaching, 871b
  young-earth creationists, 874a
  See also Evolution
Creation Research Society, 872a,b
Creative Federalism, 441a
Credit cards, 1028b, 1032a
  BankAmericard, 1032a
  Carte Blanche, 1028b, 1032a
  credit unions and, 1032a
  Diners Club, 1028b
  Interbank Card Association, 1028b
  Master Charge, 1028b, 1032a
  VISA, 1032a
Credit unions
  credit cards, 1032a
  Jewish immigrants, 1573a
Creel, George, 171a, 597a, 605a, 626a,
  698a,b, 699a

Creel Committee. *See* Committee on Public
  Information (CPI)
CREEP. *See* Committee to Re-elect the
  President (CREEP)
Creole Rhapsody (Ellington), 1602a
Crèvecoeur, Michel-Guillaume-Jean de,
  192b
Crime rates in cities, 465a, 468a
Crisis, 276b, 1597a
Crisis of the Negro Intellectual (Cruse), 1604a
Cristaller, Walter, 17a
"Criteria of Negro Art, The" (Du Bois),
  1593a,b
*Critical Elections and Congressional Policy
  Making* (Brady), 323b
Critical Realism (Sellars), 1643b
Crocker, Betty, 1025a
Croly, Herbert, 256a, 276b, 277a–b, 510b,
  521b, 863b
  Progressive Democracy, 277a
  Promise of American Life, The, 277a, 430a
Crops
  corn, 41b, 43b, 50b, 56a, 1192b, 1384b,
    1385a–b
  cotton, 63b, 72a, 1192b, *1385a–b*
  forage, 87b
  peanuts, 72a
  reductions, 68b, 1162b
  soybeans, 50b, 56a, 71a, 72a
  tobacco, 63b
  treatment, 775a–b, 792b–793a
  wheat, 44a, 45b, 47a, 1192b, *1385a–b*
Croquet, 1745b
Crosby, Bing, 1628a, 1755a
Cross Currents, 1525b
Crothers, Charles, 927b
Crouch, Stanley, 1624b
Crowley, Patrick, 1524a
Crowley, Patty, 1524a
Crown Cork & Seal, 1136b
Crucible Steel, 1135b, 1142b
Cruikshank, Nelson, 486a,b
Crumb, George, 1630a
Crumb, Robert, 1484a
Cruse, Harold, 1604a
Cryogenics, 785b
Cryptanalysis, 578a, 599b, 600a, 605a, 1148a
  Black Chamber, 599b
C-SPAN, 824b
Cuba, 621b, 676a–b
  foreign policy, 583a
  Kennedy and, 341b–342a
  refugees at Guantánamo Bay, 189a
  Revolution, 727b
  world economy, 721a
Cuban Giants, 1770b
Cuban Missile Crisis (1961), 342a, 561a,
  584b, 612b
  television, 1478b
Cubberley, Ellwood, 1806b
Cubist-Realists, 1702a
Cuff, Robert D., 597a
Culbert, David Holbrook, 1755b
Cullen, Countee, 150b, 1456a
Cullen, Michael, 1025a
Cult movements, 1557a
  scientific-technological, 1557b
Cultural activities
  and CIA, 710b–711a
  middle class, 1746a
  upper class, 1744a,b

Cultural Approach to History, The (Ware), 175b
Cultural Contradictions of Capitalism, The (Bell), 290a–b
Cultural democracy, 175b
Cultural Excursions (Harris), 1728a, 1739a
Cultural hierarchy. *See* Highbrow culture; Lowbrow culture
Cultural imperialism, 710b, 711b
  modernization theories, 695b
  resistance to, 712b
Cultural institutions, 31b, 38b
  Eastern region, 38b
Cultural interactions, **695a–717b**
Cultural nationalism, 268a
Cultural pluralism, 171a, 263a, 1577b, 1581b, 1588b, 1741b
  effect on art funding, 1738a–b
  and welfare, 1071b
Cultural studies, 1486b–1487b
Culture
  blending of national cultures, 714a–b
  changing values, 1345b
  decentralization of resources under federal programs, 1729b
  environmental revolution in, 1380a–1381b
  increasing role of courts, 377a
  racializing of, 149b
  regional issues, 30a–b
  West, 92a–98a
  white supremacy in, 1593a
Culture and Democracy in the United States (Kallen), 258a
Culture of Cities, The (Mumford), 10a, 12a
Cummins Engine, 1152b
  work reform, 1119b
Cunneen, Joseph, 1523b, 1525b
Cunneen, Sally, 1523b, 1525b
Cunningham, Imogen, 1709b
Cuomo, Mario M., 1532b
Curran, Charles, 1528b, 1531a–b
Currency
  fixed exchange rates, 1198b
  floating exchange rates, 692a
  numeraire, 1187b
  speculation, 1246a
  stabilization, 1253a–b, 1254a, 1259b
  See also Dollar; Gold standard
Current account balance, *1178a–b*
Current life expectancy, 959a–b
Curriculum, The (Bobbitt), 1806a
Curry, John Steuart, 55a, 1705b, 1706b
  Baptism in Kansas, 1706b, *1707a–b*
Curti, Merle, 258a, 506a
Curtis, Charles, 335a–b tab
Curtis, Tony, 135b
Curtis Institute, 33a, 1621a
Curtis Publishing Company, 31b, 1105b
Curtiss, Glenn, 769a,b
Curtiss Manufacturing Company, 769b
Curvin, Robert, 1778a
Cushing, Harvey, 1410a
CWA. *See* Civil Works Administration (CWA)
Cyberpunk style, 1793a
Cycles of Prosperity and Depression (Hansen), 1298a
Cyclotrons, 746a–747b, 760b
Cynical Society, The (Goldfarb), 206b
Czechoslovakia, 679a, 683a

D

Dabney, Charles, 64b
Dada movement, 1701b
  objects, 1704b
Daedalus, 209a
Dahl, Robert, 285b
Dahomey, 1596a
Dahrendorf, Ralf, 930a
Daily Graphic (New York), 1481b
Daily Word, 1546a
Daily Worker, 1601a
Dairy farming, 44a, 311b–312a
Daisetz Teitaro Suzuki, 1555a
Dakotas, 1362a
Daley, Richard, 300b, 301b, 1081a, 1748a
Dalhart, Vernon, 67b
Dalí, Salvador, 1710a
Dalkon Shield, 953b
Dallas Theological Seminary, 1499b–1500a, 1503b
Dallek, Robert, 602a
Dalton, Melville, 1111a–b
Daly, Mary, 1378a
Damage limitation strategy, 613a
Damnation of Theron Ware, The (Frederic), 1438b, 1439a
Damned and the Beautiful, The (Fass), 1825b
Dams and reservoirs, 84b, 85a, 85B, 1339a
  See also Hydroelectric power
Dana, 1141a
Dana, John Cotton, 1699a
Dance, 1741a–b
  cakewalk, 1594a
  Eastern region, 33a
  Ford Foundation, 1733a,b
  halls, 1748b
  salsa, 1632a
Dance of the Deer Foundation, 1561a
Dance Theater of Harlem, 1738a
Danforth, William, 497b
Danforth Foundation, 497b–498a
Daniels, John T., *768a–b*
Daniels, Josephus, 841a
Darby, John Nelson, 1498a, 1499b
Dare the School Build a New Social Order? (Counts), 1808b
DARPA. *See* Defense Advanced Research Projects Administration
Darrow, Clarence, 382a, 866a, *867a–b,* 1497b
Darwin, Charles, 134a, 878b, 1637b
  Descent of Man, The, 859a
  influence on gender theories, 900b
  On the Origin of Species by Means of Natural Selection, 859a
Darwinism To-Day (Kellogg), 860b
Data General, 1149a
Data processing, 809a–810b, 821b, 1148b
Daughters of the American Revolution, 163a, 254a
  immigrants, 139b
Davenport, Charles B., 864a
Davenport, Herbert, 1292a
David, Paul, 1388b
Davidson, Donald, 10a,b, 14a,b, 1660a
  "Very Idea of a Conceptual Scheme, The," 1660a
Davidson, Paul, 1304b
Davidson, Roger, 361b, 368a

Davidson, Thomas, 1645a
Davies, Arthur B., 1697a, 1698a,b
Davis, Allen, 477b
Davis, Allison, 925b
Davis, Angela, 290a
Davis, Arthur Vining, 1135b
Davis, F. James, 135a
Davis, Henry G., 335a–b tab
Davis, James J., 1093a
Davis, John W., 335a–b tab
Davis, Katherine Bement, 227b, 228a
Davis, Miles, 1624a, 1630b
Davis, Ron, 1719a
Davis, Stuart, 1699a, 1702b, 1707b, 1710b, 1713a, 1715a, 1730b
  "American Scene, The," 1706b
  The Masses, 1706b
Davis, Vincent J., 599a
Davisson, Clinton J., 844b–845a
Dawes, Charles G., 335a–b tab
Dawes Plan (1924), 632a, 723a, 1249b–1250a
Dawidowicz, Lucy, 1589b
Dawson, John William, 859a
Dawson, Manierre, 1701a
Day, Doris, 135b
Day, Dorothy, 282b, 1517b, 1519a,b, 1520a
Day, William R., 390a–b tab
  Hammer v. *Dagenhart* (1918), opinion in, 379b
Day care. *See* Child care
"Day of Atonement, The" (Raphaelson), 1580a
Day of the Locust, The (West), 1581b
D-Day, 646a–b
DDT crisis, 1366b
Dean, James, 1060a
Dearborn Independent, 1578b
Death
  changing causes, 967b–971b
  degenerative disease as cause, 967b
  external causes, 967b, 968b, 970b
  leading causes, 1900, 967b tab
  leading causes, 1930, 968b tab
  leading causes, 1960, 969a tab
  leading causes, 1989, 969b tab
Death Comes for the Archbishop (Cather), 1441b
Death of a Salesman (Miller), 115b
Death penalty
  race-based difference, 397b
  Supreme Court and, 419a
Death rates
  age-adjusted, 958b, *959a–b*
  age-adjusted, by sex, *964a–b*
  age-adjusted, by sex and race, *965a–b*
  age-specific, 959a, *962a–b*
  annual, 958b
  cause-specific, 959a
  crude death rate, 958b, *959a–b*
Death Registration Area, 957b–958a
Debentures, 1216a, 1230a
Debreu, Gerard, 1299a,b, 1300a
Debs, Eugene V., 55b, 204a, 257a, 278a, 597a, 1496b
  presidential elections, 335a–b tab
Debt, 1155b, 1160a, 1174b, *1175a–b,* 1176a, 1179a–b, 1245a, 1246b, 1257a, 1261a
  federal, 1900-1994, *1176a–b*
  reduced by inflation, 1325a

world economy, 732a, 733b
DEC. *See* Digital Equipment Corporation
De Capite, Michael, 176a
De Casseres, Benjamin, 1705a
DeCastro, Edson, 1149a
Decline and Resurgence of Congress, The
    (Sundquist), 355b, 364a
Declining Significance of Race, The (W. J.
    Wilson), 214b
Decolonization, 1253b
"Deconstructing Europe" (Pocock), 268b
Deconstruction (architecture), 1689b
Deconstructionism, 268b
Deegan, Mary Jo, 929a
Deep Ecology, 1378b–1379a
Deep South (Davis, Gardner and Gardner),
    925b
Deering, Christopher J., 360a
Defense, Department of, 333b, 526b, 609a,
    687b, 1281a
    aviation, 779b
    contracts, 1201b
    nuclear research, 750b
    Research and Development Board, 755b
    research funding, 850a, 852b
    space programs, 787a–b
Defense Advanced Research Projects
    Administration (DARPA), 853a
Defense industry, 28b, 98b, 312a
    development under Reagan, 1201b
    government intervention, 311a
    South, 72a, 457a
    West, 81a, 85a
Defense spending, 1167b, 1174b, 1309a–b
    and federal budget deficit, 1202b
    increase during Cold War, 612b
    Midwest, 57b–58a, 59a
    as percentage of GNP, 1201b
    under Reagan, 1327a
    source of revenues for universities, 613b
    South, 75a
Deficit Politics (Kettl), 358a
Deficit spending, 1162b 1163a, 1164a,
    1177a, 1321b–1322a,b, 1324a
DeForest, Lee, 803b, 804b, 1471a–b
Degas, Edgar, 1698b
Deindustrialization, 216b–217a, 1201b
    African American families, 112b
    and class mobility, 202a, 209b–210a
    labor market, 112a–b, 113a
    nativism and, 188a
Delacroix, Eugène, 1698b
Delany, Frank, 1524a
Delaware, 474b
Delaware and Lackawanna Railroad, 83b
DeLong, Bradford, 1217b
Delta Airlines, 795a
Deluge Geology Society, 868a
DeMille, Cecil B., 1473a
Democracy, 295a–b, 319a
    conflicts about authority, 321b
    continuity and quality, 296a–b
    Midwest, 49a, 53b
Democracy in America (Tocqueville), 196b,
    295a, 1067a
"Democracy versus the Melting Pot"
    (Kallen), 171a, 258a
Democratic party
    African Americans, 331b, 342b
    alliance between South and Northern
        cities, 298a

blue-collar ethnics and, 175a
Congress, 366a–b, 371a–b tab, 372a
divided by Vietnam war, 616a
fiscal policy, 1315b, 1324b
fundraising, 307a
House of Representatives, 374a
labor unions, 314a
New Deal coalition, 175a, 182b,
    300a–301a, 331b, 334b
nominating conventions, 298a
reforms, 307b
Roosevelt, Franklin, 331a, 332a
Senate, 305a
social reform, 300a
South, 64a, 74b, 429a
    See also Southern Democrats
tariffs, 1312b, 1314a
two-party system, 296b
Watergate, 313a
Democratic Promise (Goodwyn), 204b
Democratic statism, 1313a–1314a, 1317a–b
    abandoned, 1324b
    Roosevelt, F., and, 1320a
Demographic changes
    effect on poverty, 1087a
    income distribution, 1087a
Dempsey, Jack, 1768a
    appearance in vaudeville, 1463b
Demuth, Charles, 1697b, 1702a
    poster portrait of William Carlos
        Williams, 1702b
Denfeld, Louis, *611a–b,* 612a
Denison, Edward F., 1165b–1166a, 1173a
Denmark, 960b
Dennis, Michael, 746b
Den of Thieves, 1238b
Denton, Nancy, 214b
De Pauw, Gommar, 1533b
Depew, David J., *as contributor,* 1635a–1663b
Depolarization Project on Ethnic America,
    182a
Depository Institutions Deregulation and
    Monetary Control Act (1980), 531b
Depression. *See* Great Depression
Depressions and recessions: the business
    cycle, **1183a–1207b**
De Priest, Oscar, 172b
Deregulation, 531a–533b, 1283b
    airlines, 794a–795a
De Roose, Frank, 252a
Derrida, Jacques, 291a, 1454a, 1658b
    influence on architecture, 1689b
Descent of Man, The (Darwin), 859a
    racist application, 134a–b
Deserts, 81a, 91b
Desert Storm. *See* Operation Desert Storm
de Stijl movement, 1682a
Destiny of a Continent (Ugarte), 702a
Destroyer-for-bases agreement (1940), 577a,
    601b, 635a
Destruction of European Jews, The (Hilberg),
    1589b
Détente, 616a
Detergents, 1372a
Detroit, 451b
    financial crisis, 464b
    suburbs, 459b–460a, 467a
    working class evolution in, 205b
Detzer, Dorothy, 554b
Devanter, Willis Van, 381b, 382b, 390a–b
    tab

Device (Johns), 1718b
DeVoto, Bernard, 10b
De Vries, Hugo, 860b
Dew, Thomas, 134a
Dewes Act (1887), 92a
Dewey, Alice, 1641a, 1805a
Dewey, Evelyn, 1808a
Dewey, Jane M., 277b
Dewey, John, 196a–b, 257b–258a,b, 264a,
    276a, 277b–278a, 280a–b, 282b,
    292a–b, 878b, 880b, 887a, 888a,
    1496b, 1501b, 1502a, 1521b, 1574b,
    1639a–1641a, 1644b, 1651a, 1807a
    and Addams, Jane, 277b, 1641a
    "Americanism and Localism," 257b
    Child and the Curriculum, The, 1805a
    China's education system, 697a
    "Christianity and Democracy," 277b
    Committee of One Hundred Thousand,
        281b
    Common Faith, A, 277b
    in *Contemporary American Philosophy,*
        1640b
    Essays on Experimental Logic, 1642b
    Ethics of Democracy, The, 278a
    Experience and Nature, 1644b
    Freedom and Culture, 282b
    Individualism, 197b
    Individualism Old and New, 281a
    laboratory school, 1805a
    Liberalism and Social Action, 277b, 282b
    Public and Its Problems, The, 197b, 280a–b,
        287a
    Quest for Certainty, The, 281a
    Reconstruction in Philosophy, 281a, 284b,
        1639a, 1651a
    response to new realists, 1642b
    School and Society, The, 201a, 1805a
    Schools of Tomorrow, 1808a
    "Shortcut to Realism Examined, The,"
        1642b
    "Theory of Valuation," 1651a
Dewey, Thomas E., 334b, 578a–b, 580a,
    1828a
    presidential elections, 335a–b tab
DeWitt, John, 385b
Dewson, Molly, 122a
"Diagnosis by Dream" (*Good Housekeeping*),
    200a
Dial, 257b
Dialectic of Sex, The (Firestone), 913a
Diarrhea and enteritis, 960a, 961a
    leading cause of death in 1900, 968a
Dichter, Ernest, 1052b
Dick, A. B., 822a
Dick Act (1903), 595b–596a
Dickens, Charles, 1067a, 1436a, 1746a
Dickinson, Preston, 1702a
Dickinson, Robert Lou, 227b
Dickson, William K. L., 1752b
Dictionary of Races and Peoples, A, 163b
Di Donato, Pietro, 176a
Didrikson, Mildred "Babe," 1764b
Diebenkorn, Richard, 1714b
Dien Bien Phu, 664b
Dies, Martin, 1731a
Diet
    change in the end of the century, 1367a
    as obsession, 1798a
Dietrich, Marlene, 700a, 1795a
Dietz, Peter, 1515b, 1517b

Different Mirror, A (Takaki), 190b
DiGiorgio Corporation, 91a
Digital Equipment Corporation (DEC), 821b–822a, 1149a
Digitized data, 799a, 826a
Dignitatis Humanae, 1522b
Dignity, 1531b
Di Inzikhistn (The introspectivists), 1570a
Dillingham Commission (1907-1911), 163a
DiMaggio, Paul, 1462b
Dine, Jim, 1587a
Dine, Thomas, 1590a
Dingell, John D., 997a
Dingley Tariff (1897), 1246b, 1269a
Dinnerstein, Dorothy, 913a
Dinnerstein, Leonard, 138a
Dionne, E. J., 292a
Dior, Christian, 1790a,b
Diphteria, 960a, 968a,b
  antitoxin, 974a, 977a
Diplomatic power, 720a–b
Directive No. 15: Race and Ethnic Standards for Federal Statistics and Administrative Reporting (OMB), 180b
Directors of Industrial Research, 842a, 847b
Direct taxation, 1310b
Dirigibles. *See* Airships
Disabilities Act, 447b
Disability insurance, 485a–b, 1076a
Disarmament Conference in Geneva (1933), 633a
Disaster by Decree (Graglia), 388a
Disciples of Christ
  liberalism, 1500b
  population percentages, 1492b, 1493a
  schism, 1493a–b
Discrimination, 95a, 96a, 97b
  in art institutions, 1703b
  housing, 95b
  Judaism, 1578b
  See also Anti-Semitism
Disease
  chronic, 967b, 970a
  cultural and behavioral determinants, 972a
  degenerative, 967b
  ecobiologic determinants, 972a
  health and, 957a–986b
  medical, public health and political determinants, 972a
  standard of living determinants, 972a–b
  See also specific diseases
Disney, Walt, 59b, 707a, 1030a, 1468a, 1476b
Disney Studios, 703a, 1030a
  animation, 1466a
Dispensationalism, 1499b
Displaced Persons Act (1948), 165a–b tab, 178b
Displaced Persons Act (1950), 178b
Disposable diapers, 1034a
Dissent, 209b, 1831b
Distillers Securities, 1132a
Distribution of Wealth, The (Clark), 1290a–b
Distribution of Wealth, The (Commons), 1296a–b
Distribution organizations, 1129b–1130a, 1131a
District of Columbia rent control law, 407b

Disuniting of America, The (Schlesinger), 189b
Divided government, 302b–303a, 304a–b tab, 305a–b tab, 323a, 349b, 360a
  Bush and, 351a
  Eisenhower and, 349b
  Nixon and, 349b
  Reagan and, 349b
Divine, Father, 1600a
Divine Light Mission, 1552b
Divine Science, 1545b, 1546a
Divorce, 105a
  and abundance, 215b
  child poverty, 237a–b
  at end of nineteenth century, 222a
  feminization of poverty, 123a
  impact on children, 236b–237a
  law reform, 105b, 123a, 227a–b, 241a
  mutual consent, 227a, 241a
  and politicians, 233a
  rates in mid-1960s, 233a
Dixiecrat movement, 436b
Dixon, A. C., 861a
Dixon, Thomas, 150b, 1593a
Di Yunge, 1570a
DNA, 763b
Dobie, J. Frank, 10b
Dobrynin, Anatoliy, 561b
Doby, Larry, 1778a
Dobzhansky, Theodosius, 869a–870a,b
"Doctors, Economists, and the Depression" (Taussig), 1298b–1299a
Dodd, Lawrence, 357a–b, 360a, 371a–b
  "Congress and the Quest for Power," 356b
Dodd, Thomas J., 1479a
Dodge, Charles, 1630a
Dodge, Mabel. *See* Luhan, Mabel Dodge
Dodgers, 462a
Dodsworth (Lewis), 1027a
Doggie Bob (Arneson), 1720a
Dole, Robert, 306a, 350a, 488b
  presidential elections, 336a–b tab
Dollar, 1253a
  devaluation, 313a, 730a,b, 1162b, 1199b, 1235b, 1250b, 1257b, 1262b
  foreign investments, 1245a, 1265a
  and international monetary system, 728a
  loss of confidence in, 728a–729b
  valuation, 728b–729a,b, 731b, 732a–b, 1164b, 1166b, 1169b, 1176b, *1177a–b,* 1256a, 1257a
Dollard, John, 927a
Dollar Diplomacy, 721a
Domestic economy, 1264a
  foreign trade, 1262b
  government, 1167a
  investments, 1176a
Domestic policy
  versus foreign policy, 569b, 577b, 590b
  national-security, 334a–b
  presidency, 336a
  world economy, 723b, 731a, 732b
Domestic Policy Council, 529b–530a
Domestic relations courts, 395b
Domestic science, 226b
Domestic violence, 237b–238a
Domhoff, G. William, 208a,b
Dominican Republic, 679b, 682b
Dominicans, 1511b
Donagan, Alan, 1655a

Donald Duck, 1323b
Dondero, George, 1713b
Donnellan, Keith, 1659a
Donor's Forum of Chicago, 506b
Donovan, William J., *604b,* 604b
Dooley, Tom, 1524a
Doolittle, James, 641a
Doolittle Commission, 581a
Doors, 1628b
Dorfman, Ariel, 710a
Dorrance family, 1131b
Dorsey, Tommy (Thomas A.), 149b, 1621a
Dos Passos, John, 33b, 262a
Dostoyevsky, Fyodor, 1446a
Dott, Robert H., Jr., 874a
Doubleday, Abner, 1762b
Double Dealer, 67b
Douglas, Paul, 1832a
Douglas, William O., 382b, 390a–b tab
Douglas Aircraft, 773b, 795b
  Douglas DC-3, *774a–b*
  See also McDonnell Douglas Corporation
Douglass, Frederick, 143a, 145a, 1595a
  abolitionism, 133b, 134a
Douglass, Harlan Paul, 460a
Dove, Arthur, 1697b, 1698a, 1704b
Dow, Arthur Wesley, 1704a
Dow, Herbert, 1139a
Dow Chemical, 1139a, 1143a, 1145b, 1146a,b–1147a
  research, 835b
Dow-Jones Industrial Average, 1261b
Down Beat, 1624a
Downs, Anthony, 1302a
Drachsler, Julius, 1577b
Drake, Edwin, 1396b
Drake, St. Clair, 213a, 925b, 929b
Draper, Mrs. Henry, 741b
Dreadnought, 594a
Dreier, Katherine, 1700a
Dreiser, Theodore, 33b, 52a, 1437b, 1438b
  American Tragedy, An, 1359a
  Sister Carrie, 1437b
Dresser, Annetta, 1545b
Dresser, Julius, 1545b
Drew, Charles Richard, 948a
Drexel, Burnham, Lambert, 1211a, 1236a
Drexel Institute of Technology, 32b
Dreyfus, Hubert, 1658a
Drift and Mastery (Lippmann), 196a–b, 256a–b, 274a, 277a
Drinking. *See also* Prohibition
  New Deal laws, 122a
  Progressive Era laws, 122a
Dropkin, Celia, 1570a
Dropsie College for Hebrew and Cognate Learning, 1566b
Droughts, 44a, 53a
Droz, Rick, 1721b
Drucker, Peter, 1101a
Drug manufacturers. *See* Pharmaceutical industry
Dubnov, Simon, 1569a
Dubois, Rachel Davis, 174a, 183b
Du Bois, W. E. B., 129a, 144a,b, 145a, 155b, 287a–b, 1087b, 1644b
  "Black Man Brings His Gifts, The," 259b
  black sacred culture, 1594b, 1595b
  "Conservation of Races, The," 1595a
  "Criteria of Negro Art, The," 1593a,b
  criticism of Booker T. Washington, 145b

editor of *Crisis,* 1597a
education, 1810a
Niagara Movement, 146a
Philadelphia Negro, The, 922a
Souls of Black Folk, The, 259a, 276b, 1456a, 1594b
on William James, 276b
Duchamp, Marcel, 1699b, 1701b, 1715a
Nude Descending the Staircase, 1699b
Dudgeon, Richard B., 1807b
Dudley, Charles B., 832b–833a
Dudziak, Mary L., *as contributor,* 377a–399b
Duffy, Francis, 1519b
Duisberg, Carl, 835a, 838a
Dukakis, Michael, 185a, 350a, 589b
presidential elections, 336a–b tab
Duke, James B., 1042b, 1131a,b
Duke University, 75b, 506b
Dulles, Allen, 581a, *581b*
Dulles, John Foster, 560a, 581a, *582a–b,* 614b, 754b
television, 1478b
Dumbarton Oaks conference (1944), 557a
Dummer, Ethel, 236b
DuMont Laboratories, 1475b
Dunbar, Charles, 1289a, 1291a
Dunbar, Paul Laurence, 1594b
writing in dialect, 1596a,b
Duncan, Isadora, 1704b
Duncan, Robert Kennedy, 839a, 842b
Dunlop, 1249b
Dunlop, John, 1110a
Dunn, Leslie C., 870a
Dunnigan, Alice, 148a
Dupee, F. W., 1444a
du Pont, Irénée, 1414a
Du Pont de Nemours, E. I., Company, 840a, 846a, 850b, 1139a, 1143a–b, 1416b
antitrust actions, 838a, 847a–b, 849a
arts patronage, 1737a
Experimental Station, 837a,b
explosives industry, 837b–838a
fellowships, 842b
General Experimental Laboratory, 837b–838a
grants, 852a
industrial research, 837a
neoprene, 845b
nuclear research, 849b
nylon, 845b–846a, 848a–b
Patent and Process Agreement, 1145b
polymers, 845a–846a, 1146a, 1147a
research, 835b, 847a–b, 851a
Durkheim, Émile, 924b, 926b
Durr, Virginia, 71b
Dushkin, Alexander, 1576a
Dust Bowl, 84b, 88a, 1366b, 1368a–b
Dust storm, *53a–b*
Dutchman (Baraka), 1604a
Duveneck, Frank, 1694b
Dwight, John Sullivan, 1611b
Dworkin, Gerald, 1655a
Dworkin, Ronald, 423a
Dybbuk, The (Ansky), 1570b
Dyestuff industry, 840a
Dylan, Bob, 1627a,b, 1628a
Dynamic Sociology (Ward), 919b
Dynamics of Prejudice (Bettelheim & Janowitz), 1584b

E

Eakins, Thomas, 1694a, 1697b
Early music revival, 1629b
Earth Day (22 April 1970), 1371b, 1377a, 1380b
Earth First!, 88a, 1378b, 1560b
Earth from space, *1379a–b*
Earthquakes, 98b
EarthSave, 1560b
East, E. M., 869a
East, The, **25a–40b,** *26a–b*
East Coast Edison Trust, 83b
Easterlin, Richard, 1184a
Eastern Europe
after World War I, 683a
American firms in, 1205a
Eastern Liberalism, 30a
East European Jews, 1565b, 1566b, 1567a, 1572a, 1574b, 1575a,b, 1577a, 1586a
second-generation, 1578a, 1580b
Eastman, Crystal, 476a, 547b, 549b
Eastman, George, 838a–b, 1752b
Eastman, Max, 282a, 1439a
Eastman, R. O., company, 1024b
Eastman Kodak, 28a, 822a, 840a, 1021a, 1030a, 1411a, 1469a
industrial research in Japan, 854a
reliance on German chemical industry, 838a
research, 835b, 838a–b, 848b, 851a
Eastman School of Rochester, 33a
East-West Journal, 1558a
Eaton, Fred, 1362b
Eberstadt, Ferdinand, 608b
Eccles, Marriner, 1277b, 1321b
Echo Park, 1373a
Eckert, Wallace, 847a
Eco, Umberto, 1484a
Eco-Defense (Foreman), 1378b
Ecofeminism, 1560b
École des Beaux Arts (Paris), 1669a, 1679a
Ecology
artists and, 1720a
disasters, 1376b
industrial chemistry, 1372a
philosophy of the commons, 21b
regionalism and, 21a–b
Econometrica, 1299a, 1300a, 1304b
Econometrics, 1299a
Econometric Society, 1299a
Economic Analysis of Law (Posner), 1302a
Economic Approach to Human Behavior, The (Becker), 934b
Economic blocs, 733a–b
Economic Cycles (Moore), 1293b
Economic history, 1302b
Economic inequality, 1353a
ethnic antagonisms, 191b
racial antagonisms, 191b
Economic interdependence, 1187b, 1204b
Economic Interpretation of History, The (Seligman), 920a, 1291a
Economic Interpretation of the Constitution, An (Beard), 920a
Economic Justice for All (1986), 1529b
Economic leadership
after World War II, 1197a–1199a
loss in the 1970s, 1199a
Economic opportunity

popular belief in, 1072a
Economic output
during Great Depression, *1162a–b*
per sector, 1900-1913, *1160a*
Economic performance, **1155a–1181b**
Economic policies, 1249b, **1267a–1287b**
banking, 1295a,b
controversy about, 1289a–b
science and, 1289b
trusts, 1295a
Economic Principles (Fetter), 1292a
Economic Recovery Tax Act (1981), 1174a–b, 1204a–b, 1327a
Economics
consumption, 1025b
demand management, 1167b, 1203a
game theory, 1304b–1305a
general equilibrium theory, 1299b, 1302b
institutionalism, 1290b, 1294a, 1296a–b, 1303b
Keynesian, 311a, 437a, 1026a, 1299a, 1300a–b, 1302b, 1304b
marginal productivity theory, 1290a
Marxism, 1304a
mathematical, 1299a
neoclassical, 316a
Nobel prizes, 1299a
Phillips curve, 1300b, 1302b–1303a
scientific method, 1305a
utility theory, 1290a
Economics and Philosophy, 1305a
Economics of Discrimination, The (Becker), 934b
Economics of Enterprise (Davenport), 1292a
"Economics of Exhaustible Resources, The" (Hotelling), 1383b
Economics of Higher Education (1962), 1829b
Economic Stabilization Act (1970), 528a
Economic Theory of Democracy, An (Downs), 1302a
Economic thought, **1289a–1307b**
Economies of scale, 1137b, 1140a, 1147a, 1166a, 1255a
Economies of scope, 1137b, 1140a
Economist, 709b
Economists
as celebrities, 1305b
Chicago school, 1174a
Keynesianism, 1322a
New Deal and, 1420b–1421a
taxation, 1315a, 1323a
Economy
compositional changes, 1186b–1187b
Congress, 356a
Eastern region, 26a–28b, 38b
effect of rise of new industries, 1187a
foreign policy, 569b, 575b, 589b–590a
instability, 1188a
post-World War II, 1198a
private-sector agencies, 1281b
racism, 95b
regulation, 436a
secular transitions in development, 1186b–1187a
service expansion, 1422b–1423a
South, 69b, 75a–77a
structural changes, 1186b–1187b
structure, 1116a–1124b, *1157a–b*
West, 83a
Economy and Society (Weber), 199b
Ecumenical councils, 1511a, 1520b

Ecumenical movement, 1527a, 1535a, 1562b
Eddy, Arthur Jerome, 1699a
Eddy, Mary Baker, 1544a–b, 1545a,b
Eddy, Sherwood, 554b
Edge Act (1919), 1248b
Edge City, 20b
Edgeworth, Francis Ysidro, 1299b
Edison, Thomas A., *834a–b,* 841a, 1411a, 1469a, 1470b, 1752b
   laboratories, 833b–834b
Edison Electric, 1137b–1138a
Edison General Electric, 835b
   See also General Electric
Education, 438a
   accessibility, 1408a–b
   Afrocentrism, 1605a–1606a
   applied psychology in, 880b
   assimilation of immigrants, 1803b–1804a
   bias in curriculum materials, 1814b
   black institutions, 1598b
   business interest in, 1411a
   Catholics, 1521a–b, 1523a, 1528b, 1530a
   class characteristic, 199b
   federal programs, 485b, 1082a, 1325a, 1811b, 1812a, 1814b
   high schools, 201b, 1415a–b
   institutes of technology, 1407b
   intercultural movement, 174a
   jobs in, 1804a
   Judaism, 1566a, 1572b–1573a, 1576a,b, 1577b–1578a, 1585a
   management, 1111a
   mental testing, 880b–881a
   middle class growth, 201a
   music, 1611b, 1621a
   New Deal and, 1421a
   parochial schools, 1520b, 1524b
   and the professions, 1407b, 1408b
   public support of, 1417b
   regulation, 431b
   school war of 1967-1969 in New York City, 181b–182a
   separate-but-equal doctrine, 1813a
   South, 64a–b, 76b
   states and school reform, 1815a
   stratification by economic elites, 201a
   two-model approach to earth history, 872b
   use by suffragists, 117a
   vocational, 477b
   World War II, 1164b
   See also Colleges; Elementary and secondary education; Higher education; Universities
Educational Alliance, 1579a
Educational Psychology (Thorndike), 1806a
Educational Wastelands (Bestor), 1811b
Education Amendments (1972), 1780b, 1812a–b tab, 1820a–b tab, 1829a, 1833a
Education Consolidation and Improvement Act (1981), 1812a–b tab
"Education for a World of Team Players" (Snedden), 1806a
Education of All Handicapped Children Act (1974), 1812a–b tab, 1814a
Edwards, Harry, 1779a, 1782a
Edwards, Jonathan, 1502b
EEC. *See* Common Market
EEOC. *See* Equal Employment Opportunity Commission (EEOC)

Efros, Israel, 1573b
Egan, John, 1524a
Egypt, 690a
   foreign policy, 582a
Ehrenreich, Barbara, 104b
Ehrlich, Paul, 1375b
Ehrlichman, John, 345b
Eichelberger, Clark, 554a
Eichmann, Adolf, 1589a
Eilberg, Amy, 1589a
Einstein, Albert, 498b, 558b, 1584a
EIS. *See* Environmental impact statements
Eisenhower, Dwight D., 29b, 30a, 262b, 322b, 337a–340b, *338a, 647a,* 1280b
   arms control, 559b
   arts patronage, 1735a
   Big Science, 759a
   blue-collar vote, 310a
   Catholic vote, 1524b
   compensatory demand management, 1198b
   D-Day, 646a
   divided government, 349b
   farewell speech, 754a
   federalism, 438b–439b
   foreign policy, 580b–584a
   integration, 309a
   Mandate for Change, 615a
   military spending, 612b
   North Africa, 643b–644a
   preservationism, 1373a
   presidential elections, 335a–b tab
   regulatory state, 526a,b
   school desegregation, 73b, 387b
   settlement of Korean war, 661b
   social security, 483a–b
   space research, 754b–755a, 756a
   spy planes, 781a
   Supreme Court appointments, 389b
   television, 1478b
   U.S. Information Agency (USIA), 705b
   vetoes, 347a tab
Eisenhower College, 1832b
Eisenhower Doctrine, 690a
Eisenhower Institute, 506a
Eisenman, Peter, 1687a, 1689b
Eisenstein, Ira, 1582a, 1588b
Elazar, Daniel J., 49a
Elchanan, Isaac, 1575a
Eldercare, 1002a
Elections
   foreign policy, 570a–b
   fraud, 435b
   minority of popular vote, 334b
   nonpartisan, 299b
   open seat, 306a
   patterns of voting, 307a
   politics, 296a
   See also Primary elections; specific elections
Elections of 1896, 1291a
Elections of 1912, 721b
   antitrust as issue, 521a
   judicial power as issue, 379b–380a
Elections of 1916, 548a
Elections of 1920, 574b, 1274b
   radio broadcast of returns, 1755a
Elections of 1924, 380b
Elections of 1932, 281b
Elections of 1936, 331b
Elections of 1938, 334b

Elections of 1940, 577a
Elections of 1944, 577b
Elections of 1946, 725a–b
Elections of 1948, 178a, 334b
   health insurance as issue, 998a
Elections of 1952
   foreign policy, 580b
   Korean War as issue, 662a
Elections of 1964, 342a–b
Elections of 1968, 344a
   law and order, 389b, 422b
Elections of 1972, 388b–389a
Elections of 1974, 313a, 346a
Elections of 1976, 346a–b
Elections of 1980, 350a
Elections of 1984, 349a
Elections of 1992, 303a, 351b
   family as issue, 221a
   foreign policy, 590b
   health care reform as issue, 987a
   right to abortion, 393a
Elections of 1994, 303a
   family values as issue, 188b
Electoral college, 303b
Electrical industry, 28a, 1137b–1138b
Electric Bond & Share, 1138a
Electric Home and Farm Authority, 1026a
Electricity, 1019b–1020a, 1024a, 1160b, 1333b
   consumer items, 1338b
   Eastern region, 27b
   effect on health, 1338b
   hydroelectric power, 85a, 91b, 431b
   lighting, 834b
   rural, 1026a
Electric power systems
   consolidation, 1223a
   nuclear generation, 1353a
   power-plant ownership and production of electricity, 1920–1990, 1335a–b tab
   private ownership, 1334b
   regional, 1338b, 1348a
   World War II, 1343b, 1344a
Electric Storage Battery, 1138b
Electrocardiograph, 952b
Electron diffraction, 844b–845a
Electronic Data Systems, 1150b
Electronic inventory control, 814a
Electronic media
   audience-performer relationship, 1464b
   entertainment, 1465a
   foreign policy, 580a
Electronic Numerical Integrator and Computer (ENIAC), *811a–b,* 1827b
Electronics industry, 57b, 76a, 837b, 850a, 1128b, 1143a, 1144b, 1148a–1149a, 1150b, 1151b–1152a
   eroded market share, 1235b
   games, 1033a
   Germany, 835a
   imports, 1258a,b
   international competition, 1200a
   international investments, 1262a–b
   Southwest, 462b
Electronic warfare, 783b–784b, 795b
Elementary and secondary education, **1803a–1817b**
   evolution taught in, 861b
Elementary and Secondary Education Act (1965), 1812a–b tab, 1813a

Elementary Principles of Economics (Fisher), 1292a
Elements of Pure Economics (Walras), 1299b
Eli Lilly Company, 944a,b, 1147b–1148a
Eliot, Charles, 1805b
Eliot, T. S., 1441b, 1442a, 1449b
  After Strange Gods, 1444b, 1445a
  Four Quartets, 1449b
  on Nashville Agrarians, 1444b–1445a
Elitism and the arts, 1725b–1728b
Ellington, Duke (Edward Kennedy), 1602a, 1620b, 1623b, 1630b
Elliott, Carl, 72a
Ellis, Edith, 227a
Ellis, Havelock, 226b, 900a–901a
Ellis, John Tracy, 1522b
Ellis, Perry, 1791b
Ellis Island, 35a, 135b, 137b
  reception center, 1670b, *1671a–b,* 1671b–1672a
"Ellis Island Art" (Cortissoz), 1703b
"Ellis Island" (Monk), 1581a
Ellison, Ralph, 34a, 154a, 1456a, 1602b
  Invisible Man, 34a, 1450b–1451a, 1601a–b
Ellison, William, 133b
Ellman, Richard, 1453a
Ellsberg, Daniel, 562a, 587b
Ellwood, David, 239a, 709a
Elman, Mischa, 1571a
Elmslie, Geroge Grant, 1678b
Ely, John Hart, 388b
Ely, Richard T., 204b, 274b, 919a, 1289a, 1295a, 1494b, 1496b
  and Addams, Jane, 275b
  Outlines of Economics, 274b
  Socialism and Social Reform, 274b
Emancipation Proclamation, 570b
Emergence of Professional Social Science, The (Haskell), 919a
Emergency Immigration Restriction Act (1921), 165a–b tab, 172a
Emergency medical and infant care program, 995b
Emergency Peace Federation, 548b, 549b
Emergency powers, 326b
Emergency Price Control Act, 525b
Emergency Tariff (1921), 1248b
"Emerging Infectious Diseases," 983b
Emerson, Alfred, 870a
Emerson, Ralph Waldo, 9b, 204a, 1436b, 1449a, 1540a
  Mumford and, 11a–b
Emmeri, Herbert, 523a
Emory University, 75b
  Woodruff, Robert W., 1833b
Empire State Building (New York), 1673a, 1681a
Empirical naturalists, 1644b
Employee Benefit Guaranty Corporation, 1227a–b tab
Employee Retirement Income Security Act (1974), 1227a–b tab, 1234b
Employee Retirement Income Security Act (1975), 528a
Employee Stock Ownership Plan (ESOP), 1237b
Employers' organizations, 310b–311a
  Europe and U.S., 319a
Employment
  in agriculture, 1386a
  as class characteristic, 199b

per sector, 1900–1913, *1160a*
  racial aspects, 148b
  segmentation by gender, 106b, 107b–108a
  segregation in South, 66b
  South, 75a–b, 76a–b
  See also Labor force; Unemployment
Employment Act (1946), 525b, 526b, 1167a, 1278b, 1300b, 1324a
Employment regulation, 1285a
Emplumada (Cervantes), 1456b
Encyclicals. *See* Papal encyclicals
Encyclopaedia Britannica, 1099a
Encyclopedia of Social Reform (Bliss), 275a
Encyclopedia of the Social Sciences, 161b, 1296a, 1491a
Encyclopedia of Unified Science, 1651a
Endangered Species Act (1973), 1377a
End of Ideology, The (Bell), 199a, 286b, 287a, 1831b
End of the Road, The (Barth), 1452b
Energy, 1281a
  conservation, 1260a
  consumption, 1171a, *1171a–b*
  consumption and population as percentages of world totals, 1333a–b tab
  consumption tax, 1328b
  cost increase after 1970, 1346a
  crisis, 1376a
  infrastructure, 1346a, 1347b–1348a
  market restoration, 1285a
  production: market share of energy sources, 1960-1990, 1347a–b tab
  regulation, 1168a–b, 1170a
Energy Conservation and Production Act (1976), 528a
Energy Policy and Conservation Act (1976), 528a
Engagement and Marriage (Burgess and Wallin), 103a
Engels, Friedrich, 195b
Engerman, Stanley, 1302b
Engineering, 1413b–1414a
  schools in Eastern region, 32b
Engineering Council, 1416a
England. *See* Britain
English Companies Act (1900), 1224a
English Tudor style, 1679a
ENIAC, *811a–b,* 1827b
Enteritis. *See* Diarrhea and enteritis
Enterprise (ship), 641a
Entertainment
  blacklists, 1468a
  communications, 800b–801a, 827a
  consumption, 1024b
  courts as, 397b
  Eastern region, 28a, 38a
  effects on product sales, 1060a
  history, 1461a–1487a
  linked forms of, 1480b
  Midwest, 48a–b, 51b
  new kind of monopolies, 1488a
  privatization, 1470b
Entertainment and Sports Programming Network (ESPN), 824a
Enthoven, Willem, 952b
Entrepreneurs, 1129b, 1137b, 1149a, 1150a, 1152b, 1155a, 1327b
Environmental Defense Fund, 1376b, 1378b
  and McDonald's Corporation, 1377b
Environmental Impact Statements (EIS), 529a, 1377a

Environmental Protection Agency (EPA), 315b, 345a, 529a, 1170b, 1283a, 1377a
Environment and environmentalism, 88a, 1358a, 1371b–1380a
  broadening demography, 1378a
  Deep Ecology, 1378b
  Federalism, 447b–448b
  foreign trade, 1264b
  forests, 88b
  influence on energy infrastructure, 1347b–1348a
  interrelatedness of social, economic, and ecological problems, 1376b
  legislation, 1284a
  lobbyists, 314a
  Midwest, 59a
  natural scientists, 1374a
  and new age, 1558b, 1560a
  Nixon and, 345a, 442b
  photographers and, 1714b
  pollution control under Nixon, 345a
  Protestants, 1506a
  regulations, 315b, 534a, 1170b–1171a, 1173a, 1285a
  and scientists, 1426a
  South, 76b
  space program, 791b
  use of environmental impact statements, 1377a
  vs. conservationism, 1380b
  West, 81b, 91a, 98b
  See also Conservationism
EOP. *See* Executive Office of the President (EOP)
EPA. *See* Environmental Protection Agency (EPA)
Episcopalians
  liberalism, 1494a, 1500b
  population percentages, 1492b, 1493a
Epistle to the Romans (Barth), 1502a
Epstein, Jacob, 1579a
Epstein, Richard, 422a
Equal Employment Opportunity Act (1973), 528a
Equal Employment Opportunity Commission (EEOC), 120a, 527b, 1283a
"Equality between the Sexes" (Rossi), 929a
Equality League of Self-Supporting Women, 117a
Equal Pay Act (1963), 123b
Equal protection, 419a–421a
Equal Rights Amendment (ERA), 117b, 120b, 239b, 1530b
Erdrich, Louise, 59b
Erie Canal, 25b
Erie Railroad, 1217b
Erikson, Erik, 911a–b
Ernst, Max, 1710a
Ernst and Ernst, 1410a
Eros and Civilization (Marcuse), 931b
ESA. *See* European Space Agency (ESA)
Espionage Act (1917), 171b, 408a, 416a, 550a, 597a, 626a
ESPN, 1774a
Esposito, Meade, 300b
Espy, James, 741a
Esquire, 114b
Essays on Experimental Logic (Dewey), 1642b
Essex Institute of Salem (MA), 255a
Eternal City (Blume), 1708b

Eternally Wounded Woman, The (Vertinsky), 901b
Ethics, professionals, 1421b
Ethics in Government Act (1978), 530a–b, 533b
Ethics of Democracy, The (Dewey), 278a
"Ethnic Communities" (Ware), 161b
Ethnic Heritage Studies Program Act (1972), 183b
Ethnic Identity (Alba), 190a
Ethnicity and ethnic identity, 1023b
  accommodation of assimilationist demands, 168b
  affirmation of ethnic identities, 183a
  arts, 1720b, 1738a, 1739b
  assimilation, 211a
  bloc voting, 169b
  Catholics, 1512b–1514b, 1515a, 1516a, 1534a–b
  in Chicago, 206a
  and class, 195b, 196a, 210b–212a
  clubs, 1748a
  defined, 161a,b
  Eastern region, 38b
  entertainment, 1464a, 1466a
  ethnic economies, 169a
  ethnicity and immigration, **161a–193b**
  ethnic organizations and radio, 805a
  and gender, 106b
  genealogy, 183a
  historians, 184a
  Jewish neighborhoods, 1578b
  Judaism, 1581b, 1585b
  loyalties and vote, 297a–b
  mass consumption, 173a, 211b
  Midwest, 43a, 48a
  Neo-Marxism on white ethnic identity, 184b
  parochial schools, 1808a
  in politics, 300b
  popular culture, 1486b
  population distribution, 167b
  West, 92a, 93a–b, 98a
  in Woonsocket, R.I., 206a
  during World War II, 264a
Ethnic Options (Waters), 190a
Ethnonationalism, 162b–163a
Ethnoracial pentagon, 130b, 190b, 1457a
Ethologists, 892b
Eugenics movement, 161a, 256b, 863b
  justified by psychologists' view of heredity, 886a
  marriage laws, 225b
Eugenics Records Office, 864a
Eurobonds, 1262a
Eurodollars, 1256a, 1259a
Europe
  after World War I, *680a–b*
  collapse of socialist economies, 1306a
  collective-security arrangements, 610a
  currency system, 680b
  economic power, 682a, 729b
  economy post–World War I, 723a
  film industries, 707b
  Grand tour, 1744a
  health insurance, 990a
  high-speed passenger trains, 1353b
  nationalism, 702b
  reconstruction, 726b
  social insurance, 123b
  subsidies to mutual benefit societies, 990a

  and U.S. economic interests, 678b
  world economy, 726a
  before World War I, *622a–b*
European Association for American Studies, 706b
European Coal and Steel Community, 725b
European Community (EC). *See* Common Market
Europe and the People without History (Wolf), 917b
European Economic Community (EEC). *See* Common Market
European Recovery Program. *See* Marshall Plan
European Space Agency (ESA), 790a–b
European Union (EU). *See* Common Market
Evangelicalism, 1562b
  millenial religious movements, 1540b
  South, 64b, 77b
Evangelical revivals
  South, 63b
  19th century, 1539b
Evangelicals, 1491b, 1493a, 1501b, 1504a,b
  See also Fundamentalism; Protestantism: conservatives
Evans, Sara, 119b
Evans, Walker, 10a, 70a–b, 1730a
  Let Us Now Praise Famous Men, 1709b
Evans, Warren Felt, 1545b
Eveleth, Charles, 841b
Evening American, 382a
Evening Transcript, 65a
Everglades National Park, 1373a
Evergreen State University, 1831a
Evers, Medgar, 1778b
Evert, Chris, 1780b
"Everybody's Protest Novel" (Baldwin), 1601b
Evolution
  condemnation of Nazi race theory, 869b
  liberal Protestants, 1495b
  mathematical models, 869a
  natural selection, 868b
  synthetic theory, 870b
  teaching banned in public schools, 866a
  view of natural selection, 859a
Evolution and Dogma (Zahm), 859b
Evolutionary Naturalism (Sellars), 1643b
Evolutionary theory, **859a–876b**
Evolution of Civilization, The (Saint-Gaudens), 1696a
Evolution of Cooperation (Axelrod), 1305a
Evolving Role of the Joint Chiefs of Staff in the National Security Structure, The, 604a
Ewing, Oscar, 1001a
Exceptionalism, American, 264b
Excess-profits taxation, 1316a
  abolition of, 1317b
Exchange rates, *1177a–b,* 1256b
Executive branch, 315a–316a
  agencies and interest groups, 317b–318a
  importance, 361b–362a
  powers, 356b–357a, 358a
  relationship with Congress, 361a, 362b
  reorganization under Nixon, 529b
Executive Office of the President (EOP), 358b, 361a, 525a,b, 1322a
Executive Order 6174, 600a
Executive Order 8802, 95b, 1602b
Executive Order 9066, 96b, 385b, 605b

Executive Order 12291, 532b
Executive Order 12498, 532b
Executive Reorganization Act (1939), 333b, 525b
Executive Suite, 340a
Exercise, 1798b
Exile's Return (Cowley), 1442b
"Existence of an Equilibrium for a Competitive Economy" (Arrow and Debreu), 1300a
Exodus (Uris), 1587b
Experience and Nature (Dewey), 1644b
Exports, 1140a, 1159a,b, 1160b, 1163b, 1164a, 1166b, 1176b, 1201b, 1390a–b
  in 1914 and 1990, 1264b tab
  economy, 1155b
  high absolute net export growth industries, 1879–1909, *1391a–b*
  high absolute net export growth industries, 1899–1928, 1392a–b
  manufacturing, *1166b*
  as a percentage of GNP, 1247b
  pre–World War I, 721b
  during World War I, 722a, 1247b
  See also Foreign trade; Imports
Expressways. *See* Highways
Exxon Corporation, 87a, 852a, 1740b
  arts patronage, 1737b
  New York Philharmonic, 1737a
  work reform, 1119b

F

Fabric of Our Lives, The (Weiss and Socoloff), 1719b
Fackenheim, Emil, 1589a
Facsimile machines, 822b–823a
Factories, 50a, 1024a, 1129a, 1130a
  canning, 1131b–1132a
  Midwest, 55b, 57a–b
  share of U.S. market, 1979 and 1984, 1260a tab
  suburbs, 467a
Failsafe, 781a
Fairbanks, Charles W., 335a–b tab
Fairbanks, Douglas, 1465a
Fairchild Semiconductor Company, 812a
Fair Deal, 284b, 322b, 1280a
Fair Employment Practice Act, 1777b
Fair Employment Practice Committee (FEPC), 71a, 95b, 177b, 1602b
  Chicano workers and, 149a
Fair Housing Act (1968), 154b
Fair Labor Standards Act (1938), 69a,b, 122b, 123b, 1278a
  minimum hourly wage, 1750b
  Supreme Court and, 385a
  weekend, 1750a
Falk, Marcia, 1587a
Fall of Natural Man, The (Pagden), 917b
Fall of the House of Labor, The (Montgomery), 205b
Faludi, Susan, 1797a
Falwell, Jerry, 1492a, 1507a
Family, **221a–243b**
  courts, 225a
  gender in, 101b–106a
  Great Depression, 104b
  nuclear, 101b, 124a, 215b

Russell Sage Foundation, 493a
smaller, 1033b
in South, 61b, 63a,b–64a, 77b
See also African American family; Family law
Family, Socialization and Interaction Process (Parsons), 908b
Family Assistance Plan, 487b
under Nixon, 1083a–b
Family law
courts, 225a
new subjects in, 240a
revolution in, 240a, 241b
sexual equality, 240a
Family Life Bureau, 1521a
Family of Men (Steichen), 1714b
Family Rosary Crusade, 1523b
Family Support Act (1988), 489a, 1088a
Famous Funnies, 1482a
Famous Players-Lasky, 1469a
Faneuil Hall (Boston), 36b
Fan magazines, 1466b
Fanny Herself (Ferber), 1581a
Fanon, Frantz, 287b, 1603b
Farben, I. G., 835a, 1249b, 1251b
Farewell to Arms, A (Hemingway), 1440a
Faris, Ellsworth, 922b
Farley, James A., 1518a
Farley, John, 1516a
Farm, The (Bromfield), 55a
Farm Aid concerts, 57a
Farm bloc
politicians, 51a–b, 57a
vote, 309a
Farm Bureau. *See* American Farm Bureau Federation
Farmers' Alliance, 195a
Farmers and farming, 43b, 81a, 88a–b
business, 45a, 57a
changing technology, 1366b
dairy, 44a, 311b–312a
demographics, 71a,b–72a, 1386a
depression, 50b–51a
ecology of farms, 1367a
effect of AAA, 68b
energy-intensive agriculture, 1371b
expansion of acreage, 1384b
family farms, 43b, 44a, *44a–b*, 56b
fertilizers, 1367b, 1371b, 1385b–1386a
Great Depression, 1161a–b
incomes, 1160b
mechanization, 71b, 72a, *72a*, 1384b
Midwest, 41a, 59a
New Deal, 53a
parity, 51a, 53a
pesticides, 1371b
prices in world economy, 720a
prosperity, 55b–57a
South, 63b–64a
subsidies, 57a
subsistence farmers, 63b
telephones, 803a
tractors, 1366b–1367a, 1384b
during World War II, 71a
yields per acre, 1384b
See also Agriculture; Tenant farmers; Sharecroppers
Farmers' Holiday Association, 53a
Farm-Labor party, 296b
Farm Security Administration, 15a

photographs for, *1708a–b*, 1708b, *1709a–b*, 1730a
Farnham, Marynia, 110a, 288b
Farnsworth, Philo T., 815b
Farrakhan, Louis, 266b, 1548b
Farrand, Max, 495a
Farrar, Geraldine, *1612a*
Farrar, Timothy, 402b
Farrell, James T., 1443a,b
Judgment Day, 1443a
Young Lonigan, 1443a
Young Manhood of Studs Lonigan, The, 1443a
Fascism
Catholics, 1519a–1520a,b
Jewish organizations against, 1574a
Fashion design, 1789b, 1790a,b
regulated during World War II, 1790a
Fashion industry, 27b–28a, 31a, 38a, 1025b, 1788b–1791b
counterculture style, 1031b
See also Apparel industry; Clothing and appearance
Fass, Paula, 1825b
Faubus, Orval, 387b
Faue, Elizabeth, 109b
Faulkner, William, 10b, 68a, 150a,b, 706a, 1445a–b, 1604a
Absalom, Absalom!, 10a, 1445b
As I Lay Dying, 1445a
Light in August, 1445a
Sound and the Fury, The, 1445a
Fax machines. *See* Facsimile machines
FBI. *See* Federal Bureau of Investigation (FBI)
FDA. *See* Food and Drug Administration (FDA)
Federal-Aid Highway Act (1956), 72a, 465b, 1351b
Federal Aid Road Act (1916), 1751a
Federal arts programs, 30a, 32b–33a, 1725a, 1728b, 1729b, 1731b, 1734a, 1738b
hearing in the House of Representatives, 1735a
women, 1739a
Federal Arts Project (WPA), 15b, 1705b, 1730b
women in, 1731a
Federal assistance
South, 72a, 75a
Southern industry, 70b
Federal budget deficits. *See* Budget deficits
Federal Bureau of Corporations, 1219a
Federal Bureau of Investigation (FBI), 605a
Nixon, Richard M., 442a
Federal Bureau of Public Roads, 1351b
Federal Bureau of Roads, 1341a
Federal Communications Commission (FCC), 815b, 1168b, 1340a, 1472b, 1473b, 1476a, 1479a
American Telephone and Telegraph (AT&T), 820a–b
cable television, 1479b
television, 817a–b, 1476b
Federal Council of Churches, 1503b
See also National Council of Churches
Federal Council of Churches of Christ, 1516a
Federal deposit insurance, 1226a
Federal Deposit Insurance Corporation (FDIC), 524b

Federal Emergency Relief Administration (FERA), 524b, 1073b, 1729b
medical expenses, 995a
teachers' salaries, 1809a
Federal Energy Administration Act (1974), 528a
Federal Express, 1351a
Federal Farm Board, 1275b
Federal Farm Loan System (1916), 1272b
Federal Food, Drug, and Cosmetics Act, Kefauver-Harris amendments, 1031a
Federal funding, 853a
Big Science, 754a, 755a, 759b, 761a–762a
industrial research, 831a, 847a, 850a–852b
Federal government, 83a
after World War II, 333b
expansion, 198a
expenditures, *1161a–b*, 1163a
foundation involvement in, 496b
increased role in infrastructure, 1337a
intervention in economy, 1199a
as major donor to private research, 503b
Morill land-grant colleges subventions, 1821b
outlays by function, 1940-1973, *1168a–b*
revenues, *1161a–1159b*
and welfare, 1071b
West, 84a–86a
Federal grants-in-aid. *See* Grants-in-aid to states
Federal Hall (New York), 36b
Federal Highway Act, 340a
Federal Home Loan Bank Board, 1338a
Federal Housing Administration (FHA), 69a
computers, 810a
Federal Housing Authority (FHA), 1338a
discrimination, 1338a
Federalism
Cooperative Federalism, 433a–b, 436a–440a
New Federalism, 433a, 442b, 445b, 447a, 1199a
use by Supreme Court to limit congressional action, 379a–b
virtues, 427a, 428b
Federalism and the States, **427a–450b**
Federalist, The, 196b, 388b, 439a
Federalist 10, 295b, 1212a, 1311a–b
Federalist 46, 446a
Federalist 72, 515a
interest groups, 318a
Federal Jurisdiction (Friendly), 394a–b
Federal Music Project, 1619a
Federal National Mortgage Association, 1338a
Federal One. *See* Federal Project Number One
Federal Power Commission, 431b, 1168b, 1170b, 1346b
Federal power expansion, 429a–431a, 446a
Federal Project Number One, 1730a–1731a
See also Works Progress Administration
Federal Radio Act (1926), 1340a
Federal Radio Commission, 806b, 815b, 1340a, 1472a
Federal Register, 526a, 527b
Federal Reserve Act (1913), 1249a, 1271b, 1295b
endorsement by Mitchell, 1294a

Federal Reserve Banks, 31a, 1189a, 1224a, 1271b
  New York, 1224a, 1275a
Federal Reserve Board, 1168b, 1172b, 1174a–b, 1189a, 1203b, 1271b, 1327b
  professionals and, 1410b
  securities, 1162a
Federal Reserve System, 349a, 430b, 723b, 1160a, 1189a–b, 1213a, 1223b, 1224a, 1254a, 1272a, 1275a, 1314a, 1316b–1317a, 1319a, 1321b, 1322a
  increased monetary and bank regulatory powers (1935), 1227b
  and inflation, 731a, 1327a
Federal Rules of Civil Procedure, 395a–b
Federal Savings and Loan Insurance Corporation, 1338a
Federal spending. See Government spending
Federal Steel, 1135a
  See also Illinois Steel Company
Federal style, 1668a
Federal subsidies
  criticized by neoclassical economists, 316a
  cutbacks, 98b
  shipbuilding, 85b
Federal taxes
  estate taxes, 1315b, 1320a
  inheritance taxes, 1319a
Federal Technology Transfer Act (1986), 853a
Federal Telegraph Company, 746b
Federal Trade Commission Act (1914), 256a, 1271a, 1272a
  economists and, 1295a
Federal Trade Commission (FTC), 409a, 520a, 521a, 532a, 1026b, 1032a, 1160a, 1170b, 1226a, 1227a–b tab, 1314a, 1480b
  professionals and, 1410b
  radio broadcasting, 806a
Federal Water Pollution Control Amendments (1972). See Clean Water Act
Federal Writers' Project, 175b
Federated American Engineering Societies, 1414a
Federated Colored Catholics of the United States, 1515a, 1517b
Federated Department Stores and Allied Stores, 1238a
Federation of American Scientists, 558b, 559a
Federation of American Zionists, 1573b
Federation of Galician Jews, 1573a
Federation of Islamic Associations, 1549b
Federation of Reconstructionist Congregations and Havurot, 1588b
Feidelson, Charles, Jr., 1453a
Feigl, Herbert, 1645b, 1648b
Fein, Leonard, 1587a
Feinberg, Abraham, 579b
Feinberg, Joel, 1655a
Feinstein, Moses, 1585a
Feis, Herbert, 636b
F-111 (Rosenquist), 1719b
Fellig, Arthur, 1709b
Fellman, David, 437b
Fellowship of Reconciliation (FOR), 549a, 555b
  nuclear pacifism, 558b
Fellowship of Socialist Christians, 1502a

"Feminine Mind, The" (Jastrow), 903b–904a
Feminine Mystique, The (Friedan), 110b, 120a, 288b, 910a–b, 929a, 1457b
Feminism, 119b, 290b, 343b, 910a, 1567b
  arts, 1739a
  and environmentalism, 1378a
  gender as a political identity, 120a
  gender theories, 101a–b, 911a
  Judaism, 1589a
  literature, 1457a–1458a
  mass media studies, 1486b
  and neopaganism, 1557b
  and new age, 1558b
  New Left, 289a
  and postmodernism, 1453a–b
  and preservationism, 1358b–1359a
  Progressivism, 275b, 276a–b, 278b
  Protestants, 1506a
  sexual harassment, 121a
  single parenthood, 105b
  sociological research, 933a
  theory of body appearance obsession, 1799b
  See also Women
Feminist Art Program (California Institute of the Arts), 1719b
"Feminity" (Freud), 906a–b
Fenning, Daniel, 7a
Fenton, Joseph Clifford, 1522a
FEPC. See Fair Employment Practice Committee (FEPC)
Ferber, Edna, 1581a
Ferenczi, Sándor, 883a–b
Ferguson, Adam, 918a
Fermi, Enrico, 848a, 1826a
Fermi National Accelerator Laboratory, 759b–760a
Ferraro, Geraldine A., 1532a
  presidential elections, 336a–b tab
Ferrer School, 1696b–1697a
Ferriss, Hugh, 1681a
Fertilizers, 1143a,b, 1145b, 1146b, 1160b, 1192b, 1367b
Fessenden, Reginald Aubrey, 803b, 804b, 1471a–b
Festinger, Leon, 892b
Feteke, John, 1454b
Fetter, Frank A., 1292a, 1296a, 1297a, 1298a
  theory of interest, 1292b–1293a
Feyerabend, Paul, 1656a
FHA. See Federal Housing Administration (FDA)
Fiat, 709a
Fiber optics, 799a, 826a, 1031b, 1480b
Fiedler, Leslie, 1453b, 1457a
Field, Stephen J., 383a
Fields, Barbara, 129b–130a
Fierce Attachments (Gornick), 1586b
Fieser, Louis, 837a
Fifth Chinese Daughter (Wong), 1456b
Filer, John H., 505b
Filipino Americans, 97a
  immigration, 186a
  interracial relations, 153a
  during World War II, 152b
  See also Philippines
Fillmore, Charles, 1545b
Fillmore, Myrtle, 1545b
Film Europe movement, 699b

Film industry
  diversified corporations, 1470a
  global film, 714b–715a
  HUAC investigations, 1754b
  integrated vertical monopoly, 1754a
  Plan to Reorganize the Motion Picture Business of the United States, 1469a
  Production Code Administration, 1467b
  race, 150b–151a
  See also Hollywood
Films, 1021a–b, 1461b, 1462b, 1464b, 1465a, 1752a–1754b
  Age of Innocence, 1458a
  Alfie, 1468b
  American Graffiti, 1751b
  Apartment, The, 34b
  Big Sky, The, 84a
  Birth of a Nation, 96a, 151a, 699a, 1465b, 1593a
  Bonanza, 84a
  Bonnie and Clyde, 1469b
  Catholic moral rating, 1521a
  censorship for obscenity, 1468b
  Charlie Chan, 151a
  Chinatown, 1363a
  Chinatown Nights, 151a
  Chorus Line, A, 34b
  cinematic techniques, 1465b
  Coming to America, 34b
  commercials, 1034b
  costume drama, 1466a
  Country, 57a
  distribution, 1469a–1470a
  Dr. Strangelove, 781a
  Dog Day Afternoon, 34b
  domination of world markets, 699b
  Dumbo, 151a–b
  early interpretation, 1465a–b
  Eastern region, 34b, 38a
  East of Eden, 1060a
  80 Million Women Want _____?, 117a
  entertainment, 1464b–1470b
  eroticism, 1468b
  exports, 698b
  Fame, 34b
  film noir, 1468a
  fire-safety laws, 1467a
  Fort Apache, the Bronx, 34b, 84a
  Forty-Second Street, 34b
  French Connection, The, 34b
  Front Page, The, 34b
  gender stereotypes, 1466a–b
  genres, 1466a
  Godfather, The, 34b
  Goldiggers of 1933, 1466a
  Gone with the Wind, 151a, 1466b
  Goodfellas, 34b
  Grapes of Wrath, The, 1073a, 1754b
  Great Train Robbery, The, 83b, 1465b
  Gunsmoke, 84a
  High School Confidential, 1751b
  Hollywood, 1754a–b
  Hoosiers, 59b
  I Am a Fugitive from a Chain Gang, 1466a
  interpretations, 1466a
  Intolerance, 699a
  Invasion of the Body Snatchers, 1468a
  Jaws, 1469b
  Jazz Singer, The, 1467b, 1580a
  Jewish producers, 1580a
  Jurassic Park, 1469b

King Kong, 34b
Klute, 34b
Levi's 501s sales, 1060a
Lights of New York, 34b
Listen Up: The Lives of Quincy Jones,
  1488a
Little Caesar, 172b
Lone Ranger, The, 84a
Manhattan, 34b
Man Who Shot Liberty Valance, The, 84a
Maverick, 1477a
Midnight Cowboy, 34b
Mr. Deeds Comes to Town, 703b
Mr. Smith Goes to Washington, 703b
My Darling Clementine, 84a
mysteries, 1466a
New Jack City, 34b
New Spirit, The, 1323b
Pawnbroker, The, 1468b
Pink Flamingos, 34b
Platoon, 715a
profanity, 1468b
Public Enemy, The, 151a
racism, 1466a,b
Raiders of the Lost Ark, 1469b
Rambo, 715a
Rebel without a Cause, 1060a
Red River, 84a
Rifleman, The, 84a
Rio Bravo, 84a
Robocop, 715a
Rocky, 34b
Roger and Me, 57b
Royal Family of Broadway, 34b
Saludos Amigos, 703a
science fiction, 1466a
She Done Him Wrong, 1466a
She Wore a Yellow Ribbon, 84a
silent, 1473a, 1752b
Song of the South, The, 151a
Sound of Music, The, 1469b
Stagecoach, 84a
star identification, 1753a–b
Star Wars, 1469b
study of effect on youth, 1484b
Suffrage and Man, 117a
"Suggested for Mature Audiences" label,
  1468b
Three Days of the Condor, 34b
Tin Men, 115b
Tootsie, 34b
traditional family, 106a
and vaudeville, 1464b
Vote for Women, 117a
Wall Street, 34b
On the Waterfront, 34b, 1524a
West Coast producers, 83b–84a, 1752b
westerns, 1466a
Who's Afraid of Virginia Woolf, 1468b
Why We Fight, 703b
Wild One, The, 1060a
Working Girl, 34b
Yiddish, 1570b
Your Girl and Mine, 117a
Final Opus of Leon Solomon, The (Badanes),
  1589b
Financial capitalism, 1239a
  rise, 1214b–1217b
Financial centers, 1248b, 1249a
Financial disclosure, 1230b–1231a
  annual financial reports, 1219b, 1226b

quarterly earnings statements, 1226b
Financial information
  capital markets as markets of, 1210a
  computers and, 1239b
  early secrecy about, 1219b
  telecommunications technologies,
    1239b
Financial institutions, 38b
  information processing, 800a
Financial panics
  defined, 1184b
  in 1890s, 1188b
  inadequate supply of currency,
    1184b–1185a
  loss of confidence, 1185a–b
  See also Panic of 1907
Fine arts
  definition, 1725a, 1726a
  testing boundaries, 1728b
Finkelstein, Louis, 1583a–b
Finney, Charles Grandison, 1496b
Finney, Ross Lee, 1622a
Fire (gunnery) control equipment, 1148a
Fire in the Lake (F. Fitzgerald), 267b
Fire safety codes, 977a
Fireside chats, 635b
Firestone, 1142a
Firestone, Henry, 834a–b
Firestone, Shulamith, 913a
First Amendment, 447a
  extended to conduct, 417a
  secularist interpretation by Supreme
    Court, 1521b, 1522a
First Boston, 1238a
First Hague Peace Conference (1899),
  543b–544a
First International Congress of Eugenics,
  864a
First National Bank, 1216b
First U.S. Army, 628a
Fiscal policy
  bipartisan, 1324b
  as countercyclical policy, 1187b–1188a,
    1203a
  economic stabilization, 1324b
  effect on international trade, 1187b
  foundations, 497b
  Hoover, 1319a
  influence on health insurance, 999a
  Mellonism, 1274b
  and political economy, 1312a
  promotion of private construction, 1334b
  tax incentives and political economy,
    1312a
Fischel, Harry, 1567a, 1575a
Fischl, Eric, 1720b
Fish, Julia, 1718a
Fisher, Irving, 1290a, 1292a, 1293a, 1296a,
  1297a, 1298a, 1299a, 1305b
  theory of interest, 1292b
Fisher, Louis, 360a
Fisher, Ronald A., 868b–869a
Fisher, Sidney George, 402b
Fisher Body plant, 54a–b
Fishing industry, 27b
  Columbia River, 85a
  foreign policy, 570a
  West, 92b
Fishman, Joshua, 184a
Fisk University, 1598b, 1824b
Fitch, John, 1093a

Fitzgerald, F. Scott, 33b, 52a–b,
  1440b–1441b, 1457a
  Great Gatsby, The, 52a, 1440b
  This Side of Paradise, 1440b
Fitzgerald, Frances, 267b
Fitzhugh, George, 918b, 920a
Five-Power Naval Limitation Treaty (1922),
  552a, 566a–b tab, 599a
Flack, Audrey, 1718a
Flag Day, 254a
Flag desecration, 417a
Flagg, Ernest, 1674a
Flagstad, Kirsten, 1616b
Flamingo Hotel, 462b–463a
Flammable Fabric Act (1967), 527b
Flanagan, Hallie, 1730b
Flaubert, Gustave, 1137b
Fleischmann, Albert, 866b
Fleming, John, 815a
Fletcher, John Gould, 10b, 14a
Flexner, Abraham, 498b, 509b, 943b, 991a,
  1408b–1409a, 1412a, 1822a
Flexner Report, 943b, 1822a
Flood, Curt, 1775b
Floods in Midwest, 41b
Flores, Patricio, 1530a
Florida
  air conditioning, 72b
  resistance to high-speed passenger trains,
    1353b
  retirement, 72b
Florida, Richard, 852b
Flour milling, 1191a
Flowering of New England, The (Brooks), 33b
Flowerman, Stanley, 1584b
Flow of goods in the United States,
  1047a–b
Flying boats, 771a, 773b–774a
  Martin Clipper, 774a, 775a–b
FM radio, 815b, 818b, 1474b
  See also AM radio; Radio
Foch, Ferdinand, 628a
Foerster, Norman, 1827a
Fogarty, Anne, 1790b
Fogel, Robert, 1302b
Fog Horns (Man Ray), 1704b
Foley, Tom, 303a
Folk culture, 261b
Folk dances, Israeli, 1573b, 1579a, 1587b
Folker Company, 459b–460a
Folk music, 1627b
  Anglo-American, 1618b
  collecting, 1618b, 1619a
Folksbiene. *See* Fraye Yidishe Folksbiene
Follett, Mary Parker, 1101a, 1105a
Folsom, James E. "Big Jim," 72b
Folsom, Joseph Kirk, 222b
Fonda, Henry, 84a
Food Administration, 596b, 626a–b, 995b,
  1273b, 1274a
Food and Drug Administration (FDA),
  948a, 1026b, 1826b
  regulations for the testing of
    investigational drugs on humans,
    950b–951a
Food industry, 1021a, 1131a–b, 1160a,
  1164a
  fast foods, 1033b
  labels, 1027a
  packaged food, 1020b
  regulation, 430a

Food regulations, 430a
impact on health, 973b, 975a
Food stamps, 301a, 487b, 1082a, 1084a,
1085a
cost of, 1088a
cuts under Reagan, 1204a
Foot, Philippa, 1655a
Football, 38b
American Football League, 1774a
increasing teams, 1773b
National Football League, 1768b, 1769b
Super Bowl, 1774a
See also College football
FOR. See Fellowship of Reconciliation
(FOR)
Forand, Aimee, 1001b
Force, Juliana, 1729b
Ford, Gerald R., 346a, *346b*, 364b, 1283b
conditional clemency, 562b
federalism, 443a
foreign policy, 583a
inflation, 1173b–1174a
presidential elections, 336a–b tab
social regulation, 527b
vetoes, 347a tab
Vietnam War, 671a
whip inflation now, 1172a–b
Ford, Henry, 50a, 195a, 205b, 256b, 497b,
500a, *543a, 834a–b,* 1021b, 1038a,
1057b, 1058a, 1139b–1140a. See also
Ford Foundation; Ford Motor
Company
affordable cars, 1751a
anti-Semitism, 172a, 1578b
Drucker, Peter, on, 1101a
in *Encyclopedia Britannica,* 1099a
and marketing, 1045a
and mediation movement in World
War I, 547b
minimum daily wage, 1750a
Model T, 46a–b
reduction of manufacturing costs, 1098b
shorter workweek, 1749b–1750a
Wayside Inn, 37a
Ford, Henry, II, 847a
Ford, Henry Jones, 521b
Ford, John, 84a
Ford Foundation, 31b, 1734a,b, 1735a,
1737a–b, 1739b
arts support, 1732b, 1733a,b
assets, 1732a
criticism, 501b
grants, 1737a
private higher education, 503b
Public Broadcasting System, 1479b
Social Development program, 1738a
Symphony Orchestra Trust, 1734a
Fordham University, 32a
Ford Motor Company, 46b, 1140a–1141a,
1149a
automation department, 1112b
Dearborn Engineering Laboratory, 847a
distribution system, 1038a
foreign investments, 1247a
industry standard, 1098a–1099b
unions, 1108b, 1109a
Willow Run factory, 55b, 59a
See also Model T Ford
Fordney-McCumber Tariff (1922), 631b
Foreign Affairs, 1376a
Foreign aid, 1167a

World War II, 1253a–b
Foreign Bank Supervision Enhancement Act
(1991), 1263b
Foreign competition, 313a, 1176b
effect on economy, 312a, 316b
Foreign exchange, 1164b
restrictions, 1253b
Foreign Language Information Service
(FLIS), 173b, 176a
Foreign policy, **569a–592b**
Africa, 690a
assured destruction strategy, 613a
Congress, 356b
Democratic party, 302a
foundations and, 508b
imperialism, 720a
multilateral security pacts, 338a
Pacific strategy, 676b
president and, 330b, 336a
Supreme Court's interpretation of
presidential power, 411b–412a
Foreign Policy Association, 575b
functionalist approach to war prevention,
553a
Foreign trade and foreign investment,
1243a–1266b
Foreign trade and investment, 1155a, 1166a,
1176a
in 1914 and 1990, 1264b tab
foreign direct investment (FDI), 726b,
727a–b, 728a, 1244b, 1245a–1247a,
1248a, 1249a–b, 1250b, 1252a, 1254a,
1256a, 1261a, 1262a
foreign trade and, 1243a–1266b
as part of GDP, *1158a–b*
world economy, 727a
Foreman, Dave, 1378b
Forest management, 38b
fire suppression, 1363a
Pinchot, Gifford, 1362a
timber supply, 1363a
Forestry Reserves Act (1891), 1359b–1360a,
1361b
Forests, 84b, 88b, 1130a, 1132b,
1401a–1405b
national forests, 1402a
policy, 1363a
set aside by the president, 1402a
sustainable position, 1403b
wasteful cutting, 1361b
See also Logging industry
Forest Service, 84b, 88b, 1272a, 1358b,
1363b, 1402a
managing annual timber harvest, 1403b
Forest Service Organization Act (1897),
1360a
Forman, Henry James, 1484b
Forman, Paul, 850a
Forrestal, James, 608b, *609a–b,* 612a
Forrester, Jay, 812a
Forsberg, Randall, 564a
Forstmann-Little, 1236a
Fortas, Abe, 389b, 390a–b tab, 391a–b tab,
1585b
Fortune, 110b, 1058b, 1078a, 1472b, 1481b,
1831b
Forum, 282b
on urban decay, 458a
Forverts, 1569a–b, 1570b
Fosdick, Harry Emerson, 1500a, 1503b
Fosdick, James T., 553a

Foster, Rube, 1771a
Foucault, Michel, 291a, 893a, 1454a
Fouilhoux, André, 1684b
Foundation Center, 31b, 491b
Foundation Directory, 1993 (Foundation
Center), 491b–492a
Foundation for Shamanic Studies, 1561a
Foundation News, 502b
Foundations
arts support, 1725a, 1729a, 1735a, 1737a,
1738a
Eastern region, 31b
and federal government, 493b–494a,
1733b
freedom, 1733b
general purpose, 492b
health, 974b
independence of, 208b–209a
versus individual philanthropy, 1738a
industrial research, 831a, 852b
medical research funding, 943a–b
research on marriage, 228a
standard accounting in universities, 1826b
status as charities source of debate, 492b
tax deductions, 1733b
Foundations and public policy, **491a–512b**
Foundations of Economic Analysis (Samuelson),
1299b, 1305b, 1421a
Foundations of Social Theory (Coleman), 934b
Fourcalt process, 1142b
Fourier, Charles, 918b
Four-Power Treaty, 599a
Four Quartets (Eliot), 1449b
Fourteen Points, 279b, 550b, 597b, 627b,
679a
Fourteenth Street School of painting, 1704b
Fox, Daniel, 988a
Fox, Kate, 1540b
Fox, Kohn Pederson, 1688a
Fox, Maggie, 1540b
Fox, Richard Wightman, *as contributor,*
1491a–1509b
Fox, William, 1464b, 1580a, 1752b
Fox Broadcasting, 1469a
television, 1476a
Fox network, 1477b
France, 960b
arbitration treaty with, 545a
banks, 1220b
bauxite, 1395a
defense spending, 1201b
disability insurance, 485a
employers' groups, 310b
film agreement with, 707a
indicative planning system, 1281b
jazz in, 701b
nuclear electric power, 1353a
radio and television, 712b
reaction to American cultural influence,
709b
standing army, 621b
value-added tax, 1326b
World War I loan, 631b
Franchises, 1137a, 1140a, 1142a, 1160a
Franciscans, 1511b
Franco, Francisco, 634a, 1519a–b
Frank, Joseph, 1448a
Frank, Leo, 138b–139a, 1577a
Frank, Robert, 1715a
Frank, Waldo, 1567b
Franke, W. H., 112b

Frankena, William, 1655a
Frankenthaler, Helen, 1587a, 1714b
Frankfurter, Felix, 281b, 382b, 390a–b tab,
    393b, 436a, 1585b
    Brown, 387a
    on Court Act of 1922, 394a
    on Truman, 386a
Frankfurt School, 1485a–1486a, 1487a,b
Franklin, Aretha, 1631a
Franklin, Benjamin, 1384a
Franklin, John Hope, 142a
*Franklin D. Roosevelt and American Foreign
    Policy, 1932–1945* (Dallek), 602a
Franklin Mint, 1470a
Franz Ferdinand, Archduke, 573a
Fraser, Donald, 301b
Fraternal organizations
    Catholics, 1514b, 1515a
    health care insurance, 989a
Fraunces Tavern, 36b
Frazier, E. Franklin, 212b–213a, 287a, 927a,
    929b, 1087b
    Negro Family in the United States, The,
    213a, 925b
Frederic, Harold, 1438b, 1439a
Frederick, John T., 52a
Frederickson, George, 129b
Freedom and Culture (Dewey), 282b
Freedom House, 31b
Freedom of expression, 415b–417b
Freedom of religion, 417b–418b
Freedom Riders, 74a, 154a, 388a
Freedom Summers (1964, 1965), 74a, 119a
Freeman, Joseph, 1444a
Freer, Charles Lang, 1734a
Free Speech Movement, 266b, 1656a,
    1830a,b
Free Trade Agreement, U.S.-Canadian,
    1262b
Free Yiddish People's Stage, 1570b, 1574a
Frege, Gottlob, 1642b, 1646a
Freie Arbeiter Stimme, 1569b
Freiheit, 1569a
French, Daniel Chester, 1694b–1695a,
    1695a
Freud, Sigmund, 882a–b, *883a–b*
    psychoanalytic theory of gender,
    905a,b–906b
Freudianism
    americanization, 884a
    Judaism, 1586a
    and meaning of the self, 891a
    and the media, 890b
    and sexual radicals, 891a
Frey, Albert, 1682b
Friday, William, 1831a
Friedan, Betty, 110b, 120a, 288b, 910a–b,
    929a
    Feminine Mystique, The, 1457b
Frieden, Jeffry A., *as contributor,* 719a–734b
Friedlaender, Israel, 1567a, 1569a, 1574b
Friedman, Lawrence, 267a
Friedman, Milton, 1162a, 1299a, 1301b,
    1305b
Friendly, Fred W., 1478a
Friendly, Henry J., 394a–b
Friends Meeting House (Philadelphia), 37a
Friends of the Earth, 319a, 1376b
Friml, Rudolf, 1613b
Frohnmayer, John, 1736b, 1740a,b, 1741b
From Cotton Belt to Sunbelt (Schulman), 68b

Fromm, Erich, 234b, 890a
From Machine Shop to Industrial Laboratory
    (Israel), 833b
Frontier
    conservationists, 1360b
    icon, 1358a
    interpretation of, 7a
    myth, 83a, 85a, 91b, 92a
    See also West
Frost, Robert, 1450a
    at University of Michigan, 1827a
Frost Belt, 58a
Fruehauf Trailer, 1140b, 1238a
F.64 group, 1709b
FTC. *See* Federal Trade Commission (FTC)
Fuchs, Daniel, 1580b
Fuchs, Laurence, 213b–214a
Fuel Administration, 1273b, 1416a
Fugitive, 14a, 67b
Fugue-a-ditty (Ellington and Strayhorn),
    1620b
Fulbright, J. William, 585b, 586b
Fulbright Act (1946), 1820a–b tab
Fulbright program, 704b
Full Employment Act (1946), 333b,
    1420b–1421a
Fuller, Charles, 1503b
Fuller, Hoyt, 1603a, 1604a
Fuller, Margaret, 1436b
Fuller, Melville, 404b
Fuller Theological Seminary, 1500a
Fultz, F. M., *1359a*
Functionalism, 878b, 879a
Functions of the Executive, The (Barnard),
    1101a
Fundamentalism, 1491b, 1497b, 1498b,
    1499a–1500b, 1542a, 1562b
    radio, 1503b–1504a
    sociological study of, 68a
Fundamentals, The, 861a, 1499a, 1500a
Fund for the Promotion of Aeronautics,
    771b, 772b–773a
Funeral homes, Jewish, 1572b
Funk, Eugene D., 50b
Furco Glass, 1142b
Furfey, Paul Hanly, 1523a
Furia, Philip, 1619b
Furness, Frank, 1668b
Furniture industry, 452a, 1019a, 1130b,
    1150b
    South, 76a
Fussell, Paul, 1788a, 1794a
    Class, 1785b
"Future of the States, The" (Fellman), 437b

G

Gadamer, Hans-Georg, 1305a, 1657b
Gagarin, Yuri, 787b
Gaia hypothesis, 1379a–1380a
Gaia (Lovelock), 1379a
Galanos, James, 1790a
Galaxy exploration, 744b
Galbraith, John Kenneth, 1031a, 1195a,
    1301a, 1305b
    Affluent Society, The, 199a, 285a
    American Capitalism, 285a
    Americans for Democratic Action, 285a
Galenson, 132a

Galilee (ship), 743a
Galileo space mission, 790a
Gallico, Paul, 1767a
Galli-Curci, Amelita, 1616b
Gallo, Robert, 949a
Gallup, George, Jr., 1492b, 1533a,b
Galton, Francis, 863b
Gamble, Vanessa Northington, *as contributor,*
    987a–1007b
Gambling, 91b
Games and Decisions (Luce and Raifa), 1305a
Gamma globulin, 945a
Gamoran, Emanuel, 1576a, 1577b
Gannett, Henry, 7b
Gannett newspapers, 1481b
Gans, Herbert, 183a, 190a
Gantt, Harvey, 75a
GAO. *See* General Accounting Office
    (GAO)
Gap (store), 1034a
Garcia, Mario, 140b
Garden cities, 12a,b, 460a
Garden City, Mich., 459b–460a
Garden State Parkway, 35b
Gardner, Burleigh, 925b
Gardner, Isabella Stewart, 1726a, 1728a
Gardner, John, 487a, 503b, 504a
Gardner, Mary R., 925b
Garfinkel, Harold, 927b, 928b
Garland, Hamlin, 1437b, 1438a,b
Garland, Judy, 1626a
Garment-making industry. *See* Apparel
    industry
Garner, John N., 335a–b tab
Garnier, Tony, 1667a
Garreau, Joel, 20b
Garrison, William Lloyd, 10a, 546b
Garroway, David, 1476a, 1477a
Garvey, Marcus, 96a, 145a,b, 259b, 260a,
    1598b, 1599a–b
    Africa, 146a
Gary, Elbert, 475b, 844a
Gas industry, 1164b
    South, 72b
Gaslight-fixture industry, 27b
Gates, Frederick T., 943a
Gates, Henry Louis, Jr., 156a, 1456a
Gateway Arch (Saint Louis), 1673a
GATT. *See* General Agreement on Tariffs
    and Trade (GATT)
Gauguin, Paul, 1698a, 1705a
Gaulle, Charles de, 690b
Gayle, Addison, 1603a,b
Gay Liberation (Segal), *1718a*
Gay pride, 266b
Gay rights, 304b
    Protestants, 1506a
Gay student organizations, 1835a
GDP. *See* Gross Domestic Product (GDP)
GE. *See* General Electric
Geddes, Patrick, 12a–b
Gee, Samuel, 941a
Geertz, Clifford, 291a, 933b, 936a–b
    Interpretation of Cultures, The, 936a
Gehry, Frank, 1689b
Geiger, Roger, 850b
Geigy, 1367b
Gellner, Ernest, 252b, 255a, 268b
Gemini space program, 788a
Gender
    arts, 1720b, 1739b

Gender (*cont.*)
  as category of social inquiry, 933a
  and class, 196a, 214b–215a
  and clothing, 1794b–1797a
  feminist theory of, 289a
  liberalism divided by, 1506a
  missionaries, 696a
  as political identity group, 120a
  popular culture, 1486b
  and race, 139a
  realism and, 1437b–1438a
  strategy, 263b
  Supreme Court, 420b
Gender: An Ethnomethodological Approach
  (Kessler and McKenna), 912b
Gender Advertisements (Goffman), 929b
Gender issues, **101a–127b**
Gender theories, **899a–915b**
General Accounting Office (GAO), 358a,
  362a, 523a, 1318a
General Agreement on Tariffs and Trade
  (GATT), 575b, 725a, 726a, 1166a,
  1253a, 1254a, 1263a
  Kennedy Round, 726b
  Tokyo Round, 730b, 1259b
  Uruguay Round, 732b, 1262b
General aviation, 774b, 792b–794b, 796a
General Chemical, 835b
General Competitive Analysis (Arrow and
  Hahn), 1300a, 1305b
General Dynamics, 786b, 795b, 796b
General Education Board, 493a, 943b,
  1729a
General Education Bureau, 1409a,b
General Electric, 803b, 804a, 835b, 837b,
  846a, 849b, 1137b–1138a,
  1142b–1143a,b, 1148b–1149a, 1152b,
  1411a, 1471b, 1475a
  Aircraft Engine Division, 1145a
  foreign investments, 1247a
  repurchase of stock, 1201b
  research, 835a–836b, 848b, 851a
  unions, 1109a
General Electric Research Laboratory,
  835b–836b, 843b, 1138a
General Electric Theater, 817a
General Foods, 1119b
General Intelligence Division, 598a
General Land Office, 84b
General Mills, 45b, 1025a
General Motors, 46b, 57b, 1021b–1022a,
  1038b, 1058b, 1140a–1141a, 1150b
  Corvair safety, 312b
  Flint plant, 57b
  investment in Mexico, 1201b
  motor bus, 1337b
  ouster of chief executive, 1239a
  Technical Center, 848b
  unions, 1108b, 1109a
  work reform, 1119b
General Motors Acceptance Corporation,
  1022a
General Munitions Board, 597a
General Revenue Sharing, 441b
General Services Administration, 526b
*General Theory of Employment, Interest, and
  Money* (Keynes), 1026a, 1299a, 1300a,
  1322a, 1421a
General Tire, 1142a
Generation gap after World War II, 1059b
Generation without Memory (Roiphe), 1586b

Genesis Flood, The (Whitcomb and Morris),
  872a, 873b, 874b
Genetical Theory of Natural Selection, The
  (Fisher), 868b
Genetic material, 739b, 762b–763b
Genetics and the Origin of Species
  (Dobzhansky), 869a
Geneva Conference (1927), 552a
Geneva Conference (1954), 664b
Geneva Protocol (1925), 552a
Geneva Summit (1955), 559b
Genius of American Politics, The (Boorstin),
  265b, 285b
Gentleman's Agreement (1907), 572a
Geographers, 27a
Geology, 757a
Geophysical Laboratory (Carnegie
  Institution), 743b, 754a
Geophysics, 743b
George, Henry, 274a, 1068a, 1313b
Georgetown University, 1528b
Gerard, Ralph, 870a
Germain, Richard, 1046b
German American Bund, 175b
  anti-Semitism, 1578b
German Americans
  foreign policy, 574a
  Hitler and, 175b
  Midwest, 43a
  World War II, 176b
German American Turner societies, 1748a
German Breuer Community, 1585a
German Central Verein, 1517b
German Jews, 1565a–b, 1566b, 1567a,
  1577a
  and banking, 1214a
Germany, 350b, 679a, 960b
  armament, 684a
  banks, 1220b
  chemical industries, 835a, 838a–b, 839b,
    840b
  competition from, 1084b
  cooperative role of banks, 1217a
  defense spending, 1202a
  economy, 1200a, 1284a
  exports, *1166b*
  foreign policy, 573a–b
  German Reich, 325a
  industrial research, 834b–835b, 842b,
    853b–854b
  jazz in, 701b
  labor productivity, *1156a–b*
  Lincoln Center, 1734b
  manufacturing productivity, 1202a
  national compulsory sickness insurance,
    989b
  occupation, 608b
  radio and television, 712b
  real GDP per person, *1156a–b*
  reparations bill after World War I, 630b
  research universities, 840b
  social insurance, 1071a
  space programs, 790a
  standing army, 621b
  as threat, 595a
  trade with, World War I, 623a
  unification, 693a
  withdrawal from the League of Nations,
    633a
  See also Nazi Germany
Germ theory of disease causation, 973b

Germ warfare. *See* Biological weapons
Geronimo with His Spirit (Brown), 1720b
Gershwin, George, 1581a, 1615b, *1616a,*
  1619a
Gershwin, Ira, 1619a
Gersten, Bertha, 1570b
Gerstle, Gary, 260b, 262b–263a
  Working-class Americanism, 206a
Gerth, Hans, 926b
Gestalt psychology, 888a–b
Getty Center for the History of Art and the
  Humanities, 1737b
Getty Trust, 1737b
Ghetto as term, 168a
Giacosa, Giuseppe, 1788b
Giants, 462a
Gibbon, John, 952b
Gibbons, Green, 1236a, 1238a
Gibbs, Josiah Willard, 1637b
GI Bill, 110b, 499a,b, 1077a, 1107b, 1421b,
  1820a–b tab, 1827b
  art students, 1713a
  Catholics, 1522b
  educational services, 1198b
  housing, 1198b
  infrastructure development, 1345a
Gibson, Althea, 1778a
Gibson, Hoot, 84a
Gibson, Josh, 1771a, *1771a–b*
Gibson girl, 1795b
Giddens, Anthony, 932a, 933b
  *Class Structure of the Advanced Societies,
    The,* 207a
Giddings, Franklin, 274b, 920b
Gilbert, Cass, 1674a, 1680a
  Woolsworth Building (New York), *1700b*
Gilbert and Sullivan, 1613b
Gilbreth, Frank, 1094a,b–1095a
Gilded Age, 11b, 274a
Gilkey, Langdon, 873b
Gill, Irving, 1679a
Gillespie, Dizzy (John Birks), 1602a, 1623b,
  1624a
Gillette
  Cavalcade of Sports, 1029b
  razors, 1034a
Gilliam, Franklin D., 366b
Gilliam, Junior, 1777b
Gilliam, Sam, 1719a
Gilligan, Carol, 912a–b
Gillis, James, 1519b
Gillispie, Charles C., 747b
Gilman, Charlotte Perkins, 275b, 1438b
  economic theory of gender, 905a–b
  Herland, 1458a
  Man Made World, 275b, 905b
  Women and Economics, 905a
  Yellow Wall-Paper, The, 1438b
Gilman, Daniel Coit, 1495b
Gimbel, Sophie, 1790a
"Gimpel the Fool" (Singer), 1588a
Gingrich, Newt, 303a, 305a–b, 306a,
  374a,b
Ginn, Edwin, 545a
Ginsberg, Allen, 1555a, 1587a
Ginsburg, Douglas H., 391a–b tab
Ginsburg, Ruth Bader, 391a–b tab
Ginzburg, Louis, 1574b
Giovanni, Nikki, 1603b
Girls' Protective Leagues, 223b
GIs' cultural influence, 703b–704a

Glacier National Park, 1365b
Glackens, William, 1696a
Gladden, Washington, 275a, 1494b, 1496b
Gladstone, William, 542b
Glanz-Leyeles, Aaron, 1570a
Glasgow, Ellen, 63a, 1458a
Glasnost, 617b
Glass, Carter, 1226b, 1295b
  racism, 131a, 147b
Glass, Philip, 1629a
Glass industry, 1132a, 1133a, 1142a–b
Glass-Steagall Act (1933), 1227a–b tab
Glatshteyn, Yankev, 1570a
Glatzer, Nahum, 1585b
Glazer, Nathan, 181a, 184a, 290a, 1588b
Gleason, Jackie, 151b, 1477b, 1756b
Gleason, Philip, 262b, 267a, 1523a, 1529a
  on Horace Kallen, 258a–b
Glendon, Mary Ann, 291b, 292a
Glengarry Glen Ross (Mamet), 115b
Glenmary Sisters, 1530b
Glenn Martin Company, 1145a
Glennon, John Joseph, 1516a
Glick, Henry, 396b
Global economy, 1245b
  competition, 1264b–1265b
  industrial research, 853b–854b
  transformation, 691b
  See also World economy
"Global village," 1486a
Glueck, Nelson, 1585b
GNP. See Gross National Product (GNP)
Goals 2000: Educate America Act (1994),
  1812a–b tab
"God Bless America" (Berlin), 1581a
Goddard, Henry H., 881a, 885b
Goddard, Robert, 785b, 786a
Godfather, The (Puzo), 183b
Godkin, E. L., 1102b
God's Own Junkyard (Blake), 1665a
God's Presence in History (Fackenheim),
  1589a
Goethe, Johann Wolfgang von, 1436b
Goff, Bruce, 1689a
Goff, Frederick H., 495a
Goffman, Erving, 927b, 928a–b, 929b
Gold, 86a
  inflow during World War I, 1190b
Gold, Michael, 1442b, 1444a, 1580b
  Jews without Money, 1442b–1443a
Goldberg, Arthur J., 390a–b tab, 1585b
Goldberger, Joseph, 942b
Gold Dust Twins, 1024b
Golden Bowl, The (H. James), 1439b
Golden Day, The (Mumford), 11a–b
Goldfaden, Abraham, 1570b
Goldfarb, Jeffrey, 206b
Goldfield, David R., as contributor, 61a–79b
Goldin, Claudia, 202a
Goldman, Emma, 226b, 257a, 1439b, 1568a
Goldman, Sachs, 1214a
Goldschmidt, Richard B., 874a
Goldsmith, James, 1236b
Gold standard, 681b, 719b–720a, 724a,
  725a, 728b–729a, 1155a, 1161b, 1162a,
  1163b, 1167a, 1249b, 1250a, 1251a
Goldstein, Herbert, 1575b
Goldstein, Israel, 1585a
Goldwater, Barry, 25a, 74b, 342a, 348a,
  585a–b, 586b
  presidential elections, 336a–b tab

on Supreme Court, 389a
Goldwyn, Samuel, 1580a, 1752b
Goldy and Dusty, 1024b
Golf, 1768a
  in country clubs, 1763b
  influence of television, 1775a
Golub, Leon, 1719b
Gomery, Douglas, 1484a–b
Gompers, Samuel, 167a, 204b, 257b, 309b,
  697a, 990b, 1071b
Goodbye, Columbus (P. Roth), 34a
Goode, William, 929a
Good Housekeeping, 200a
Goodhue, Bertram Grovesnor, 1679b
Goodman, Andrew, 153b
Goodman, Benny, 702b, 1620b–1621a,
  1630b
Goodman, Paul, 1581a
Goodnow, Frank J., 522a
Goodrich, B. F., 1133b, 1142a
Goodrich, Lloyd, 1699a, 1714a, 1735a
Good Society, The (Lippmann), 282a
Goodwin, Hannibal, 1752b
Goodwin, Philip L., 1684b, 1684b
Goodwyn, Lawrence, 204b
Goodyear, 1142a
  research, 835b
  unions, 1109a
Goodyear Aircraft, 457a
Gorbachev, Mikhail S., 564a, 589a, 617a,
  617b
  summit meetings with Reagan, 564b
Gordin, Jacob, 1570a
Gordis, Robert, 1586b
Gordon, George A., 1495a
Gordon, Linda, 123b
Gordon, Milton, 161a, 184a
Gore, Al, 800b
  presidential elections, 336a–b tab
Gorky, Arshile, 1712b, 1722a
Gornick, Vivian, 1586b
Gosden, Freeman, 152a, 1473a
Gospel music, 67b, 1624b
Gospel of Americanism, 698a
Go Tell It on the Mountain (Baldwin), 1601b
Gothic Revival, 1668a
Gottlieb, Adolph, 1579a, 1587a, 1712b
Gottmann, Jean, 18b–19b, 27a
Gottschalk, Louis Moreau, 1612a
Gould, Howard, 769a
Gould, Jay, 1215a
Gould, Mark, 933b
Gould, Stephen Jay, 874a
Goulden, Joseph, 662b
Gouldner, Alvin, 931a
Government
  bonds. See Bonds
  centralization, 429b–432a, 436b, 437b,
    438b, 439b, 446b, 1309a, 1310a
  commission form of, 64a
  decentralization, 427a–429a
  divided. See Divided government
  employment, 1082a, 1106b
  family welfare, 229b, 230a
  growth, 361a, 1158a, 1309a–1310a,b
  income, 1167b, 1244a
  power. See Governmental power
  and private philanthropy, 503a, 505b
  reorganization during Great Depression,
    1164a
  securities. See Securities

spending. See Defense spending;
    Government spending
Governmental power, 355a, 360b
  Constitution and, 401a
  judicial restriction, 408a–410a
  role of the courts in containing, 377a
Government by Judiciary (Berger), 388a
Government Operations Committee, 338b
Government spending, 310a, 1160a, 1167a,
  1170a, 1309a, 1325a–b, 1327a–b
  defense. See Defense spending
  general administration, 1309a–b
  health and welfare, 1309b
  human resources, 1167b
  increase, 1309a
  New Deal, 433a
  opposition, 1326a
  South, 300b
  World War II, 1163b, 1322b
Goya, Francisco, 1698b
Grable, Betty, 263b
Grade, Chaim, 1569b
Grady, Henry, 77a
Graebner, William, 430a
Graff, Gerald, 1453b
Graglia, Lino, 388a
Graham, Billy, 1504a–b
Graham, Frank Porter, 68a
Graham, John, 1712b
Graham, Margaret, 851b–852a
Graham, Martha, 1710a,b
  influence on Abstract Expressionism,
    1713a
Grain Futures Act (1922), 1275b
Grain processing, 1131a
Gramm-Rudman-Hollings Balanced Budget
  Act (1985), 1174b, 1327b
Gramsci, Antonio, 931a
  Prison Notebooks, 208b
Grand Army of the Republic, 254a
Grand Canyon National Monument, 1360a
Grand Central Terminal (New York),
  1671b, 1673a
Grand Coulee Dam, 85b, 1026a, 1373a
"Grand Old Opry," 1626b
Grange movement, 49a, 53b, 309a, 310b
Grant, Madison, 137b, 138a, 187b
Grant, Ulysses S., 652a
Grants, 852a
  arts, 1728a, 1729a, 1737a–b
  federal, 429a, 433a–b, 439a,b, 440b–441b,
    442b, 443a, 444b–445a, 446a
  Ford Foundation, 1733a
  matching funds, 1736a
  Midwest, 48b, 58a
Grants-in-aid to states, 480b, 481b, 1271a,
  1325b
  aid to crippled children, 997a
  aid to the aged, 997a
  aid to the blind, 997a
  categorical help, 230a
  conditional, 408b, 411a
  maternal and child care, 997a
Grapes of Wrath, The (Steinbeck), 10a, 262a,
  1443a
Grasslands, 1361a
Grattan, Hartley, 633a
Gratz College, 1566b
Gravenites, Linda, 1790b
Graves, Michael, 1687a, 1689b
Graves, Morris, 1714b

Graves, Nancy, 1720b
Gray, Asa, 859a
Gray, C. Boyden, 351a
Gray, Hanna Holborn, 1835b
Gray Panthers, 1083a
Gray-Pecora investigation, 1225a
Grazing Service, 84b
Great American Universities (Slosson), 1822b
Great Basin, 81a
Great Crusade, 322b
Great Depression, 432b, 1072b–1073b,
    1161a–1163b, 1162a–b, 1193b–1197b,
    1275b
  African American families, 229b
  agriculture, 1160b
  arts organizations, 1729b, 1731b
  automobile industry, 1139b, 1140a
  Catholics, 1516b, 1517b
  consumption, 1023b–1028a, 1197a
  diplomacy, 683a–685b
  Eastern region, 27b, 31a
  economic regulation, 409a–b
  education, 1808b
  family, 228a–230a, 229b
  family income pooling, 104b, 229b
  foreign policy, 575a,b
  immigrants, 174b–175a
  imperfect markets, 1195b–1196a
  industrial production, 1153b
  investment behavior, 1196a
  Judaism, 1586a
  long-run perspective, 1195a–1196a
  middle class, 199a
  Midwest, 52a–55a
  policy-error theories, 1195a
  professions, 1419a
  ranchers, 87b
  senior citizens, 229b
  short-run theories, 1194b–1195a
  taxation, 1319a–1322b
  technological stagnation theories, 1195b
  weekend as result of, 1750a
  women in work force, 109a
  world economy, 723a
Great Gatsby, The (Fitzgerald), 52a, 1440b
Great Lakes, 41b
  transportation, 45a,b
Great Migration, 67a
  and school segregation, 1810a–b
  Washington, Booker T., and, 1595b
Great Northern Railroad, 1365b
Great Performances, 1740b
Great Plains, 44a, 53a
  cattle grazing, 1362a
  soil erosion, 1368a–b
  women, 51b
Great Plains, The (Webb), 10a
Great Society, 322b, 342b, 362a, 440b–442a,
    503a, 504b, 586a, 1082a, 1167b,
    1199a, 1282a
  criticism of programs, 1083b
  higher education, 1829a
  social and economic cost, 1235a
  status of foundations, 507b, 509b
Great Wall of Los Angeles, The (Baca), 1719b
Great War. *See* World War I
Greece, 608a
Greek Orthodoxy, 1546b
Greek Revival, 1668a
Greeley, Andrew M., 1527b, 1531a
Green, Gerald, 1589b

Green, Martin, 33b
Green, Paul, 1827a
Green, Pumpsie, 1778a
Green, T. H., 1640a
Green Bank Observatory, 753a
Greenbelt program, 460b
Greenberg, Clement, 1587a, 1712a–b
Greenberg, Hank, 1579b, 1773b, 1774b
Greenberg, Hayim, 1582a
Greenberg, Irving, 1589a
Greene, Balcomb, 1710b
Greene, Charles S., 1679a
Greene, Harold, 821a
Greene, Henry M., 1679a
Greene, Herbert, 1689a
Greene, John C., 871a
Greenewalt, Crawford, 848a
Greenfield, Kent Roberts, 604a
Greenlee, Gus, 1771a
Green parties, 1560b
Greenpeace, 1378b, 1560b
Greenstein, Fred I., 338b, 339a
Greenwich Village, 1699a
Greer, 636a
Gregory, George, 1771b
Grenada invasion, 589a
Grene, Marjorie, 1657b
Grew, Joseph, 632b, 637b, 638a
Grey, Thomas, 291b
Grice, Paul, 1653b
  "In Defense of a Dogma," 1654a
Griffin, Susan, 1378a
Griffin, Walter Burley, 1678b
Griffin-Landrum Labor Management
    Reform Act, 338b
Griffith, D. W., 96a, 699a, 1465b, 1593a
Griffiths, Martha W., 1004b
Griggs, Sutton, 1594b
Grine Felder (Green fields) (Hirschbein),
    1570b
Grooms, Red, 1716b
Gropius, Walter, 1681b, 1682b, 1684a
Gropper, William, 1704b, 1707a, 1714a
Gross, Mimi, 1716b
Gross Domestic Product (GDP), 1155a
  foreign investment, *1158a–b*
  government as a share of, *1157a–b*
  Great Depression, 1163a
  per man-hour, *1165a–b*
  per person, *1156a–b*
Gross Kundes, 1569b
Grossman, Allen, 1587a
Grossman, David, 1588a
Gross National Product (GNP), *1159a–b,*
    1159b, 1160b, 1161a, 1164a, 1165a,
    1170a
  1860–1980, *1189a–b*
  1929–1940, *1194a*
  1938–1973, *1163a–b*
  components, 1973–1990, *1170a–b*
  foreign investments, 1167a
  foreign trade, 1246a–b, 1247a,b, 1264a
  Great Depression, 1163a
  Great Society, 1167b
  Social Security taxes, 1325a
Gross private domestic investment, 1929-
    1940, *1194b*
Groton, 1808a
Group, The (McCarthy), 34a
Group Health Cooperative of Puget Sound,
    1004b

Grover & Baker, 1044a,b
Groves, Leslie, 847b, 849a
Growing Up Absurd (Goodman), 1581a
Growth of Cities in the Nineteenth Century
    (Weber), 454b
Gruber, Carol, 1822b
Gruen, Victor, 1030b
Grumman Aerospace, 796b, 1145a
Grunge style, 1793a
Gruzen and Partners, 1690b
Grzywinski, Ronald, 504b
G-3 powers, 678a
  disarmament, 682a
  relations, 684b
Guadalcanal, 641b
Guam, 551b, 595a, 621a, 720b
Guantánamo Bay naval base, 189a
Guaranty Trust, 1216b
Guard of Honor (Cozzens), 1445b, 1446b
Guernica (Picasso), 1708a
Guerrero, José, 1719b
Guest, Edgar A., 1441b
Guest, Robert, 1112b
Guggenheim, Daniel, 771b, 772b–773a
Guggenheim, Peggy, 1712b, 1728b
Guggenheim Foundation, 507b
Guilbaut, Serge, 706b
Gulf of Tonkin incident, 784a
Gulf of Tonkin resolution, 585b, 586b
Gulf Refining Company, 111b–112a
Gulf War, 565a, 590a–b, 672a–b, 693a
  aircraft, 784b
  Bush and, 351a
  campus peace activism, 1835a
  Catholics, 1532a
  television, 1478b
Gulf + Western, 1470a
Gunboat diplomacy, 326a, 721b
Guru Maharaj Ji, 1552b
Gurumayi Chidvilasananda, 1552b
Gurvitsch, Aaron, 1657a
Guston, Philip, 1587a, 1714b, 1721b
Gutenberg Galaxy, The (McLuhan), 1486a
Guth, Charles G., 1055b
Guthrie, Edwin, 887b
Guthrie, Woody, 1619a, 1627a, *1627a–b*
Gutiérrez, Ramón, 132b
Gutman, Herbert, 205a, 1095b

H

Haas, Francis, 1517b, 1518a, 1519a
Habad houses, 1585a
Haber, Samuel, 1103a
Haberdashery industry, 27b
Habits of the Heart (Bellah et al.), 197a,
    290b, 1507a
Hacker, Helen, 910a
Hackman, Gene, 268b
Hackney, Sheldon, 191a
Hadassah, 1567b, 1568a, 1573b, 1577b,
    1587b–1588a
Hadley, Arthur, 1291b
HaDoar (The Post), 1573b
Haesler, Otto, 1684a
Hagood, Margaret J., 13b
Hague Peace Conference (1899), 552a
Hahn, Frank, 1300a, 1305b
Haiti, 679b

Halachic Man (Soloveichik), 1589a
Haldane, J. B. S., 868b–869a, 1072b
Hale, Edward Everett, 544a
Hale, George Ellery, 743b–745b, 761a,
    840b–841a, 842b–843a
Hale, Philip, 1611b
Hale and Rogers, 1672b
Hale Telescope (Palomar Mountain), 756b
Haley, Alex, 183b
Halfeld, Adolf, 702a
Halkin, Simon, 1573b
Hall, G. Stanley, 226a, 880b, 882b, *883a–b*
    on coeducation, 1809a
    gender theory, 902a, 903b
Hall, Jacquelyn, 138b
Hall, Kermit, 416b
Hall, Stuart, 932a
Haller, John, 134b
Hallmark, 1737a
Halper, Albert, 1580b
Halpern, Ben, 1582a
Halpern, Moshe Leyb, 1570a
Halsey, William F., Jr., *609a–b*
Halsted, William S., 1410a
Hamilton, Alexander, 388b, 515a, 1311b,
    1332a
Hamilton, Walton Hale, 924a, 1296a
Hamilton College, 32a
Hammack, David C., *as contributor,* 25a–40b
Hammerstein, Oscar, II, 1581a, 1619a,
    1625b
Hammer v. Dagenhart (1918), 379b, 408a, 432a
    overruled, 385a, 410b
Hammond, Phillip E., 1539a
Hammons, David, 1720b
Hampshire College, 1830b
Handicapped children, public education,
    1813b, 1814a
Handy, W. C., 48a
Hanford, Benjamin, 335a–b tab
Hanford Engineer Works, 847b, 849b
Hanford Nuclear Reservation, 98b
Hanford Works, 85b
Hanks, Nancy, 1736b
Hanna, Mark, 308b
Hannah, John, 59b
Hanoi, 586b–587b
Hansberry, Lorraine, 1602a
Hansen, Alvin, 1298a,b, 1322a
    review of Keynes' *General Theory,* 1300a
Hanson, Duane, 1721a
    Janitor, 1716b
    Vietnam Scene, 1719b
Hanson, Howard, 1622a
"Happy Days Are Here Again,"
    1025b–1026a
Haraway, Donna, 913b
Hardin, Garrett, 1374b, 1375b–1376a
Harding, Sandra, 913b
Harding, Warren G., 328a, *328b,* 523a,
    1274b
    foreign policy, 575a
    isolationism, 631a–b
    presidential elections, 335a–b tab
    return to normalcy, 842b, 846a, 847b
    segregation, 260a
    vetoes, 347a tab
Hardy, Thomas, 702a
Hare, R. M., 1655a
Hare Krishna. *See* International Society for
    Krishna Consciousness

Hargrove, Erwin, 346b
Haring, Keith, 1716b
Harkness, Edward S., 495a,b
Harkness, Stephen, 495a
Harlan, John M., II, 390a–b tab
Harlan, John Marshall, I, 406a
    Lochner v. *New York* (1905), dissent in,
        378a
Harlem Globetrotters, 1771a,b
Harlem Renaissance, 34a, 150b,
    1596b–1599a
    failure of the movement, 1600b
Harlem Rens, 1771b
Harlem School for the Arts, 1738a
Harlow, Bryce, 313a
Harmon Foundation, 1703b
Harmonic Convergence, 1560b
Harner, Michael, 1561a
Harper, Frances E. W., 1594b, 1595b
Harper, William Rainey, 1495b, 1640b
Harper's, 1481b, 1508b
    cities, 458a
    on Los Angeles, 456b
*Harper's Anthology of 20th Century Native
    American Poetry* (Niatum), 1456a
Harper's Bazaar, 976a
Harper's Magazine, 744b, 1298b
Harper's Monthly, 1481a
Harrigan, Ann, 1524a
Harriman, W. Averell, 586b, 654b
Harrington, Michael, 1078a, 1079a–b,
    1086a, 1087a
Harris, Abram, 929b
Harris, Chauncy D., 18a
Harris, Howell John, 1108b, 1109b
Harris, Joseph P., 361b
Harris, Neil, 1027a, 1030a, 1728a, 1739a
Harrison, Abramovitz and Harris, 1686a,
    1686b
Harrison, Benjamin, 519a
Harrison, Beverly, 1506a
Harrison, Wallace K., 1684b, 1685b
Harrison Act (1914), 406b
Harris Teachers College, 1822b
Hart, Albert Bushnell, 276b, 355b
Hart, Lorenz, 1619a–1620a
Hart, Moss, 1578b, 1581b
Hart, Philip, 1283b
Hart, William S., 84a
Hartford Appeal, 1534a
Hartigan, Grace, 1714a
Hartley, Marsden, 1697b, 1698a, 1701b,
    1703a
    Adventures in Art, 1703a
Hartley, Robert, 1067b–1068a
Hartmann, Heidi, 118a
Hartmann, Heinz, 890a
Hartmann, Sadakichi, 1693b
Hartsfield, William B., 69b, 72b
Hartshorne, Charles, 1652b
Hartz, Louis, 196b, 264a, 267b, 285b–286a
Harvard Business Review, 850b, 1298b
Harvard Business School, 1111a
Harvard College Observatory, 741a–b, 742a
Harvard Medical School, 943a
    guidelines for conduct in medical
        research, 949a
Harvard School of Design, 1682b
Harvard University, 32a, 944b, 1819a,
    1820b, 1821a, 1823b

arts education, 1729a
    coeducation, 1824b
    Fogg Museum, 1729a
    general education courses, 1831a
    law school, 31a
    public relations, 1822b
    segregation, 1825b
    Unitarianism, 1493b
Harvey, David, 1454b, 1455a
Harvey, William H., 1291a
Hasidic Jews, 1584b–1585a, 1589a
    clothing, 1791b–1792a
    Lubavitch community, 1585a
    Satmar community, 1584b–1585a
Haskalah, 1444a
Haskell, Thomas, 919a
Haskins and Sells, 1110a
Hassam, Childe, 1695b
    Brooklyn Bridge, 1701b
Hassan, Ihab, 1453b
Hatch Act (1887), 942a, 1825a
Hatcher, Richard, 58b
Hatfield, Mark, 306a, 951b
Hauerwas, Stanley, 1506a
Haugen, Gilbert N., 51a
Havemeyer, H. O., 1220a
Haverford College, 32a
Hawaii, 595a, 676b
Hawkins, Chauncey, 222a
Hawkins, Hugh, *as contributor,* 1819a–1839b
Hawks, Howard, 84a
Hawley, Ellis W., *as contributor,* 1267a–1287b
Hawley, Frederick B., 1297a
Hawthorne, Nathaniel, 1436b
Hay, John, 544b, *571a,* 571a–b, 621a, 720b,
    1669b
Hayakawa, S. I., 188a, 571b
Hayden, Tom, 287a
Hayek, Friedrich von, 289b, 924b, 1304a
Hayes, Carlton, 252a,b, 261a
Haymarket bombing, 1290b
Haynes, George Edmund, 920a
Haynsworth, Clement F., Jr., 391a–b tab
Hays, W. M., 864a
Hays, Will, 699b, 700b, 1467a–b
Haywood, "Big" Bill, 204b
Hayworth, Rita, 135b, 263b, 264a
Hazard of New Fortunes, The (Howells),
    1437a
HBO. *See* Home Box Office (HBO)
Headphones, 1471a
Headquarters Nights (Kellogg), 862a, 865b
Head Start, 238a, 1081a,b, 1813b
Heald, Henry, 1733b
Health and disease, **957a–986b**
    regulations, 534a
Health care
    cost control, 1005a
    escalating costs, 1003b–1004b
    federal programs, 1325a
    government programs, 988a
    grants-in-aid to state agencies, 995a
    growth of services, 1309a–b
    merchant seamen, 989b
    South, 76b
Health care delivery, **987a–1007b**
Health House, 1682b
Health insurance, 1084b
    campaign for state-administered, 476b
    corporate, 1005b, 1078a
    medical profession and, 1417a

Health insurance (*cont.*)
  on national policy agenda, 1205a
  voluntary, 992b–995a, 998b
Health Insurance Plan (New York City),
  1004b
Health Maintenance Organization Act
  (1973), 996a–b tab, 1004b
Health maintenance organizations (HMOs),
  1004b
Healy, Bernardine, 949a
Hearing aids, 1028b
Hearst, 1482b
Heart disease, 968a,b, 969a, 970a
  evolution of diagnosis and care,
  952b–953a
Heartland, 42b, 43b, 58a
  industrial, 45b
  traditional values, 56a
  See also Midwest
"Heartland Is Hot, The," 59b
Hearts of Men, The (Ehrenreich), 104b
Heart surgery, 952b, 953a
Heath Anthology of American Literature
  (Lauter), 1458a–1459b
Heat-Moon, William Least, 41b, 59b
Heavy industries, 45b, 54a, 57b
Hebrew culture, 1573b
Hebrew language, 1573b, 1575a, 1587a
Hebrew Language and Culture Association,
  1573b
Hebrew Sheltering and Immigrant Aid
  Society (HIAS), 1573a, 1576a
Hebrew Union College, 1566a, 1585b,
  1590a
Hecht, Ben, 1581b
Heckscher, August, 1735b–1736a
Heclo, Hugh, 1317a
Hegel, Georg Wilhelm Friedrich, 1635a,b,
  1639b–1640a
Heidegger, Martin, 926b, 1454b, 1657a–b
  Being and Time, 1657a
Heifetz, Jascha, 1571a, 1616b
Heilbron, John, 746a
Heinz, 1020b, 1022b, 1052a
Heinz, Henry John, 1131b–1132a
Held, Al, 1714a
Helicopters, 783a–784a, 796a
  general aviation, 793a–b, 794b
Helios project, 790a
Heller, James, 1582b
Heller, Joseph, 1452a
Heller, Walter, 199a, 1080a, 1086a, 1300b
Hellman, Lillian, 1581b
Helmholtz, Hermann von, 1639a
Helms, Jesse, 1740a–b
Helmsley, Leona, 1329a
Helsinki meeting of CSCE (1975), 692b
Hemingway, Ernest, 706a, 1440a,b, 1441b
  Farewell to Arms, A, 1440a
  Sun Also Rises, The, 1440a
Hempel, Carl, 1645b, 1655b
Henderson, Stephen, 1603a
Henderson, W. J., 1611b
Hendrix, Jimi, 1628b
Henle, Robert J., 1528b
Henri, Robert, 1696a,b–1697a
Henri Bendel, 1789b
Henry, Joseph, 741a
Henry, Merton G., 602a
Henry Street Settlement, 1567b
  Dewey, John, and, 277b

Hepburn, Katharine, 1466b, 1795a
Hepburn Act (1906), 519a
Herald Tribune, 31a
Herberg, Will, 179b, 264a, 1492b, 1523a,
  1586a, 1588b, 1589a
Herbert, Victor, 1613b
Hercules, 1146a, 1147a
Heredity, Race, and Society (Dobzhansky and
  Dunn), 870a
Heredity laws, 860b–861a, 862a, 864a
Her First American (Segal), 1589b
Heritage Foundation, 507b, 1739b
Herland (Gilman), 1458a
Herman, Woodrow "Woody," 1623b
Hermeneutics, 1305a
Hermeneutics and Economics (Lavoie), 1305a
Herring, George C., *as contributor,*
  651a–674b
Herrnstein, Richard, 894a
Herron, George, 1494b
Herschberger, Ruth, 910a
Hertzberg, Arthur, 1590a
Hertzberg, Frederick, 1119a
Herzog (Bellow), 1450a
Hesburgh, Theodore, 1528b, 1831a
Heschel, Abraham Joshua, 1589a
Hess, Alfred F., 949a
Hess, Harry H., 757a
Hesse, Eva, 1721a, 1722a
Heston, Charlton, 1739b
Hetch Hetchy, 1364b
Hewlett-Packard, 1149a
Heyward, Carter, 1506a
HIAS. *See* Hebrew Sheltering and
  Immigrant Aid Society (HIAS)
Hickenlooper Amendment (1962), 585a
Hidden-Hand Presidency, The (Greenstein),
  339a
Hidden Persuaders, The (Packard), 265b,
  1031a
Hier, Marvin, 1589b
Higginbotham, A. Leon, 132a
Higgins, George, 1524a, 1525b
Higginson, Francis Lee, 1669b
Higginson, Henry Lee, 1726a
Higginson, Thomas Wentworth,
  1761b–1762a
High, Jack, *as contributor,* 1289a–1307b
Higham, John, 172b, 188a, 190a, 597a
  on Horace Kallen, 258a
Highbrow culture, 1462b–1463a
Higher education, 201b, 1407b
  accreditation, 1821b
  African Americans in, 1828a–b, 1832a
  area studies, 1831a
  Asian Americans, 1832a
  Catholic institutions. *See* Catholic
    colleges and universities
  civil rights activism, 1830a
  coeducation, 1834b
  college vs. university, 1824b
  diversity in faculty, 1835a–b
  ethnic barriers after World War I,
    1825b
  extension programs, 1822a
  extracurricular activities, 1823a
  federal sponsorship of research, 1828b
  freshman orientation programs, 1826b
  fundraising, 1825b, 1833b
  general education courses, 1831a
  Hispanics, 1832a

landmark legislation affecting, 1820a–b
  tab
loans, 1829a, 1832a–b
Louis Harris survey, 1837b
Marxist faculty, 1827a
national organization by institutions,
  1822a
normal schools, 1819b
political correctness, 1834a
professional schools, 1821b
rising business influence, 1832b
sabbatical leave, 1824a
scholarly specialization, 1823b, 1826a
scholarships, 1832a–b
secularization, 1825b
student loans, 1204a
student militancy, 1830a–b
tuition, 1833b
unionized staff, 1836a
violence on campus, 1835a
women in, 102a, 902b, 1828a, 1832a
work-study programs, 1829a
  See also Business administration; Colleges;
    Liberal arts colleges; Medical schools;
    Universities
Higher Education Act (1965), 1820a–b tab,
  1829a
Higher Education for Business, 1423b
High fidelity recordings, 1471a
High-tech industries, 57b–58a
High voltage technology, 746b
Highways, 90a, 91a, 458b, 465a–b
  deterioration, 1352a
  development, 458b, 465a–b, 465b–466a
  federal aid, 1341b
  federal-aid highway systems construction
    and funding and total road mileage,
    1917-1970, 1342a–b tab
  interstate, 56b, 439b
  national system, 1341b
  parkways, 1337b
  railroads decline, 1341a
  state-controlled toll roads, 1351b
  transportation, 1351a
  user charges, 1318b–1319a
Highway Trust Fund, 1351b
Hilberg, Raul, 1589b
Hill, Anita, 156b–157a, 393a
Hill, James, 1005b
Hill, Lister, 1000b
Hillbilly music, 67b, 73b
Hill-Burton Act. *See* Hospital Survey and
  Construction Act (1946)
Hillel Foundation, 1577a, 1585b
  See also B'nai B'rith
Hillman, Sidney, 69b, 175a, 206a
Hillquit, Morris, 1568a
Hinckle, Beatrice, 903b
Hindemith, Paul, 1621a
Hindenburg, 1473b
Hinduism, 1541b, 1550a–1553a
  ethnic manifestation, 1552b–1553a
  export manifestation, 1550b–1552b
  temple, 1553a
Hindus, Milton, 1585b
Hine, Lewis, 1697b, 1702a
Hippie culture
  clothing style, 1793a
  and fashion design, 1790b
Hiroshima, 647b, 750a, 779a
Hirsch, Stefan, 1701b

Hirschbein, Peretz, 1569b, 1570b
"Hispanic Presence, The," 1530a
Hispanics, 95a
    artists, 1738a,b
    Catholics, 1512a, 1513a, 1530a–b, 1534b
    Congress, 365a
    Eastern region, 37b
    ethnicization, 181a
    in higher education, 1832a
    Los Angeles riots, 97b
    music, 1631b–1632a
    population percentages, 29a–b
    poverty and, 1086a
    public education, 1813b
    radio broadcasts, 818a
    sunbelt, 463a–b
    television programming, 1032b
    West, 81a, 93b–94a
Hiss, Alger, 178b, 334a
Historical Evolution of Modern Nationalism
    (Hayes), 261a
Historical peace churches, 541b, 549a
Historical research on foundations, 506a–b
Historical Research on Social Mobility
    (Kaelble), 207a
Historical sociology, 932b
Historic preservation, 35b–37b
    Midwest, 59b
History
    importance in the South, 61b, 63a
History and Philosophy of the Social Sciences, A
    (Manicas), 917b
History of Labor in the U.S. (Commons),
    204b
*History of Military Mobilization in the United
    States Army, 1775–1945* (Kreidberg and
    Henry), 602a
Hitchcock, Henry-Russell, 1681a–b
Hitchcock, James, 1533b
Hitler, Adolf, 602b, 632b, 1163a
    and German economy, 1298b
    holocaust, 1583b
    persecution of Jews, 576b
HIV infection, 969b
    See also AIDS
Hmong refugees, 186a
HMOs. *See* Health maintenance
    organizations (HMOs)
Hoagland, Hudson, 946b
Hobart, Garret A., 335a–b tab
Hobsbawm, Eric, 252b, 268b, 269b
Ho Chi Minh, 586b, 666a
Hochschild, Arlie, 116a
Hockey, 1768b, 1773b
Hoddeson, Lillian, 748a
Hodsoll, Frank, 1736b
Hoechst, 835b, 852a
Hoeckner, Carl, 1701b
Hoff, Marcian "Ted," 812a
Hoffman, Frederick J., 1441a
Hoffman, Joyce, 155a
Hoffman, Paul, 705b
Hoffmann, Abbie, 290a
Hofmann, Hans, 1710a, 1712b
Hofstadter, Richard, 286a
    on Sumner, 919b
Hogan, Ernest, 1596a
Hoge, Vane M., 1000a
Hoggart, Richard, 932a
Holabird and Roche, 1675b
Holabird and Root, 1681a

Holiday, Billie, 141b
Holistic health movement, 1558a
Holland, 960b
Holland, Maurice, 843b
Hollander, John, 1587a
Hollander, Stanley C., 1046b
Hollerith, Herman, 809b–810a
Hollinger, David A., 130b, 190a,b, 264b,
    267a
    as contributor, 1435a–1460b
Hollingworth, Leta, 903a
Hollywood, 456a, 1462a, 1464b, 1465b,
    1466a
    direct distribution, 699a
    entertainment, 1468a
    foreign ownership of studios, 715a
    Jewish producers, 1580a
    television, 1476b
    trade organization, 1467a–b
    See also Film industry
Hollywood Ten, 1468a
Holman, Nat, 1776a
Holmes, Ernest, 1545b
Holmes, Oliver Wendell, Jr., 390a–b tab,
    1436b
    Abrams v. *United States* (1919), dissent in,
        416a
    Black and White Taxicab Co. v. *Brown and
        Yellow Taxicab Co.* (1928), dissent in,
        383b
    eugenics, 864b
    Lochner v. *New York* (1905), dissent in,
        378a
    Schenck v. *United States* (1919), opinion
        in, 416a
Holocaust, 1583b, 1587b, 1589a–1590a
    cartoons, 1484a
    impact on American Jews, 1589a–b
    museums, 1589b–1590a
    survivors, 1566a
Holt, Hamilton, 544b, 550a
Holt, L. Emmett, 976a
Holty, Carl, 1710b
Holzer, Jenny, 1721a
Homans, George, 934b
Home Box Office (HBO), 824a, 1032b,
    1479b
Home economics, 226b, 1021a
Homeless people, 1085a
    men, 123a
    political art, 1719b
Home Owners Loan Corporation, 524b,
    1322a, 1338a
Homer, Winslow, 1694a
Home shopping
    Home Shopping Network (HSN), 824b
    television, 1480a
Homestead, Pa., 107b
Homestead Act, 1362a
Homestead (Byington), 215a
Homestead Works, 1135a
Home to Harlem (McKay), 1600b
Homosexuals, 103b–104a, 907b–908a
    Catholics, 1531a,b–1532a
    in the military, 304b
    popular culture, 1462a
    repression of, 104b
Honest to God (Robinson), 1504b
Honeywell, 1148b, 1149a
Hong Kong, 693b
Hood, Leroy, 763a

Hood, Raymond, 1680a, *1680b,* 1681a,
    1682b, 1684a
    McGraw-Hill Building, 1681b, *1682a*
Hook, Sidney, 281b, 282b, 1444a, 1644b,
    1648b
Hooker, J. D., 744b
Hooker telescope, 744b
Hookworm, 942b
Hoos, Ida, 1115a, 1123a
Hoover, Herbert C., 29b, 281b, 328b, *329b,*
    632b, 1072a, 1073b, 1274b, 1276a
    about radio, 1472a
    administrative state, 523a–b
    American Individualism, 197b, 279b
    balanced budget, 600a
    capital market reform, 1225a
    Challenge to Liberty, The, 282a
    champion of pure science, 843a–b
    consumption, 1025b
    disarmament, 552a
    experimental telecast, 1475a
    federalism, 432b
    fiscal activism, 1319a–b
    Food Administrator, 596b, 626a–b
    foundations and federal government, 496b
    global economic activities, 683b
    gold standard, 1250b
    Great Depression, 1161b–1162a
    mining engineer, 1389b–1390a, 1395b
    post-war relief coordination, 495b
    presidential elections, 335a–b tab
    radio broadcasts, 806a, 807b
    revisionist history of, 328b–329a
    vetoes, 347a tab
Hoover, J. Edgar, 171b, 598a, 605a
    racism, 155a
Hoover Commissions, 499a, 525b–526a,b,
    1193a
Hoover Dam, 91b
Hope, Bob, 1474a
Hopi tribe, 93a
Hopkins, Emma Curtis, 1545b
Hopkins, Harry, 479a, 1074a, 1321b, 1729b
Hopkins, Pauline, 1594b, 1595a
Hopper, Edward, 1704b, 1710b
    Nighthawks, 1710b
Horkheimer, Max, 1485a–b, 1486a, 1584b
Horney, Karen, 890a, 909a
Horowitz, Daniel, 1018b
Horowitz, Helen Lefkowitz, 1825b
Horowitz, Vladimir, 1616b
Horsley, David, 83b
Horton, Willie, 77a
Hospers, John, 336a–b tab
Hospitals
    before 1920, 988b
    Commonwealth Fund, 495b
    denominational, 992a
    medical centers, 38a
    Mount Sinai, 1413b
    racial discrimination, 991b
    religious discrimination, 991b
    Saint Vincent, 1413b
    segregation, 1000a
    teaching, 38a
    transformation, 990b–992b
    Veterans. *See* Veterans hospitals
Hospital Survey and Construction Act
    (1946), 996a–b tab, 999b, 1000a
Hostages, 588b, 589a
Hotchkiss, 1808b

Hotelling, Harold, 1383b
Hot Line Agreement, 561a, 613a
Houdini, Harry, 1463b
Hounshell, David A., *as contributor,* 831a–857b
House, Edward M., 596a, 597b, 626a
House behind the Cedars, The (Chesnutt), 129a, 130a
House of Mirth, The (Wharton), 1438b
House of Representatives
   committees, 355b–357b, 361b–363b
    See also Congress: committees
   Democrats by region, 370a–b tab
   religious affiliations, 368a–b tab
   and Republican party, 302b
   revolt against Joseph Cannon, 297b–298a, 355b–356a
   Speaker of the House, 303a, 355b–356a, 370b, 373b
   See also Congress
House Un-American Activities Committee. *See* Un-American Activities Committee (House)
Housing, 1029a
   covenants, 168a
   federal policies, 1345b–1346a
   federal programs in South, 69a
   owner-occupied and renter-occupied housing units (nonfarm), percent, 1910-1991, 1334b tab
   private investment, 1334a, 1338a
   public. *See* Public housing
   rent-subsidy programs, 1346a
   single-family, 47b, 1334a
Housing Act (1949), 1345b
Houston, Tex., 456b–457a
Howard, Ebenezer, 12a,b, 460a
Howard Hughes Foundation, 508a
Howard Hughes Medical Institute, 947a
Howard University, 947b
Howe, George, 1682a, 1684a
Howe, Irving, 282a, 1453b, 1585b, 1586b, 1601b
Howell, Joel, 952b
Howells, John Mead, 1680a
Howells, William Dean, 33b, 1437a,b, 1438b
   Hazard of New Fortunes, The (Howells), 1437a
   and James, Henry, 1439a
   on Twain, 1438a
Howison, George Holmes, 1635a, 1636b
How the Other Half Lives (Riis), 168a, 1068b
"How to Counter Alienation in the Plant" (Walton), 1119a
How to Read Donald Duck (Mattelart and Dorfman), 710a
How to Win Friends and Influence People (Carnegie), 1102a, 1496a
Hruska, Roman, 391b
HUAC. *See* Un-American Activities Committee (House)
Hubbard, L. Ron, 1557b
Hubble, Edwin P., 744b
Hubble Space Telescope, 761a–b, 790a
Hudson Review, 1447a
Hudson River school, 35a
Huggins, Nathan, 1456a
Hughes, Charles Evans, 381b, 382b, 390a–b tab, 410a, 434a, 551b, 599a
   on Constitution, 423b

NLRB v. *Jones & Laughlin Steel Corp.,* opinion in, 410a–b
   presidential elections, 335a–b tab
Hughes, Langston, 150b, 176a, 1456a, 1597b, 1598b, 1599a, 1601a
   Big Sea, The, 1597b, 1601a
   "Negro Artist and the Racial Mountain, The," 1597b, 1603a
"Hugh Selwyn Mauberley" (Pound), 1450a
Hull, Clark, 887b–888a, 891a
Hull, Cordell, 575b, 637a,b, 685a, 724a
Hull House, 49b, 256b, 453b, 1068b
   Dewey, John, and, 277b
   and University of Chicago, 922a,b
Human Action (Mises), 1305b
Human Capital (Becker), 934b
Human Genome Project, 739b, 763a–b
Human Geography of the South (Vance), 13b
Human immunodeficiency virus infection. *See* HIV infection
Humanistic psychology, 234b, 896a, 1558a
Human mind and personality, The, **877a–898b**
   See also Psychology
Human Radiation Interagency Working Group, 951b
Humason, Milton, 744b
Hume, David, 918a
Humphrey, Hubert H., 301a, 586a–b, 613b
   "Political Philosophy of the New Deal, The," 283a
   presidential elections, 336a–b tab
Humphrey-Hawkins Act (1978), 1284a
Hungary, 350b, 679a
Hunger of Memory (Rodriguez), 187b, 1456b
Hungry Hearts (Yezierska), 1578a
Hunt, Alfred E., 1135a
Hunt, Richard, 1714a
Hunt, Richard Morris, 1665a, 1669a, 1671a
Hunter, James Davison, 1562b
Hunter, Robert, 1068b–1069a,b, 1070a, 1087a
Hunthausen, Raymond, 1528b
Huntington, Henry, 455a
Huntington, Samuel P., 187a, 364b–365a, 367b, 607a
Hurd, Peter, 1706b
Hurok, Sol, 1574a
Hurst, Fannie, 1568a
Hurston, Zora Neale, 150b, 262a, 1456a, 1599a
   Mules and Men, 1599a
   Their Eyes Were Watching God, 1599a
Hussein, Saddam, 590a, 672b
Husserl, Edmund, 926b, 1642b, 1656b, 1657a
Hutton, E. F., 483b
Huxley, Julian, 870b
Hyatt, Alpheus, 860a
Hyde, Henry, 1532b
Hydroelectric power, 85a, 91b, 431b
Hygeia, 941b
Hygiene culture, 975b–976a
Hygienic Laboratory of the Marine Hospital Service, 942b

I

I. M. Singer. *See* Singer Sewing Machine Company

Iacocca, Lee, 57b, 185a
IBM. *See* International Business Machines
Ibsen, Henrik, 1437b
Icahn, Carl, 1236b, 1237a, 1238a
ICC. *See* Interstate Commerce Commission (ICC)
Iceland, Reuben, 1570a
Ickes, Harold, 281b
Identity politics, 154a, 155a–b
   and vocabulary, 156a
Ideology and politics, 285b, 308b, 312a
"If We Must Die" (McKaye), 1600b
Ignatov, David, 1570a, 1581a
I Know Why the Caged Bird Sings (Angelou), 1772b
I Learn from Children (Pratt), 1808a
Illinois
   invalidation of reform legislation, 405a–b
   mothers' pension legislation, 473a
Illinois Institute of Technology (IIT), 1682b, 1685a
Illinois (ship), 625a
Illinois Steel Company, 1135a
I'll Take My Stand (Twelve Southerners), 10a, 14a, 68a, 1444b, 1445a
IMF. *See* International Monetary Fund (IMF)
Immigrants and immigration, 1084b
   Americanization, 1513a–b, 1515a, 1516a, 1520a, 1804a
   anglicization of names, 135b
   apparel industry, 1020b
   Arabic speakers, 186a
   Asia, 96a–97b
   assimilation through public education, 1803b–1804a
   auto industry, 46b
   Buddhists, 186a
   Catholics, 254b, 1511a–1512a,b, 1512b–1513b, 1516a, 1534a–b
   Chinese, 571b
   cosmopolitan technocratic elite, 186b
   countries of origin, *164a–b*
   cultural conflict of second generation, 174a
   Eastern region, 29a–b, 33b, 37b
   effect on poverty, 1068a
   employment, 1173a
   and ethnicity, 161a–193b
   family patterns, 223b–224a
   and gender, 168a–b tab
   Hindus, 186a
   Hispanic, 1493a
   illegal, 94b, 96b, 98a
   increase and change after 1965 Act, 185a–186a
   Irish and racism, 137b
   Jews, 254b, 1565a–1567a, 1568a, 1571b, 1572a–1573a
   liberal Protestants, 1494b
   literature, 34a
   Midwest, 58b
   Muslims, 186a, 1547b–1548a
   nationalism, 254a–b, 255b, 260a–b
   new ethnic districts, 186b
   New York City, 453a
   non-Protestants, 1497a
   organized crime, 169b
   origins, 98a
   Persian speakers, 186a
   politics, 299a

poverty, 1071a
pre-World War I policy, 163a–b
quotas, 1578a, 1582a, 1583a
and race, 137a, 168a–b tab
reduction in the 1920s, 205b
religions, 1550a
restriction in the 1920s, 211b, 256b, 575a
restriction laws justified by heredity, 886a
in rural areas, 167b
second generation, 174a, 1578a
silent films, 1021b
silent narrative films, 1752b
sports, 1766a,b
1980s–1990s, 212a, 217a–b
sunbelt, 463a
survivance, 260b
to the United States, 1821–1993, *162a–b*
West, 81a–b, 83b, 94a
women, 107b, 902a
working class composition, 205b
during World War I, 625a–b tab
Immigration Act (1891), 165a–b tab
Immigration Act (1903), 165a–b tab
Immigration Act (1917), 165a–b tab
Immigration Act (1924), 94a, 96b, 139b
Asian Indians, 141a
Immigration Act (1986), 94b
Immigration Act (1990), 166a–b tab, 185b
Immigration and Nationality Act (1952),
166a–b tab, 178b
Immigration and Nationality Act
Amendments (1965), 166a–b tab, 185a,
1548a, 1556a
Immigration and Naturalization Service,
94b, 144b
West, 97b–98a
"Immigration Backlash," 191a
Immigration quota law (1921), 631b
Immigration Reform and Control Act
(1986), 166a–b tab, 185b
Immigration Restriction Act (1924)
eugenics and, 864b–865a
Immunization, 977a
Immunology research, 974a
Impeachment, 589a
Imperial Chemical Industries (Great
Britain), 847b, 1145b
Imperialism, 593b–595a
and presidential power, 325a
Imperial Preference System (Great Britain),
724b
Imports, 1163b, 1166b, 1176b
in 1914 and 1990, 1264b tab
economy, 1155b
and high dollar, 731b
minerals, 1392a–b
as a percentage of GNP, 1247b
petroleum, *1172a–b*
United States net mineral imports as a
percentage of consumption,
1870–1970, *1393a–b*
world economy, 727a
during World War I, 1247b
See also Exports; Foreign trade
Impressionism, 1695b
In a Different Voice (Gilligan), 912a–b
Income
as class characteristic, 199b
distribution, 1313b
Eastern region, 28a, 38b
increase in South, 72b

inequality, 1071a, 1085a, 1086a, 1197a
Midwest, 59b
Income taxes, 439b, 1167b, 1313a–b,
1314a–b, 1315a, 1318a–1319a
corporate, 1315a
farming, 57a
federal, 1314a
government reliance on, 1309b
legislation, 429a, 430a
less progressive, 1317b
mass-based, 1323a–1324a
mass taxation, 1323a
mortgages, 1029a
reform, 1328a
and Sixteenth Amendment, 1314b
state, 49a
Incumbency, 302b, 305b–306a
"In Defense of a Dogma" (Grice and
Strawson), 1654a
Independence Hall, 37a
Independence National Historical Park, 37a
Independent, 1698b
Independent Counsel, 530b, 533b
Independent Sector, 504a
Independent voters, 306b, 308a
Index of American Design (Federal Art
Project), 15b
India, 707b
Indiana University, 506b
Indian Claims Commission, 92b
Indian Education Act (1972), 1812a–b tab,
1814a
Indians. *See* Native Americans
Indians, Asians. *See* Asian Indians
Individual autonomy protection, 421a–422a
Individualism, 437a, 745b
Catholics, 1517a, 1534b–1535a
Midwest, 49b
redefined for mass society, 197a
Individualism (Dewey), 197b
Individualism Old and New (Dewey), 281a
Individual rights
as focus of constitutional jurisprudence,
401b
Supreme Court and, 384a, 401a–b,
413a–414a
Indonesia, 693b
In Dubious Battle (Steinbeck), 1443a
Industrial capitalism
immigrants as labor reserve, 163b
managerial practices and ethnic
categories, 164a
nationalism, 252b, 253a
owner-employers, 1100b
supported by colleges and universities,
1822a
Industrial Chicago, 1675b, 1676a
*Industrial Discipline and the Governmental Arts,
The* (Tugwell), 1298b
Industrialization, 1263b
Congress, 356a–b
Eastern region, 27a–28b, 37b
employment for artists, 1693b
export markets, 720a,b
family, 222a
foreign trade, 1255a
liberal Protestants, 1494b
nationalism, 255b
natural resources and, 1390a–1392a
poverty, 1068a
second revolution, 1128b–1139b

South, 63b–64a
West, 90a
women and, 902a
Industrial research and manufacturing
technology, **831a–857b**
Industrial Research Institute (IRI), 843b
Industrial Workers of the World, 86b, 171b,
204b, 549b
immigrant workers, 167a
Industry
driving method of supervision,
1096b–1097a
funding of university research, 852a
laboratories, 835a, 836a–b, 853b
marketing, 1064b–1065a
Midwest, 43b, 50a, 52b, 54a, 59a
policy, 1264a
prices, 1162b
production, **1127a–1154b**
psychological testing, 885b
safety, 976b
sector variations in recovery from Great
Depression, 1196a–b
society reform, 1314a
Inequality
concern with, 195a, 202a
in death rates, 210a
motive for social action, 195a
See also Income: inequality; Wealth:
inequality
Infant and Maternal Health program, 478b
Infant Care (Children's Bureau), 976a
Infant mortality, 225b, *964a–b*
race differential, 970b
rates, defined, 959a
Infectious diseases
as causes of death, 967b
resurgence, 969b
Inflation, 730b, 1163b, 1169b, 1171a,
1172a–b, 1174b, 1257a, 1259b
and disinflation, *1173a–b*
under Johnson, 728b
world economy, 731a
World War II, 1322b–1323a
Influenza, 969b
1918 epidemic, 959b
Information processing, 799a, 821b
business institutions, 800a–801a
Information technologies, 27b, 28a
Information technologies, 1118a
fundamental work change, 1120b–1122b
general upgrading of skill requirements,
1124a–b
professions in, 1422b
Infrastructure, The, **1331a–1355b**
economic performance and, 1158a,
1160b
five industrial countries compared, 1990,
1332a–b tab
Ingalls Hockey Rink (Yale U.), 1689b,
1690a–b
Ingres, J.-A.-D., 1698b
Inheritance taxes, 1320a
Inherit the Wind, 1497b
"Inner and Outer Space" (Erikson), 911a–b
Innes, Stephen, 132b
In New York (Halpern), 1570a
Innis, Harold, 1486a–b
Innocents Abroad, The (Twain), 1746a
Inquirer (Philadelphia), 257b
Inquiry, 597b

Inquiry into Meaning and Truth, An (Lewis), 1650b
In re Debs (1895), 404b
Insane asylums, 472b
In Sickness and in Wealth (Stevens), 995a
Inside of the White Slave Traffic, The, 223a
Institute for Creation Research, 872b
Institute for Medical Research (Rockefeller University), 493a
Institute for Public Administration (IPA), 497a, 499b
  social sciences application, 496a
Institute for Research in the Social Sciences (Graham U.), 68a
Institute for Social and Religious Research, 1501b
Institute for Southern Studies, 76b
Institute of Medicine, 947a
Institute of Social Research, 931b
Institute on Pluralism and Group Identity, 182a
Institute on Religion in an Age of Science, 871a
Institute to Coordinate Women's Interest (Smith College), 102b
Institutional change, 314a–316a
Institutional Economics (Commons), 1296b
Institutional investors
  and restrictions, 1231a–b
  rise, 1229b
  use of security analysts, 1231a
Institutional Investor Study (SEC), 1232b
Insulin, 944a
Insull, Samuel, 1223a, 1335a
Insurance industry, 31a
  as institutional investors, 1231b
Intel Corporation, 812a, 823b
Intellectual Craftsmen (Weiland), 936a
Intelligence, 614a
Intelligence community, investigation of, 616b
Intelligence testing. *See* Mental testing
Intercollegiate athletics
  corruption, 1776a–b
  Knight Commission, 1777a
Intercontinental ballistic missiles (ICBM), 786b, 787b
Interest, Theory of, 1292a
  Fetter-Fisher, 1292b
Interest Equalization Tax (1964), 1255b
Interest groups
  in balance, 312b
  cause groups, 296a, 309a, 310a, 319b
  changes in the 1960s, 314b
  and congressional committees, 317b–318b
  and courts, 315a–b
  defined, 308b, 312a
  economic decline in the 1970s, 316b
  institutional environment, 316a
  parties and, 295a–320b
  power versus visibility, 317a–318a
  producer groups, 296a, 310a, 311a,b, 311b, 314b, 316b, 317a–b, 319a–b
  public, 314b, 316a–317a
  single-issue groups, 317a
  specialized interests representation, 295b–296a
  at start of century, 308b–309a
  temporary coalitions, 318b
  visibility versus power, 317a–318a
Interest rates, 1176a–1177a

federal regulation of maximum, 1226a–b
  monetary policy, 1261b
"Interest Theory and Price Movements" (Fetter), 1298a
Intergenerational culture of poverty, 1079b, 1087a
Intergovernmental relations, 439a
Interim agreement on strategic arms, 563b
Interior, Department of the, 81a, 84b, 1281a
  Bureau of Land Management, 312a
Intermediate-range Nuclear Forces (INF) Treaty (1987), 552b, 564b, 566a–b tab, 617a
Internal-combustion engine, 1159a, 1160b, 1334a
Internal improvements, 402b, 1332a
Internal Revenue Service (IRS)
  expanded role after Tax Act of 1969, 507a
  professionals and, 1410b
Internal Security Act (1950), 178a
International Association of Physical Oceanography, 757b
International Association of Seismology and Physics of the Earth's Interior, 757b
International Atomic Energy Agency, 561b
International Bank for Reconstruction and Development, 687a, 725a, 726a, 727a, 1166a, 1198b, 1252b, 1253a
  and developing countries, 726b
International Banking Act (1978), 1259a
International Bimetallism (Walker), 1291a
International Brotherhood of Teamsters, Chauffers, Warehousemen, and Helpers of America. *See* Teamsters
International Business Machines (IBM), 809b–810b, 812b–814b, 819a, 821a–b, 826b, 1148b–1149b, 1150b, 1284a
  Air Force computers, 812b
  arts patronage, 1737a
  heart-lung machine, 953a
  ouster of chief executive, 1239a
  personal computers, 823b
  research, 847a, 848b, 851a
  research cuts, 854a
  Watson, Thomas J., Research Center, 848b
  weapons early warning systems, 850a
International commerce. *See* International trade
International Composers' Guild, 1617a
International Congress of Religious Liberals, 1551a
International economic integration, 729b
International economy, 1158a, 1160a
International Education Board, 745a
International Exhibition of Modern Art (1913). *See* Armory Show (1913)
International Geological Congress, 1390a, 1394a
International Geophysical Year, 755a–b, 787a
International Harvester, 1137a, 1141b, 1386a
  unions, 1109a
International Houses, 498a
International Institutes, 173b
Internationalism, 724a,b, 1249b–1250a
  after World War I, 679b
  linked with geopolitical goals, 725b

post-World War I, 722b, 723a
International Labour Organization, 1115a
International Ladies Garment Workers Union, 1108b, 1574a
International Metaphysical League, 1546a
International Monetary Fund (IMF), 575b, 687a, 713a, 725a, 726a, 1166a, 1198b, 1252b, 1253a
International Paper Company, 1132b
International Polar Year, 755a
International Society for Krishna Consciousness, 1552a
International style (architecture), 1681b, 1682b
  1920s, 1679a
International trade, 312b, 1155a,b, 1166a, 1200a–b
  Bretton Woods Conference (1944). *See* Bretton Woods Conference (1944)
  foreign competition, 1166b, 1235b
  global restructuring of commerce, 1201b
  most-favored-nation reciprocity, 1166a
  See also Exports; Imports
International Trade Organization (ITO), 725a
International Typographical Union, 1096a
International Ultraviolet Explorer, 753a
International Union of Geodesy and Geophysics, 757b
International Woman's Suffrage Alliance, 547a
International Women's Congress (1915), 547a
International Worker's Order, 1574a
Interorganization Council on Disarmament, 552b
Interparliamentary Union, 544b
Interpretation of Cultures, The (Geertz), 936a
Interracial relations
  Asian Indians, 152b–153a
  Filipinos, 153a
Interstate Commerce Act (1887), 379a, 429a, 518a, 1269a
Interstate Commerce Commission (ICC), 315a, 518a, 1272a, 1281b
  professionals and, 1410b
  during Progressive Era, 519a
  and separation of powers, 518b–519a
Interstate Highway Act (1956). *See* Federal–Aid Highway Act (1956)
Interstate Oil Compact, 1398a
Intervenor Funding Program (Federal Trade Commission), 529a
Interventionism, 676a
  foreign policy, 578b
In the Days of Simon Stern (Cohen), 1589b
In Tune with the Infinite (Trine), 1496a, 1546a
Inventors
  patents, 833a–b
  railroad technology, 833a
  versus scientists, 832b
Inventors of the Promised Land (Friedman), 267a
Investment Bankers Association, 1224b–1225a
Investment banks
  concentration of U.S. investment banks of members of the Investment Bankers Association, by city, 1912, 1220b tab
  on corporate boards, 1215a, 1216b–1217a

fees, 1221a
influence over corporate strategy and
    policy, 1219a
merchants as, 1213a–b
private, 1213b–1214a
and railroad companies, 1215a
Second Bank of the United States, 1213a
separation from commercial banking,
    1226a
Investment behavior
    accelerator model, 1184a–b
    and Great Depression, 1196a
    post–World War II, 1198a
Investment Company Act (1940), 1227a–b
    tab, 1228b
Investments, 1164a, 1167a, 1174b
    broadening of demographic base, 1222b
    Great Depression, 1161a, *1162a–b,* 1163a
    international position, 1970–1990,
        1179a–b
    telephones, 802a
    trusts, 1223a
    underwriting syndicates, 1216b
    See also Institutional investors; Savings and
        investments
Invisible Man (Ellison), 34a, 154a,
    1450b–1451a, 1601a–b
IPA. *See* Institute for Public Administration
    (IPA)
"I Paid My Income Tax Today" (Berlin),
    1323b
Ipana Troubadours, 1024b
IQ tests. *See* Mental testing
Iran, 689b
    foreign policy, 588b, 589a
    revolution of 1979, 692b
Iran-Contra affair, 533b, 589a, 617a
Iranian Jews, 1566a
Iran-Iraq War, 1258a
Iraq, 689b, 690a
Ireland, John, 1514a
IRI. *See* Industrial Research Institute
Irish American Gaelic Athletic Association,
    1748a
Irish Americans, 570b
    foreign policy, 574a
    politics, 169a
    popular culture, 1462a
Irish Melodies (Moore), 1462b
Iriye, Akira, *as contributor,* 675a–694b
Ironmaking, 1092b
Iron ore, 1387b, 1392b, 1393b–1394b
    world iron-ore reserves by continent
        (estimated), 1910, 1955, 1985, *1394a–b*
Irony of American History, The (Niebuhr),
    284a
Irrigation, 1164b
IRS. *See* Internal Revenue Service (IRS)
Irving, Washington, 1436b, 1744b
Isaacs, Susan, 34a
Is America Safe for Democracy? (McDougall),
    885b
Is Curly Jewish? (Jacobs), 1586b
Iseman, M. S., 137a, 138a
"Is Female to Male as Culture Is to
    Nature?" (Ortner), 912a
Isham, Samuel, 1693b
Islam, 1547b–1550a
    Ahmadiyya Movement in Islam, 1548a
Islamic Center (D.C.), 1549b
Islamic Conference in America, 1549b

Islamic fundamentalism, 692b
    reaction to American culture, 712b
Islamic Society of North America, 1549b
Island Within, The (Lewisohn), 1581b
Isolated State, The (Thünen), 16b
Isolationism, 554a, 555a, 575a, 633a,
    1249b–1250a, 1251b
    Catholics, 1520a, 1524a
    foreign policy, 578b
    during Great Depression, 684a
    Midwest, 55b
    post–World War I, 722b, 723b
    post–World War II, 725a
Israel, 690a
    American Jewish support, 1584a, 1586a,
        1587b, 1590b
    Israeli Jews, 1566a
    recognition, 579b
    War for Independence, 580a
Israel, Paul, 833b
Italian Americans, 137b
    anti-Italian violence, 138a–b
    fascism, 175b
    foreign policy, 576b
    popular culture, 1462a
    World War II, 176b
Italy, 960b
    film agreement with, 707a
    nuclear electric power, 1353a
    radio and television, 712b
ITO. *See* International Trade Organization
    (ITO)
Ives, Burl, *1627a–b*
Ives, Charles, 1610b, 1612b, *1613a,* 1617a,
    1622b
Ivy League, 32a,b
"I Want to Hear a Yankee Doodle Tune"
    (Cohan), 1614a
"I Was Marching" (Le Sueur), 1443a
Iwo Jima, 642a
I.W.W.. *See* Industrial Workers of the World
Izaak Walton League, 58b, 1370b, 1371a

J

J. M. Kaplan Fund, 504a
J. Paul Getty Trust, 1737b
Jack, Homer, 559a
Jackson, Andrew, 324a, 402a
Jackson, Carol, 1523b
Jackson, Jack, 1484a
Jackson, Kenneth, 31a
Jackson, Mahalia, 149b, 1624b
Jackson, Michael, 1631a,b
Jackson, Robert, 526a
Jackson, Robert H., 382b, 390a–b tab
    Korematsu v. *United States* (1944), dissent
        in, 385b, 387a
    West Virginia State Board of Education v.
        Barnette (1943), opinion in, 386a
Jackson State University, 1830b
Jackson-Vanik Amendment (1974), 585a
Jacobs, Aletta, 547a
Jacobs, Jane, 179a
Jacobs, Paul, 1586b
Jacobson, Eddie, 579b
Jacobson, Gary C., 324b
Jacoby, Sanford, 1103b
Jahn, Helmut, 1688a

Jahoda, Marie, 200a
Jamaica, 1395a
James, Charles, 1790b
James, D. Cleighton, 663a
James, Henry, 163a, 1439a,b, 1455a, 1744a
    Ambassadors, The, 1439b
    American Scene, The, 1439b
    Golden Bowl, The, 1439b
    Wings of the Dove, 1439b
James, William, 258a, 276a, 878b, 1439a,
    1455a, 1635b, 1636b, 1637a,b–1638b
    Dewey, John, on, 1640b
    Pragmatism, 1638a
    Principles of Psychology, 1638a
    review of *Studies in Logical Theory,* 1641a
Jane Fonda's Workout Book, 1798b
Janitor (Hanson), 1716b
Janowitz, Morris, 1584b
Janowitz, Tama, 34a
Japan, 325a–b, 678a, 688b, 690b, 691b, 960b
    air warfare, 778a–779a
    armament, 684a
    automobile industry, 58a, 731b–732a
    competition from, 1084b
    cooperative role of banks, 1217a
    cultural protectionism, 702b
    defense spending, 1202a
    East Asian sphere of influence, 732b
    economy, 693b, 729b, 1200a, 1284a
    employers' groups, 310b
    exports, *1166b*
    film industry, 707b
    five industrial countries compared, 1990,
        1332a–b tab
    foreign policy, 589a–b
    high-speed passenger trains, 1353b
    industrial research, 853b, 854a–b
    labor productivity, *1156a–b*
    manufacturing productivity, 1202a
    nuclear electric power, 1353a
    peace treaty with, 688b
    real GDP per person, *1156a–b*
    reconstruction, 726b
    as threat, 595a
    withdrawal from the League of Nations,
        632b
    world economy, 726a
Japan as Number One (Vogel), 1259a
Japanese Americans, 135a
    internment during World War II, 152b,
        176b–177a, 231a, 263a–b, 385b, 605b
    segregation, 572a
    West, 96a
Jarrell, Randall, 1449b
Jaspers, Karl, 926b
Jastrow, Joseph, 880a, 903b–904a
Javits, Jacob, 30a, 307b, 951a, 1735a
Jazz, 149b, 150a, 1601b–1602a,
    1615b–1616a, 1623b, 1630b
    cultural export, 701b, 706b
    important art form, 1630b–1631a
    Southern origin, 67b
Jazz Review, The, 1624a
Jeanes Fund, 1803b
Jeans, 1792b, 1795a
Jefferson, Thomas, 324a, 1332a
    Southerners versus Northerners, 61b
Jeffries, Jim, 143a,b, 1770a
Jehovah's Witnesses, 1498b, 1501b
    absolutists, 556a
    and freedom of expression, 417b, 419b

Jenks, Jeremiah W., 1268a–b, 1291b, 1295a
Jenner, William, 338b
Jenney, Neil, 1716b, 1720a
Jenney, William Le Baron, 1674a–b, *1674b*, 1675b
Jennings, Herbert Spencer, 865a
Jensen, Arthur, 894a
Jensen, Jens, 47b
Jensen, Michael, 1237a, 1296b
Jersey Standard, 1145b, 1146a
Jessel, George, 1025a, 1755a
Jesuits, 1511b, 1517b, 1522a
Jevons, William Stanley, 1289b
    Coal Question, The, 1387a–b
Jewelry industry, 27b
Jewett, Frank B., 837b, 841b, 844a–b
Jewish Center, 1577b
Jewish Chronic Disease Hospital, 950b
Jewish Cultural Reconstruction, 1584b
Jewish Currents, 1586b
Jewish Exponent, 1566b
Jewish Frontier, 1582a
Jewish Institute of Religion, 1579a, 1585b
Jewish journals, 1566b, 1567b, 1568b, 1580a, 1581b–1582a, 1586b–1587a, 1588a
Jewish King Lear (Gordin), 1570a
Jewish Labor Committee, 1574a, 1583b
Jewish literature, 1580b–1581b, 1586a–b
    translated from Hebrew, 1588a–b
    See also Jewish journals
Jewish People's Fraternal Order, 1574a, 1582a
Jewish Publication Society, 32a, 1566b, 1588b
Jewish Social Studies, 1579b
Jewish Spectator, 1582a
Jewish Teacher, 1577b–1578a
Jewish Theological Seminary, 32a, 1574b, 1575a,b, 1585b, 1588b
Jewish United Federation of Teachers, 181b
Jews
    antiprovincial movement, 1444a
    Congress, 365b
    evolution, 859b
    Harvard University, limitation at, 1825b
    immigration of, 137b–138a, 254b, 1578a–b
    and immigration restrictions, 575a
    institutions, 32a
    intellectuals, 1443b, 1444a
    Landsmanshaft, 1573a, 1580a
    organizations, 1566a–b, 1571b–1577b
    popular culture, 1462a
    population percentages, 1492b
    vote and foreign policy, 578a–b, 582a
Jews without Money (Gold), 1442b–1443a, 1580b
Jim Crow. *See* Segregation
Jiménez, Luis A., 1720b
Jimmy Carter as President (Hargrove), 346b
Job Corps centers, 1080b
Jobs. *See* Employment
Jobs, Steven, 823a
Jodo Shinshu, 1553a, 1554b
John XXIII, Pope, 1520b, 1522a, 1528a
John D. and Catherine T. MacArthur Foundation. *See* MacArthur Foundation
John Deere, 1141b, 1152b
John Hancock Center (Chicago), 1686a

John Hancock Tower (Boston), 1686b
John Paul II, Pope, 1528a, 1534a
John Reed Club, 1601a
Johns, Jasper, 1715a,b, 1716a
    According to What, 1718b
    Device, 1718b
Johns Hopkins University, 32b, 741b–742a, 1495b, 1639a, 1820b
    Applied Physics Laboratory, 749a, 752a
    medical school, 1834b
    as model of graduate school, 1408a
Johnson, Betsey, 1790b, 1797b
Johnson, Charles S., 1597a
Johnson, Earvin "Magic," 1773a
Johnson, Gerald, 68a
Johnson, Hiram W., 554a, 631a
    presidential elections, 335a–b tab
Johnson, Hugh S., 1026b
Johnson, Jack, 143a–b, 1770a, *1770a–b,* 1772a
Johnson, James Weldon, 1596a, 1598b
Johnson, Judy, *1771a–b*
Johnson, Louis, *611a–b*
Johnson, Lyndon B., 209b, 301a, 322b, 331b, 334b, 342a–344a, *343a–b, 344a,* 466a, 1199a, 1282a
    antiwar movement, 562b
    arms control, 560b, 561b
    arts patronage, 1736a
    balance of payments, 1255b–1256a
    Big Science, 760a
    budget deficit, 1169a
    Catholic vote, 1524b
    civil rights, 74b, 301b
    and Congress, 362b
    consumer protection, 1031a
    Corporation for Public Broadcasting, 1479b
    education policy, 1813b
    and Eisenhower, 349b
    fiscal policy, 1167b, 1203a, 1324b
    foreign policy, 585a–b, 585a–586a
    Great Society, 440b–442a
    housing policy, 1346a
    imperial presidency, 362a
    inflation, 728b
    Latin America, 690a–b
    Medicare, 486b
    Mohole project, 758a
    presidential elections, 336a–b tab, 342a–b
    social regulation, 527b
    Sputnik, 754b
    Supreme Court appointments, 389b
    television, 1478b, 1479a
    vetoes, 347a tab
    Vietnam War, 363b, 664a, 669a
    war on poverty, 1078b, 1080a–1081a
Johnson, Marietta, 1808a
Johnson, Miriam, 929a
Johnson, Philip, 1681b, 1688a, 1689a
    American Telephone & Telegraph Building (New York), 1687b, *1688a*
    Seagram Building (New York), 1685a, *1685b*
Johnson, Richard, 1487a
Johnson, Robert Underwood, 1359b
Johnson, Robert Wood, 497b, 500b
Johnson, Tom L., 49b
Johnson, William H., 1703b, 1704b, 1710b
Johnson Act (1934), 1251a,b
Johnson & Johnson, 1052a

name recognition, 1052a
Johnson-O'Malley Act (1934), 1810b–1811a, 1812a–b tab
Johnson-Reed Act. *See* National Origins Act (1924)
Johnston, John, 844b
Joint Board (1903), 594b, 602a
Joint Chiefs of Staff (JCS), 333b, 603b, 612a
    National Security Act (1947), 612a
Joint Committee on the Reorganization of Congress, 373b
Joint Planning Board of the War and Navy Department, 601a, 635a
Jolson, Al, 1580a
Jonas, Hans, 1657a
Jones, Ernest, *883a–b*
Jones, Fay, 1689a
Jones, Howard Mumford, 1695a
Jones, Jacqueline, 102b, 108a
Jones, LeRoi. *See* Baraka, Amiri
Jones, Quincy, 1488a
Jones, Samuel M. (Golden Rule), 49b
Jones, Walter B., 335a–b tab
Jones Act (1916), 621b
Joplin, Janis, 1628b
Joplin, Scott, 48a, 58b, 1596a,b, 1614b–1615a, *1615a*
Jordan, Barbara, 189a
Jordan, David Starr, 861b, 862b, 863b, 864a
Jordan, Louis, 1625a
Jordan, Michael, 1773a
Jordan, Winthrop, 129b
Jorstad, Erling, 1493a
Josiah Macy Foundation. *See* Macy Foundation
Journal for Symbolic Logic, 1648b
Journalism, sensational, 1484a
Journal of American History, 211b
Journal of Economic Issues, 1303b
Journal of Law and Economics, 1301b
Journal of Philosophy, 1641b, 1642b, 1644b
Journal of Political Economy, 1291b–1292a, 1298a
Journal of Politics, 328b
Journal of Post-Keynesian Economics, 1304b
Journal of Social Forces, 13b
Journal of the American Medical Association, 238a, 990a
Journal of the American Society of Naval Engineers, 1094b
Joyce, James, 1441b, 1442a
    Portrait of the Artist as a Young Man, A, 1448b
Judaism, 1586b
Judaism and Jewish culture, **1565a–1592b**
    literature, 34a
Judaism as a Civilization, 1582a
Judd, Donald, 1717a
Judeo-Christian tradition, 1534a, 1583a–b
Judge, William Q., 1540b, 1543b
Judges
    election of, 396a
    judicial law clerks, 394b–395a
    Missouri plan, 396b
    rent-a-judge, 394b
Judges Bill (1925), 394a
Judgment Day (Farrell), 1443a
Judicial review, 377a, 402a
Judiciary. *See also* Courts, The; Supreme Court
    affirmative action policies, 529a

and Congress in policy making, 528b
Judiciary Act (1789), 383a,b
Judith (Chadwick), 1612b
Juglar cycle, 1184a
Juilliard Musical Foundation, 1729a
Juilliard School, 33a, 1621a, 1734b
Julien, Claude, 709b
Julius Rosenwald Foundation, 974b
Julius Rosenwald Fund, 494b
    medical research, 943b
    schools for southern blacks, 1803b
Jump for Joy (Ellington), 1602a
Jung, Carl G., *883a–b,* 909a
    influence on Abstract Expressionism,
        1713a
Jungle, The (Sinclair), 1359a, 1438b, 1440b
Junk bonds, 1236a–b, 1261b
Juno rockets, 755b
Just and the Unjust, The (Cozzens), 1446b
Justice, 1574a
Justice, Department of, 1281a
    American Telephone and Telegraph
        (AT&T), 819a
    Civil Liberties Unit, 413b, 435b
    civil rights, 440b
    computers, 813a, 821a, 827a
    radio, 806a–b
Justices of the peace, 395b–396a
Juvenile courts, 225a, 395b
JVC, 825a
    Video Home System (VHS), 1032b

K

"Kaddish" (Ginsberg), 1587a
Kaelble, Hartmut, 207a
Kaestle, Carl F., *as contributor,* 1803a–1817b
Kafka, Franz, 1446a
Kahn, Albert, 820b
Kahn, Herman, 612b, 613a, 663b
Kahn, Louis I., 1689b, 1691a
Kahn, Otto, 1727b
Kaibab National Forest, 1370b
Kaiser, Henry J., 85a–b, 1004b
Kaiser Aluminum & Chemical, 1136a
Kaiser Permanente, 1004b
Kalecki, Michal, 1186b
Kales, Albert, 396b
Kallen, Horace, 210b, 258a,b, 259b, 1577b,
        1581b, 1588b, 1656b
    "Democracy versus the Melting Pot,"
        170b–171a
Kallet, Arthur, 1027a
Kallmann, McKinnell and Knowles, 1690a
    Boston City Hall, *1691a–b*
Kaltenborn, H. V., 807a, 1755b
Kamali, Norma, 1788b
Kammen, Michael, 254b, 261a
Kandinsky, Wassily, 1700a, 1713a
Kansas, 1362a
Kansas Blue-Sky Law (1911), 1227a–b tab
Kansas State College, 1822b
Kant, Immanuel, 1635a,b, 1637a–b
Kanter, Rosabeth
    Men and Women of the Corporation,
        1111b–1112a
    secretarial function, 1115b–1116a
Kantowicz, Edward R., 1515b

Kaplan, Mordecai, 1567a, 1574b, 1577a–b,
        1581b, 1582a, 1588a
Kaplan Fund, 504a
Kapleau, Philip, 1555b
Kappell, William, 1621a
Karan, Donna, 1797a
Karenga, Maulana (Ron), 1603a, 1604a
    Black Community Development, 1604a
Kargon, Robert, 745a
Karl, Barry D., 208b, 1729a
    as contributor, 491a–512b
Karp, David, 1757a
Katz, Michael, 472b
    "Underclass" Debate, The, 210b
Katz, Mickey, 1571a
Katz, Shlomo, 1586b
Katz, Stanley, 208b, 1729a
Katzenbach, Nicholas deB., 364a
Katzmann, Robert, 363b, 364b
Katznelson, Ira, 203b–204a
Kauffman, Mark, *611a–b*
Kaufman, Burton, 657a, 659b
Kaufman, George S., 1581b
Kaye, Danny, 1323b, 1578b
Kazin, Alfred, 15b, 34a, 1440b, 1446b,
        1449b, 1586a
    On Native Grounds, 1446a
K1 C2 (Korea, Communism, and
        Corruption), 580b
Kearny, 636b
Kedourie, Elie, 252a,b
Kefauver, Estes, 1280b
    presidential elections, 335a–b tab
Kehilla, 1576a, 1577b
Kehillah, 1576a–b
Keidanren, 1734b
Keillor, Garrison, 1736a
Keith-Albee-Orpheum Company, 1464b
Keith-Albee Vaudeville Circuit, 1463b,
        1464a
Kekkonen, Urho, 710a
Keller, Evelyn Fox, 913b
Keller, Helen, 1463b
Keller, James, 1523b
Kelley, Florence, 117b, 121b, 477b, 1068b
Kellogg, Frank, 553b
Kellogg, M. W., 846a
Kellogg, Paul, 547b, 549b
Kellogg, Vernon L., 860b, 863b
    Headquarters Nights, 862a, 865b
Kellogg-Briand Pact (1928), 553b, 566a–b
        tab, 575b, 599b, 632a
Kellogg's, 1022b
Kellor, Frances, 170b
Kelly, Ellsworth, 1717a
Kelly Bill. *See* Air Mail Act
Kelso & Company, 1237b
Kelvin, Lord, 279a
Kemmerer, Edwin, 697a
Kempe, C. Henry, 237b
Kendall, Donald, 1060b
Kendall, Sue M., 1706b
Kennan, George F., 591b, 607b, 608a, 618a,
        624b, 688a
Kennedy, Anthony M., 391a–b tab, 392b,
        393a
Kennedy, David M., *as contributor,*
        621a–649b
Kennedy, Edward M., 30a, 185b, 316a,
        347b, 588b, 951a,b, 1004b, 1283b
Kennedy, Jackie, 503b

Kennedy, John F., 265b, 322b, 340b–342a,
        341a, 343a–b, 1199a, 1281b
    and academics, 503b
    arms control, 560b
    arts patronage, 1735b
    assassination, 342a, 1477a, 1478b
    Big Science, 759a–b
    Catholics, 1520b, 1524b, 1525a, 1526a–b
    consumer protection, 1031a
    Cuban missile crisis, 561a, 584b
    economic development of Third World
        countries, 690a
    federal education policy, 1813b
    fiscal policy, 1167b, 1203a, 1324b
    foreign policy, 583a–584a, 585a
    housing policy, 1346a
    Look interview 1960, 1526b–1528a
    Mohole project, 758a
    New Frontier, 503a
    and poverty, 1078b, 1080a
    presidential elections, 336a–b tab
    social welfare, 485b
    space flight, 787b–788a
    Supreme Court appointments, 389b
    on television, 1478b–1479a
    vetoes, 347a tab
    and Vietnam war, 664b
    world economy, 728a
Kennedy, Joseph P., 1225b, 1464b, 1518a
Kennedy, Robert F., 30a, 301a, 487a
    assassination, 442a
Kennedy, William, 34a, 114b
Kennedy Center (Washington), 1734a
Kenner, Hugh, 1448a, 1450a
Kent, George, 1604a
Kent, Rockwell, 1713b, *1713b*
    World War I, 1701b
Kent State University, 1830b
Kentucky Derby, 1770a
Kenya, 713a
Keppel, Frederick, 1729a, 1732b
Kerby, William, 1515b
Kerkut, Gerald A., 874a
Kern, Jerome, 1619a, *1619b*
Kern, John W., 335a–b tab
Kernell, Samuel, 324b
Kerner Report, 180b
Kerouac, Jack, 1555a, 1715a
Kerr, Clark, 1831a
    Uses of the University, The, 1829b
Kerr, Robert S., 1001b
Kerr-Mills bill, 1001b
Kesey, Ken, 1452b
Kesselring, Albert, 646a
Kessler, Suzanne, 912b
Ketchel, Stanley, *1770a–b*
Kettering, Charles, 848b, 1414a
Kettl, David, 359b
Kettl, Donald, 358a, 360a,b
Kevles, Daniel, 749a, 751a, 763a, 840b,
        846b, 847a, 849a, 850a, 852a
Kevorkian, Jack, 952a
Key, Ellen, 226b–227a
Key, Francis Scott, 785a
Keynes, John Maynard, 724b, 1026a,
        1162b–1163a, 1163a, 1277b, 1299a,
        1300a, 1321b, 1421a
Keynesianism
    as culmination of corporate liberalism,
        1324a
    Reorganization Act (1939), 1322a

Keyserling, Leon, 1280a
Key West Agreement, 612a
Khomeini, Ayatollah Ruhollah, 588b
Khrushchev, Nikita, 265a, 341b, 583a–b,
    583b, 584b, 1030b–1031a, 1478b
    arms control, 560a
    spy planes, 781a
Kidder, Drexel, 1214a
Kidder, Peabody & Company, 1215a, 1216b
Kidwell, Claudia B., 1788b
Kienholz, Ed
    Portable War Memorial, 1719b
    State Hospital, The, 1719a
Kilgore, Harley M., 759b
Killers of the Dream (Smith), 71b, 147b
Killian, James R., 1828b
Killingsworth, Charles, 1114b
Kimball, Justin Ford, 993b
Kimball, Moses, 1748b
Kim Il-sung, 656a,b
Kinder Care, 1033b
Kinetoscope, 1752b
King, Billie Jean, 1775a
    equal rights in sports, 1780a
King, Carole, 1471a
King, Cecil, 1001b
King, Ernest, 603b
King, Larry, 1756a
King, Martin Luther, Jr., 74a, 118b, 153b,
    180b, 266a, 287a,b, 1600a
    assassination, 442a
    holiday, 97b
    nonviolent resistance, 1505a–b
    SANE, 559b
King, Rodney, 97b, 154a, 188b, 398a–b,
    825b
King, Stephen, 1482b
King, Willford, 1071a
King-Anderson bill, 1001b–1002a
King Kullen stores, 1025a
Kingsley, Clarence, 1805b
Kingston, Maxine Hong
    China Men, 1456b
    Woman Warrior, The, 1456b
Kinnock, Neil, 319a
Kinsey, Alfred, 103b, 908a
Kipling, Rudyard, 678a
Kirk, Russell, 1525a
Kirkland, Edward C., 1291a
Kirkpatrick, George R., 335a–b tab
Kirstein, Lincoln, 1727b
Kirzner, Israel, 1304a
Kissinger, Henry, 584a, 587a–b, 588a–b,
    616b, 691b, 1832a
    antiwar movement, 562b
    Middle East, 692a
    Vietnam War, 669b
Kistiakowsky, George, 759a
Kitchin, Claude, 1315b, 1316a
Kitchin wave, 1184a
Kitt Peak National Observatory, 753a,
    758b
Kitty Hawk, N.C., 768a
Klamer, Arjo, 1306b
Klein, Calvin, 1791a
Klein, Lawrence, 1300b
Klein, Melanie, 909a
Klepfisz, Irena, 1587a
Klezmer music, 1571a, 1580a
Kline, Franz, 1712b
Klineberg, Otto, 886b

Kloppenberg, James T., as contributor,
    273a–294b
Knickerbocker Club (New York), 1743b
Knight, David, 740a
Knight, Frank, 1297a–b, 1298b
    review of Keynes' General Theory, 1300a
Knights of Columbus, 114b, 1519b
Knights of Labor, 274a
Knopf, Alfred A., 1373b
Knowledge advancement, 1165b–1166a
Knox, Frank, 578a, 635a
    presidential elections, 335a–b tab
Knox, Philander C., 594b
Koch, Kenneth, 1587a
Koch, Robert, 944a
Kochner, A. Lawrence, 1682b
Kodak. See Eastman Kodak
Koffka, Kurt, 888a
Kohl, Helmut, 352a
Kohlberg, Lawrence, 911b
Kohlberg Kravis Roberts & Company,
    1211a, 1236a
Kohler, Wofgang, 888a
Kohn, Eugene, 1582a
Kohn, Hans, 252a, 264b
Kolmer, John, 946a
Kolodney, William, 1579a
Komarovsky, Mirra, 910a, 929a
Kondratieff, N. D., 1184a
Konoye, Fumimaro, 637b, 639b
Kooning, Willem de, 1712b, 1722a, 1730b
Korea
    economic power, 693b
    Joint Soviet-American occupation, 654b
    Korean Democratic party, 656a
    United Nations goal, 658a
    United Nations Peace-Keeping
        Operations (PKO), 693a
Korea Association of Creation Research,
    874a
Korean Americans, 96b–97a, 186a
Korean National Association, 96b–97a
Korean War, 336b, 611a–b, 612b, 654a–b,
    654b–663a, 688b, 1167b, 1253b, 1280a
    aircraft industry in Los Angeles, 462a
    airplanes, 782a
    arms race, 849b
    causes, 656a–b
    economic stimulus, 1077b, 1198b
    foreign policy, 580b–581a
    higher education, 1829a
    limited war, 651a
    national security state, 1281a
    nuclear research, 750b
    settlement negotiations, 660a–661a
    taxation, 1325a
Kornblum, William, 209b
Kosher laws, 1572b, 1575b
Kosinski, Jerzy, 1756a
KOS (Kids of Survival), 1716b
Kotler, Aaron, 1585a
Koussevitzky, Serge, 1616b
Kovacs, Ernie, 1477b
Kracauer, Siegfried, 1484a
Krasner, Lee, 1710b, 1731a
Kraus, Adolph, 1566b
Krehbiel, Henry E., 1611b
Kreidberg, Marvin A., 602a
Kreisler, Fritz, 1616b
Kripke, Saul, 1659a–b
    "Naming and Necessity," 1659a

Krishnamurti, Jiddu, 1544a
    influence on Abstract Expressionism,
        1713a
Kristol, Irving, 290a, 1586a
Kroc, Ray, 1757a
Krock, Arthur, 383b
Kropotkin, Petr, 862b
Kruger, Barbara, 1587a, 1721a
Krugman, Saul, 950b
Krupa, Gene, 1571a
Krupat, Arnold, 1456a
Krutch, Joseph Wood, 1501a
Kuhlman, Kathryn, 1501a
Kuhn, Loeb, 1214a, 1216b
Kuhn, Thomas, 267a, 291a
    Structure of Scientific Revolutions, The,
        1655b
Kuhn, Walt, 1698a
Ku Klux Klan, 55a, 139b
    anti-Semitism, 1578b
    Black, Hugo L., 382b
    Catholics, 1516b
    Garvey, Marcus, meeting with, 260a,
        1599b
    Midwest, 52a
    1920s revival, 68a, 172b
    West, 96a, 97b
Kulp, J. Laurence, 868a
Kumin, Maxine, 1587a
Kunitz, Stanley, 1579a, 1580b
Kurys, Sophie, 1779b
Kutler, Stanley, 1450a
Kuwait, 693a, 1478b
    invasion, 590a
Kuznets, Simon, 1159b, 1184a, 1421a
Kwanza, 1604a
Kyle, James H., 1268a

L

L. L. Bean, 1064a
Labor, 29b, 1264a
    after World War I, 1193a
    collective bargaining, 1108a
    division by ethnicity, 166a
    Eastern region, 28a–b
    expansion, 1173a
    new production conditions, 1096a–1098a
    occupational profile, 1107a, 1118a
    productivity, 1156a–b, 1172b
    Russel Sage Foundation, 493a
    sectoral shifts, 1107a
    skill levels, 166a, 205a,b
    turnover rate in early century, 1098a
    unrest, 254b–255a, 1193a, 1290b
    World War II, 1109a, 1164b
    See also specific unions
Labor, Department of, 1272b, 1281a
Labor and Monopoly Capital (Braverman),
    200b
Laboratory Animal Welfare Act (1966),
    949b
Labor costs, 1166b, 1176b, 1178a–b
Labor Health Institute (Saint Louis), 1004b
Labor-Management Relations Act. See
    Taft–Hartley Act
Labor unions, 30a, 83b, 86b, 95a, 309b,
    310a–b, 430a, 431a, 435b
    architects opposed to, 1667a

changed work force, 1117a
college faculties, 1835b
Democratic party, 314a,b
federal policy, 311b
and foreign direct investments, 727b
Jewish, 1574a
leaders and immigration restrictions, 167a
loss of bargaining power in 1990s, 473a
membership, 1109b
Midwest, 54a, 57b, 58a
multiethnic coalitions, 167b
musicians, 1733b
nativist sentiments prior to 1930s, 167a
political action committees, 313b
racism prior to 1930s, 167a
regulation, 431b
and revolutionary radicalism, 204a
and saloons, 1748a
South, 69a–b, 71a
Taft-Hartley Act, 311b
white collar, 1108b
women in, 107a, 109b, 112a
world economy, 727b
See also specific organizations
Labor withholding, 1097b
Labor Zionists, 1582a
Labour party (Britain), 308b, 319a
Lacey, John D., 1360a
Lacey Act, 1360a
Laconia (ship), 1746a
Ladies Home Journal, 37b, 114b, 976a,
  1677b, 1787b
Laemmle, Carl, 1580a, 1752b, 1753a
LaFarge, John, 1517b
La Follette, Robert M., 49a, 299b, 380b,
  548b, 548b
  presidential elections, 335a–b tab
La Gallienne, Eva, 1727b
La Guardia, Fiorello, 172b, 1734b
Lakota, 134b
Lamar, Joseph R., 390a–b tab
Lamarck, Jean Baptiste, 859b
Lammerts, Walter E., 872a
Lamphere, Louise, 933a
Land development, 1160a
Land distribution
  Mexican Americans, 95a
  West, 84a–b, 88a, 92b
Landis, James, 437a,b, 1420b
Landis, James M., 393b
  on Court Act of 1922, 394a
Landis, Kenesaw Mountain, 1769a–b
Land O'Lakes Statement, 1528b
Landon, Alfred M., 481b
  presidential elections, 335a–b tab
Landscape
  architecture, 35b–37a
  Eastern region, 34b–35b
  Midwest, 41b, 43a, 47b, 56a–b
Land's End, 1064a
Land Withdrawal Act (1910), 1397b
Lang, Fritz, 700a
Lang, Jack, 713a, 714b
Lang, Pearl, 1579a
Langdell, Christopher, 1408b
Lange, Dorothea, 261b, *1708a–b,* 1708b,
  1730a
Lange, Oskar, 1306a
Langley, Samuel Pierpont, 767a–b
Langley Field, VA, 772a
Langmuir, Irving, 836b, 841b, 844b

Language, Truth, and Logic (Ayer), 1646b
Language Loyalty in the United States
  (Fishman), 184a
Lansing, Robert, 596a
Lansky, Meyer, 462b, 1579b
Laotians, 97a, 186a
Lapp, Ralph E., 754a
Lapson, Dvora, 1573b, 1576a
Lapson, Judah, 1576a
Lardner, Ring, 1767a
Large-scale scientific enterprise, **739a–765b**
Larkin, Oliver, 1712b
Larson, Edward J., 861b
Larson, Nella, 150b
Las Casas, Bartolomé de, 132a
Lasers, 1031b
Lashley, Karl, 888a, 892b
Laski, Harold, 924b
Lassaw, Ibram, 1712b, 1722a
Last Hurrah, The (O'Connor), 34a
Las Vegas, Nev., 462b–463a
Late George Apley, The (Marquand), 1788a
Lathrop, Julia, 121b, 477b
Latin America
  Good Neighbor policy, 724a
  reaction to Americanization, 710a
  trade with, 733a
  world economy, 721b, 722a, 724a–b,
    726b
Latin American Confederation of Labor,
  705a
Latinos
  Catholics, 1493a
  evangelical Protestantism, 1492b–1493a
  poverty, 210a
  West, 93b–94a
Latter-day Saints. *See* Mormons
Laughlin, Harry H., 864b
Laughlin, J. Laurence, 1291a, 1293a
  banking reform, 1295b
Laura Spelman Rockefeller Memorial, 495a
Lauren, Ralph, 1791a
Lausanne Conference (1923), 682b
Lauter, Paul, 1458a
Lavoie, Don, 1305a
Law, Ruth, 770a
Law, Sylvia A., 993b
Lawrence, D. H., 1447b
Lawrence, Ernest, 745b–748a, 750b, 752a
Lawrence, Florence, 1753a
Lawrence, Jacob, 1710b, 1714a
Lawrence, Mass., 107b
Lawrence Laboratories (Harvard), 1408a
Lawrence Livermore laboratory, 85b
Lawson, Ernest, 1697a, 1721b
Lawson, John Howard, 1581b
Lawyers. *See* Legal profession
Lazarsfeld, Paul, 1485a
Lazarus, Emma, 163b
Lazzeri, "Poosh 'Em Up Tony," 173a, 1766b
Lead, 1387b, 1392b
Leaf, June, 1714b, 1721b
League of Composers, 1617a
League of Conservation Voters, 1376b
League of Nations, 328a, 550b, 574a–b,
  630a, 722b, 1249b
  admission of Soviet Union, 684b
  American refusal to join, 723b
  covenant, 630b
  Film Europe movement, 699b
  mandates, 679b

League of Nations Association, 553a
League of United Latin American Citizens
  (LULAC), 95a, 140b, 144b
  education, 1811a
League of Women Voters, 120b
League to Enforce Peace, 550a
Leahy, William D., 603b, *609a–b*
Lear, Norman, 1477b
Lear, William, 794a
Learning From Las Vegas (Venturi), 1665a
Least Dangerous Branch, The (Bickel), 388b
Leather industry, 1130a,b, 1132b, 1150b
  trade performance, 1200b
Leaves of Grass (Whitman), 427b
Lebanon, 679b
Lebedoff, Aaron, 1570b
Le Bourget airport (France), *772a–b*
Le Brun, Napoleon, 1675a
Le Conte, Joseph, 860b
Le Corbusier, 1684a, 1685b, 1689b
Lectures on Modern History (Acton), 427b
Lederer, Susan E., *as contributor,* 941a–956b
Lee, Benjamin, 957a
Lee, Don L.. *See* Madhubuti, Haki
Lee, Helen Jackson, 147b–148a
Lee, Higginson, 1216b
Lee, Ivy, 1411a
Lee, Russell, 1708b
Leeser, Isaac, 1566b
Lefebvre, Marcel, 1533b
Leffingwell, William Henry, 1105a–1106a
Leffler, Melvyn P., 607b, 608a
Left
  architects and the, 1667a
  cultural values, 304b
  literary culture of, 1442b–1443a
  See also New Left
Legal Aid Society, 1417a
Legal cases
  Abington School District v. *Schemp* (1963),
    418a
  Abrams v. *United States* (1919), 416a
  Adair v. *United States* (1908), 405b
  Adamson v. *California* (1947), 436a
  Adkins v. *Children's Hospital* (1923), 378b,
    381b, 409a
  American Power and Light Co. v. *S.E.C.*
    (1947), 435a
  Bailey v. *Drexel Furniture Co.* (1922),
    408a, 432a
  Baker v. *Carr* (1962), 365a, 388a, 419b
  Barron v. *Baltimore* (1833), 414b
  Betts v. *Brady* (1942), 440a
  Black and White Taxicab Co. v. *Brown and
    Yellow Taxicab Co.* (1928), 383a–b
  Brandenburg v. *Ohio* (1969), 416b
  Brown v. *Board of Education* (1954). *See*
    Brown v. *Board of Education* (1954)
  Brown v. *Board of Education II* (1955), 387a
  Buck v. *Bell* (1927), 864b
  Burstyn v. *Wilson* (1952), 1468b
  Buttfield v. *Stranahan* (1904), 522b
  Califano v. *Goldfarb* (1977), 421a
  Carter v. *Carter Coal Company* (1936),
    380b, 409b
  Chambers v. *Florida* (1940), 435b
  Champion v. *Ames* (1903), 379b, 406a
  *Cincinnati, New Orleans, and Texas Pacific
    Ry. Co.* v. *I.C.C.* (1896), 519a
  Civil Rights cases (1883), 404a, 410b
  Clark v. *Jeter* (1988), 421a

Cohens v. Virginia (1821), 402a
Cohen v. California (1971), 416b
Cook v. Ochsner Foundation Hospital,
    1000a
Cooper v. Aaron (1958), 387b
Coppage v. Kansas (1915), 378a, 405b
Craig v. Boren (1976), 420b
Davis v. Beacon (1890), 1542a
Dennis v. United States (1951), 416b
Eaton v. Grubbs, 1003a
Eisenstadt v. Baird, 240b
Employment Division v. Smith (1990), 418a
Engel v. Vitale (1962), 418a
Erie Railroad Co. v. Tompkins (1938),
    383a,b
Euclid v. Ambler Realty Company (1926),
    409a
Everson v. Board of Education (1947), 417b,
    1521b
Field v. Clark (1892), 522b
Furman v. Georgia (1972), 419a
Garcia v. San Antonio Metropolitan Transit
    Authority (1985), 411a, 444a
Gibbons v. Ogden (1823), 402a
Gideon v. Wainwright (1963), 418b, 440a
Gitlow v. New York (1925), 415a, 436a
Gregg v. Georgia (1976), 419a
Griswold v. Connecticut (1965), 240b, 387b,
    421b, 440a
Hammer v. Dagenhart (1918). See Hammer
    v. Dagenhart (1918)
Hampton, J.W., Jr., and Co. v. United States
    (1928), 522b
Harris v. New York (1971), 419a
Home Building and Loan Association v.
    Blaisdall (1934), 434a
Houston, East and West Texas Railway Co.
    v. United States (1914), 379a
Hurtado v. California (1884), 415a
Immigration and Naturalization Service v.
    Chadha (1983), 412b, 533b
Inland Steel case (1949), 999a
Ives v. South Buffalo Railway Co. (NY Ct
    App, 1911), 405b
Katzenbach v. Morgan (1966), 411b
Keyes v. School District No. 1 (1971), 388b
Korematsu v. United States (1944), 385b,
    387a
Lau v. Nichols (1974), 1814a
Lee v. Weisman (1992), 418a
Levy v. Louisiana (1968), 421a
Lochner v. New York (1905), 310a, 377b,
    405a
Loving v. Virginia (1967), 154b, 420a
Lucas v. South Carolina Coastal Council
    (1992), 534b
Lucas v. Forty-Fourth General Assembly
    (1964), 422b
McCray v. United States (1904), 406b
McCulloch v. Maryland (1819), 402a
McLaughlin v. Florida (1964), 420a
McLaurin v. Oklahoma (1950), 386b
Mapp v. Ohio (1961), 418b
Marbury v. Madison (1803), 387b, 402a
Martin v. Hunter (1816), 402a
Massachusetts v. Mellon (1923), 408b, 432a
Mendez case (1945), 1811a
Minersville School District v. Gobitis (1940),
    385b–386a
Miranda v. Arizona (1966), 388a, 418b
Missouri v. Canada (1938), 386b, 435b

Missouri v. Holland (1920), 408b
Moran v. Burbine (1986), 419a
Morehead v. New York ex rel. Tipaldo
    (1936), 381b
Morrison v. Olson (1988), 533b
Muller v. Oregon (1908), 378b
Myers v. United States (1926), 408b
National League of Cities v. Usery (1976),
    411a, 443b
Nebbia v. New York (1934), 434a
New York Times v. Sullivan (1964), 416b
New York v. United States (1992), 411a–b
NLRB v. Jones & Laughlin Steel Corp.
    (1937), 382a, 384b, 410a–b
Nollan v. California Coastal Commission
    (1987), 534b
Northern Pacific Railway Company v. North
    Dakota (1919), 407b
Northern Securities Co. v. United States
    (1904), 406a, 1271a
Ohio v. Standard Oil Co. of Ohio (1892),
    1269a
Ozawa v. United States, 141a
Palko v. Connecticut (1937), 414a,
    435b
Paramount case (1948), 1467a, 1468b,
    1469a,b, 1754a
Planned Parenthood of Southeastern
    Pennsylvania v. Casey (1992), 421b
Planned Parenthood v. Danforth (1976),
    240b
Plessy v. Ferguson (1896), 142a,b, 386b,
    1770b, 1812b
Pollock v. Farmer's Loan and Trust Co.
    (1895), 1314a
Powell v. McCormack (1969), 412b
Reed v. Reed (1971), 420b
Regents of the University of California v.
    Bakke (1978), 1836b
Reynolds v. Sims (1964), 419b
Reynolds v. United States (1879), 417b,
    1542a
Roe v. Wade (1973). See Roe v. Wade
    (1973)
Sacco and Vanzetti case, 172b
Scenic Hudson Preservation Conference v.
    Federal Power Commission (Ct App. NY,
    1966), 1373b
Schechter Poultry Corp. v. United States
    (1935), 327a, 380b, 409b, 435a, 528b,
    1277a
Schenck v. United States (1919), 408a, 416a
Scottsboro case (1931), 1601a
Shelley v. Kraemer (1948), 419b
Sherbert v. Verner (1963), 418a
Sierra Club v. Morton, 1374a
Simkins v. Moses H. Cone Memorial
    Hospital, 1002b–1003a
Slaughterhouse cases (1873), 404a, 415a
Smith v. Allwright (1944), 71a
Smith v. Barlow (1953), 501a,b
Smith v. Illinois Bell (1930), 819b
South Dakota v. Dole (1987), 411a
Southern Railway Co. v. United States
    (1911), 435a
Stafford v. Wallace (1922), 408b
Standard Oil Co. of New Jersey v. United
    States (1911), 521a, 1271a
Swann v. Charlotte-Mecklenburg Board of
    Education (1971), 388b
Sweatt v. Painter (1950), 386b, 1813a

Swift & Co. v. United States (1905), 406a,
    1271a
Swift v. Tyson (1842), 383a
Texas v. Johnson (1989), 417a
Texas v. White (1869), 428a
Tinker v. Des Moines School District (1971),
    417a
Twining v. New Jersey (1908), 415a
United States v. American Tobacco Co.
    (1911), 1271a
United States v. Bhagat Singh Thind (1923),
    97a, 141a
United States v. Butler (1936), 381a, 409b,
    411a, 434a
United States v. Carolene Products (1938).
    See United States v. Carolene Products
    (1938)
United States v. Classic, 435b
United States v. Cohen Grocery Company
    (1921), 408a
United States v. Curtiss-Wright Export Corp.
    (1936), 330b, 411b
United States v. Darby (1941), 385a–b,
    410b, 516a
United States v. Doremus (1919), 406b
United States v. E. C. Knight Co. (1895),
    379a, 404b, 520b, 1269a
United States v. Grimaud (1911), 522b
United States v. Harris (1883), 404a
United States v. Leon (1984), 419a
United States v. Nixon (1974), 412b
United States v. O'Brien (1968), 417a
United States v. One Package of Japanese
    Pessaries, 228a
United States v. Peters, 387b
United States v. Trans-Missouri Freight
    Association (1897), 1269a
volume, 393a
Wallace v. Jaffee (1985), 418a
Webster v. Reproductive Health Services
    (1989), 421b
Wesberry v. Sanders (1964), 365a
West Coast Hotel v. Parrish (1937), 381b,
    410a, 434a
West Virginia Board of Education v. Barnette
    (1943), 386a, 417a
Wickard v. Filburn (1942), 310a, 384b,
    410b, 435a, 516a
Wilson v. New (1917), 405b, 519b
Wisconsin v. Yoder (1972), 418a
Wooley v. Maynard (1977), 417a
Yeshiva case (1980), 1835b
Younger v. Harris (1971), 444a, 448a
Youngstown Sheet & Tube Company v.
    Sawyer (1952), 412a
Legal Foundations of Capitalism, The
    (Commons), 1296b, 1305b
Legal profession
    bar examination, 1412b
    corporate law, 1410a, 1411a
    Eastern region, 31a
    education, 1408b
    evolution, 1410a
    Great Depression, 1419a
    New Deal, 1420b
    new services and organization, 1428a–b
    restricted access to, 1416b
    standardization of practice, 1420b
    stratification, 1413a
Legal Realism, 435b
Léger, Fernan, 1701a, 1710a

Legion of Decency, 1467b, 1521a
Legion of Mary, 1518b
Legislative Reorganization Act (1946), 359a, 361a,b, 368b
    amendments (1970), 362a
Legislative veto, 530b
    Supreme Court, 412b, 533b
Lehar, Franz, 1613b
Lehigh University, 32b
Lehman Brothers, 1214a
Leijonhufvud, Axel, 1304b
Leisure
    and consumption, 1017a, 1021a, 1030b, 1757b
    democratization, 1757a–1758b
    gender in, 113a–116a, 124a
    link to sexuality, 114a
    new attitudes in 1920s, 1768a
    personal-consumption expenditures, 1033a
    privatization, 1756b, 1757b
    traditional gender roles, 115a
Leisure and recreation, **1743a–1759b**
Leivick, H., 1570a
Leman, Christopher, 481a
LeMay, Curtis E., 336a–b tab
Lemke, William, 335a–b tab
Lend-Lease Act (1941), 525b, 577a, 601b, 635b, 686a, 724b, 1251b–1252a
Lennon, John, 1628a
Leo XIII, Pope, 1514b, 1515b, 1517a
Leonard, Benny, 1579b
Leonard, Buck, 1771a
Leonard, Karen, 152b
Leonard, Richard, 1373a
Leontief, Wassily, 1299a
Leopold, Aldo, 58b, 1370b, 1371a–b, 1374b, 1380b
Leopold, Nathan, 865b
Leprosy, 942a
Lerner, Abba, 1299a
Lerner, Michael, 1587a
Lesbian student organizations, 1835a
Lescaze, William, 1680a, 1682a,b, 1684a
"Lessons" of the Past (May), 607b
Le Sueur, Meridel, 1443a
"Letter from a Birmingham Jail" (King), 266a, 287b–288a
Let Us Now Praise Famous Men (Agee and Evans), 10a, 1709b
Leuba, James H., 865b
Leukemia, 85b
Leveraged buyouts, 1236a, 1261b
Lever Food and Fuel Control Act (1917), 326b, 407a, 408a
Lever House (New York), 1685b
Levey, Samuel, 1005b
Levi, Leo, 1567a
Levin, Meyer, 1580b, 1587b
Levine, Donald, 930a
Levine, Jack, 1714b
Levine, Lawrence, 1462b, 1595b, 1597b–1598a
Levine, Peter, as contributor, 1761a–1783b
Levine, Philip, 1587a
Levine, Sherrie, 1587a
Levinson, Barry, 115b, 1477b
Levinson, Salmon O., 553b
Levinthal, Bernard, 1572b, 1575b
Lévi-Strauss, Claude, 893a, 926b, 935b–936a, 1454a

Levi Strauss & Co., 1060a, 1065a, 1792b
Levitt, Helen, 1709b
Levitt and Sons, 1029a
Levitt brothers, 466b
Levittown (Long Island), 466b, 1029a
Lewis, C. I., 1650b
    Inquiry into Meaning and Truth, An, 1650b
Lewis, Earl, 190a
    as contributor, 129a–160b
Lewis, Jerry, 136a
Lewis, Jerry Lee, 73b
Lewis, John L., 206a, 1108b
Lewis, Meriwether, 1048a
Lewis, Oliver, 1770a
Lewis, R. W. B., 1451a
Lewis, Sinclair, 52a,b, 115b, 279a, 702a, 1027a, 1435b–1436a, 1440a–b, 1441b, 1457a
    Arrowsmith, 1440b
    Babbitt, 1440a
    influence on Grant Wood, 1706a
    Main Street, 1440a
Lewis, Ted, 1615b
Lewis, Thomas, 952b
Lewis and Clark expedition, 1048a–b
Lewis-Beck, Michael S., 328b–329a
Lewisohn, Ludwig, 1581b, 1585b
Lewitt, Sol, 1717a
Leyb, Mani, 1570a
Libby, E. C., 1133a
Libby, McNeill & Libby, 1132a
Libby-Illinois, 1133a
Libby-Owens, 1133a
Liberal arts colleges, 1820b–1821a
    national organization, 1822a
Liberal capitalism, 1314a
Liberal democracy, 436b
Liberalism, 1311a
    Catholic, 1525a, 1534a
    gender division, 1506a
    governmental programs for families, 239b–240a
    religious, 1491b, 1492a, 1497b
    secular, 1491b–1492a, 1497b
Liberalism and Social Action (Dewey), 277b, 282b
Liberal party (Britain), 295a
Liberal Tradition in America, The (Hartz), 196b, 285b
Liberation theology, 1505b, 1506a,b
Libertarians, 290b
Liberty Bond drives, 596b
Liberty loans, 1316b–1317a
Liberty University, 1832b
Libraries
    Eastern region, 32b
    Midwest, 48a–b
Library of American Literature (Stedman), 1436b
Library of Congress
    Archive of Folksong, 1619a
    Congressional Research Service, 362a
Lichtenstein, Roy, 1716a, 1718b
Liebman, Max, 1578b
Liessin, Abraham, 1569b
Life, 708b, 1481b, 1482b, 1710a, 1811b
Life Adjustment Education, 1811a–b
Life and Death of Great American Cities, The (Jacobs), 179a
Life and Times of Frederick Douglass, The (Douglass), 1595b

Life expectancy
    at birth, 960a–b
    negative impact of new developments, 977b
    rise in, 957b
    South, 76b
Light in August (Faulkner), 1445a
Lilienthal, David, 10a, 668b, 748b
Lilienthal, Otto, 767a
Lilith, 1587a
Lilly, Eli, 493b, 497b, 500a, 501b
Lilly Endowment, 501b
Lima, Agnes de, 1808b
Lima Conference (1938), 685a
Limbaugh, Rush, 188b, 1756a
Limerick, Patricia Nelson, as contributor, 81a–99b
Limited Test Ban Treaty (1963), 561a, 566a–b tab, 613a
Limited War (Osgood), 663b
Limited War Revisited (Osgood), 672a
Limited wars, **651a–674b**, 653a–b
    Korean War, 611a
"Limits to growth" theorists, 1376a
Limon, José, 1456b
Lincoln, Abraham, 42b, 324a, 570b
    presidential power, 402b
Lincoln Center, 1734b, 1735a
Lincoln Laboratories, 28a
Lincoln Portrait (Copland), 1617b
Lind, Jenny, 1612a
Lindbeck, George, 1506a
Lindbergh, Charles A., 55b, 176b, 576b, 700b, 701a, 771b, 772a–b, 953a
Linde, Hans, 444b
Linde cooling compressor, 1132a
Lindheim, Irma, 1568a
Lindsay, John, 487a
Linen, 1786a
Linguistic analysis, 1645b–1646b
Link, Arthur, 596b, 597b
Linton, Ralph, 926a
Lipartito, Kenneth J., as contributor, 1407a–1430b
Lipchitz, Jacques, 1701a
Lippmann, Walter, 202a, 256a, 257b, 258b, 276b, 279b, 808b, 885b, 1567b, 1568a, 1581b, 1644b, 1651b, 1807a
    Drift and Mastery, 196a, 274a, 277a
    Good Society, The, 282a
    Preface to Morals, A, 281a, 1501a
    Preface to Politics, A, 277a
Lippold, Richard, 1714a
Lipset, Seymour Martin, 290a, 934b
Lipsey, Robert, 1264b
Lipsky, Louis, 1567a, 1584a
Lipsyte, Robert, 1778b
Liquor industry, 1132a
Liston, Sonny, 1778b
Literacy
    popular culture, 1481a
    racism, 64b
    tests, 94a
Literary culture, **1435a–1460b**
Literary Digest, 621b, 1019a
Literary Guild, 1482b
Literature
    black dialect, 1596a
    black group unity, 1593b
    black stereotypes, 1593a
    defined, 1435a

INDEX

Literature (*cont.*)
  Eastern region, 33a–34b
  Ford Foundation, 1733a
  gender-specific markets, 114b
  Harlem Renaissance, 150b
  Midwest, 52a–b, 55a
  race in, 150a–b
  Southern, 61a, 67b–68a
  West, 83b
  women, 48a
Littauer Center (Harvard), 496a
Little, Arthur D., 836a, 839a,b, 1411a
Little, Frank, 86b
Little, Malcolm. *See* Malcolm X
Little House series (Wilder), 55a
Little Rock crisis, 387b
Litton Industries, 821a
Liturgical movement
  Catholic, 1516b, 1517a,b, 1525b, 1533b
  McCarthy, Eugene, 1525b
Livermore Laboratory (Calif), 849b
Livingston, M. Stanley, 746a, 750a
Living Wage, A (Ryan), 1069a
Llewellyn, Karl, 435b
Lloyd George, David, *598a–b*
Loans, 1160b, 1248b, 1250b–1251a, 1252a
  foreign investments, 1244b–1245b
  foreign policy, 573a–b, 575b
  world economy, 721b, 727a
  World War I, 723a
Lobbyists, 313b–314a
  contract, 318b
  corporation, 313b
  medical research, 947a
Local government, 1160a
  fiscal policy during Great Depression, 1321b
  human services, 1318a
  property taxation, 1321b–1322a
  services, 1325b
  taxation, 1312b–1313a, 1314b
Localism
  and categorical-assistance programs, 1075a
  nationalism, 260b–261a
  World War II, 264a
Locarno treaties (1925), 680b
Locke, Alain, 130a–b, 155b, 259b, 1656b–1657a
  New Negro, The, 1597a, 1598b
Lockheed Corporation, 795b, 796a,b, 1145a
Lodge, Henry Cabot (1850–1924), 137b, 163a, 574a, *574b,* 593b, 630b–631a, 720a
  Treaty of Versailles, 551a
  at Washington Conference (1921–1922), 599a
Lodge, Henry Cabot, Jr. (1902–1985), 662b
  presidential elections, 336a–b tab
Loeb, Jacques, 879a
Loeb, Richard, 865b
Loew, Marcus, 1464b, 1469a, 1580a
Loew's/MGM, 1469a
Logan, Rayford, 71b
Logan-Walter bill, 526a
Logging industry, 27b, 63b–64a, 76a, 81a, 88b, 1130b, 1150b, 1164b
  health insurance, 989b
  labor unions, 86b
  Midwest, 44a
  trade performance, 1200b
  See also Timber

Logical Positivism, Pragmatism, and Scientific Empiricism (Morris), 1649a
Logical Structure [Aufbau] of the World, The (Carnap), 1648b
Lollapalooza '92, 1464b
Lönberg-Holm, Knud, 1682a
London, Jack, 143b, 1438b
London, Meyer, 1568a
London Conference (1930), 682a
London Naval Treaty (1930), 552a–b, 599b
London Naval Treaty (1936), 552b
Lonely Crowd, The (Riesman et al.), 179b, 197a, 265b, 285b, 1831b
Long, Huey, 282a, 1320a
  radio broadcasts, 807b
  "Share Our Wealth Campaign," 199a
Long, Russell B., 389a, 1326b
Longfellow, Henry Wadsworth, 1436b, 1437a
Long telegram, 607b
Look, 1482b, 1590b
Lookstein, Joseph, 1575b
Lopiano, Donna, 1781a
Lord and Taylor, 1790a
Los Alamos
  computers, 811b
  laboratory, 85b, 98b, 849b
  weapons laboratory, 748a–b
Los Angeles, *89a–b, 90a–b,* 455a–456a,b
  Dodgers, 462a
  during Great Depression, 457b
  immigrants, 212a
  muralists, 1719b
  riots, 97b–98a, 188b, 214b
  suburbs, 455a
Los Angeles Power and Water Department, 89b
Lösch, August, 17a
Losing Ground: American Social Policy, 1950–1980, 1087b
Losing Ground (Commoner), 1375a
Lost Cause, 74a
Lost Colony, The (Green), 1827a
Los Tejanos (Jackson), 1484a
Lost Paradise, A (Chotzinoff), 1586b
Lott, Trent, 306a
Lotus Corporation, 1150a
Louis, Joe, 1772a, 1781b
Louis, Morris, 1587a, 1714b
Louis, Pierre, 948a
Louisiana, 872b
Louisiana Pacific, 1364a
Love, Alfred H., 542a
Love Canal, N.Y., 1377b
Lovejoy, Arthur O., 1644a
  in *Contemporary American Philosophy,* 1644a
Lovelock, James, 1379a
Lovins, Amory, 1376a
Low, J. O., 1112b
Low, Seth, 254a
Lowbrow culture, 1462b–1463a
Lowe, Anne, 1790a
Lowell, A. Lawrence, 1825b
Lowell, Amy, 1439b
Lowell, James Russell, 1436b, 1437a, 1440a
Lowell Historic District, 37b
Lowenthal, Leo, 1485b
Lowenthal, Mark M., *as contributor,* 593a–619b
Lowi, Theodore, 312a

Lowry, W. McNeil, 1732a,b, 1733a,b, 1734a, 1735a, 1737a
Lozowick, Louis, 1579a, 1701a
Lubell, Samuel, 176b
Lucas, George, 1469b
Lucas, Robert, 1303a
Luce, Henry, 708b, 1481a
Luce, R. Duncan, 1305a
Lucey, Patrick J., 336a–b tab
Lucey, Robert, 1517b, 1518a, 1519a,b, 1524b
Lucic, Karen, 1702a
Ludlow, Louis, 555a
Ludmerer, Kenneth, 943a
Lugar, Richard, 445b
Luhan, Mabel Dodge, 1698a, 1699a, 1704a, 1728b
Lukacs, John, 33b
Luks, George, 1696a, 1697a
LULAC. *See* League of United Latin American Citizens (LULAC)
Lumber industry. *See* Logging industry; Timber
Lumière, Auguste, 1752b
Lumière, Louis, 1752b
Lunar voyage, 788a–b, *789a–b*
Lundberg, Ferdinand, 110b, 288b
Lunn, Arnold, 1525a
Lurton, Horace H., 390a–b tab
Lusitania (ship), 595a, 623b, 624a
Lutherans
  liberalism, 1494a, 1500b
  population percentages, 1492b
Lyme disease, 960b, 970a
Lynch, David, 1477b
Lynchings
  Midwest, 52a
  sociological study, 68a
  South, 64b, 431b
Lynd, Helen Merrell, 202b, 924a, 1018a–1019a, 1020a, 1021b, 1022a, 1024a,b, 1026a, 1501b, 1807b
Lynd, Robert, 202b, 924a, 1018a–1019a, 1020a, 1021b, 1022a, 1024a,b, 1026a, 1501b, 1807b
Lyon, Leverett S., 459b
Lyotard, François, 510a
  Postmodern Condition, The, 510b
Lyotard, Jean-François, 936b–937a
Lytle, Andrew Nelson, 14a

M

Ma, Yo-Yo, 1629a
Maastrict Treaty (1991), 853b
Mabie, Hamilton Wright, 1437a
McAdoo, William G., 625b, 626a, 630a, 1315b, 1316a–1317a
MacArthur, Douglas, 337a, 580b, 595b, 669a–b, 686b
  Korean War, 611a–b, 612a, 657b–659a
  occupation of Japan, 704a
  World War II, 641b, 642a
MacArthur Fellowships, 507b
MacArthur Foundation, 507b, 508a, 1737b
Macbeth Gallery, 1697a
McBride, Henry, 1699a
McCain, Franklin, 74a
McCall's, 231b

INDEX

McCardell, Claire, 1790a
McCarran-Walter Act. *See* Immigration and Nationality Act (1952)
McCarthy, Eugene, 301a, 1525a–b
McCarthy, Joseph, 178b, 265a, 284b, 334a, 338b, 361b, 502a, 614b, 1518b, 1524b–1526a
   television, 1478b
McCarthy, Kathleen D., *as contributor*, 1725a–1742b
McCarthy, Mary, 34a, 1444a
McCarthyism, 1478a, 1525a, 1526a
   Army-McCarthy hearings, 338b
   as attack on Anglo-American supremacy, 178b
   pluralism, 286a
McCartney, Paul, 1628a
McClellan, George, 595b
McCloskey, Donald, 1302b, 1305a
McCloskey, Robert, 442a
McCloy, John J., 177a
McConnell, Grant, 433b
McConnell, Mitch, 395a
McConnell, Stuart, *as contributor*, 251a–271b
McCormick, Cyrus, 1669b
McCormick, Edith Rockefeller, 1727b
McCormick, Harold, 1727b
McCormick, Katherine Dexter, 946b
McCormick, Robert R., 55b
McCormick Harvester, 1136b, 1137a–b
McCormick Reaper Plant, 1095a–b
McCullers, Carson, 1457a
McDaniel, Hattie, 1466b
McDill, Bob, 1631a
Macdonald, Dwight, 503a, 1444a, 1485b–1486a
McDonald's, 1757a
McDonnell-Douglas, 786b, 796a, 1144b
McDougall, Walter, 751b
McDougall, William, 885b
MacDowell, Edward, 1612b
McEvoy, Arthur F., *as contributor*, 1357a–1382b
McGee, W. J., 12a, 1360b
McGerr, Michael, 116b
McGill, Ralph, 73a
McGovern, George, 182b, 301b, 314a, 587a
   Family Assistance Plan, 487b
   presidential elections, 336a–b tab
McGovern-Fraser Commission, 301b
McGowan, William, 820b
McGraw, John, 1766a
McGraw-Hill, 1064b
McGraw-Hill Building (New York), 1681b, 1682a
Mach, Ernst, 781b, 1647b
McHarg, Ian, 21a,b
Machen, J. Gresham, 1500a–b, 1501a
Machine-Age Exposition (1927), 1702a
Machine politics, 297a, 299a, 300b
   See also Political bosses
Machinery industry, 1136a–1137a, 1164a
   continuous process, 1130b, 1131a,b
   foreign trade, 1243b
   operators, 1130a
   World War I, 1191a
Machine tool technology, 1112a
McIntire, Carl, 1503b, 1504a
Macintosh computers. *See* Apple Computers
MacIntyre, Alasdair, 291a, 1655a
McIntyre, James, 1530b

MacIver, Robert, 924a
McKay, Claude, 150b, 1600b, 1601a
McKay, Douglas, 1373a
MacKaye, Benton, 10a,b, 11b, 12a–13a, 16b, 21a
McKenna, Joseph, 390a–b tab
McKenna, Wendy, 912b
McKenzie, R. D., 17b–18a
McKeon, Richard, 1644b, 1648b
McKeown, T. R., 972a–b
McKim, Charles F., 1669b
McKim, Mead and White, 1665a, 1669a
   Neo-Renaissance style, 1669b
   Pennsylvania Station, 1673a
   Public Library (Boston), 1687a
McKinley, William, 135a, 255a, 325a–b, 325b, 570b–571b, 720a, 801a
   presidential elections, 335a–b tab
   presidential power, 406b
   vetoes, 347a tab
Mack Truck, 1140b
MacLean, Nancy, 139a
McLeod, J. J. R., 944b
McLuhan, Marshall, 818a, 1480b, 1481a, 1482a, 1486a–b, 1487a,b
McMath, Sid, 726b
McMillan, Neil, 142a
McNally, Dave, 1775b
McNamara, Robert, 612a, 613a, 668a,b
McNary, Charles L., 335a–b tab
McNeill, John J., 1531b
McNutt, Paul V., 603a–b
McPherson, Aimee Semple, 1415b, 1501a, 1503b
McPherson, Harry, 670b
McReynolds, James C., 382b, 390a–b tab
Macy Foundation, 943b
   medical research, 952b
Mad, 1437a, 1470a, 1483b
Maddison, Angus, 1165b, 1166a
Madhubuti, Haki, 1603b, 1604a
Madison, James, 196b, 197a, 295b, 318a,b, 402a, 427a, 446a, 570a, 1212a, 1311a–b
Madison, James H., *as contributor*, 41a–60b
Madonna, 1631a, *1632a*
Madsen, Richard, 290b
Magazines, 38a, 1023a
   for black audiences, 1594a, 1597a–b
   circulation, 1483a
   literary, 33b–34a
   New York City, 31b
   popular culture, 1481a
   publishers, 1482b
   See also specific magazines
Magnes, Judah, 1567a, 1569a, 1576a
Magnesite, 1387b
Magnesium plants, 85b, 91b
Magnetic fields, 742b–743a, 755b
Mahan, Alfred Thayer, 593b
Maharishi International University, 1551b
Maharishi Mahesh Yogi, 1551b
Mahayana Buddhism, 1554a
Mahony, Marion, 1678b
Maier, Charles, 705b
Mailer, Norman, 34a, 706a, 1450a
   Naked and the Dead, The, 1450a
Mail order industry, 452b
Mainbocher, 1790b
Maine, Henry, 918b
Main Street (Lewis), 52a, 1027a, 1440a

Maistre, Joseph de, 918a
Major, John, 352a
Major Agenda Committee, 373b
Major League Professional Baseball Players' Association, 1775b
Making America Corporate (Zunz), 107b
Making a New Deal (Cohen), 206a
Making It (Podhoretz), 1586a
Making of an American, The (Riis), 33b
Making of an Economist, The (Colander and Klamer), 1306a–b
Making of the English Working Class, The (Thompson), 205a, 932b
Malamud, Bernard, 34a, 1457a, 1586b
Malaysia, 693b
Malcolm, Janet, 1458a
Malcolm X, 266b, 287b, 288a, 1548b, 1792a
   Ali, Muhammad, friendship with, 1778b
Malden, Karl, 1524a
Mallinckrodt, 852a
Mall of America, 1034a
Maloney Act (1938), 1227a–b tab, 1228a
Mamet, David, 115b
Man, Economy, and State (Rothbard), 1304a
Man, Paul de, 1834a
Managers, 1107b, 1116b, 1134b, 1143a, 1144b, 1149a, 1416a–b, 1423b, 1424a
   Eastern region, 28a
   executive compensation, 1234b
   executive golden parachutes, 1237a
   executives, 1118a
   growth, 1101b
   information technologies and, 1123b–1124a
   managerial opportunism, 1233b, 1234a
   middle, 1094b, 1102a
   middle class, 198a, 200b
   new managerial hierarchies, 1107b
   production, 1129b
   professional, 1110b, 1424a
Man and Woman (Ellis), 900a 901a
Manchurian Crisis, 576a
Mandate for Change (Eisenhower), 615a
Manhattan, *35a–b, 36a–b*
Manhattan Engineer District, 749a
Manhattan Project, 85b, 605b, 846a, 847b, 848b, 849a, 1144b, 1421b
   computers, 810b
Manhattan Transfer (Dos Passos), 33b
Manhattanville College, 32b
Manicas, Peter, 917b
Manifest Destiny, 133b
Man in Reciprocity (Becker), 927a
Man in the Gray Flannel Suit, The (Wilson), 179b–180a
Manly, Charles M., 767a–b
Man Made World, The (Gilman), 275b, 905b
Mann, Michael, 937b
Mann, Sally, 1720a
Mann, Thomas, 1441b
Mann, Thomas E., 367b, 374b
Mann Act, 1772a
   Johnson, Jack, 143b
Manne, Henry, 1296b
Mann-Elkins Act (1910), 519a
Mannheim, Karl, 926b
Man Nobody Knows, The (Barton), 115b
Manufactured products, 1019a, 1264a
   foreign trade, 1243b
   imports, 1246b

Manufacturers Hanover Trust Building (New York), 1686a
Manufacturing
  conflict with marketing, 1039b
  continuous-process machinery, 1052a–b
Manufacturing industry, 57a–b, 1022b–1023b, 1025b, 1151b, 1155a, 1164b, 1173a
  capital intensity, 1128b
  Eastern region, 27a–28b, 30b
  economic performance, 1159b
  economies of scale, 1129a–b
  foreign investments, 1262a–b, 1264b
  imports from developing countries, 732a
  Midwest, 45b, 451b–452a
  Northeast, 451b–452a
  tariffs, 1312a
  value added, 1127b–1128a, 1129a–b tab, 1139b, 1144a, 1146a, 1151b, 1164a
  world economy, 730b
  world trade, 1166b
Man with a Briefcase, 2,970,882 (Borofsky), 1717b
Man with the Blue Guitar, The (Stevens), 1449b
Mao Zedong, 611a, 658b, 659a
  limited war in Korea, 660a
  Vietnam War, 666a
Maple Leaf Club, 48a
"Maple Leaf Rag" (Joplin), 48a, 1596a, 1614b
Mapplethorpe, Robert, 1721a, 1740a
Marburg, Theodore, 550a
Marchand, Roland, 111b, 1025b
March of Dimes, 509a
"March of Time" newsreels, 1252a
Marciniak, Edward, 1524a
Marconi, Guglielmo, 803b, 1461b, 1471a–b, 1754b
Marconi Company, 1250a
Marcos, Imelda, 1787a
Marcus, Ralph, 1579a
Marcuse, Herbert, 290a, 931b, 1485b, 1585b, 1586a, 1657b
  Eros and Civilization, 931b
  One-Dimensional Man, 931b
Margin of Hope, A (Howe), 1586b
Margolies, Moses, 1575b
Margolin, Anna, 1570a
Marin, John, 1698a, 1701a, 1702a
  Brooklyn Bridge, 1701b
Marin, Peter, 123a
Marin County Civic Center, 1677b
Marine Protection Research and Sanctuaries Act (1977), 528a
Marino, Eugene, 1530a
Marital adjustment, 907b–908a
Marketing, **1037a–1066b**
  bonds, 1316b
  consumer frustration, 1017a–b
  consumption, 1018a, 1022b, 1034a
  history, phases I, II, and III, 1062a–b tab
  history, phases I and II, 1054a–b tab
  information technology, 1061b
  mass marketing, 1022b, 1024a
  micromarketing, 1062a
  organizations, 1129b–1130a, 1131a, 1138a,b, 1143b
  telemarketing, 58a
  See also advertising
Market research, 1019a

Markets
  fragmentation, 1050b
  global integration, 1120b
  psychographic segmentation, 1061a
  restoration, 1285a
Markey Charitable Trust, 947a–b
Markle Foundation, 509a
Markoe, William, 1517b
Marks, Carole, 148b
Marks, Harry, 948b
Marley, Étienne-Jules, 1752b
Marquand, John P., 34a, 1788a
Marriage
  changed roles, 235a
  companionate, 103a, 227a, 228a, 232a
  counseling funded by foundations, 228a
  evolution, 103a
  legal innovations, 225b
  training for, 227a
Marsalis, Wynton, 1631a
Marsh, George Perkins, 12a
Marsh, Reginald, 1704b, 1710b
Marshall, George C., 578a, 579b, 603b, 604a, 608a, 611b, 725b
  Abstract Expressionist art tour, 1713a
  at Yalta, 606a–b
Marshall, John, 387b, 402a, 435a
Marshall, Louis, 1567a,b, 1560a, 1571b, 1576b
Marshall, Paule, 1602b
Marshall, Robert, 1369b
Marshall, T. H., 926a
Marshall, Thomas R., 335a–b tab
Marshall, Thurgood, 143a, 389b, 390a–b tab, 392b, 1813a
Marshall Islands, 85b
Marshall Plan, 579b, 608a, 688a, 705b, 707b, 725b, 1167a, 1198b, 1253a, 1264a
  Freedom Trains, 705b
Martin, Agnes, 1717a, 1721b
Martin, Albro, 519b
Martin, Fletcher, 1708a
Martin, Joseph, 659b, 662b
Martin, Robert F., 1159b
Martin Act (New York, 1921), 1227a–b tab
Martin Clippers, 774a, 775a–b
Martines, Lauro, 1669b–1670a
Glen L. Martin Company, 769b
Martin Marietta, 786b, 1145a
Martone, Michael, 59b
Marx, Alexander, 1574b
Marx, Groucho, 1473a
  television, 1476a
Marx, Harpo, 1464a
Marx, Karl, 251b, 1068a, 1289b, 1455b
  Capital, 202b
Marx, Minnie, 1464a
Marxism
  Jews, 1581b, 1582a
  nations, 252b–253a
  sociology and, 931a–932a
  working class, 202b
Marxist fiction. *See* Left: literary culture of the
Maryland, 476b
Maslow, Abraham, 234b, 896a, 1119a
Mason, Bobbie Ann, 1034b
Mason, Charles, 1500b
Mason, Charlotte, 1601a
Mason, Edward S., 1297b

Massachusetts
  bureaucracy, 1270b
  welfare, 474b
Massachusetts Institute of Technology (MIT), 32b
  Division of Defense Laboratories, 1828b
  Servomechanisms Laboratory, 850a
Massachusetts Metaphysical College, 1544b
Mass audience, 1476a
Mass communications, 799a, 827a
  networks, 805a–809a, 814a–819a
  and presidents, 332b, 356b
  public policy, 800b
"Masscult & Midcult" (Mcdonald), 1486a
Mass culture, 1485b–1486a
  effect on ethnic groups, 173a
  exports, 700b
  New Yorkers and, 208a
Mass distribution, 1158b
Masses, The, 1706b
Massey, Douglas, 214b
Massive retaliation, doctrine of, 612b
Mass media, 1023a, 1024a
  analysis, 1486a–b
  during Cold War, 687b
  interpretation, 1484a–b
  versus mass culture, 1488a
  rock 'n' roll, 1628a
  during World War II, 264a
Mass media and popular culture, The, **1461a–1490b**
Masson, André, 1710a
Mass politics, 295a, 298b, 318b
Mass production, 1132a, 1144b, 1148a, 1158b
  consumer goods, 1020b
  democratization of leisure, 1757a
  effect on craftwork, 1092b–1093b
  effect on ethnic communities, 211b
  increase in size of enterprise, 1095a
  new jobs for middle class, 107b
  power machinery accidents, 1095b
  replacement of craft labor with semi-skilled labor, 1096a–b
  resource abundance, 1391b
  and scientific management, 1092a–1096a
  See also Assembly lines
Mass society, 197a–b
Mass tourism, 701a, 707b
Mass transportation
  cuts in grants under Reagan, 1204a
  mass-transit systems, 465b, 1337b, 1351b
  West, 89b–90a
Masters, Edgar Lee, 52a
Material Policy Commission, 1392b
Materials Testing Accelerator (MTA), 750a–b
"Maternalist" welfare state, 477b–478a
Maternal mortality
  race differential, 970b
  rates, defined, 959a
Mathematical Investigations into the Theory of Value and Prices (Fisher), 1290a
Mather, Frank, 1729a
Mather, Stephen, 1365a–b
Mathers, Jerry, 232b
Mathewson, Stanley, 1097b
Matisse, Henri, 1697b, 1698a, 1699a
Mattelart, Armand, 710a
Matter of Color, A (Higginbotham), 132a
Matthews, Fred, 921a

Matthiessen, F. O., 1446a, 1449a
Maurer, Alfred, 1697b, 1698a, 1702b–1703a, 1722a
Maurer, James A., 335a–b tab
Maurer, Louis, 1702b
Maurin, Peter, 1517b
Maury, Matthew, 740b–741a
Maus (Spiegelman), 1484a
Maverick, Maury, 69b
Maxwell, James Clerk, 1637b
Maxwell School (Syracuse U.), 496a
May, Elaine, 105a
May, Ernest R., 607b
May, Ernst, 1667a, 1684a
May, Henry F., 1439b
Maybeck, Bernard, 1671b
Mayer, Louis B., 1468a, 1580a, 1752b
Mayhew, David, 297a, 307b
Mayo, Charles, 1410a
Mayo, Elton, 475a, 885b, 1111a, 1119a
Mayo, William, 1410a
Mayr, Ernst, 869a
Mays, Benjamin, 144b
Mc. *Names beginning with this prefix are alphabetized as if spelled Mac.*
MCA-Universal, 715a
MCI. *See* Microwave Communications Incorporated
Mead, George Herbert, 276a, 904a, 920a, 927b–928a, 1640b
Mead, Lucia Ames, 546b
Mead, Margaret, 908a–b, 922a
  Sex and Temperament in Three Cultures, 908b
Mead, William Rutherford, 1669b
Meaney, George, 314a
Meaning of Evolution, The (Simpson), 871a
Means, Gardiner C., 1296a,b
  Modern Corporation and Private Property, The, 1233a
Meany, George, 1110a
Measles, 960a, 968a,b, 970a
Measurement of Intelligence, The (Terman), 903a
Meat Inspection Act (1906), 1026b, 1272a
Meat-packing industry, 452a, 1132a–b, 1141a–b
  turnover rate, 1098a
Mecca Temple (New York), 1734b
Mechanical industries, 1127a–b, 1130b, 1131a
Meckel, Richard A., *as contributor,* 957a–986b
Meckling, William, 1296b
Media
  consultants, 1478b
  political campaigns, 308a–b, 319a
  and psychoanalysis, 884a
  religion, 1535a
  scholarly analysis, 1484a–b
Media Monopoly, The (Bagdikian), 1487b
Medicaid, 30a, 123a, 445b, 486a,b, 1002a, 1082a, 1084a,b, 1085a, 1425a,b
  cuts under Reagan, 1204a
Medical Device Amendments (1976), 953b
Medical profession
  evolution, 1409b
  fee-for-service, 988b
  Great Depression, 1419a
  medical schools, 1408b, 1412a
  restricted access to, 1416b

specialization, 1410a
stratification, 1413b
Medical research
  agricultural experiment stations, 942a
  animal subjects, 949a–b
  collaboration, 948a
  Commonwealth Fund, 495b
  debate on federal funding, 947a
  foundations, 496a
  foundations dedicated to a disease, 509a
  funding, 941b–943a, 943a–944a, 945a, 946b–947b
  human subjects, 949b–950a
  laboratories federally funded, 942b
  Rockefeller, John D., Sr., 495a
  social organization, 947b–949a
Medical schools
  Flexner Report, 991a–b, 1822a
  and hospitals, 991a
  reform, 943b
  specialization, 991b
  standardizing, 1822a
Medical science and technology, **941a–956b**
Medical technology
  concern about, 952a–981–954a
  Midwest, 59a
  mortality decline, 978b
  protection of public from unsafe devices, 953b
  spiraling cost of medical care, 952a, 954a
Medicare, 30a,b, 123a, 441a, 471b, 485b, 486a,b, 488b, 1001b, 1002a, 1076a, 1082a, 1425a,b
  reimbursement system, 1003b–1004a
Medina, Harold, 1229b
Mees, C. E. Kenneth, 838b, 841b, 842a, 843b
Meese, Edwin, 446b–447a
Megalopolis, 25b–28b, 30b
Megalopolis (Gottmann), 18b–19b
Meharry Medical College, 947b
Meher Baba, 1550a
Meier, Richard, 1687a, 1689a
Meiklejohn, Alexander, 924a
Meinong, Alexius, 1642b, 1646a, 1656b
Meir, Golda, 1587b
Mellencamp, John Cougar, 59b
Mellon, Andrew, 839a–b, 843a, 1317b–1318a
  and Gray-Pecora investigation, 1225b
  Taxation, 1318a
Mellon, Andrew W., 995b, 1274b, 1734a
Mellon, Richard, 839a–b
Mellon Foundation, 31b, 1737b
Mellon Institute, 839a–b, 842b
Melman, Seymour, 1110b–1111a
Melosh, Barbara, 109b, 1708a
Melting Pot, The (Zangwill), 163b, 1568b
Melville, Herman, 1436b, 1440a, 1449a
Memoirs of Hecate County (Wilson), 33b
Memorex, 1149b
Memorial Day Massacre, 1108b
Men and Brethren (Cozzens), 1446b
Men and Women of the Corporation (Kanter), 1111b–1112a
Mencken, H. L., 67b, 150b, 279a, 1436b, 1439b, 1440a, 1441b, 1497b
Mendel, Gregor Johann, 860b–861a
Mendelowitz, Shraga Feivel, 1575b
Menger, Carl, 1289b, 1299b, 1303b–1304a
Meningitis, 232b, 968a, 977a

Menominee termination policy, 1814a
Menorah Journal, 1581b
Menotti, Gian Carlo, 1737a
Mental Cure, The (Quimby), 1545b
Mental hygiene movement, 884a, 890b
Mental illness
  government health care, 989b
  psychotherapy, 881b–882a
  treatment of, 881b
Mental testing, 880b–881a, 885a, 894a
  cultural factors, 886b
  education, 1806a
  masculinity-feminity tests, 907b
  Revised Binet-Simon Intelligence Scale, 903a
Mental Traits of Sex, The (Thompson), 903b
Men Who Manage (Dalton), 1111a–b
Merbold, Ulf, 790b
Mercedes-Benz distribution system, 1038b–1039a
Merchandise trade, 1244a, 1246a, 1260a
Merchant, Carolyn, 1378a
Merck & Co., 848b, 1147b
Mercury, 1387b
Mercury space program, 788a
Meredith, Don, 1774b
Meredith, James, 119a, 1828b
Mergenthaler Linotype, 1136b
Meriam Report (1928), 1810b
Merleau-Ponty, Maurice, 1657b
Mermaid and the Minotaur, The (Dinnerstein), 913a
Merriam, Charles, 281b
Merriam, John C., 743b
Merrick, George, 459a
Merrick, John, 66a
Merrill Lynch, 1231a, 1236b
Merriman, Frank, 135a
Merritt Parkway, 1751a
Merton, Robert K., 927b, 1485a
Merton, Robert K. (Crothers), 927b
Merton, Thomas, 1523b
Mesifta Torah V'daath, 1575b
Mesmerism, 877b, 1540a
Messenger, 1597a
Messersmith, Andy, 1775b
Messiah of Stockholm, The (Ozick), 1589b
Messter, Oskar, 1752b
Metallgesellschaft, 1135b
Metalworking industry, 1127a–b, 1128b, 1134b–1136a
  World War I, 1191a
Metaphysical beliefs, 1539b
Metaphysical Club, 1546a
Metaphysical Club (Harvard), 1637a
Metaphysical Society of America, 1652b
Metaphysics of Logical Positivism, The (Bergmann), 1652b
Meteorology
  airplanes, 772b–773a
  network, 741a
Methodists
  Congress, 365b
  liberalism, 1494a, 1500b
  population percentages, 1492b
Method of Attaining Extreme Altitudes, A (Goddard), 785b
Methodus, 1305a
Metro-Goldwyn-Mayer, 1754a
Metropolis of Tomorrow (Ferriss), 1681a

Metropolitan Community, The (McKenzie), 17b–18a

Metropolitan District Commission (Boston), 27a

Metropolitan Life Insurance Company
health programs, 974b–975a
job segregation by sex, 107b–108a

Metropolitan Museum of Art (New York), 33a, 1671a, 1693b, 1699a, 1726b, 1727a,b
"Great Age of Fresco, The," 1737a
Great Depression, 1731b
women artists, 1739a
women donors, 1728a

Metropolitan Opera (New York), 33a, 1611b, 1629a, 1727b, 1734a, 1737a
Great Depression, 1731a
Lincoln Center, 1734b
Opera Guild, 1731a

Metropolitan regionalism, 13a, 16b–19b
arts, 38b
population percentages, 38a

Mexican American Movement (MAM), 144b

Mexican Americans, 83a, 94a,b, 95a, 140a–b, 144b–145a, 186a
in film, 151a
music, 67b, 150a
public education, 1803b, 1811a
self-organization, 149a
West, 91a

Mexico, 679b
border policy, 94b
film industry, 707a–b
free trade with, 733a, 1205b
labor, 94b
nationalization of U.S. oil properties, 724b
privatization of television, 713a
Revolution, 94a, 724b, 1247a
world economy, 721a

Meyer, Adolf, 881b, 888a, 890a

Meyer, Cord, Jr., 558b

MGM, 1468a, 1470a
television, 1476b

MGM (United Artists)
foreign ownership, 715a

Miami, 456b
immigrants, 212a

Miami Herald, 456b

Michel, Virgil, 1517a

Michelin, 1249b

Michigan school of electoral studies, 306b

Michigan State, 1821a

Microbiologic developments, 974a

Microelectronic and Computer Technology Corporation (MCC), 852b

Microsoft Corporation, 823b, 826b–827a, 1150a

Microwave Communications Incorporated (MCI), 820a–b, 821a

Microwave technology, 820a–b, 826a, 1344a

Middle class, 81a, 196b–202a, 1158a
African Americans, 214b
consumption, 1018a–b, 1018b, 1024a, 1029a
East, 25a
growth, 195a–b
independent entrepreneurs, 198a
leisure, 1744a–1747a
taxation, 1323b

Tax Reform Act (1986), 1328a
Victorian home, 1746b
women leisure activities, 1746b–1747a

Middle-class housing, 1679a
residential developments, 1679b
suburbs, 1688b

Middle East, 693a
after World War I, *681a–b,* 682b
petroleum, 683a, 692a, 1398b–1399a *See also* Organization of Petroleum Exporting Countries (OPEC)
Wilson and, 679b

Middletown in Transition (Lynd and Lynd), 1024a

Middletown (Lynd and Lynd), 202b, 924a, 1018a–1019a, 1021b, 1022a, 1501b

Middletown Revisited (Lynd and Lynd), 1807b

Midgeley, Thomas, Jr., 1414a

Midland, The, 52b

Midnight Ride of Paul Revere, The (Wood), 1706a

Midstream, 1586b

Midway, Battle of, 641a

Midwest, **41a–60b,** *42a–b*
cities, 451a
Congress, 365b–366b
World War II defense industry, 457a
World War II housing, 1343a

Midwest, The, 56a

Midwestern Universities Research Association, 759b–760a

Midwest Governors Conference, 58a

Midwest Living, 60a

Midwives, 225b

Mies van der Rohe, Ludwig, 1667b, 1681b, 1682b, 1684a, 1685a
Seagram Building (New York), 1685a, *1685b*

Migrant laborers, 95a

Migration
outmigration, 71b
to the South, 77a
to suburbs, 467a
West, 81b
See also African Americans

Migrations to cities, 458b–459a
influence on hospitals, 991a
shift from self-employment to wage-earning status, 1091b

Miklis, Sidney, 358b

Milbank, Caroline, 1791a, 1796b

Milbank Memorial Fund, 228a, 493a
health programs, 974b
medical research, 943b

"Mile High" skyscraper, 1677b

Miles, Catherine Cox, 907b

Military
administrative system, 594a
airplanes, 769a, 770b, 773b, 776b–779b
airships, 777a–b
bases and local economic development, 1202a–b
budgets, 584a
computers, 810b
conscription as instrument of Americanization, 171b
funding of basic research, 847a
homosexual men during World War II, 104a
homosexuals, 304b
radio, 1471b–1472a

television, 815b

Military force
Caribbean, 721a
Central America, 721a

Military-industrial complex, 339b, 503b, 572a, 584a, 589b–590a, 613b, 754a
and power elite, 207b

Military installations
South, 70a–b, 72a
West, 85a

Military Training Camps Association, 601b

Militia of the Immaculate Conception, 1518b

Milken, Michael, 1236a–b, 1238b

Milkis, Sidney M., 326b

Milk pasteurization, 973b

Mill, John Stuart, 1455b

Millar, John, 918a

Millay, Edna St. Vincent, 1441b

Millennialism, 1498a–b, 1540b
dispensationalists, 1499b

Miller, Arthur, 115b, 1581b

Miller, Frieda, 110a

Miller, Glenn, 1621a

Miller, Kenneth Hayes, 1704b

Miller, Kerby, 137b

Miller, Marvin, 1775b

Miller, William, 1498a

Miller, William E., 336a–b tab

Millers, 1131a

Millett, Kate, 288b, 913a

Millikan, Robert A., 840b–841b, 842b–843a
and U.S. Steel, 844a–b

Millis, Walter, 633a

Mills, C. Wright, 287a, 340a, 610b, 926b, 930a
Power Elite, The, 207b–208a, 1830b
Sociological Imagination, The (Mills), 930a
White Collar, 200a, 1111b

Mills, Kerry, 1614b, 1619a

Mills, Wilbur D., 486a,b, 1001b

Mill towns, 27b

Millwork, 1130b

Milward, Alan, 708b

Milwaukee, 451b
public schools, 1807a
suburbs, 460b

Mind-cure movement, 1545a–b, 1546a

Mind That Found Itself (Beers), 884a

Mineral Leasing Act (1920), 1397b

Minerals, 977b, 1387a–1390a
purposeful exploration, 1388b
U.S. share of world mineral production, 1913, *1388a–b*
U.S. share of world mineral production, percent 1913 and 1989, *1394a–b*
worldwide exploration, 1395a

Minimalist sculpture, 1717a

Mining, 27b, 38b, 81a
cancer, 86a
coal, 87b, 91a
copper, 86a
education, 1389b
health insurance, 989b
labor unions, 86b
legal environment, 1388b
network, 1390a
South, 69b
United States Geological Survey (USGS), 1389a

Mining Law of 1872, 1388b–1389a
Ministerial Association of Greater Houston, 1526a
Ministry, 1415b
Minkoff, N. B., 1570a
Minneapolis-Saint Paul
   Census Bureau study (1940), 109a
   Eastern rite Catholics, 1514a
Minnesota Committee on Public Safety, 171a
Minnesota Council on Foundations, 506b
Minnesota Mining and Manufacturing
      Company, 822a, 1028a
Minnow, Newton, 1479b, 1480b
Minorities
   protection though freedom of religion, 418a
   in service sector, 1201a
Minstrel shows, 134a, 1461b, 1462a
   African Americans, 1594a, 1595b
Minton, Sherman, 390a–b tab
Mintz, Steven, as contributor, 221a–243b
Mirabal, Nancy, 138a
Miranti, Paul J., Jr., as contributor, 1407a–1430b
Mirele Efros (Jewish Queen Lear), 1570a–b
Mises, Ludwig von, 924b, 1299a, 1304a, 1305b, 1306a
Mishkin, 1612a
Miss, Mary, 1721a
Missiles, 778b, 783b–784b, 786b, 787b, 850b, 1145a
   Atlas, 788a
   nuclear, 787b
   Titan, 788a
Missionaries
   Catholics, 1520b, 1523b–1524a
   liberal Protestants, 1495a–b
   social reform, 696b
Mission to Planet Earth, 739b
Mississippi River, 41b
   transportation, 45a, 56b
Missouri, 473a
Missouri River, 41b
   transportation, 45a
Missouri (ship), 647b
Miss Porter's School, 1808b
MIT. See Massachusetts Institute of
      Technology (MIT)
Mitchell, Arthur, 1738a
Mitchell, Charles, 1225b
Mitchell, Joan, 1714a
Mitchell, Lucy Sprague, 276a
Mitchell, Wesley C., 279a, 1293b–1294a, 1296a, 1298a
Mitchell, William (Billy), 776b, 776b–777a
Mitman, Gregg A., as contributor, 859a–876b
Mitterand, François, 352a
Mix, Tom, 84a
Mixter, Russell L., 868a
Mlakar, Frank, 176a
Mobil Corporation, 1737a
Mobility
   geographical, 206b
   as illusion of class advancement, 207a
   upward intergenerational, 199b
Mobilization Committee, 562b
Moby Dick (Melville), 1440a
Model Cities program, 466a, 1081b
Model T Ford, 46a–b, 48a, 455b, 1021b–1022a, 1057b–1058a, 1059a, 1140a, 1751a

Modern Age, 1525a
Modern Architecture-International
      Exhibition (Museum of Modern Art, 1932), 1683b–1684a
Modern Corporation and Private Property, The
      (Berle and Means), 1233a, 1296b
Moderne style, 1681a
Modernism (architecture), 1680a
   neo- or late, 1689a
Modernism (literature), 1441a–b
   African American writers, 1450b
   defined, 1447b–1448a
Modernist art, 1698b–1699a
   influence on cultural values, 1703b
Modern Language Association, 1458a, 1831a
Modern Maturity, 1483a
Modern Music, 1617b
Modern Schoolman, 1517a
Modern Temper, The (Krutch), 1501a
Modern Tradition, The (Ellman and
      Feidelson), 1453a
Modern Woman (Farnham and Lundberg), 110a, 288b
Modigliani, Franco, 1299a
Moelin distillery, 1132a
Mohole project, 757a–758a
Moholy-Nagy, Lazlo, 1710a
Mohorovicic Discontinuity, 757a
Molloy, John T., 1794a, 1797a
   Woman's Dress for Success Book, The, 1785b, 1796a
Molnar, Thomas, 1525a
Molodovsky, Kadia, 1570a
Molotov, Vyacheslav, 685a
MoMA. See Museums: Museum of Modern
      Art
Momaday, N. Scott, 1456a
Moment, 1587a
Mona (Parker), 1612b
Mondale, Walter, 307b
Mondale, Walter F., 951a
   presidential elections, 336a–b tab
Mondrian, Piet, 1712b
Monetary History of the United States
      (Friedman and Schwarz), 1301b
Monetary policy
   anti-inflationary under Reagan, 1204b
   as countercyclical policy, 1187b–1188a, 1203a
   effect on international trade, 1187b
   reform, 1271b
Monetary theory
   bimetallism, 1291a
   in economic thought, 1292a–1293a
Money, 1481b
Money Machine, The, 1238a
Money Trust, 1216b
   and Pujo committee, 1220a
Monk, Meredith, 1581a
Monk, Thelonious, 1630b
Monkey-Wrench Gang, The (Abbey), 1378b
Monopolies
   entertainment, 1465b, 1472b
   media, 1488a
Monopolies and Trusts (Ely), 1295a
Monopoly Capital (Baran and Sweezy), 1304a
Monroe, Hornet, 1678a
Monroe, James, 402a
Monroe Doctrine, 675b

preserved by the United Nations, 557b
Roosevelt Corollary, 721a
Monsanto, 1143b, 1146a, 1147a
   research, 852a
Monsky, Henry, 1583b
Montagu, M. F. Ashley, 263a, 869b, 870a
Montague, William Pepperell, 1641b
Montevideo (1933), 685a
Montgomery, David, 107a, 166b–167a, 1093a
   Fall of the House of Labor, The, 205b
   Workers' Control in America, 205b
Montgomery Ward, 452a, 700b, 1022b, 1030b, 1051a
   catalog, 48b, 1019a
   1955 proxy war, 1233b
Monthly Review, 1304a–b
Mood Indigo (Ellington), 1620b
Moody, 1231a
Moody, Dwight, 1498a
Moody, William H., 390a–b tab
Moody Bible Institute, 1499a, 1503a,b
Moore, Barrington, Jr., 932b
Moore, Charles, 1689b
Moore, Deborah Dash, as contributor, 1565a–1592b
Moore, G. E., 1642b, 1653b
Moore, Harry Estill, 13b
Moore, Henry L., 1293b, 1299a
Moore, Joan, 210b
Moore, John Bassett, 550b
Moore, Marianne, 1458a
Moore, Michael, 57b
Moore, Thomas, 1462b
Moqui tribe, 93a
Moral Equivalent of War, The (W. James), 258a
Moral Majority, 182b, 184b, 309a, 1492a, 1507a
Moral Man and Immoral Society (Niebuhr), 282b, 287b, 1502a
Morawska, Ewa, 168a
Morawski, Jill, as contributor, 899a–915b
Morbidity and Mortality Weekly Report, 983b
Morbidity increase, 979b
Moreland, Bob, 1625b
Morgan, Arthur E., 15b
Morgan, Barbara, 1710a
Morgan, H. Wayne, 1695b
Morgan, J. P., & Company, 1214a, 1216b, 1217b, 1218a
   on concentration of banks in New York, 1220b
   creation of U.S. Steel, 1218b
   Glass-Steagall Act, 1226a
   international loans to Europe, 723a
   World War I loans, 722a
Morgan, Jay, 1672b
Morgan, John Pierpont, 802a, 1135b, 1193b, 1214a, 1215a, 1218b, 1219b, 1727a, 1730b
   on corporate disclosures, 1223b
   Pujo committe, 1220a
Morgan, Lewis Henry, 918b
Morgan, Thomas Hunt, 865a, 869a
Morgan Library, 33a, 1726a
Morgan Stanley investment bank, 1226a
Morgenstern, Oskar, 1304b
Morgenthau, Henry, Jr., 603a, 637a, 1252a, 1277b, 1320a–b, 1322b, 1583b
Morgen Zhurnal, 1569a,b

Morgolies, Moses, 1575b
Morin, Alexander, 842b, 846a, 847b, 851a,b
Mormons, 81a, 93b, 1540a, 1542a–b
 population percentages, 1492b, 1501b
 Reynolds v. United States (1878), 417b
Morrill, Justin S., 1820a
Morrill Act (1862), 429a
Morrill Land-Grant College Act (1862),
 1021a, 1408b, 1820a–b tab
Morrill land-grant colleges
 federal subventions, 1821b
 national organization, 1822a
Morris, Charles, 1648b
 *Logical Positivism, Pragmatism, and Scientific
 Empiricism,* 1649a
Morris, George L. K., 1710b
Morris, Henry M., 872a, 873a
Morris, Henry O., 382a
Morris, Robert, 1717a
Morris, William, 1700a
Morrison, Charles Clayton, 1501b
Morrison, De Lesseps, 72b
Morrison, Jim, 1628b
Morrison, Toni, 150b, 1456a, 1604b
Morse, Chandler, 1383b
Morse, Jedidiah, 7a–b
Morse, Samuel F. B., 833a, 1697b
Morse, Wayne, 110b
Morse code, 803b, 1471a, 1755a
Mortality
 Death Registration Area, 957b–958a
 decline, 961a–963a, 963a–b, 977a
Mortgages, 1028b–1029a, 1161b, 1209a,
 1322a
 bonds, 1230a
 taxation, 1325b
Morton, Ferd "Jelly Roll," 1615b
Moses, Robert, 458b, 1734a–b
Mosk, Stanley, 444b
Mosques, 1549b
Mother Earth, 1568b
Mothers of the South (Hagood), 13b
Mothers' Pensions, 122a, 225a
 state legislation, 473b–474a
Motherwell, Robert, 1728b
Motion Picture Export Association
 (MPEA), 707a
Motion Picture Patents Company (MPPC),
 1469a
Motion Picture Producers and Distributors
 Association (MPPDA), 699b, 1467a
Motion Picture Production Code, 1754b
Motion Picture World, 1482a
Motley, Archibald, 1703b, 1704b, 1710b
Motor bus, 1337b
Motor Carrier Act (1980), 531b
Motorola, 462b
 microwave technology, 820a
Motor Vehicle Theft Act (1919)
 upheld by Supreme Court, 408b
Mount Holyoke College, 102a, 1819b,
 1836a
Mount Wilson Solar Observatory,
 744a–745b
Movies. *See* Films
Movie stars, 1465b, 1473a
Movie theaters, 1021b, 1465a
 chains, 1469a
 commercials, 1034b
 Roxy Theatre (New York), *1753a–b*
 urban decline, 464a

 See also Nickelodeons
Moving Picture Story, 1482a
Mowery, David, 839b, 843b, 844b
Moynihan, Daniel P., 30a, 184a, 185b, 489a,
 504a, 1081a, 1083a, 1086b, 1088a,
 1328a
 Negro Family, The, 210a, 235b, 1605a
Mozambique, 692b
MPPC. *See* Motion Picture Patents
 Company
MPPDA. *See* Motion Picture Producers and
 Distributors
 Association
MTA. *See* Materials Testing Accelerator
MTV. *See* Music Television
Mubarak Ali Khan, 152b
Muck, Karl, 257a
Muggs, J. Fred, 1477a
Muhammad, Elijah, 287b, 288a, 1548a
Muhammad, Wallace D.. *See* Muhammad,
 Warith
Muhammad, Warith, 1548b
Muir, John, 1358b, 1359a, 1359b, 1364a,b,
 1380b
 and Pinchot, Gifford, 1359b, 1360a
Mules and Men (Hurston), 1599a
Mulholland, William, 89a–b
Muller, Hermann J., 865a, 869b
Mulroney, Brian, 352a
Multiculturalism
 extreme form on campuses, 189a–b
 in higher education, 1836a
 literature, 1457a
 and postmodernism, 1453a–b
Multinational corporations, 726b–727a,
 1245b, 1246a, 1248a,b–1249b, 1254b,
 1255a, 1257b, 1261a
 European, 729b
 Japanese, 729b
 in Latin America, 727b
Mumford, Lewis, 10a, 11a–13b, 14a, 16b,
 18a, 1651b
Muncie, Ind. *See Middletown; Middletown in
 Transition; Middletown Revisited*
Muncy, Robyn, 122a
Mundelein, George William, 1516a, 1518a
Muni, Paul, 1570b
Munich crisis (1938), 634a
 radio coverage, 1755b
*Municipal and Private Operation of Public
 Utilities,* 1295b
Munitions Investigating Committee. *See*
 Nye Committee
Munk, Max, 772b
Munk, Walter, 757a
Munsey, Frank, 1730b
Munsey's Magazine, 256b, 1764a
Münsterberg, Hugo, 1484a, 1638b
MURA. *See* Midwestern Universities
 Research Association
Murals, 42b, 55a, 1719b
 post office, 54b
Murdoch, Rupert, 715a
Muroc Air Base, 781b
Murphy, Arthur, 1655a
Murphy, Edgar Gardner, 65a
Murphy, Frank, 382b, 390a–b tab, 413b,
 435b, 1518a
Murphy, Gardner, 888b
Murphy, George, 1468a
Murphy, Gerald, 1702b

Wasp and Pear, 1704b
Murphy, Isaac, 1770a
Murphy, Paul, 414b
Murray, Charles, 238b–239a, 1087b
Murray, Henry A., 888b
Murray, James E., 997a
Murray, John Courtney, 1522a–b, 1526a,
 1532b
Murray, Pauli, 66a
Murrow, Edward R., 807a, 1473b, 1478a
Musar (moral) movement, 1572a
Muscle Shoals dam, 1369b
Museums, 38a, 1463a, 1725b, 1726a, 1728b,
 1731b, 1732a,b, 1737a, 1739a
 Abby Rockefeller Folk Art Center, 1728b
 Art Institute of Chicago, 33a, 48a, 1693b,
 1726b, 1731a
 Boston. *See* Boston Museum of Fine Arts
 Brooklyn. *See* Brooklyn Museum
 Cincinnati, 1726b, 1731b
 Clark Museum (Williamstown, MA), 33a
 Cleveland Museum of Art, 33a
 corporate funding of exhibits, 1737a
 de Menil Museum (Houston), 33a
 Eastern region, 33a, 37a
 endowment linked to professionalization,
 1728a
 Farmers' Museum, 37a
 Field Museum of Natural History
 (Chicago), 48a, 1714b
 Fogg Museum (Harvard), 1729a
 Frick Collection (New York), 33a, 1726a
 Gardner Museum (Boston), 33a, 1726a,
 1728a
 Getty Museum (Los Angeles), 33a
 Guggenheim Museum (New York), 33a,
 1677b, 1712b–1713a
 Hagley Museum, 37b
 Hancock Shaker Village, 37b
 High Museum of Art (Atlanta), 33a
 Holocaust Memorial Museum, 1589b
 Jewish Museum (New York), 1590a
 Judah L. Magnes Museum (Berkeley),
 1590a
 Kimball Museum (Fort Worth), 33a
 Los Angeles County Museum, 33a
 Metropolitan Museum of Art. *See*
 Metropolitan Museum of Art(New
 York)
 Midwest, 48a
 Museum of Modern Art (MoMA) (New
 York), 33a, 1684a, *1684b,*
 1684b–1685a, 1700b, 1704b–1705a,
 1706b, 1728b
 Museum of Science and Industry
 (Chicago), 494b
 National Gallery (Washington), 1734a
 Old Sturbridge Village, 37a
 patronage, 1738a
 Philadelphia. *See* Philadelphia Museum
 Shelburne Museum (of folk art), 1728b
 Skirball Museum (Cincinnati), 1590a
 Spertus Museum of Judaica (Chicago),
 1590a
 Strong Museum, 37b
 village museums, 37a
 Whitney Museum (New York), 33a,
 1690b, 1706b, *1715b,* 1718a, 1728a
 Whitney Studio Club, 1739a
 Williamsburg, Va., 494b
 women patrons, 1728a

Music, **1609a–1634b**
  African American. *See* African American
    music
  counterculture clothing, 1793a
  Eastern region, 38b
  federal programs, 1730a
  Ford Foundation, 1733b, 1737b
  Jewish immigrants and, 1571a
  Judaism, 1581a, 1584a
  Mexican American, 150a
  Midwest, 48a, 55a, 58b
  racializing of culture, 149b
  Southern contribution, 61a, 67b
  South in 1950s, 73b
  Yiddish culture, 1571b
Musicals, 1462a, 1463a
  Annie, Get Your Gun, 1625b, *1626a–b*
  Hair, 235a
  My Fair Lady, 1625b
  Oklahoma!, 1581a, 1625b
  Sound of Music, The, 1625b
  South Pacific, 1584b, 1625b
  Sunday in the Park with George, 1631a
  On the Town, 1586b
  West Side Story, 1586b, 1625b
Music for the Theater (Copland), 1617b
Music Project, 15b
Music publishing, 1462b, 1614a
  See also sheet music
Music Television (MTV), 1480a
Music videos, 1034a
Musiker, Sammy, 1571a
Muskie, Edmund S., 363a
  presidential elections, 336a–b tab
Muslim American community, 1548a
Muslims, 1541b
  See also Islam
Muslim Students Association, 1549b
Mussolini, Benito, 576b, 1519b
Muste, A. J., 558a, 559a
Mutation theory, as alternative to evolution,
  860b, 862a
Mutual aid societies, 168a
Mutual Broadcasting System, 807a, 1504a
Mutual funds
  and democratization of capital markets,
    1210b
  as institutional investors, 1231b
  restrictions by Investment Company Act
    (1940), 1228a
Mutualistas, 95a
Muybridge, Eadweard, 1470b, 1752b
My Antonia (Cather), 52a, 1441b
Mydans, Carl, 1710a
Myrdal, Gunnar, 153b, 177b, 263a, 927a,
  929b
  American Dilemma, An, 214a
"Mysterious Stranger, The" (Twain), 1438a
Mystic Seaport, 37a
"Myth of the Modern Myth, The"
  (Stauffer), 1447b
"Myth of the Postmodernist Breakthough,
  The" (Graff), 1453b

N

NAACP. *See* National Association for the
  Advancement of Colored People (NAACP)
Nabokov, Vladimir, 1452a

NACA. *See* National Advisory Committee
  on Aeronautics (NACA)
Nader, Ralph, 312b, 1031a, 1835a
Nader's Raiders, 1031b
Naess, Arne, 1378b
NAFTA. *See* North American Free Trade
  Agreement (NAFTA)
Nagasaki, *647b,* 647b, 750a, 779a
Nagel, Ernest, 1644b, 1648b, 1655b
  Structure of Science, The, 1649a
Nagel, Thomas, 1655a
Naked and the Dead, The (Mailer), 1450a
Naked Lunch (Burroughs), 1452b
Naked Public Square, The (Neuhaus), 1507a
"Naming and Necessity" (Kripke), 1659a
Napalmed Head (Golub), 1719b
Narrative of the Life of Frederick Douglass, The
  (Douglass), 1595a
NAS. *See* National Academy of Sciences
  (NAS)
NASA. *See* National Aeronautics and Space
  Administration (NASA)
Nash, Gary B., 190a
Nashville Agrarians, 10a,b, 14a–b, 1444b
Nasser, Gamal Abdul, 582a
Nathan, George Jean, 1581b
Nathan, Richard, 359a
Nation, 31a, 279a, 281b, 1102b, 1597b,
  1827a
  on Miami, 456b
National Academy of Design, 1695a
National Academy of Sciences (NAS),
  748b, 757b, 840b, 841a, 842b, 873b,
  947a
National Advisory Cancer Council, 747a
National Advisory Commission on Civil
  Disorders, 180b
National Advisory Committee for
  Aeronautics (NACA), 771b–772b,
  778a, 781a–b, 841b
  See also National Aeronautics and Space
    Administration
National Advisory Council of Economic
  Opportunity, 122b–123a
National Aeronautics and Space
  Administration (NASA), 75b, 710a,
  755a–756b, 761a, 787b–791b, 796a,
  841b, 850a, 851a
  satellite transmission of data, 1348b
  See also National Advisory Committee for
    Aeronautics
National Aero–Space Plane, 796a
National American Woman Suffrage
  Association, 117a, 309a
  African American women, 118a
National Arts Club, 1697a
National Arts Stabilization Fund, 1737b
National Association for Constitutional
  Government, 380a
National Association for the Advancement
  of Colored People (NAACP), 50a, 96a,
  118b, 145a, 146a, 178a, 260a, 276b,
  309a, 1567b, 1597a
  on *Amos 'n' Andy* show, 1473a
  education, 1813a
National Association for the Study and
  Prevention of Tuberculosis, 943b, 974b
National Association of Broadcasters, 1479a
National Association of Evangelicals, 1503b
National Association of Governors, 489a
National Association of Manufacturers

(NAM), 310b, 1109b–1110a, 1272b,
  1280a
National Association of Marriage
  Counselors, 228a
National Association of Scholars, 1834a
National Association of Securities Dealers
  (NASD), 1227a–b tab, 1228a
National Baptist Convention, 145a
National Broadcasting Company (NBC),
  262a, 806b, 1472a,b, 1475a,b, 1755a
  blue network, 807a, 816a, 1472a,b, 1473a
  See also American Broadcasting
    Company
  news, 1478a
  red network, 806b, 1472a
  revenues, 1474a
  sportscast, 1773b, 1774a
  television, 1476a
National Brotherhood of Professional
  Baseball Players, 1775b
National Bureau of Economic Research,
  495a, 496a
National Bureau of Standards, 1826b
National Cancer Institute, 945a
National Capital Planning Commission, 20a
National Cash Register, 1148b
  foreign investments, 1247a
National Cash Register Company, 809a
National Catholic War Council, 1516a,
  1517b, 1521a
National Catholic Welfare Council, 1516a
National Christian Science Association,
  1544b
National Citizens' League, 1295b
National City Bank, 654a, 1216b
  example of full-service bank, 1222b
  foreign branches, 1249a
National Civic Federation, 1269b, 1295a,b
National Civil Liberties Bureau, 597a
National Collegiate Athletic Association,
  1776a,b, 1834a
  women's sports, 1780a
National Commission for the Protection of
  Subjects of Biomedical and Behavioral
  Research, 951a
National Committee for a Sane Nuclear
  Policy (SANE), 584b–585a, 1505b
  antinuclear movement, 559a, 564a
National Committee to Study the Antitrust
  Laws, 1280b
National Community Relations Advisory
  Council, 1582b
National Competitiveness Technology
  Transfer Act (1989), 853a
National Conference of Catholic Charities,
  1515a
National Conference of Christians and Jews,
  176a
National Conference of Commissioners,
  1270b
National Conservation Commission, 1272a
National Consumers' League, 115a, 117b,
  121b, 1026b
"National Conversation on American
  Pluralism and Identity, A," 191a
National Cooperative Research Act (1984),
  852b
National Council for Prevention of War,
  553b
National Council for the Limitation of
  Armaments, 553a–b

National Council of Churches, 31b, 1503b
See also Federal Council of Churches
National Council of Churches of Christ, 1516a
National Council of Jewish Women, 1566b, 1587b
National Currency and Banking Acts (1863–1864), 1213a
National Defense Act (1914), 596a
National Defense Act (1920), 598b
National Defense Advisory Council, 602a
National Defense Education Act (1958), 72a, 340a, 503b, 583a, 787a, 1811b, 1812a–b tab, 1820a–b tab, 1829a
National Defense Research Committee, 605b, 945a
National Defense Tax Bill (1940), 601b
National Dental Institute, 945b
National Distillers Products, 1132a
National Education Association, 1805b, 1835b
National Endowment for the Arts (NEA), 30a, 1424b, 1629a, 1721a, 1725a, 1735a, 1736a–b, 1737a, 1739b, 1740a
    antiobscenity pledge, 1740b
    Expansion Arts and Community Cultural Programs, 1738b
    grants, 1736b
    Hispanic Task Force, 1738b
    Office of Minority Concerns, 1738b
National Endowment for the Humanities (NEH), 30a, 189b, 1424b
    projects reflecting American diversity, 183b
National Energy Act (1978), 1171a, 1172a
National Energy Conservation Policy Act (1978), 528a
National Environmental Policy Act (1969), 527b, 1376b–1377a
National Farmers' Organization, 310b
National Farmers' Union, 310b
National Farmers' Union (Britain), 310b–311a
National Forest system, 1358b
National Foundation for Infantile Paralysis, 945b, 946a
National Guard, 595b, 598b, 599a
National Heart Institute, 945b, 953a
National Highway Act (1956), 582b
National Historical Publications and Records Commission
    projects reflecting American diversity, 183b
National History Standards Project, 189b
National Housing Act (1934)
National Industrial Recovery Act (1933), 432b, 433a, 435a, 523b, 524a, 600a, 1108a, 1251a–b, 1276b, 1398a
    invalidated by Supreme Court, 380b, 409b
    and professions, 1420a
National Institute for Mental Health, 945b
National Institutes of Health (NIH), 1424b
    guidelines for federally funded human experimentation, 950b
    Office of Scientific Integrity, 949a
    research, 945a,b, 1828b
National Invitational Tournament, 1776a
Nationalism, **251a–271b,** 575b, 731b
    and Judaism, 1567a, 1568b
National Jewish Welfare Board, 1582b

National Laboratories, 849b, 853a
National Labor Relations Act (1935). *See* Wagner Act (1935)
National Labor Relations Board (NLRB), 69a, 310b, 311b, 524b, 1108a
National Lawyers Guild, 413b
National Liberation Front (NLF), 664a
National Linseed, 1132a
National Medical Association, 1000a
National Military Establishment, 609a
National Monetary Commission, 1188b, 1271b, 1295b
National Organization for Women (NOW), 120a, 288b
National Origins Act (1924), 165a–b tab, 172a, 260a, 261a
National Park Service, 37a, 84b, 1358b, 1365a–b, 1373a
National Peace Conference, 554a
National Polish Catholic Church, 1514a
National Press Club, 656b
National product and income, 1860–1980, *1190a–b*
National Radio Astronomy Observatory, 753a–b
National Railroad Passenger Corporation. *See* Amtrak
National Recovery Administration (NRA), 68b–69b, 262a, 310a, 479a, 523b, 524b, 1026b, 1277a
    Blue Eagle codes, 310a
    See also Consumer Advisory Board
National Religious Broadcasters, 1504a
National Research Act (1974), 951a
National Research Council (NRC), 840b, 841b, 842b–843a,b, 1416a, 1651b
    Committee for Research on Problems of Sex, 228a, 946b
    permanent charter post-World War I, 842a
National Research Endowment, 843a–b
National Resources Planning Board, 283a, 1322a
    NRPB Report, 283a–b
National Review, 289b, 1525a
National Rifle Association, 308b, 317b
National Rural Life Conference, 1517b
National Safety Council, 475a
National Science Board, 752b, 852a
National Science Foundation (NSF), 752a–753a, 757a, 759b, 847a–b, 849a, 852a, 1424b, 1812a
    Big Biology, 758b
    grants to scientists, 1828b
    R&D in 1993, 831a–b
National Sculpture Society, 1695a
National Security Act (1947), 333b, 609a, 779b
National Security Adviser, 615a
National Security Agency, 614a
National Security Council (NSC), 333b, 345b, 527a, 580a, 589a, 608b, 609a–b, 615a, 687b, 704b, 757b
    importance under Nixon, 616b
    Vietnam, 666a
National Security Resource Board (NSRB), 608b, 609a, 1279a
National security state, The, 333b, **593a–619b,** 739b, 1167b, 1264b, 1281a
    Eisenhower and, 339b, 340a

foreign investments, 1263a
foreign policy, 569b, 576a, 581a–b, 586b
industrial research, 850b–851a
and preservation of "the American way of life," 688a
National Socialism, Germany. *See* Nazi Germany
National Spiritualist Association of Churches, 1543a–b
National Sports Broadcasting Act (1961), 1774a
National Standards for United States History, 189b
National System of Interstate and Defense Highways Act (1956), 1751a
National Tax Association, 1315a
National Traffic and Motor Vehicle Safety Act (1966), 1031a
National Tribune, 255a
National Tube, 1135a
National Tuberculosis Association, 943b
National Urban League, 145a, 146a, 1597a
National War College, 751a
National War Labor Board, 262b, 1278a
National Welfare Rights Organization, 1083a
National Wildlife Federation, 1370b
National Women's Party, 117b
    African American women, 118a,b
National Youth Administration, 1808b, 1825a
Nation at Risk, A (1983), 1814b
Nation of Islam, 180a, 266b, 1548a
    Ali, Muhammad, 1778b
Nation of Vipers, A (Wylies), 910a
Native Americans, 132a, 134b, 139b–140a
    art, 1703a, 1738b
    boarding schools, 1810b
    cultural assimilation, 134b
    environmental politics, 1378a–b
    ethnicization, 181a
    Federal policy, 92a
    in film, 151a
    health care for, 989b
    Indian Nations at Risk advisory committee, 1814b
    Indian New Deal, 92a
    Indian Welfare League, 152b
    literature, 1456a
    Midwest, 50b, 58b
    military elimination, 134b
    music, 1618b, 1631b
    Oklahoma, 140a
    pan-Indian consciousness, 140a
    poverty, 1086b
    public education, 1803b, 1810b, 1813b
    Red Power, 266b
    reservation day schools, 1810b
    salmon industry, 1378a
    spirituality, 1558a
    termination policy, 1814a
    tribal identity, 92b, 93b
    West, 83a, 92a–b, 92a–93b
Native Son (Wright), 154a, 1450b, 1601a,b
Nativism, 254b
    deindustrialization, 188a
    fluctuation with economy, 188a
    immigration, 137b, 172a, 187b
    marriage laws, 225b
    poverty, 188a

NATO. *See* North Atlantic Treaty Organization (NATO)
Natural gas, 1333b
    appliances, 1338b
    effect on health, 1338b
    utilities, 1346b–1347a
Natural Gas Policy Act (1978), 528a
Naturalization Act (1906), 165a–b tab, 169a
Natural resources, 1155a, 1158a, 1165a, 1272a, **1383a–1406b**
    conservationism, 1361a
    mass production, 1158b–1159a
    regulation, 1275a
    renewable vs. nonrenewable, 1383b
    West, 81b, 84b, 86a–88b
    See also raw materials
Natural Resources Defense Council, 1376b, 1378b
Nature and Destiny of Man, The (Niebuhr), 282b–283a, 1502b
"Nature of Cities, The" (Harris and Ullman), 17a
Naughty Marietta (Herbert), 1613b
Nauman, Bruce, 1720a
Navajo, 93a
    resistance to government schooling, 1810b
Naval Consulting Board (NCB), 841a,b, 1416a
Naval Observatory, 740b
Naval Research Laboratory, 749a, 841a
Naval War College, 594b
Navy
    aircraft, 771a–b, 777b, 779a, 782b
    Big Navy, 594a
    build-up, 543b, 720a
    Bureau of Aeronautics, 599a
    Caribbean Squadron, 594b
    Depot of Charts and Instruments, 740b
    exploration, 740a
    funding of basic research, 849a
    General Board, 594a
    industrial research, 837b
    missiles, 786b
    nuclear aircraft carriers, 849b
    nuclear ships, 849b
    radio, 1471b
    War Plans, 637a
Navy League, 543b, 572a
Naylor, Gloria, 1604b
Nazarene, The (Asch), 1569b
Nazerman, Sol, 1589b
Nazi Germany, 1519b
    Catholics, 1519b–1520a
    refugees, 1566a
    See also Holocaust
Nazi race-hygiene movement, 865a
NBC. *See* National Broadcasting Company (NBC)
NEA. *See* National Endowment for the Arts (NEA)
Neal, Charlie, 1777b
Neal, Larry, 1603a, 1604b
Nebraska, 1362a
NEC, 1149a
Needell, Allan, 749b, 752a
Neel, Alice, 1710b
"Negro Artist and the Racial Mountain, The" (Hughes), 1597b, 1603a
Negro at Work in New York City, The (Haynes), 920a

Negro Business League, 145b
Negro Digest, 1604a
Negro Ensemble Company, 1738a
Negro Factories Corporation, 259b
Negro Family, The (Moynihan), 210a, 235b, 1086b, 1605a
Negro Family in the United States, The (Frazier), 213a, 925b
Negro spirituals, 1594b, 1618b
Negro World, 146a, 1599b, 1600a
NEH. *See* National Endowment for the Humanities (NEH)
Nelson, Barbara, 122b
Nelson, Daniel, 1094b, 1095b, 1097a
Nelson, Gaylord, 1377a
Nelson, Michael, 326b
Nelson, Richard, 850b–851a
Nelson, Willie, 1631a
Neo-Darwinism, 860a
Neo-Expressionism (architecture), 1689a
Neo-Lamarckianism, 859b
Neonatal mortality, *964a–b*
    rates, defined, 959a
Neopaganism, 1557a–b
Neo-Renaissance style, 1669b
Ner Israel Yeshiva, 1585a
Nestor Film Company, 83b
Neuhaus, Richard, 1507a–b
Neumann, Emmanuel, 1584a
Neumann, John von, 1304b
Neurath, Otto, 1647a
Neustadt, Richard E., 338b, 339a, 340a–b
Neutra, Richard, 1680a, 1682b, 1684a
    Philip Lovell residence, *1683a*
Neutrality, 621a
    foreign policy, 573a
    policies of differential, 635b
    rights of neutrals on the high seas, 595a
    World War I, 595a
Neutrality laws, 633b–634a, 636b, 684b
    Neutrality Act (1935), 600b
    Neutrality Act (1937), 600b
    Neutrality Act (1939), 600b
Nevada test site, 91b, 98b
Nevelson, Louise, 1579a, 1715b, 1721b, 1731a
New Age Journal, 1539a
New Age movement, 1558a–1562a
    followers, 1561b–1562a
    New York Times 1991 survey, 1562a
    ritual, 1560b–1561a
New American Right, The (Bell), 286a
Newark, 180b
New Beginning, 322b
Newberry Library, 48a
Newby, Robert G., 930b
"New Colossus, The" (Lazarus), 163b
Newcomb, Simon, 1289a, 1293a, 1299a
Newcombe, Don, 1777b
New Conservatism (Jewish), 1586a
New Constellation, The (Bernstein), 291b
New Deal, 1073b, 1276b–1279b
    arts programs, 1705a–b, 1728a, 1729b, 1732b, 1733a
    bureaucratic state, 523b
    Catholics, 1518a
    change of the social order, 300b
    conservationism, 1366a–1371b, 1380b
    conservative reactions, 282a, 1074a
    consumption, 1026a–b
    education, 1808b

    Eisenhower and, 339b
    ethnic workers and, 175a
    family, 230a
    federal bureaucracy, 332a
    federalism, 432b–436a
    and foundations, 497a
    government-professional relations, 1420a
    health insurance, 997b
    interest groups, 310a–312a
    multiple-use watershed development, 1369b
    political reform, 299b–301a
    presidential role, 322b, 323b, 330a, 331a
    regionalism, 15a–316a
    responsibilities of government, 331b, 332a
    social insurance state, 332a
    social welfare, 471a
    South, 68b–70a
    Supreme Court and, 380a–381b, 409a–b, 524b
    tax reform, 1320a–1321a
    tensions in Democratic party, 300b
    West, 85a, 87b
    women's role, 122a
New Deal Wealth Tax (1935), 500a
New Dimensions of Political Economy (Heller), 199a
New Economic Policy, 1283a
Newell, Frederick, 1272b
New England, 37a
    Congress, 365b
New England Conservatory, 33a, 1612b
New England Idylls (MacDowell), 1612b
New England Journal of Medicine, 948a, 950a
New Exploration, The (MacKaye), 10a
"New Face of America" (Time), 191a
New formalism (architecture), 1689a
New Foundation, 322b
New Freedom, 1271a, 1316a
    Brandeis' influence on, 278a
New Frontier, 322b, 340b, 342a, 1199a, 1203a
New Industrial State, The (Galbraith), 1301a
New International Economic Order, 1257b
New Jersey, 474a–b
New Jersey Holding Company Act (1889), 1215b
New Labor historians, 205a–b, 206b
Newlands, Francis G., 1362b, 1364b
Newlands Reclamation Act (1902), 84b, 90b, 1362b, 1363a
New Left, 205a, 206b, 286b, 287a, 931b, 1586a
    Anti Vietnam War movement, 562a, 668a
    and feminism, 289a
    and military-industrial complex, 1425b
    scholars, 207a–b
    women, 119b
Newman, Barnett, 1579a, 1587a, 1712b
New Masses, 1601a
New Mexico Quarterly, 10b
New Music, 1617a
New Nationalism, 256a, 327b, 1271a
    Croly's influence on, 277a, 278a
New Negro, The (Locke), 259b, 1597a, 1598b
New Negro concept, 212b, 1596b
New People (Williamson), 212b
New Realism, The, 1641b
New religious Right, 871b

New Republic, 276b, 278a, 281b, 1442a,b, 1568a, 1807a, 1808b, 1827a
News broadcasts
  radio, 1473a–b
  television, 1477a,b, 1477b–1478a
  See also Newsreels
New Scholasticism, The, 1517a
New School for Social Research, 1577b, 1657a, 1826a
News Corp. Ltd., 1482b
Newspapers, 38a, 1023a
  facsimile editions, 815a
  Midwest, 48a
  musical critics, 1611b
  New York City, 31a
  popular culture, 1481a
  publishers, 1482b
Newsreels, 1473a–b
Newsweek, 31b, 59b, 191a, 388b, 714a, 1284a, 1305b, 1481b, 1720b, 1788b
New System of Geography, A (Fenning and Collyer), 7a
New Theater, 1727b
New Thought, 881b, 1540a, 1542b, 1545a,b–1546b
  International New Thought Alliance, 1546a
  International New Thought Congresses, 1546a
Newton College of the Sacred Heart, 32a
New World of Science, The (Hale and Millikan), 843a
New York, Lower Manhattan (Hirsch), 1701b
New York Association for Improving the Condition of the Poor, 1067b
New York Athletic Club, 1743b, 1744a
New York Century Club, 1743b
New York City, 452a,b, 456b, 1067a
  bureaucracy, 1270b
  cultural center, 1586a, 1714b
  financial crisis, 464b, 467b
  immigrants, 212a
  Jewish culture, 1567a–1571b, 1586a–b
  Lower East Side, 453a
  money center, 725a, 1213a
  poverty, 453a
  public schools, 1807a, 1815b
  skyscrapers, 1681a
  suburbs, 458b, 467a
  subway, 453a
  urban decline, 463b
  vaudeville, 1463a,b
  welfare, 487a
  women in work force, 107b
  Yankee Stadium, 1775b
  See also Wall Street
New York City Ballet, 1733a–b, 1734b
New Yorker, 462a, 1458a
  map, 41b
New York Giants, 1766b, 1774b
New York Herald, 143b
New York Intellect (Bender), 33b
"New York intellectuals," 1831b
New York Jockey Club, 1743b
New York magazine, 468a
New York Mets, 1774a–b
New York Post, 1102a
New York Psychoanalytic Society, 882b
New York Public Library, 32b, 1671b, 1673b
  Lincoln Center, 1734b

New York Regional Association of Grantmakers, 506b
New York Shakespeare Theater, 1733a
New York state
  invalidation of reform legislation, 405a–b
  welfare, 487a
New York State Council of the Arts (NYSCA), 1736b, 1738b, 1739b
  Ghetto Arts Program, 1738a
New York State Theater, 1734b
New York State Thruway, 25b
New York Stock Exchange, 1161a, 1209a, 1218a, 1232a, 1249a–b
  volume of trading, 1900–1990, 1232a–b tab
New York Stock & Exchange Board, 1211b
New York Telephone Company, 1102a
New York Times, 31a, 117a, 202a, 279b, 381b, 453b, 713a, 966a, 1670b, 1740b, 1765a
  on bombing of Cambodia, 587b
  on consumer confusion, 1062b
  on *Erie* case, 383b
  on New York city, 468a
  on science, 760b
  Sunbelt, 75b
  on Thomas, Clarence, 393a
New York Times Magazine, 1237a
New York Union Club, 1743b
New York University, 32b
New York Yacht Club, 1743b
New York Yankees, 1766b, 1768b–1769a, 1775b
New Zealand, 689a
Ngo Dinh Diem, 664b
Nguyen Cao Ky, 667b
Nguyen Van Thieu, 667b
Niagara Movement, 146a
Niatum, Duane, 1456a
Nicaragua, 654a, 682b
  foreign policy, 589a
  Sandinista regime, 692b
Nichiren Shoshu, 1553b, 1556a
Nicholas II, Tsar, 543b
Nichols, J. C., 454b, 466b
Nickel, 1387b
Nickelodeons, 1021b, 1465a
  Midwest, 48a
Nicklaus, Jack, 1775a
Niebuhr, H. Richard, 282b, 1502a–b
  "Protestantism," 1491a
Niebuhr, Reinhold, 282b–283a, 284a, 1446a, 1497a, 1501b–1503a, 1504a,b, 1507b–1508a, 1644b
  Americans for Democratic Action, 285a
  Children of Light and the Children of Darkness, The, 284a
  Irony of American History, The, 284a
  Moral Man and Immoral Society, 282b, 287b, 1502a
  Nature and Destiny of Man, The, 1502b
Nielsen, Waldemar A., 492a, 505a
Nietzche, Friedrich Wilhelm, 1427a, 1448b, 1452a, 1454b
Nighthawks (Hopper), 1710b
Nightingale, Florence, 1414a
Night (Wiesel), 1589a
NIH. *See* National Institutes of Health (NIH)
Niles, David, 579b

Nimitz, Chester W., *609a–b,* 641b, 642a, 686b
Nine-Power Treaty, 599b
1984 (Orwell), 851a
Nineteenth Amendment, 117a
Nintendo, 1033a
Nishi Hongwanji movement, 1554b
Nissan, manufacturing system, 1061b
Nitze, Paul, 610b
Nixon, Richard M., 155b, 265a, 341a, 344a–346a, *344b,* 388b, 616a, 820b, 1199a, 1468a
  administrative presidency, 359a, 360b, 362a
  antiwar movement, 562b
  Arms Control and Disarmament Agency (ACDA), 560b
  and bureaucratic politics, 517a
  Comprehensive Child Development Bill, 123b
  versus Congress, 362b, 364a, 372b
  divided government, 349b
  dollar devaluation, 730a, 1256b
  economic controls, 1283a
  Family Assistance Plan, 487a–b
  federal aid, 441b
  federal commitment to termination, 92b
  federal executive power, 442a
  foreign policy, 583a–584a, 585a, 586a–587b
  foreign trade, 1256a, 1257b
  gold convertability (1971), 692a
  gold standard, 1167a
  Graham, Billy, 1504a
  Guam Doctrine, 691a
  health policy, 1004b
  Keynesian economics, 311a
  kitchen debate, 1030b–1031a
  law and order, 422b
  New Federalism, 440a–443a
  presidential elections, 335a–b tab, 336a–b tab
  and presidential government, 528b
  public approval, 336b
  Silent Majority speech, 587a
  social regulation, 527b
  stagflation, 1169a–b
  Supreme Court appointments, 389b, 391a–392a, 418b
  television, 1478b, 1479a
  vetoes, 347a tab
  Vietnam War, 669b
  on Warren Court's criminal procedure rulings, 418b
  Watergate. *See* Watergate affair
  working class vote, 302a
NLRB. *See* National Labor Relations Board (NLRB)
Nobel Prize, 52a
  Chamberlain, Owen, 750a
  Compton, Arthur H., 842a
  Davisson, Clinton J., 844b–845a
  Langmuir, Irving, 836b, 841b, 844b
  Lawrence, Ernest, 747b
  Lewis, Sinclair, 1435b, 1440b
  Millikan, Robert, 844a–b
  Pauling, Linus, 1374b–1375a
  Richards, Theodore W., 742a
  Segrè, Emilio, 750a
Noguchi, Isamu, 1710b
Noland, Cady, 1720a

Noland, Kenneth, 1714b
   at Black Mountain College, 1715b
Nominating conventions, 298a–299b, 300b
   Chicago, 301a–b, 587a
Nondomestic service workers, 1107a
Noneconomic freedoms, 415a
Nonfortification agreement, 682a
Nonpartisan League, 49b
Nonprofit organizations, 504a–b
   arts, 1726b
   broadcasting, 1473b
   Eastern region, 31b
   scholarly interest in, 505b, 506b
Non-Proliferation agreement, 565a–b
Nontraditional religions, **1539a–1564b**
Norell, Norman, 1790b, 1795a
Norman, Jessye, 1629a
Normandy (France), 786b
Norris, Frank, 1438b, 1503b
   Octopus, The, 1438a
Norris, George W., 51a, 554a, 1369b
Norris, J. Frank, 866a
Norris, town of, 15b–16a
Norris, William, 1148b
Norris-La Guardia Act (1932), 1108a
North, Douglass, 1302b
North, Oliver, 589a
North American Aviation, 1145a
North American Free Trade Agreement
   (NAFTA), 693b, 1263a
North American Rockwell, 795b
North Atlantic Treaty Organization
   (NATO), 337b, 558a, 579b, 610a,
   688a, 725b
   nuclear weapons, 787b
   and Warsaw Pact, 692a
North Carolina Mutual Life Insurance
   Company, 66a
North Carolina poor laws, 472b–473a
North Dakota, 474b
Northeast-Midwest Congressional Coalition,
   58a
Northeast region
   cities, 451a
   World War II defense industry, 457a
Northern Pacific Railroad, 1217b
Northern Securities, 1218a
Northgate Shopping Center, 1030b
Northrop Aviation, 796a,b, 1145a
   computers, 812a
Northrup loom, 1130a
Norton, Charles Eliot, 1439a
Norton, Edwin, 1131b
Norton, Mary, 110b
Norton, O. W., 1131b
Norway, 960b
Notes toward a Supreme Fiction (Stevens),
   1449b
Nott, Josiah, 134a
Novak, Michael, 155b, 182b
NOW. *See* National Organization for
   Women (NOW)
Noyce, Robert, 812a
Noyes, A. A., 840b–841b, 843a
Nozick, Robert, 290b
NRA. *See* National Recovery
   Administration; National Rifle
   Association
NRC. *See* National Research Council
   (NRC)
NSC-68, 610b, 688b

Nuclear fallout, 1374b
Nuclear fission, 1372a
Nuclear freeze movement, 564a–b
Nuclear Non-Proliferation Treaty (1968),
   561b, 566a–b tab
Nuclear pacifism, 558a–559b
Nuclear power, 1144b
   aircraft carriers, 781a
   plants, 1346b
   submarines, 786b
Nuclear reactors, 749b, 753b
Nuclear research, 849a
Nuclear science, 747a–b
Nuclear strategy, 613a
Nuclear test ban treaty, 342a
Nuclear-waste disposal
   West, 98b
Nuclear weapons, 85b–87a, 750a b, 754b,
   779a, 781a
   arms race, 610b
   Atomic bomb, 739a, 748a–b
   atomic bomb, 846a, 849b, 1144b, 1253a
   Catholics, 1532a
   foreign policy, 579a, 581a–b, 589a
   H-bomb, 559a
   hydrogen bombs, 849b
   Jewish researchers on atom bomb, 1584a
Nucor company, 1151b
Nude Descending the Staircase (Duchamp),
   1699b
Nullification controversy, 402b
Numbers, Ronald L., 990a
   as contributor, 859a–876b
Nuremberg Laws (1935), 576b
Nursing profession, 1414a–b
Nussbaum, Martha, 1655a
Nutt, Jim, 1719a
Nye, David, 1021a
Nye, Gerald P., 55b, 554a,b, *554b,* 600b,
   633b
Nye Committee, 555a, 633b, 1251a
Nylon, 847b, 848a,b, 1786a

O

Oak Ridge National Laboratory, 753b–754a
OAO. *See* Orbiting Astronomical
   Observatory (OAO)
OAS. *See* Organization of American States
   (OAS)
Oberlin College, 1819b
Obermann, Julian, 1579a
Objectivists (poets), 1580b
O'Boyle, Patrick, 1524b
O'Brien, David, 389b
O'Brien, Thomas C., 335a–b tab
Obscenity
   films, 1468b
   and public art support, 1740b–1741a
Occupational health, 1377b
Occupational safety, 976b, 1377b
Occupational Safety and Health
   Administration (OSHA), 315b, 1283a
Ockrent, Christine, 714b
O'Connell, William, 1516a
O'Connor, Frank, 34a
O'Connor, James, 932a
O'Connor, John, 1532b
O'Connor, Sandra Day, 391a–b tab, 393a

on Constitution, 401a
Octopus, The (Norris), 1438a
Odets, Clifford, 1581b
O'Donnell, John M., 879a
Odum, Howard W., 10a,b, 11a, 13b–15a,
   68a, 69b, 71a
Office, The, 1115b
Office equipment industry, 809b
Office-machine industry, 28b
Office Management Principles and Practice
   (Leffingwell), 1105a
Office of Defense Mobilization, 1280a
Office of Economic Opportunity,
   1080b–1081b
   compared to New Deal, 1080b
   conservative reaction, 1081b–1082a
Office of Economic Stabilization, 603b
Office of Emergency Management, 525b,
   1322a
Office of Federal Contract Compliance,
   527b
Office of Indian Education, 1814b
Office of Information and Regulatory
   Analysis, 531b
Office of Inter-American Affairs, 703a
Office of Management and Budget (OMB),
   315a, 345a, 349a, 359b, 529b, 532b
   See also Bureau of the Budget
Office of Naval Research (ONR), 750b,
   849a
Office of Price Administration, 262b, 602b,
   1028a, 1278a
Office of Price Administration and Civilian
   Supply, 602b
Office of Production Management, 602b
Office of Research on Women's Health,
   947a
Office of Scientific Research and
   Development, 605b, 752a, 945a, 1000b
Office of Strategic Services (OSS), 604b
Office of the Coordinator of Information,
   604b
Office of the Secretary of Defense, 612a
Office of War Information, 605a, 703b,
   1323b
   Bureau of Motion Pictures, 703b
   inclusive pluralism, 178a
Office of War Mobilization, 603b, 1278a
Office scientific management, 1114b
Office workers
   suburbs, 467a
   turn of the century, 1104b
Official Catholic Directory, 1511b–1512a
Official English laws, 97b, 98a
Of Mice and Men (Steinbeck), 1443a
O'Gara, James, 1525b
Ogburn, William F., 279a, 920a, 923a,b
O'Hagan, Ann, 1764a
Ohain, Hans von, 781b
O'Hara, John, 34b
Ohio, 1353b
Ohio Mattress Company, 1238a
Ohio River, 41b
   transportation, 45a
   Valley, 44a
Oil embargos, 57b
Oil industry, 72b, 86b–87a, 1130a,
   1133b–1134b, 1141b–1142a, 1144a,
   1145b, 1147a, 1160b, 1164b
   domination of energy infrastructure,
   1347a

Oil industry (*cont.*)
  early mergers, 1218a
  Federalism, 438b
  foreign investments, 1251a, 1254a
  foreign policy, 579b
  global economy, 1254b, 1258a
  Great Depression, 1161b
  in Los Angeles, 456a
  price decline, 30b
  regulation, 1168b, 1170b–1171a
  urban growth, 463a–b
Oil prices, 1169b, 1170a, 1172a, 1244a
  impact on the American balance of
    payments, 1199b
  oil shock of 1973, 692a, 730a, 1155b,
    1168b, 1199a, 1345a,1397b
  oil shock of 1979, 692a, 730a, 1199a,
    1259b, 1345a, 1397b,1400a
O'Keeffe, Georgia, 1702a, 1704a, *1704a,*
    1704b
  Brooklyn Bridge, 1701b
Okin, Susan, 290b
Okinawa, 642b
Olcott, Henry, 1540b, 1554a
Old age. *See* also Senior citizens
  assistance, 1075a
  as defined stage in life, 226a
  insurance, 230a, 1075b–1076a
  negative perception of, 226a–b
  as social problem, 226b
Old-age and survivors insurance. *See* Social
    security
Old Bunch, The (Levin), 1580b
Old Country Store, The (Carson), 1049b
Oldenburg, Claes, 1715b, 1722a
Old Jules (Sandoz), 10a
Old North Church (Boston), 36b
Olds, Ransom E., 1139b, 1751a
Oldsmobile, 1058b, 1139b
Old World influences, 168b
Old World in the New, The (Ross), 171a,
    256b
Old World Traits Transplanted (Thomas), 173b
O'Leary, Hazel, 951b
Oleszek, Walter, 361b
Oligopolies, 1188b
Oliver, Paul, 1024b
Oliver, Ruth, 770a
Olivetti, 1737a
Olmsted, Frederick Law, 1669a,b, 1744b
Olney, Richard, 594b
Olsen, Ken, 1149a
Olsen, Kenneth, 821b
Olsen, Tillie, 1586b
Olympic Games, 1477a
  politics, 1781b–1782a
OMB. *See* Office of Management and
    Budget (OMB)
Omnibus Budget Reconciliation Act
    (1981), 996a–b tab
Omnibus Trade and Competitiveness Act
    (1988), 1259b
"On Denoting" (Russell), 1646a
One-Dimensional Man (Marcuse), 931b
100,000,000 Guinea Pigs (Kallet and
    Schlink), 1027a
O'Neill, Eugene, 1443b
O'Neill, Tip, 305b
One-party politics, 64a, 67b, 68b, 71b
One World (Willkie), 556b
On Human Nature (Wilson), 871a

*On Keynesian Economics and the Economics of
    Keynes* (Leijonhufvud), 1304b
Only Yesterday (Allen), 1699a
On Native Grounds (Kazin), 1446a
ONR. *See* Office of Naval Research
    (ONR)
"On Referring" (Strawson), 1653b
*On the Origin of Species by Means of Natural
    Selection* (Darwin), 134a, 859a
On the Shore (Halper), 1580b
"On the Teaching of Modern Literature"
    (Trilling), 1448b–1449a, 1452b
"Ontological Relativity" (Quine), 1650a
Oozwald (Noland), 1720a
OPEC. *See* Organization of Petroleum
    Exporting Countries (OPEC)
Open Door policy, 594b, 599b, 1250a
  China, 571a–b, 572a, 720b
Open skies, 559b
Opera, 33a
  entertainment, 1462b
  patronage, 1727b, 1731a, 1737a, 1738a
Opera companies
  Chicago Opera Company, 1727b
  Houston Grand Opera, 33a
  Lyric Opera of Chicago, 33a
  San Francisco Opera, 33a
  Seattle Opera, 33a
  See also Metropolitan Opera (New York)
Operation Desert Storm, 364b, 784b
  congressional approval, 413a
Operation Paperclip, 786b
Operation Ranch Hand, 784a–b
Operation Wetback, 94b
Opinion polls, 307a, 319a
  use by F. Roosevelt, 577a
O Pioneers (Cather), 52a
Oppen, George, 1580b
Oppenheim, James, 1567b
Oppenheimer, Bruce, 371a–b
Oppenheimer, J. Robert, 85b, 748a–b
Opportunity: Journal of Negro Life, 1597a
Optics, 1417b
ORANGE Plan, 595a, 600a
  revision, 600b, 601a
Orbiting Astronomical Observatory (OAO),
    756a, 760b
Orchestra Hall (Chicago), 1611b
Orchestras, 1463a, 1611b, 1725b, 1732b,
    1738a, 1741a
  Baltimore, 33a
  Boston Symphony, 33a, 1629a, 1726a
  Chicago Symphony, 33a, 48a, 1727b
  Cleveland Orchestra, 33a
  Eastern region, 33a
  Ford Foundation, 1733b, 1737b
  Los Angeles Philharmonic, 1726a
  Midwest, 48a
  New York Philharmonic, 33a, 1727a,
    1734b
  nonprofit, 1726b
  Philadelphia Orchestra, 33a, 1727b
  Pittsburgh, 33a
  profit organizations, 1726b
  San Francisco Symphony, 1737a
  women in, 1739a
  women patrons, 1728a
Ordinary language philosophy, 1652a–1656a
Organic architecture, 1689a
Organization for Black American Culture,
    1604a

Organization for Economic Cooperation
    and Development (OECD), 1176b
Organization Man, The (Whyte), 198b, 265b,
    340a, 1111a–b
Organization of American States (OAS),
    610a
*Organization of Industrial Scientific Research,
    The* (Mees), 838b
Organization of Petroleum Exporting
    Countries (OPEC), 87a, 692a, 730a,
    1169b, 1170b, 1172a, 1283a, 1376a,
    1397b, 1400a
  oil prices, 1199a–b
  prices, 1256b–1259a, 1257b,
    1259b–1260a
Organized crime
  immigrants, 169b
  Jewish gangsters, 1579b
Oriental Institute, 496b–496a
Origins of American Social Science, The (Ross),
    902b, 920b
Origins of Behaviorism, The (O'Donnell),
    879a
Origins of Totalitarianism, The (Arendt), 284b,
    1584b
Orlando, Fla., 463a
Orlando, Vittorio, *598a–b*
Orloff, Ann Shola, 476b
Ornstein, Norman, 367b
Orozco, José Clemente, 1707a
Orphan in History (Cowan), 1586b
Orphans
  orphanages, 472b
  subjects for medical research, 949b–950a
Orpheum theaters, 1464a
Ortega y Gasset, José, 197b
Orthodox Church, 1546b–1547b
Orthodox Judaism, 1574b, 1575a–1576a,
    1582a–b, 1583b, 1585a,b, 1589b,
    1590b
  adaptation to America, 1572a
Orthodox Presbyterian Church, 1500b
Ortner, Sherry, 911b, 933a
Orwell, George, 851b
Osborn, Charles, 1669b
Osborn, Henry Fairfield, 862a–b
Osgood, Robert, 663a–664a, 671b–672a,b
OSHA. *See* Occupational Safety and Health
    Administration (OSHA)
OSS. *See* Office of Strategic Services (OSS)
Osteopathy, 1417b
Ostriker, Alicia, 1587a
Ostrovsky, Abba, 1579a
Ostwald, Wilhelm, 836a
O'Sullivan, John, 1765b
Oswald, Lee Harvey, 1478b
Other America, The (Harrington), 1078a
Other Bostonians, The (Thernstrom), 206b
"Other People's Money" (Brandeis), 1221b
Otis Elevator, 1136b
Ottaviani, Alfredo, 1522a, 1528b
Ottoman Empire, 679b
Oud, J. J. P., 1684a
Our Country (Strong), 254b
Our Movie-Made Children (Forman), 1484b
Outdoor relief, 473a–b
Outer Space Treaty (1967), 561b, 615a
Outlines of Economics (Ely), 274b
Outlook, 456b
Out-of-wedlock childbearing, 233b–234a
Overland journey as metaphor, 262a

Overlap Group, 1833a
Overman Act (1918), 523a
Overnight mail services, 1351a
Owen, Chandler, 1597a
Owen, Robert, 918b
Owens, Jesse, 1772b–1773a, 1781b
Owens, Michael, 1133a
Owens-Illinois, 1142b
Owsley, Frank, 10b, 14b
Oz, Amos, 1588a
Ozick, Cynthia, 1586b, 1589b

P

Paar, Jack, 1477a
Pabst distillery, 1132a
PACH. See Public Administration Clearing
    House (PACH)
Pach, Walter, 1698a
Pacific Electric Railway, 455a
Pacific Islanders, 365a
Pacific Ocean
    air warfare, 778a–779a
    exploration, 740a
Pacifism and arms limitation, **541a–567b**
Pacifist movement. See Peace movement
Packard, Alpheus, 860a
Packard, Vance, 265b, 1031a
Pact of Paris (1928). See Kellog–Briand Pact
    (1928)
Pagden, Anthony, 917b
Page, Charles Hunt, 920a
Page, Kirby, 554b
Page, Walter Hines, 8a
Pahlevi, Reza (Shah), 712b
Paige, Leroy "Satchel," 1771a, *1771a–b*
Paine, John Knowles, 1612b
Paine, Robert Treat, 543b
Paine, Thomas, 918a
Painting, 1729b, 1733a
    cultural export, 706b
    murals in post offices, 1730a
Painting and Sculpture, Section of (Treasury
    Department), 1705b
Pak Hon-yong, 656b
Pakistan, 689b
Palace Theater (New York), 1464b
Palestine, 679b
    Jewish state, 1583b–1584a
Paley, Grace, 1586b
Paley, William, 1472b
Paley Commission. See Material Policy
    Commission
Palmer, A. Mitchell, 257a, 597b
Palmer, Arnold, 712a, 1775a
Palmer, Olive, 1024b
Palmer and Hornbostel, 1671b
Palmer raids, 257a, 597b
Palmolive Company, 1024b
Pan-Africanist vision, 1599a–b
Panama Canal, 571b, 588b, 594a, 676b,
    720b–721a, 1340a
    zone, 621b
Pan American Airways, 773b–774a
Pan American Federation of Labor in the
    Western Hemisphere, 697a
Panic of 1907, 1188b, 1271b, 1295b
    solved by bankers, 1223b–1226a
Pan-Pacific Exhibition, San Francisco, 802a

Papal encyclicals, 1518a, 1525a–b
    Divini Redemptoris, 1518b
    Humanae Vitae, 1531a
    Mit brennender Sorge, 1519b
    Non abbiamo bisogno, 1519b
    Quadragesimo Anno, 1517b
    Qui Pluribus, 1518b
    Rerum Novarum, 1515b, 1517a–b
    Testem Benevolentiae, 1514b
Papashvily, George, 176a
Paper industry, 1132b, 1151b, 1164b
Paperwork Reduction Act (1980), 531b
Papp, Joseph, 1733a
Paramount Communications, Inc., 1470a
Paramount Pictures, 1466b, 1469a, 1470a,
    1472b, 1754a
    television, 1476b
Paredes, Americo, 1456b
Parents and Teachers Association (PTA),
    1731a
Pareto, Vilfredo, 1290a, 1299b
Parish councils, 1533a
Paris Peace Conference (1919), 550b, 630a
Paris peace talks, 586b
Paris Summit, 583a
Paris Treaty, 630b
Park, Robert, 17a, 161a, 173b, 213b, 922b,
    923a, 925a
Park, William H., 946a
Parke-Davis, 840a
Parker, Alton B., 335a–b tab
Parker, Charlie "Bird," 1602a, 1623b
Parker, Dorothy, 1581b
Parker, Everett, 1503b
Parker, Horatio, 1612b, 1613a
Parker, John J., 389a, 391a–b tab
Parker, William, 1302b
Parkinson, Donald, 1681a
Parkinson, John R., 1681a
Parks, Gordon, 1709a, *1709a–b*
Parks, Rosa, 118b, 153b, 388a
Parochial schools, 1803a, 1808a
Parran, Thomas, 1000a
Parsees, 1550a
Parsons, Elise Clews, 904a–b, 922a
Parsons, Talcott, 908a,b–909a, 924a–925a,
    926b
    criticism of, 930a
    Social System, The, 927a–b
Partch, Harry, 1622b
Partial Test Ban Treaty (1963), 584b, 690b
Particle accelerators, 739a,b, 746a–b,
    750a–b, 751a, 758b–759a,b–760b
Parties and interest groups, **295a–320b**
Partisan Review, 1444a, 1485b, 1581a, 1588a
    black writers in, 1601a
Partisanship, 306b
Parton, Dolly, 1631a, 1792b
Party bosses, 295b, 298a, 299a–300b
    See also Machine politics
Party loyalty, 306b, 308a
    and divided government, 307a
    states, 437b
Paschke, Ed, 1716b
Passenger airlines, 773a–774b, 792a–b, 795a
Passenger Car Design and Highway Safety,
    1031a
"Passing of Evolution" (Wright), 861a
Passing of the Great Race, The (Grant), 137b,
    187b
Pasteur, Louis, 1132a

Pastor, Tony, 1463b
Pastoralism, 58a
Pastoral letters, 1511b, 1520b, 1521b, 1522b,
    1529b, 1532a
Patchen, Loral, *711b*
Patent Office, 741a
Patents, 1145b, 1249b
    airplanes, 769a–b, 771b
    Bell System, 837b
    film industry, 1469a
    inventors, 833a,b
    medical discoveries, 944a,b
    radio, 804a, 1471a
Paterson, Donald G., 1388a
Paterson Strike Pageant, 1697a
Paterson (Williams), 1449b
Patman, Wright, 504a
Patrick, G. T. W., 902a
Patriotism: A Menace to Liberty (Goldman),
    257a
Patronage of the arts, **1725a–1742b**
Patten, Gilbert, 1762a
Patten, William, 861b, 863a,b
Patterson, David S., *as contributor,* 541a–567b
Patterson, James T., *as contributor,*
    1067a–1090b
Paul VI, Pope, 1528a, 1531a
Paul, Alice, 117a
Paul, John R., 946a
Pauling, Linus, 558b, 1374b
Paulist Press, 1533b
Pavlov, Ivan, 880a
Pawnbroker, The (Wallant), 1589b
Payne, Oliver, 1669b
Payne-Aldrich Tariff (1909), 721b, 1271b
Payne Study and Experiment Fund,
    1484b–1485a
Payroll taxes, 1320a, 1323b, 1324a
PBS. See Public Broadcasting System (PBS)
PCA. See Production Code Administration
    (PCA)
Peabody, Francis, 1215a
Peabody, George, & Company, 1214a
Peabody Conservatory (Baltimore), 33a
Peabody Fund, 493a
Peace Corps, 504a, *711b*
Peaceful Nuclear Explosions Treaty (1976),
    561b
Peace Mission, 1600a
Peace movements
    approaches to war prevention, 553a
    Catholics, 1520a
    development, 541a–542a
    and disarmament, 552b
    influence on U.S. government policy,
        541a
    liberal Protestants, 1501b
    and new age, 1558b
Peale, Norman Vincent, 1496a, 1546a
Pearce, Diana, 122b
Pearce, T. M., 10b
Pearl, Raymond, 861b, 862a, 864a, 865a
Pearl Harbor, 96a,b, 578a, 602b, 638b,
    639a–b, 686a, 778a, 808b
    isolationism, 55b
Pearl Harbor: Warning and Decision
    (Wohlstetter), 602b
Pearson, Karl, 1651b
Peat Marwick and Mitchell, 1410a
Pechman, Joseph, 1326a, 1328a
Peckham, Rufus W., 377b–378a

Pecora, Ferdinand, 1225a, 1419b
Pediatrics, 226a
Pedophilia, 1527a
Pei, I.M., 1665a
   John Hancock Tower (Boston), 1686b
Peirce, Charles Sanders, 1637a–b
Peiss, Kathy, 114a, 1748b
Pekar, Harvey, 1484a
Pekelis, Alexander, 1584a
Pell, Claiborne, 30a, 1736a, 1739b
Pellagra research, 942b
Pelli, Cesar, 1689a
Pelly, William Dudley, 175b
Pelton Waterwheel Company, 746b
Pembroke College, 32a
Pendleton Act (1883), 326b
Pène du Bois, Guy, 1698b
Penicillin, 945a
Penney, J.C., 1065a
Pennock, J. Roland, 514b
Pennsylvania, 487a
Pennsylvania Academy of Fine Arts, 1694a
Pennsylvania Coal Company, 1217b
Pennsylvania Law Review, 395a
Pennsylvania museum. *See* Philadelphia
   museum
Pennsylvania Railroad, 35b, 802a,
   832b–833a
Pennsylvania Turnpike, 25b, 35b
Pension Benefit Guaranty Corporation,
   1234b
Pension funds
   and democratization of capital markets,
     1210b
   as institutional investors, 1231b
Pentagon Papers (Ellsberg), 562a, 587b
Pentecostalism, 1491b, 1493a, 1498b–1499a,
   1500b–1501b
   Catholics, 1533a
People, 1481b
People of Plenty (Potter), 199b–200a, 285b
People's Bicentennial Commission, 268a
People's Council for Peace and Democracy
   in America, 549b
People's Religion, The (Gallup and Castelli),
   1492b
People's Republic of China, 689a, 691a
   rapprochement, 691b
   Tiananmen Square, 712a
   See also China
Pepper, Claude, 110b, 488b, 1735a
Pepsi-Cola, 1030a, 1055b–1057b
   Pepsi Generation, 1059b, 1060a
   radio advertising, 808a
Pepsodent, 1039a
   Amos 'n' Andy show sponsor, 1025a
Percy, Walker, 1457a
Pereira, Irene Rice, 1714b
Pereria, William, 1687b
Perestroika, 617b
Performing arts
   airlines, 795a
   Ford Foundation, 1733a
   live performances, 1463a, 1464b–1465a
   music, 1614a
Performing Arts, The (Rockefeller Brothers
   Fund), 1735b
Performing Arts (Baumal and Bowen), 1735b
Perkins, Carl, 73b
Perkins, Frances, 122a, 479a
Perkins, George W., 802a, 1221a

Perlman, Selig, 204b–205a
Permanent Court of International
   Arbitration, 544a
Permanent Court of International Justice
   (World Court), 551a
   United States and, 553b
Pernick, Martin, 952a
Perot, H. Ross, 308a, 321b, 322a, 1150b
   presidential elections, 336a–b tab
   third-party politics, 296b, 306b
Perry, Harold, 1530a
Perry, Ralph Barton, 1641b
Pershing, John J., 627a, 627a–b, 628a
Persian Gulf War. *See* Gulf War
Personal computers, 799a, 823a–b, 826b,
   1031b, 1148b, 1149a–b
Personality
   Protestant liberalism, 1496a
   religious pursuit of, 1496a–b
   theory, 888b
Pesotta, Rose, 1574a
Pesticides, 1371b–1372a
Peterson, Esther, 1031a
Pethick-Lawrence, Emmeline, 546b
Peto, John F., 1694b
Petrochemical industry, 72b, 463a, 1128b,
   1133a–1134b, 1141b–1142a, 1144a,
   1397b
   See also Oil industry
Petroleum, 1396a–1401a
   early uses of, 1335a
   imports, 1172a–b
   prices, 1172a–b
   world and U.S. oil reserves, 1937–1990,
     1400a
   world crude oil reserves, 1948 and 1988,
     1399a–b
   world oil production, 1890–1988,
     1398a–b
Pew Trust, 507b, 1737b
Peyton, Patrick, 1523b
Pfeffer, Leo, 1584a
Pfeiffer, Hardy Holzman, 1689a
Pfizer, 1147b
Pharmaceutical industry, 28a, 45b, 840a–b,
   1026b, 1143a,b, 1144b, 1147b–1148a
   dependent on pre-World War I Germany,
     840a
   international investments, 1262a
   medical research funding, 943b–944a
   Midwest, 59a
   regulation, 430a
   research, 839b, 944a, 1000b
Phelps, William Lyon, 1745b
Phelps-Dodge Company, 86b, 1135b
Phi Beta Kappa, 1824a
Philadelphia, 456b
   financial crisis, 467b
   during Great Depression, 457b
   schools, 1807a, 1810a
   subway, 453a
Philadelphia Centennial Exposition, 1726b
Philadelphia convention, 401b–402a
Philadelphia (Lukacs), 33b
Philadelphia Museum, 33a, 1726b, 1731b
   Great Depression, 1731b, 1732a
Philadelphia Negro, The (Du Bois), 922a
Philadelphia Record, 632b
Philanthropic organizations
   health, 974b
   Jewish, 1576a

modern foundation roots, 492a–b
scholarly interest in, 505b, 506b
See also Foundations; Private
   philanthropy; specific organizations
Philco, 1148b, 1149a
Philip Morris, 1131a, 1739b
   arts patronage, 1738b
Philippines, 551b, 595a, 599a, 621a,b, 676b,
   720b
   foreign policy, 572a
   immigration, 97a
   insurrection, 593b–594a, 654a
   mutual defense agreement with, 689a
Philippine Sea, Battle of the, 642a
Phillips, A. W., 1300b
Phillips, Duncan, 1699a
Phillips, Kevin, 28b
Phillips, William, 1444a
Philosophy, **1635a–1663b**
Philosophy and Phenomenological Research,
   1657a
Philosophy of John Dewey, The (Schlipp),
   277b
Philosophy of Science Association, 1658b
Phonographs, 1461b, 1462a, 1470b–1471a
   Amberola, 1023a
   Edison, 1023a
Photocopiers, 822a–b
Photographers, 1714b
   Farm Security Administration, 1730a
   Resettlement Administration, 1730a
   in World War II, 1710a
Photography, 851a, 1021a
   airplanes, 792b–793a
   Eastern region, 35a–b
   and environmental politics, 1373a–b
   impact on American artists, 1697b
   industry, 28a
Photojournalism, 1481b, 1730a
Photoplay, 1482a
Photoplay, The (Münsterberg), 1484a
Photorealist painters, 1718a–b
Phrenology, 877b
Physical Review, 845a
Physicians for Social Responsibility, 564a
Physicists, 837b
Physicists, The (Kevles), 840b, 850a
Physics, 1127a
   big science, 739a–b, 740a, 745b–746a
   high-energy, 751a, 753b, 759b,
     761b–762a
   technology, 1138a
"Physiographic Regions of the United
   States" (Powell), 8a
Piaget, Jean, 892b, 893a
Piano Concerto (Copland), 1617b
Picabia, Francis, 1701a,b
Picasso, Pablo, 1697b, 1698a, 1699a, 1728b
   Guernica, 1708a
Pickens, T. Boone, 1236b
Pickering, E. C., 741a–b
Pickett, Clarence, 559a
Pickford, Mary, 1465b
Picon, Molly, 1570b
Picture Stories from the Bible, 1482a
Piehl, Mel, 1517b
Piercy, Marge, 1587a
Piggly–Wiggly chain, 1025a
Pillsbury, 45b, 1020b, 1131a
Pincas, Gregory, 228a
Pinchback, P. B. S., 141b

Pinchot, Amos, 547b
Pinchot, Gifford, 84b, 1272a, 1358b,
     1363a–1364a, 1380b, 1402a
   and Muir, John, 1359b, 1360a
   opposed by Ballinger, Richard A., 1364b
Pincus, Gregory, 946b
Pinderhughes, Raquel, 210b
Pine Ridge Reservation, 93a
Pingree, Hazen, 49b
"Pink-collar" ghettos, 109b
Pinski, David, 1567a, 1570a
Pinza, Ezio, 1616b
Pioneers
   democracy, 55a
   isolation, 51b
   Midwest, 41b–43b, 47a, 58b, 60a
   values, 54b–55a
Pioneer space program, 788b
Piore, Michael, 855b
Pious, Richard, 330b
Pipelines, 1160b, 1342a–b
   Alaskan pipeline, 1347b
   Big Inch, 1343a
   federal aid during World War II, 1343b
   Little Inch, 1343b
   petroleum and natural gas pipeline
      infrastructure, 1921–1987, 1344a–b tab
   Standard Oil of New Jersey, 1335b
   World War II, 1344b
Piper, Adrian, 1721a
Piper Cub airplane, 776a, 779a
Pippin, Horace, 1701b
Pisan Cantos (Pound), 1450a
Piston, Walter, 1622a
Pitcairn, John, 1133a
Pitkin, Walter, 1641b
Pitney, Mahlon, 390a–b tab
   Coppage v. Kansas (1915), opinion in,
      378a–b
Pittsburgh, 451b
   revitalization, 1346a
Pittsburgh Crawfords, 1771a–b
Pittsburgh Plate Glass Company, 1133a,
     1142b
Pittsburgh Platform, 1566a–b, 1582b
Pittsburgh Survey, 215a
Pius IX, Pope, 1518b
Pius XI, Pope, 1517b, 1518b, 1519b
Piven, Frances Fox, 1080a, 1082b
Place No One Knew, The, 1373b
Plagiarism, 1834a
Plague, 942b
Plains, 88a
   homesteaders and droughts, 1362a
Plan BLACK, 595a
Planetary exploration, 756b, 790a
Planned Parenthood, 946b
Plant design, 1130b
Plaskow, Judith, 1589a
Plastics, 1372a
Plastics industry, 1146a
   See also Polymers
Plath, Sylvia, 1458a
Plattsburg movement, 596a
Playboy, 713a, 1481b
Playboy Channel, 1479b
Player pianos, 1470b
Playground Association of America, 1762b
   immigrants and sports, 1766a
Playwrights, 1733a
Pledge of Allegiance, 254a

Plessy, Homer Adolph, 142a
Plimoth Plantation, 37b
Plot That Failed, The (Nathan), 359a
Pluralism
   arts patronage, 1735a–1741b
   Catholicism, 1526b, 1534a
   and class, 195b
   cultural. See Cultural pluralism
   ethnic, 258a, 259b
   and interest groups, 318b
   and McCarthyism, 286a
   during World War II, 263a
Plutonium, 85b
Pneumonia, 959b, 968b, 969a,b, 977a
   leading cause of death in 1900, 968a
Pnin (Nabokov), 1452b
Poalei Zion, 1573b
Pocho (Villarreal), 1456b
Pocock, J. G. A., 268b
Pocono Mountains, 1578b
Podhoretz, Norman, 1586b
Poe, Edgar Allan, 1436b
Poetry, 1733a
   Hebrew, 1573b
   Jewish poets, 1569b–1570a, 1579a, 1581a,
      1587a
   Midwest, 52a–b
   South, 67b
   translated from Hebrew, 1587a
   translated from Yiddish, 1587a
Point Four programs, 579b
Poland, 350b, 679a, 683a
Polanski, Roman, 1363a
Polaris missiles, 786b
Polaroid, 28a
Polenberg, Richard, 603a, 605b
Polhemus, Ted, 1791b, 1792b, 1793a
Policies Plan for the Year 2000, A (National
   Capital Planning Commission), 20a
Polio, 232b, 960a
Polish Americans, 577b
Polish Peasant in Europe and America, The
   (Thomas and Znaniecki), 922b, 923a
Political action committees (PACs), 308a–b,
     313b–314a, 316a, 318a
   See also Campaign contributions
Political art, 1719b, 1720a
   Jews, 1587a
Political ideas and movements, **273a–294b**
Political parties
   divided government, 304a–b tab, 305a–b
      tab
   and interest groups, 295a–320b
   and interest groups in 1980s and 1990s,
      317b–318a
   machines, 297a
   and national unity, 319a%308%319b
   New Deal, 299b–301a
   new immigrants, 298a
   1960s protest movement, 301a
   presidents as party leaders, 324a
   and Progressive movement, 298b–299a
   reform, 296b–301b, 298b–301b
   at start of century, 297a–b
   two-party system, 296b
Political patronage, 298b
   New Deal programs, 300b
"Political Philosophy of the New Deal,
   The" (Humphrey), 283a
Political reform
   and professional experts, 1410b

under Theodore Roosevelt, 327b
Political satire, 1477b
Political Science Quarterly, 1291b
Politics
   Catholics, 1511a, 1516b, 1518a–b,
      1524b–1526b, 1525a,1528a, 1532a
   communications technology, 799b–800a,
      806a–b
   Eastern region, 28b–31a
   farming, 51a, 52b, 57a
   gender in, 116a–121b, 124b
   increasing role of courts, 377a
   Midwest, 41a, 49a–b
   racism, 66b, 76b–77a
   television, 1478b, 1479a
   religion, 1590b
      See also Separation of church and state
   South, 65b
   sports and, 1781b–1782b
Politics of Military Unification, The (Caraley),
   609a
Politics of Propaganda, The (Winkler), 605a
Polk, James Knox, 570a
Pollock, Jackson, 1712b, 1713a, 1715a,
     1728b, 1730b
Pollyanna (Porter), 1438b
Polner, Murray, 1587a
Polsby, Nelson, 356a
Polyester, 1028b
Polygamy, 93b
Polymers, 845a–b, 1128b, 1143b, 1144a,
     1145b–1147a
Pond's beauty products, 1025b
Ponselle, Rosa, 1616b
Pontiac, 1058b
Poole, Elijah. See Muhammad, Elijah
Poor houses, 472a,b, 473a
Poor laws, 471b, 474b, 480a
Poor People's Campaign, 288b
Pop artists, 1483b, 1716a–b
   Jewish, 1587a
Popes, 1511a, 1528a
   See also Papal encyclicals; individual popes
Pop music, 1631a
Popper, Karl, 873a, 1648a
Popular culture, 1462b
   audiences, 1488b
   choice, 1488a–b
   consumer ethic, 1462b
   critics, 1484b
   definition, 1461a
   environmentalism in, 1377b
   Frankfurt School studies
   and mass media, 1461a–1490b
   origins in discriminated groups, 1462a
   study of, 1484a–b, 1485a
   two worlds, 1488b
Popular Front, 1519a
Popular Mechanics, 114b
Population
   California cities, 455b
   changing age composition, 972a
   cities, 451b, 456a–461a
   Eastern region, 28b–31a
   explosion, 1375b
   growth in South, post-World War II, 72b
   infrastructure, 1331b, 1336b
   Midwest, 41a, 46b, 54a, 57b
   movement. See African Americans: Great
      Migration; Migration
   movement in South, 71a, 75a

Population (*cont.*)
  percentage by race in selected cities,
    147a–b tab
  problems research funded by foundations,
    228a
  ten largest cities in the U.S., 1950 and
    1980, 461a–b tab
  ten largest metropolitan areas in the U.S.,
    1950 and 1980, 462a–b tab
  twenty largest cities in the U.S., 1900,
    452a–b tab
  of the United States by Region,
    1890–1990, *73a–b*
  World War II, 1028b
Population Bomb, The (Ehrlich), 1375b
Populism, 274a, 297b, 308b, 429b
  anti-imperialism, 721b
  Midwest, 49a, 53b
  South, 64a,b
  taxation, 1313b
Populist party, 64a
Pork expenditures, 305b
Portable Faulkner, The (Cowley), 1445b
Portable War Memorial (Kienholz), 1719b
Porter, Cole, 1619a, *1620a,* 1631a
Porter, Edwin S., 83b, 1465b
Porter, Eleanor Hodgman, 1438b
  Pollyanna, 1438b
Porter, Eliot, 1373b, 1714b
Portfolio investments
  foreign trade, 1244b, 1245a–1246a,
    1247b, 1248a,1249a–b, 1251a, 1252a,
    1254a, 1255a, 1257a, 1258b,1261a–b
Port Huron Statement, 287a, 1830a
Portnoy's Complaint (Philip Roth), 1457a
Portrait of the Artist as a Young Man, A
  (Joyce), 1448b
Posner, Richard, 394b, 1301b–1302a
Post, George B., 1672b, 1675a
Post-Analytic Philosophy, 1658b
Postmodern Condition, The (Lyotard), 1454b
Postmodernism, 268b, 1486b
Postmodernism (architecture), 1688a,
  1689a–b
Postmodernism (art), 1720b
Postmodernism (literature), 1435a–b,
  1451b–1455b
Postneonatal mortality, *964a–b*
  rates, defined, 959a
Post Office
  air mail, 773a
  employees, 361a
Poststructuralism, 1454a, 1486b
Postsuburban cities, 468a
Potawatomis, 135b
Potsdam, 647a
Potter, David, 199a, 264a, 267b, 285b,
  808b, 817b
  People of Plenty, 199b–200a
Pottery industry, 27b
Pound, Ezra, 1441b, 1444a, 1448a,
  1449b–1450a
  Pisan Cantos, 1450a
  "Provincialism the Enemy," 1444a
Pound, Roscoe, 378a, 396b
  court reform, 393b
Pound Era, The (Kenner), 1450a
Poverty
  absolute, 1070a, 1077b, 1085a
  culture of, 1079b
  deserving poor, 1067b

  feminization, 122b–123a
  line, 1078b–1079a
  long-term, 1079b
  low wages as cause of, 1079a
  minorities and, 1086a–b
  nineteenth century, 1068a
  relative, 1070a
  South, 63a, 76b
  undeserving poor, 1067b
  urban, 1068b
  and wealth, 1067a–1090b
Poverty (Hunter), 1068b
Povich, Shirley, 1777b
Powell, John Wesley, 8a, 1360b, 1362a
Powell, Lewis F., Jr., 390a–b tab, 392b
Power dressing, 1796b
Power elite, 207b–209a
Power Elite, The (Mills), 207b–208a, 340a,
  610b, 1830b
Power-granting provisions of the
  Constitution, 401a
  broad interpretation by Supreme Court,
    402a, 405b
Power of Positive Thinking, The (Peale),
  1496a, 1546a
Pragmatism, 1636b, 1637a
  Progressivism, 276a, 279a
  renewal, 291a
Pragmatism in Law and Society (Williams and
  Grey), 291b
Pragmatism (W. James), 1638a
Pragmatists, American
  influence on psychology, 878b
Prairie farm auction, 60a
Prairie house, 1677a,b, *1678a–b*
Prairie School, 1667b
  followers, 1678b
PrairyErth (Heat-Moon), 41b, 59b
Pratt, Caroline, 1808a
Pratt and Whitney, 786b
Pratt & Whitney, 1145a
Prayer in public schools, 306b, 418a
Precisionists, 1702a
Predators' Ball, The, 1238a
Preface to Democratic Theory, A (Dahl), 285b
Preface to Morals, A (Lippmann), 281a, 1501a
Preface to Peasantry (Raper), 13b
Preface to Politics, A (Lippmann), 277a
Preisand, Sally, 1588b
Preminger, Otto, 1587b
Prendergast, Maurice, 1697a
Preparing for the Next War (Sherry), 607b
Preponderance of Power, A (Leffler), 607b
Presbyterians
  Auburn Affirmation of 1924, 1500a
  Congress, 365b
  fundamentalism, 1500a
  liberalism, 1494a, 1500b
  population percentages, 1492b, 1493a
"Present Crisis, The" (Lowell), 1437a
Present Tense, 1587a
Preservationist movement, 1358b
  revival under environmental movement,
    1372b
Presidency, United States, **321a–353b**
  budget process, 358a–361a
  Congress, 372b–373a
  Constitution II (3), 515a
  impoundment of funds, 359a
  inherent powers, 407a
  polling, 332b–333a

  power restrained by Congress, 413a
  presidential elections, 335a–b tab
  public approval, *337a–b*
  rejection of supremacy, 528b
  use of power for antiregulatory ends,
    528b
  See also Executive branch
President, Congress, and the Constitution, The
  (Pyle and Pious), 330b
Presidential Power (Neustadt), 339a, 340a
Presidential Task Force on the Arts and
  Humanities, 1739b
President John Smith (Adams), 382a
President's Commission for the Study of
  Ethical Problems in Medicine, 951b
President's Commission on Excellence,
  1814b
President's Committee on Administrative
  Management. See Brownlow
  Committee
President's Committee on Higher
  Education, 1827b
President's Committee on Social Trends,
  227b
President's Conference on Home Building
  and Home Ownership, 1020a
Presley, Elvis, 73b, 1471a, 1488b, 1625a,
  1625b, 1628b, 1792b
Press, Petersburg, *1699b*
Price, Don K., 499a
Price, George McCready, 866b–867a, 868a,
  873b
Prices, 1129b, 1130b
  controls during World War II, 603a,
    1322b
  during Great Depression, *1162a–b*
Price Waterhouse, 1410a, 1411b
Primary elections, 299a–b, 301a–b, 307b,
  308a, 319a
  labor unions, 314a,b
Princeton University, 32a, 1819a, 1823b
  art education, 1729a
  Institute for Advanced Study, 498b,
    811b
  segregation, 1825b
Principal-agent problem, 1233a–b
Principia Mathematica (Russell and
  Whitehead), 1647a
Principles of Economics (Seager), 1292a
Principles of Economics (Seligman), 1292a
Principles of Economics (Taussig), 1292a
Principles of Political Economy (Newcomb),
  1293a
Principles of Psychology (W. James), 878b,
  1638a
Printing industry, 27b, 28a, 1130a,b, 1130b,
  1150b
Print media, 1481b
  increased concentration in large
    corporations, 1482a
Prison Notebooks (Gramsci), 208b
Pritchett, Henry S., 1821b
Privacy rights in family law, 240a
Private institutions
  Eastern region, 31a–33a
  industrial research, 839a–b
Private philanthropy
  nationalization, 491a, 493b
  universities, 1821b
Private Power and American Democracy
  (McConnell), 433b

Private schools
    academies, 1803a
    child-centered schools, 1808a
    conservative Protestant Christian, 1815a
    nonreligious, 1808a
    prep schools, 1808a
    religious, 1807b–1808a
    Roman Catholic, 1815a
Privatization, 531a–b
Problem of Boston, The (Green), 33b
"Problem of Social Cost" (Coase), 1301b
Process art, 1718b
Processing industries, 1215b
Process of Education, The (Bruner), 1812a
Procter & Gamble, 313a, 1022b, 1023a,
    1028b, 1048a, 1052a
    PertPlus, 1063a–b
    work reform, 1119b
Production Code Administration, 1468b,
    1469b, 1470a
Production processes, 1139b, 1141b, 1144a,
    1146b, 1152a
    goods, 1129a–1130a
    unit system, 1139a
Production technologies, 1262a
Productivity, 1155b, *1165a–b,* 1165a–1166a,
    1170a, 1172b, 1173a, *1178a–b*
Product policy, 1037a
Product variety, 1039b
Professional Golfers Association, 1775a
Professionalization
    foundations, 502b
    philosophy, 1636a
Professional sports
    economics, 1775b
Professional standards review organizations,
    1005a
Professions, The, 1107a, 1118a,
    1407a–1430b
    certification process, 198a
    codes of ethics, 1413a
    income, 1423a
    middle class, 200b
    national associations, 198a
    professional associations, 198a, 1411b
    South, 76a
"Program and First Platform of Six
    Realists," 1641b
Program for Economic Recovery, 1204a
"Program of Social Reconstruction"
    (Ryan), 1515b
"Progress before Precedent," 1667b
Progressive capitalism, 1313b
Progressive democracy, 274a–278a
Progressive Democracy (Croly), 277a
Progressive Education Association, 1808b
Progressive Era
    domestic violence, 237b
    education reform, 1804b–1807b
    female reformers and social welfare, 477b
    foreign policy, 570b–574a
    governmental power, 405a–406b
    government expansion and professionals,
        1410b
    health problems, 225b
    Interstate Commerce Commission, 519a
    middle-class reform politics, 116b
    poor law alternatives, 473b–476b
    society defined, 920a
    specialized knowledge, 1408a
    women consumers and reform, 115a

Progressive party, 178a, 296b, 298b
Progressive reform
    child labor, 224b
    immigrants and sports, 1766a
    legislation invalidated by state judges,
        405a–b
    regulation of the workplace, 378a
    restructuring immigrant family according
        to middle-classnorms, 224a
    social welfare, 471a
    Southern, 65b
    Southern blacks, 65b
    state-administered health insurance, 476b
    youth organizations, 224b
Progressive taxation, 1317b, 1320a
Progressivism, 49a–b, 51a,b, 55a, 274a–278a,
    297b, 298b–299b, 309a,b, 429a,b,
    1314a, 1497a
    and activism in the Third World, 676a
    conservation, 1358a
    conversationism applied to other fields,
        1380b
    legislation, 1026b
    liberal Protestants, 1494b–1495a
    nationalism, 256a
    new economy, 1269a–b
    political economy, 1270a–1273a
    political parties, 298b–299a
    poverty, 1071a
    presidential power, 325a, 326b
    racism, 256b
    Rauschenbusch, 1496b
    South, 64a–67b
Prohibition, 309a, 431a, 1132a
    Catholics, 1516b
    organized crime, 1579b
    South, 64b–65a
    xenophobia, 172a
Project Camelot, 710b–711a
Project Whirlwind, 811b, 812b
Prokofiev, Sergei, 1728b
Proletarian realism, 1442b–1443a
Promised Land, The (Antin), 33b, 1578a
Promise of American Life, The (Croly), 256a,
    277a, 430a
Propaganda
    Europe, 808b
    films, 1467b
    World War II, 1027b–1028a
    during World War II, 262b
Property rights, 415a
Property taxes, 1310b, 1312b–1313a,
    1318b–1319a, 1325b
    assessment, 1313a, 1314a–1315a
    constitutional limitation on national
        government, 1311a
    Jacksonian reforms, 1313a
    real estate, 1313a, 1318b
    reform, 1314b–1315a
Proskauer, Joseph, 1584a
Prostitution
    New Deal laws, 122a
    Progressive Era laws, 122a
    as threat to family, 223a
Protecting Soldiers and Mothers (Skocpol),
    215b
Protectionism, 312b, 720a, 724a, 725a,
    732a, 1254b, 1256a, 1257a, 1258b,
    1263a
Protective Mobilization Plan (1939),
    601a

Protestant, Catholic, Jew (Herberg), 179b,
    1492b, 1588b
"Protestantism" (Richard Niebuhr), 1491a
Protestants and Other Americans United for
    the Separation of Church and State,
    1521b
Protestants and Protestantism,
    1491a–1509b, 1562a
    anti-Catholicism, 1491a
    Catholics and, 1534b–1535a
    division, 278b
    Eastern region, 31b, 32a
    evolution, 859b
    importance in American life, 1492a–b
    liberals, 1491b, 1492a, 1493a–1498a,
        1501b–1503a,1504b–1506a
    missionary movement, 696a
    national mission and identity, 1491b
    population percentages, 1492a–1493b
    religious debates within, 1491a
    See also specific denominations
Protest movements of the 1960s, 301a–b
Protocol of Peace, 1574a
"Protocols of the Elders of Zion, The," 1578b
Proton synchrotron. *See* Particle accelerators
Proud Shoes (Murray), 66a
Proust, Marcel, 1441b, 1442a
Provincetown Players, 1727b
Pruitt-Igoe Houses (Saint Louis), 1689a
Pryor, Arthur, 1613b
Psychiatry
    biological, 894b
    and psychoanalysis, 889b
Psychoanalysis, 882a, 884b–885a
    and American avant-garde, 884b
    criticism by psychologists, 883a–884a
    doubts about efficacy of, 895a
    and the media, 884a
    middle class and, 200a
    psychiatry and, 889b–890a
Psychoanalytic Review, 903b
Psychology, 877a–898b
    developmental, 909b
    education, 1806a
    gender studies, 902b–903a, 904a, 907a–b
    heredity and environment, 885b–887a
    humanistic, 234b, 896a, 1558a
    safety movement, 475a
    as scientific discipline, 878a
    usefulness to society, 880a
"Psychology as the Behaviorist Views It"
    (Watson), 879b
Psychology of Women, The (Patrick), 902a
Psychotherapy, 881b, 895b
    psychoanalysis, 889b
    self-realization, 234b
PTL Club, 824b
Public administration
    as branch of political science, 521b
    framers and, 515a–b
    presidential supremacy theory, 515a
    Spelman Fund, 496a
Public Administration Clearing House
    (PACH), 497a, 499b
    social sciences application, 496a
Public and Its Problems, The (Dewey), 197b,
    280a–b, 287a
Public Broadcasting System (PBS), 817a,
    1479b, 1740b
    Great Performances, 1737a
    Masterpiece Theater, 1737a

Public domain, 84a–b
Public health, 438a
  activities, 974a
  reformers, 454a
  regulation, 431b
Public Health Service, 1421a
Public Health Service Amendments (1972),
  996a–b tab
Public housing, 438a, 458b, 1334b,
  1345b–1346a
  federal housing-finance programs and
    new public residential construction, in
    millions of dollars peryear, 1935-1988,
    1343a–b tab
Public Interest, 290a
Public Interest Research Group, 1835a
Public Opinion (Lippmann), 279b–280a,b
  review by Dewey in New Republic, 280a
Public policy
  broadening of, 492a
  foundations and, 502a
Public relations, 1411a, 1416b
Public resources, 83a
Public schools
  centralization, 1806b
  control and organization, 1806a
  instrument of assimilation, 170a
  music education, 1621a–b
  superintendents, 1807a
  ward-based committees, 1806b–1807a
  See also Education; Elementary and
    secondary education
Public social welfare expenditures, 472a–b
  tab
*Public Speaking and Influencing Men in
  Business. See How to Win Friends and
  Influence People*
Public Utilities Regulatory Policies Act
  (1978), 528a
Public Utility Holding Company Act
  (1935), 1227a–b tab, 1227b
Public Works Administration (PWA), 69a,
  70a, 1026a
  traditional family and, 122b
Public Works of Art Project (PWAP),
  1705b, 1729b
Publishers Weekly, 31a
Publishing industry, 31a–b, 1130a,b, 1130b,
  1150b
  small companies, 1488a
  specialty niches, 1483a
Pucinski, Roman, 183b
Pueblo nation, 1810b
Puerperal septicemia, 968a,b
Puerto Rico, 186a, 621a, 676b, 720b
Pujo, Arsène, 1220a, 1295b
Pujo Committee, 1221a, 1295b
Pulitzer Prize, 52a
  Baxter, James P., 846b
  Lewis, Sinclair, 1440b
  Maus, 1484a
Punk style, 1793a
Purcell, William, 1678b
Purchasing Power of Money, The (Fisher),
  1293a
Pure Food and Drug Act (1906), 996a–b
  tab, 1026b, 1272a
  upheld by Supreme Court, 406a
Pure science, 832a–b, 842b, 843a, 846b,
  849a
  best science, 842b–843a, 846b, 854b

Puritan Boston and Quaker Philadelphia
  (Baltzell), 33b
Puryear, Martin, 1720a
Putnam, Hilary, 1659a,b
  Realism with a Human Face, 1650a
Putnam, James Jackson, 881b
Puyallup, 1378a
Puzo, Mario, 34a, 183b
PWA. *See* Public Works Administration
  (PWA)
PWAP. *See* Public Works of Art Project
  (PWAP)
Pyle, Christopher, 330b
Pynchon, Thomas, 1453b
  V, 1452b

Q

Quaker Oats, 1020b
Quakers
  conscientious objection, 549a
  peace movement and, 541b
Quarterly Journal of Economics, 1290b, 1291b
Quayle, Dan
  on court reform, 395a
  presidential elections, 336a–b tab
Quest for an American Sociology (Matthews),
  921a
Quest for Certainty, The (Dewey), 281a
Quigley, Martin, 1467b
Quimby, Harriet, 770a
Quimby, Phineas P., 1545a–b
Quine, W. V. O., 1648b,
  1649b–1650a,b–1651a, 1652a
  "Ontological Relativity," 1650a
  "Two Dogmas of Empiricism,"
    1649b–1650a
Quinn, John, 1699a
Quiz shows, 1476b–1477a
  scandals, 816b, 1029b, 1479a
Quota Law. *See* Emergency Immigration
  Restriction Act (1921)

R

RA. *See* Resettlement Administration (RA)
Rabbi Isaac Elchanan Theological Seminary
  (RIETS), 1575a–b
Rabbinical Assembly, 1574b
Rabbinical Council of America, 1575b
Rabin, Yitzak, 693a
Rabinowitz, Howard, 142b
Race, **129a–160b**
  arts, 1739b
  and class, 195b, 196a
  differentials in mortality, 965a–b tab
  diversity in Eastern region, 38b
  diversity in Midwest, 43a
  equality in Midwest, 55a
  and gender, 106b
  humor, 1473a
  impact on criminal justice system,
    397b–398a
  issue in Democratic coalition, 334b
  minorities and Congress, 365a, 372b
  missionaries, 696b
  mortality decline, 963a–b
  popular culture, 1486b

  riots. *See* Race riots
  sociology of class and, 930b
  Southern myths and theories, 61a
  from southern to national problem, 1597a
  stereotypes and art, 1720b
*Race Questions, Provincialism, and Other
  American Problems* (Royce), 258a
Race relations, 71b, 72b, 97a,b
  South, 65a,b, 75b–76a
  State government, 428b
  West, 95a–98a
Race riots, 144a, 343a, 463b, 465a
  Atlanta (1906), 66b
  Cleveland, 180b
  Harlem, 180b
  Los Angeles (1992), 97b–98a, 188b, 214b,
    398b
  in 1968, 180b
  in South during World War II, 71a–b
  television coverage, 1478b
  Watts, 96a, 180b
  Wilmington, N.C. (1898), 66a
  during World War II, 177b
Races and Immigrants in America (Commons),
  137a
Race Suicide (Iseman), 137a,b
Racial pentagon. *See* Ethnoracial pentagon
Racial uplift, 1594b–1595a, 1598a
Racial violence, 153b–154a
  in cities, 464b–465a
  See also Race riots
Racism, 161a, 163a, 435b, 439b
  Boas, Franz, and, 1567b
  Catholics, 1517b, 1524a–b
  and class, 195b
  education in South, 64a–b
  marriage laws, 225b
  Midwest, 50a
  modernist art and, 1703b
  nationalism, 255b
  Northern prejudice, 75b
  in preservationism, 1359b
  in professions, 1426a
  Progressivism, 256b
  quota programs, 302a
  scientific justifications of, 261a
  society, 922b
  in Southern politics, 66b
  Wallace, George, 344b
  See also Ku Klux Klan; Segregation;
    White supremacy
Radar, 28a, 782a, 783a, 786b, 841a, 1148a
  computers, 812a
Radburn, N.J., 460b
Radcliffe-Brown, A. R., 926b
Radcliffe College, 32a, 102a
Radiation Laboratory
  Berkeley, U. of California, 745b–748b,
    759b
  MIT, 748a, 749a, 809a
Radiation testing, 950a
  during Cold War, 951b
Radicalism
  Jews, 1568b
  as results of financial panics of 1890s,
    1188b
  and unionism, 204a
"Radical Perspectives in Sociology," 930a
Radio, 38a, 1160b, 1250a, 1339a–b, 1461b,
  1462b, 1470b, 1471a–1475a,
  1754b–1756a

advertising, 1059b
arts patronage, 1737a
broadcasting, 803a–805a, 818b–819b
call-in talk shows, 1756a
consumption, 1024a,b
educational, 1474b
effect on phonographs and records, 1471a
1920 election returns, 1472a
in Europe, 712b
fireside chats, 332b
format standardization, 1474b
game shows, 1473a
industry, 700a
Jews, 1571a
legislation, 1471b
licensing, 1475b
music, 1474b, 1616b–1617a
mysteries, 1472b–1473a
networks, 805a–809a, 827b, 1472b
New York City, 31b
nonprofit, 1474b
programming, 1024b–1025a
    See also Radio programs
public, 1473b
radio, television, and cable television, 1921–1990, 1227a–b tab
regulation, 431b
religion, 1503b–1504a
rock 'n' roll, 1628b
special interest programming, 1473b
specialized markets, 1756a
special markets, 1474a,b
syndicated shows, 1474b
transformation due to television, 1755b–1756a
use by presidents, 332b
vacuum tubes, 836b
World War II, 1473b
See also AM radio; FM radio
Radio Act (1927), 1275b, 1472a, 1475a
Radioactive pollution, 1372a
Radioactive waste, 98b
Radioactivity, 86a
Radio astronomy, 752a–753a
Radio Board, 803b, 804b
Radio City (New York), 1475a
Radio Corporation of America (RCA), 700a, 804a–b, 805b, 806b–807a, 821a, 1143a,b, 1145a, 1148b, 1250a, 1471b–1472a, 1472a–b, 1473b, 1475a
    communications technology, 800a
    industrial research, 851a
    RCA Laboratories, 848b
    research, 849a
    45rpm records, 1471a
    television, 815a–b, 1475b
Radio Free Europe, 614a
Radio-Keith-Orpheum. *See* RKO
Radio Liberty, 614a
Radio programs
    Americans All, 176a
    American School of the Air, 262a
    Amos 'n' Andy. See Amos 'n' Andy show
    Chase and Sanborn Hour, 1025a
    Fibber McGee and Molly, 1473a, 1755b
    Hit Parade, 708a
    Hour of Decision, The, 1504a
    Housekeeper's Chat, 1025a
    Jack Benny Show, 708a
    Lux Radio Theater, The, 1473a
    Major Bowes' Original Amateur Hour, 262a

Ma Perkins, 1473a
National Homemaker's Club, 1025a
National Vespers, 1503b
Old Fashioned Revival Hour, 1503b
Rise of the Goldbergs, The, 1755a
Shadow, The, 1473a
Whistler, The, 1473a
You Bet Your Life, 1473a
Radio stations, 804b
    first commercial, 1755a
    first network, 1339b
    KDKA radio, 804b, 805b, 1472a
    KYW radio, 804b
    number, 1475a
    segmentation, 1474a–b
    small companies, 1488a
    WCFL radio, 1473b
    WEAF radio, 804b, 807b
    WJZ radio, 804b
Rad Lab. *See* Radiation Laboratory
Radtke, Sandee, *711b*
Radway, Janice, 115b
Ragtime music, 48a, 149b, 1462a, 1614b
    African Americans, 1594a, 1595b
Rahv, Philip, 1444a, 1585b
Raiffa, Howard, 1305a
Railroads, 431a, 452a, 1128a, 1129a, 1130b, 1141b, 1349b
    coal, 87b
    consolidation, 1217b
    deregulation, 1283b
    development prior to the Great Depression, 1340b
    economic performance, 1160a, 1291b, 1350b
    electric interurban, 45a, 48a, 455a
    foreign investments, 1246b
    freight hauling, 1350a–b
    health insurance, 989b
    high-speed passenger trains, 1353b
    interurban railways, 1337b
    investment bankers, 1213b, 1215a
    locomotives, 1141a, 1160b
    and marketing, 1048a, 1050b–1051a
    Midwest, 45a, 56b
    passenger services, 1350a
    photography, 35a–b
    railway network, 1336a
    regulation, 64b, 309a, 405a, 429a, 430a,b, 431b, 518a–b,519b, 1314a, 1336a–b
    research and development, 832b–833a
    securities, 1214b
    South, 64a,b
    steel, 1135a
    terminals architecture, 1673a
    transcontinental, 88b
    World War II, 1344a
Railroad Transportation (Hadley), 1291b
Railroad Workers, 1110a
RAINBOW plans, 601a, 685b
Rainbow Warrior, 1378b
Rainey, Ma, 1597a
Raisin in the Sun, A (Hansberry), 1602a
Rajneesh Foundation International, 1552b
Ramakrishna, 1550b
Ramaz Day School, 1575b
Ramberg, Christina, 1719a
Ramm, Bernard, 871b
Ramo, Simon, 850a
Ranching industry. *See* Cattle
Randall, John Hermann, 1644b

RAND Corporation, 499b, 613a
Randolph, A. Philip, 177b, 214a, 1597a, 1602b
Rand School, 1578b
Rankin, Jeannette, 625a, 638b
Ransom, John Crowe, 10a,b, 14a,b, 1444b, 1445b
Rap
    culture, 1606b
    music, 150a, 1631a–b
Raper, Arthur, 10b, 13b, 14b, 15a
Raphaelson, Samson, 1580a
Rapid Transit facilities, 35a–b
Raskob, John, 198b–199a
Rate of Interest, The (Fisher), 1298a
Rationing, 1027b–1028a
    ration cards, 1164a
    World War II, 1322b
    during World War II, 603a
Ratzinger, Joseph, 1534a
Rauschenberg, Robert, 1715a,b, 1716a, 1717a, 1718b
Rauschenbusch, Walter, 478a, 1494b
    on Ely, 275a
    personality concept, 1496b
Ravage, Marcus, 1578a
Rawidowicz, Simon, 1585b
Rawls, John, 290b–291a, 1655a–b
    Theory of Justice, A, 1655a
Raw materials, 1164b, 1248b, 1264a–b
    See also natural resources
Ray, Man, 1701a,b, 1718a
    Cadeau, 1704b
    Fog Horns, 1704b
    Rope Dancer Accompanies Herself with Her Shadow, The, 1704b
Rayburn, Sam, 349b, 611a–b
Raytheon, 1145a, 1148b, 1149a
Raza Unida, La, 266b
RCA. *See* Radio Corporation of America (RCA)
Reader's Digest, 31b, 1481b, 1482b
Reader's Digest Foundation, 1737b
Reagan, Nancy, 589a
Reagan, Ronald, 155b, 239a, 268a, 290a, 322b, 346a, 348a–350a, *348b,* 617a, *617b,* 707a, 1085a, 1284b, 1468a, 1476a
    abortion, on, 392a
    administration agenda, 317b
    administrative management, 532b–533a
    antitrust policy, 532a
    appointments, 532b
    armed services expansion, 563b–564a, 1201b
    arts patronage, 1739b–1740a
    Big Science, 762a
    budget cuts, 315a, 317a
    budget deficit, 1155b
    and bureaucratic politics, 517a
    call to private philanthropy, 508b
    Congress, 371a, 372a
    control of House of Representatives, 305a
    court appointments, 392a–b
    defense spending, 617a
    deregulation, 531a,b–533a, 1259b
    economy, 30b, 1174a–b
    education, 1816a
    federalism, 58a, 445a–447b
    fiscal policy, 1327a–1328b
    foreign policy, 588a–589b

Reagan, Ronald (*cont.*)
hostages release, 412a
industrial research, 851b, 852b, 853a
labor unions, 312a
moral majority, 184b
presidential elections, 336a–b tab
and presidential government, 528b
social security, 488b
summit meetings with Gorbachev, 564b
Supreme Court appointments, 418b
television, 1479a
vetoes, 347a tab
versus Walter Mondale, 307b
welfare, 489a
working-class vote, 302a
world economy, 731a–733a
Reagan Doctrine, 617a
Reaganomics. *See* Supply–side economics
Real estate development, 1029a–1031a, 1030b
California, 455a
cities, 456b, 465a
consumption, 1025b, 1029a
eminent domain, 458b
garden cities, 460a–461a
suburbs, 454b, 460a, 466b, 1338a
Real estate taxes, 1314b–1315a, 1318b
See also Property taxes
Realism and the Background of Phenomenology (Chisholm), 1657a
Realism (literature), 1437b
Realism (philosophy), 1636b
critical, 1643a
new realists, 1641b–1642b
Realism with a Human Face (Putnam), 1650a
Rebel without a Cause, 340a
Rebuilding Europe (Ellwood), 709a
Recent Economic Changes (Wells), 1291a
Recent Social Trends (Committee on Social Trends), 496b
Recent Sociological Theories (Sorokin), 924a
Recessions, 573a, 589b, 1172a, 1174a–b, 1259b
1890, 1313b
1920–1921, 1192a, 1318a
1937–1938, 1228b
1974–1975, 730b
1980–1982, 731a, 1199a
arts patronage, 1740b
effect on 1992 elections, 303b, 304a
World War II, 1164a
Reciprocal Trade Agreements Act (1934), 684a, 724a, 1250b, 1312a
Reclamation Service, 84b, 1362b
Reconstruction, 74a, 428a, 429a
Reconstruction Finance Corporation, 1251b, 1276a
no loans to colleges, 1825a
Reconstruction in Philosophy (Dewey), 281a, 284b, 1639a, 1651a
Reconstructionism, 1588b, 1590b
Reconstructionist, 1582a, 1588a
Reconstructionist Rabbinical College, 1588b
Records, 1470b–1471a, 1616b
small companies, 1488a
Recycling, 315b
Red Badge of Courage, The (Crane), 1438a
Red Cross, 495b
Red Hot Mama. *See* Tucker, Sophie

Redistributional taxation, 1315b–1316a, 1320a, 1323a
attacked by Mellon, 1317b
Redlich, Fritz, 1216b
Red Nightmare, 265a
Red Power, 266b
Red River Valley, 47a
Red Scare (1919), 171b, 257b, 279a, 574a, 597b, 598a
Red Scare (post–World War II), 178a, 579a, 1109b
Redstone rocket, 786b, 787a
Reece Committee, 502a
Reed, Adolf, 156a
Reed, Donna, 232b
Reed, Ishmael, 1456a
Reed, James, 626b
Reed, John, 1439b
Reed, John Shelton, 77b
Reed, Stanley F., 382b, 390a–b tab
Reed, Walter, 942a, 949b
Reese, Charles, 841b, 842a,b
Reflections on Gender and Science (Keller), 913b–914a
Reform, Roman Catholic
ecclesiastical, 1526b–1528a
liturgical, 1527a
Reform Judaism, 1566a–b, 1567b, 1574b, 1576a, 1585b, 1590b
translation of prayerbook, 1588a–b
Refrigeration, 1024b, 1132a–b, 1141b
Refugee Act (1980), 166a–b tab, 185b
Refugees
European artists, 1710a
European musicians, 1621a
quotas, 185b
Regionalism, **7a–23b**
economic interests, 30b
loyalty vote, 297a–b
Midwest, 54b, 55b, 59b
Southern, 77b
Regional planning, 12a–13b
computer-based systems analysis, 19b
New York and New Jersey, 27a
planned sprawl, 20a
Radial Corridor Plan, 20a
Regional Plan of New York, 13a
Regional Planning Association, 13a, 460b, 1679b
Regulation
bipartisan basis, 525b
budgetary impact, 532b
challenge in court by interest groups, 315b
communications, 799b, 801a, 806a–b, 815a, 817a,b, 819a,826b
consumption, 1024b
economy, 1173b
government, 1168a, 1173a
Great Depression, 1163a
and neoclassical economists, 316a
persistence of, 534a–535b
prices, 1160a
in the public interest, 514b
radio licenses, 1472b
reduction under supply-side economics, 1204a
reform, 516b
Supreme Court, 385a
television, 1475a,b
See also Federal Communications

Commission (FCC); Federal Trade Commission (FTC); Supreme Court decisions
Rehabilitation Act (1973), 1812a–b tab, 1814a
Rehnquist, William H., 390a–b tab, 391a–b tab, 416b, 420b
Reich, Leonard S., 747b, 831a, 837b
Reich, Robert, 319b, 854a, 1264b
Reich, Steve, 1630a
Reichenbach, Hans, 1645b, 1648b
Reid, J. W., 1675a
Reid, M. J., 1675a
Reid, Thomas, 877a, 1642a
Reiki, 1561a,b
Reinhardt, Ad, 1717a
Reisen, Abraham, 1569b
Reisman, Philip, 1714a
Relation of the State to Industrial Action, The (Adams), 1291b
Relief and Recovery Act (1935), 1277b
Relief and Recovery Act (1938), 1277b
Religion
Eastern region, 29a–b
ethnicity and, 169b–170a
fundamentalism, 693b
institutions and cultural development, 1726a
literary campaigns against persecutions, 1518b
loyalty vote, 297b
nontraditional, 1539a–1564b
and race, 139a
South, 61a, 63a
unchurched, 1539a
working-class women, 1748b
See also specific religions
Religion and Science Association, 868a
Religious liberty, 1516b, 1517a, 1518b
Religious orders, 1511b, 1514a, 1524b, 1530b
decline, 1527b
social justice, 1529b
Religious Science, 1545b, 1546a
Remington, Frederic, 83b, 1694b
Remington Arms Company, 85b
Remington-Rand, 809b, 810a–b, 1148b, 1149a
Reminiscing in Tempo (Ellington), 1620b
RENEW, 1533a–b
Rensselaer Polytechnic Institute, 1820a
Rent supplements, 1082a
Renunciation of War as an Instrument of National Policy (1928), 566a–b tab
Reorganization Act (1939), 1322a
Report of the President's Committee on the Impact of Defense and Disarmament, 850b–851a
Report on Administrative Procedure (Jackson), 526a
Report on Economic Conditions in the South (Odum), 69b
Report on the Lands of the Arid Region of the United States (Powell), 8a, 1360b, 1362b
Representation of the People Act (Britain), 295a
Reproduction of Mothering, The (Chodorow), 913a
Republican party
Congress, 365b, 367b, 374a–b

congressional elections, 302b
"Contract with America," 305b, 374a
family values as 1992 campaign theme,
  221a
financial strategy after World War I,
  1317b
fiscal policy, 1315b, 1324b
fundraising, 307
isolationism post-World War II, 725a–b
political strategies, 302a–b
and social insurance state, 332a
South, 74b, 77a
tariffs, 1314a
taxation, 1312a–b
two-party system, 296b
Watergate. *See* Watergate affair
Republic Steel, 1135b
Research
  in 1993, 831a–b
  basic versus applied, 831b
  industrial production, 1129b–1130a
  interdisciplinary, 743b, 747a
  laboratories, 1138a, 1142b–1143b
  programs abroad, 498a
  scholars, 493a
  universities, 498b, 832b, 835a, 840b,
    847a, 849a, 852a–b, 854b
Research Triangle Park, N.C., 75b
Reserve Officers' Training Corps (ROTC),
  1822b
Resettlement Administration (RA), 15a
  photographers, 1730a
Residential design, 1676b–1680a
Resource allocation, 1155b, 1165b–1166a
Resource Conservation and Recovery Act
  (1976), 1377b
Resources for Freedom, 1392b
*Restriction of Output among Unorganized
  Workers* (Mathewson), 1097b
Retailing
  brand. *See* Brand
  brokerage firms, 1231a
  chain stores, 1022a–b, 1025a–b, 1032a
  department stores, 464a, 1017a, 1020b,
    1022b, 1030b, 1333b
  general store, 1049b–1050b
  home video stores, 1033a
  mail-order catalog firms, 1333b
  mass retailers, 1022b
  supermarkets, 1024a, 1025a–b, 1030b,
    1032a
Retirement
  benefits cut under Reagan, 1204a
  South, 72b, 75b
Retton, Mary Lou, 1780b
Reuben James, 636b
Reuter, Edward, 236b
Reuther, Walter, 206a, 1110a,b
Revco, 1238a
Revel, Bernard, 1575a
Revels, Hiram, 141b, 142a
Revenue Act (1932), 1319b
Revenue Act (1935), 1320a–b, 1750b
Revenue Act (1937), 1321a
Revenue Act (1938), 1321a
Revenue Act (1943), 1323b
Revenue Act (1948), 1279a
Revenue Act (1978), 1326b
Revenue Act (1981), 1284b
Revenues
  income tax revenues, 1318a

by type of tax in major industrial nations,
  1987, 1310a–b tab
by type of tax in U.S., 1310a–b tab
Revenue sharing, 439a, 442b, 446a, 1325b
  See also General Revenue Sharing
Revenue Sharing Act (1972), 443a
Review of Radical Political Economics, 1304a
Revivalism radio preaching, 1503b
Revlon, 1039b, 1063a
"Revolt against the City" (Wood), 55a
Revolt of the Masses, The (Ortega y Gasset),
  197b
Revolution in the Development of Capitalism
  (Gould), 933b
Rexford, Nancy, *as contributor,* 1785a–1801b
Reynolds Metals, 1136a
Rezrikoff, Charles, 1580b, 1581a
RFD. *See* Rural Free Delivery
Rhapsody in Blue (Gershwin), 1581a,
  1615b–1616b
Rhee, Syngman, 656a, 661b, 685a
Rhetorical presidency, 332a
Rhetorical Presidency, The (Tulis), 328a
Rhetoric of Economics (McCloskey), 1305a
Rhodes, Richard, 59b
Rhythm and Blues, 1625a
Ricardo, David, 1289b
Rice, Edwin, 836a
Rice, Elmer, 1581a
Rice, Grantland, 1767a, 1773a
Rice, John, 1503b
Rice University, 75b
Rich, Adrienne, 1587a
Richards, A. Newton, 945a
Richards, Bernard, 1567a
Richards, Theodore W., 742a, 761b
Richardson, Henry Hobson, 1665a, 1667b,
  1669b
  Trinity Church (Boston), *1670a,* 1687a
Richmond, Mary Ellen, 1414b
Rickenbacker, Eddie, 770b
Rickey, Branch, 1777b
Rickover, Hyman, 849b
Ricks, Willie, 1602b
Ricoeur, Paul, 291a
Ride, Sally, 790b
Ridgway, Matthew, 659a, 663a
Riesman, David, 179b, 197a, 265b, 285b,
  1486a, 1743a
RIETS. *See* Rabbi Isaac Elchanan
  Theological Seminary
Riggs, Bobby, 1780a
Rights of criminal defendants, 418b–419a
Rights Talk (Glendon), 291b
Right-to-work laws, 311b
Riis, Jacob, 33b, 168a, 1068b
Riley, James Whitcomb, 52a
Riley, William Bell, 866a
Rimbaud, Arthur, 1448b
Rimmer, Harry, 866b
Rio Pact (1948), 610a
Ripley, William Z., 137a
Rise of David Levinsky, The (Cahan), 33b,
  34a, 1578a
"Rise of the Bureaucratic State, The"
  (James Q. Wilson), 361a
Rise of the Unmeltable Ethnics, The (Novak),
  182b
Risk, Uncertainty, and Profit (Knight), 1297a
Ritter, Joseph, 1524b
Ritter, William Emerson, 861b, 862b

Rivera, Diego, 1707a
  mural destroyed at Rockefeller Center,
    1708b
Rivera, Iris, 120b
Rivers, L. Mendel, 72a
Rivers, Larry, 1587a, 1715b
Rivers and Harbors bill, 1312b
Rivers in Midwest, 41b, 45a, 56b
Rivlin, Alice, 359b
RJR-Nabisco, leveraged buyout, 1236a,
  1237b
RKO, 1464b, 1466b, 1469a, 1754a
  television, 1476b
Roach, Max, 1602a
Roads, 431b, 438a
  construction, 1751a
  South, 70a, 72a,b
  See also Highways
Road to Serfdom, The (von Hayek), 289b
Road to War, The (Millis), 633a
Roberts, Jeanne, 478a
Roberts, Jon H., *as contributor,* 877a–898b
Roberts, Owen J., 381b, 390a–b tab, 409b,
  410a, 434a–b
Roberts, Randy, *as contributor,* 1743a–1759b
Robertson, Pat, 188b, 824b, 1492a, 1507a,
  1740a
Robert Wood Johnson Foundation, 501b,
  510a
Robeson, Paul
  All-American footballer, 1771b
  Communist Party, 1601a
Robinson, Bill "Bojangles," 151b
Robinson, Edward G., 1466a
Robinson, Jackie, 173b, 263b, 1771b,
  1777b, 1778a
Robinson, Joan, 1297b
Robinson, Jo Ann, 118b
Robinson, John, 1504b
Robinson, Joseph T., 335a–b tab
Robinson, Theodore, 1695b
Robotics, 790a, 1120a
Roche, Dinkeloo and Associates, 1686b
Rochester Institute of Technology, 32b
Rock, John, 228a
Rockburne, Dorothea, 1718b, 1721b
Rockefeller, Abby Aldrich, 496b, 1684b,
  1728b
Rockefeller, John D., III, 500a, 505b, 506a,
  1725a, 1734a, 1735b, 1741b
  Lincoln Center, 1734b
Rockefeller, John D., Jr., 494a, 496b, 1370b,
  1501b
Rockefeller, John D., Sr., 195a, 493b, 862b,
  1134a–b, 1495b
  medical research, 943a
Rockefeller, Nelson, 703a, 1725a, 1736a
Rockefeller Archive Center, 506a
Rockefeller Brothers Fund, 1734b
  Performing Arts, The, 1735b
Rockefeller Center (New York), 1263a
Rockefeller fellowships, 1826b
Rockefeller Foundation, 31b, 491b, 493b,
  496b, 500a, 697b, 1734b
  astronomy, 744b–745a
  cultural grants, 1729a
  cyclotrons, 746b
  health programs, 974b
  marriage, 228a
  research fellowships, 842b
  research programs abroad, 498a

Rockefeller Institute for Medical Research, 943a, 1000b
Rockefeller Sanitary Commission, 493a, 943a
Rocketdyne, 786b
Rocket technology, 784b–792b
Rockman, Bert A., *as contributor,* 321a–353b
Rockne, Knute, 173a
Rock 'n' roll, 73b, 1464b, 1625a, 1627b–1628a
   censorship, 1483b
   in China, 712a
   radio, 1474a
   in Soviet Union, 711b–712a
Rockwell International, 786b, 795b, 1145a
Rocky Mountain Arsenal, 85b
Rocky Mountain spotted fever, 942b
Rodeo (Copland), 1617b
Rodgers, Cal, 770a
Rodgers, Daniel, 1093b
   Work Ethic in Industrial America, 1850–1920, The, 207a
Rodgers, Jimmie, 1626a
Rodgers, Richard, 1581a, 1619a–1620a, 1625b
Rodgers and Hammerstein, 1469b
Rodia, Simon, *1719a,* 1719a
Rodriguez, Richard, 187b
   Hunger of Memory, 187b, 1456b
Roeder, George H., Jr., *as contributor,* 1693a–1723b
Roentgen, William, 952b
Roe v. Wade (1973), 120b, 240b, 392a, 421b, 422a, 1532a
   Bork on, 392b, 422b–423a
Rogers, Carl, 234b, 896a
Rogers, Jimmie, 67b
Rogers, Roy, 84a, 1792b
Rogers, Will, 150b, 1073a
Rohde, David D., 367a
Rohm and Haas, 1146a, 1147a
Roiphe, Anne, 1586b
Rolling Stone, 1628b
Rolling Stones, 1628a
Rollins, Tim, 1716b
Roman Catholicism. *See* Catholics and Catholicism
Romania, 350b
Romer, Christina, 1161b–1162a
Roof, Wade Clark, 1539a–b
Roofless gable, *1666a*
Roosa bonds, 1255b, 1262a
Roosevelt, Eleanor, 122a, *343a–b,* 1601b
Roosevelt, Franklin D., 29b, 279b, 281b, 322b, 323b, 327a, 329b–330a, *330a,* 337b, 1073a,b, 1074a, 1276a,b, 1705a
   administrative state, 523b
   "Appeal to the Nations of the World for Peace and for the End of Economic Chaos," 633a
   at Argentia Bay, 602a
   on banking, 1228b
   brain trust, 331a
   budget balancing, 600a, 1319b
   budget process, 358b, 361a
   in Casablanca, 644a–b
   Catholic vote, 1518a, 1520a, 1524b
   at Commonwealth Club of San Francisco, 524a
   conservation, 1368b–1369a
   dollar devaluation, 1250b

   economic policy, 1026a
   Executive Orders, 95b, 96b
   farms, 1369a
   Federalism, 432b, 434b, 435a
   fireside chats, 1473a
   Great Depression, 1162b–1163a
   isolationism, 576a,b–577b
   Jewish aid, 1583a
   Korea, 654a
   Lend-Lease program, 1252a
   neutrality proclamation, 634b
   New Deal, 68b–69b, 299b
   and pacifists, 555a
   postwar organization, 556b
   presidential elections, 335a–b tab, 356a
   racial discrimination, 214a
   radio, 332b, 807b, 808b
   rationing, 1027b
   secret naval talks with Britain, 600b
   shipbuilding, 600a
   Social Security Act, 478b–479a, 480a, 481a
   and Supreme Court, 380b–381b
   tariffs, 1247b
   taxation, 1320a–1324a
   in Teheran, 646a
   telecast, 1475b
   vetoes, 347a tab
   War Refugee Board, 1583b
   world economy, 684a, 724a
   at Yalta, *606a–b,* 687a
Roosevelt, Theodore, 29b, 254b, 256a, 274a, 322b, 326a, *326a,* 326b, 521a, 1744a
   antitrust legislation, 1271a
   antitrust suit against Northern Securities, 1218a
   assistant secretary of the Navy, 593b
   conservation, 1358b, 1362b
   corollary to the Monroe Doctrine, 676b
   courts as campaign issue, 379b–380a
   diplomacy, 720a
   farming, 51a
   foreign policy, 571b–572a
   forests, 84b, 1360b
   land withdrawal, 1360a
   melting pot concept, 163b, 1568b
   national authority, 429b–430a
   naval buildup, 543b, 594a
   Panama Canal, 571b
   Pelican Island, 1360a
   presidential elections, 335a–b tab
   presidential power, 406b, 522a
   Progressivism, 296b, 1314a
   race, 137a, 142b, 222b
   recall of judicial decisions, 405b
   reform legislation, 378a
   sports justification, 1762a
   state role in family affairs, 224b
   vetoes, 347a tab
Root, Elihu, 430a, 544b, 545a, 594a, 595b, 720a
   at Washington Conference (1921-1922), 599a
Root, John, 1677a
Roots (Haley), 183b
Rope Dancer Accompanies Herself with Her Shadow, The (Man Ray), 1704b
Rorty, Richard, 291a, 1660b–1661b
   "World Well Lost, A," 1660b
Rosaldo, Michelle, 911b, 933a

Rose, Hillary, 913b
Rose, Phyllis, 1441b
Rose, Wickliffe, 744b–745a
Rosen, Norma, 1589b
Rosenberg, Charles E., 991a
Rosenberg, Emily S., *as contributor,* 695a–717b
Rosenberg, Harold, 1444a, 1587a, 1712b, 1715a
Rosenberg, Rosalind, 904b, 922a
Rosenblatt, Yosele, 1571a
Rosenfeld, Morris, 1569b
Rosenfeld, Paul, 1567b, 1581b
Rosenquist, James, 1716a, *1717a–b*
   F-111, 1719b
Rosenthal, Joe, 1710b, *1711a–b*
Rosenwald, Julius, 843a
Rosenwald, Lessing, 1584a
Rosenwald Foundation, 974b
Rosenwald Fund. *See* Julius Rosenwald Fund
Rosenzweig, Roy, 260b
Rosie the Riveter, 264a
Ross, Dorothy, 902b, 920b
Ross, E. A., 163a, 171a, 222b
Ross, Edward A., 256b, 274b, 920a, 921a, 922b
Ross, Michael, *1682a, 1685b, 1686b, 1688a, 1698a, 1715b, 1718a*
Rossi, Alice, 929a
Rosten, Leo, 1756b
Rostenkowski, Dan, 304b
Rostow, Walt W., 584a, 615a, 690a
Roszak, Theodore, 1712b, 1721b
Rotary clubs, 697a
ROTC. *See* Reserve Officers' Training Corps
Roth, Henry, 176a, 1443b, 1444a, 1580b
   Call It Sleep, 1443b
Roth, Philip, 34a, 1587b
   Portnoy's Complaint, 1457a
Rothapfel, S. L. "Roxy," 1753b
Rothbard, Murray, 1304a
Rothenberg, Jerome, 1587a
Rothko, Mark, 1578b, 1587a, 1712b, 1721b
Rothman, David, 950b
Rothschild enterprise (Europe), 1134b
Rourke, Constance, 10b, 262a
Rouse, Christopher, 1630a
Rousseau, Henri, 1698a
Rowan, Edward B., 1705b, 1708a
Rowland, Henry T., 832a–b, 834b, 835a, 840a, 842b
Royal Dutch enterprise (Asia), 1134b
Royce, Josiah, 258a, 1635b–1636a
   Conception of God, The, 1635b
   professionalism, 1636b
Rozelle, Pete, 1774b
Rubber Goods Manufacturing, 1133b
Rubber industry, 57b, 70b, 85b, 1130a, 1133b, 1142a, 1143b, 1144a, 1164a
   international investments, 1262a
   South, 69b
Rubenstein, Richard, 1589a
Rubin, Alvin B., 394b
Rubinow, I. M., 476a, 477a
Rubinstein, Anton, 1612a
Rubinstein, Artur, 1571a, 1616b
Rudd, Daniel, 1517b
Ruderman, Jacob, 1585a
Rudolph, Paul, 1689b

Rugg, Harold, 1808a
Ruggles, Carl, 1617a
Ruiz, Vicki, 149a
Rukeyser, Muriel, 1581a
Ruland, Richard, 1452b
Ruml, Beardsley, 494b, 495a, 1824b
Rummel, Joseph Francis, 1524b
Runyon, Damon, 1767a
Rural economy
    African American women in, 108a
    Eastern region, 36a
    Midwest, 43a, 51a, 53b, *56a–b*, 56b
Rural Electrification Administration, 70a,
    1026a
Rural Free Delivery (RFD), 48b
Rural Life and Education (Cubberley), 1806b
Rushdie, Salman, 1455b
Rusk, Dean, 561b, 668a
Ruskin, John, 1668b, 1700a, 1746a
Russell, Bertrand, 1641b, 1646a–1647a
    "On Denoting," 1646a–b
Russell, Charles, 83b, 1694b
Russell, John, 1714a
Russell, Morgan, 1701a, 1704b
Russell, Richard B., 72a
Russell Sage Foundation, 31b, 215a, 476a,
    491b, 493a, 506a, 1414b, 1679b
Russian Constructivism, 1701a
Russian Jews, 1565a–b
Russian Orthodox Church, 1514a, 1546b
Rustbelt, 43b, 57b, 58a, 60a
    African American poverty in, 210a–b
Rutgers University, 32b, 1819a
    back salary to underpaid minorities,
    1833a
    medical school, 30a
Ruth, Babe (George Herman), 173a, 1766b,
    1768b, 1768b–1769a
    appearance in vaudeville, 1463b
Rutherford, Ernest, 746a
Rutledge, Wiley B., 390a–b tab
Ryan, John A., 1069a,b, 1515b, 1517b,
    1518a, 1519a,b
Rybczynski, Witold, 1749a
Ryder, Albert Pinkham, 1694a
Ryle, Gilbert, 1653b

S

Saarinen, Eero, 848b, 1689a
    Ingalls Hockey Rink (Yale U.), 1689a,
    1690a–b
Saarinen, Eliel, 1681a
Sabbath, Jewish
    adapted to American life, 1566b, 1572b
    rituals, 1575a
Sabel, Charles, 855b
SAC. *See* Strategic Air Command (SAC)
Sacco, Nicola, 172b
Sachar, Abram, 1577a, 1585b
Sachs, Paul, 1729a
Sackville-West, Lionel, 570b
"Sacred Service" (Bloch), 1581a
Sadat, Anwar, *588a–b*
Safety movement, 471a, 475a
    regulations, 534a, 1285a
    U.S. Steel Corporation, 475b
Safeway grocers, 700b
Safire, William, 1740b

Sagan, Carl, 871a
SAGE. *See* Semi-Automatic Ground
    Environment
Sage, Margaret Olivia, 493a
Sage Foundation. *See* Russell Sage
    Foundation
Saint-Gaudens, Augustus, 1693a, *1694a–b,*
    1694b, 1721b
Saint-Gaudens, Homer, *Evolution of
    Civilization, The,* 1696a
Saint Gobain, 1249b
St. John's University, 32a
St. Lawrence Seaway, 58a, 1351a
    transportation, 56b
"St. Louis Blues" (Handy), 48a
St. Louis Committee for Nuclear
    Information, 1374b
St. Louis Post Dispatch, 467a
Saint Louis, Mo.
    during Great Depression, 457b
    suburbs, 458a, 459b, 467a
Saint Louis Exposition of 1904, 1638b
St. Patrick's Cathedral, 35a
"Saints and Their Bodies" (Higginson),
    1761b–1762a
Saks, Michael, 395a
Saks Fifth Avenue, 1789b
Salanter, Israel, 1572a
Saldívar, Ramon, 1456b
Sales forces, 1136a,b, 1138a, 1141b
Sales taxes, 1314a, 1317b–1319a, 1321b
    eschewed by federal government, 1324b
Salinger, J. D., 1451a
Salk, Jonas, 946a, 954b
Salk vaccine, 232b
Salle, David, 1587a, 1720b
Salomon Brothers, 1236b, 1239a
"Salon des Refusés" (Chicago), 1700b
Saloons, *1747a–b*
    male-oriented culture, 1748a
    working-class equivalent of clubs, 1747b
SALT (Strategic Arms Limitation Talks) I
    (1972), 563a–b, 566a–b tab, 616b, 692a
SALT (Strategic Arms Limitation Talks) II
    Treaty (1979), 563b, 566a–b tab, 588a,
    692a
Salvatierra case (Texas, 1930), 1811a
SAM. *See* Surface-to-air-missiles
Samaras, Lucas, 1720a, 1722a
Samoa, 551b
    magnetic observatory, 743a
Samuel, Maurice, 1582a
Samuel, Raphael, 1092b
Samuels, Warren, 1303b
Samuelson, Paul, 1299a,b, 1305b, 1421a
    on Keynes' *General Theory,* 1304b
Sánchez, George, 144b, 150a
Sanchez, Sonia, 1603b
Sandburg, Carl, 47a, 175b
Sand County Almanac, A (Leopold), 58b,
    1371a
Sandel, Michael, 290b
Sanders, Scott, 59b
San Diego, Calif., 212a
Sandino, Augustino, 654a
S&Ls. *See* Savings and loan institutions (S&
    Ls)
Sandoz, Mari, 10a
SANE. *See* National Committee for a Sane
    Nuclear Policy (SANE)
Sanford, Edward T., 390a–b tab

Gitlow v. New York (1925), opinion in,
    415a
San Francisco Chronicle, 633a
San Francisco Conference (1945), 557a,
    1252b
San Francisco Peace Conference (1951),
    688b
Sanger, Margaret, 226b, 228a
Sanitariums, 472b
Santa Fe Railroad, 1215a
Santayana, George, 1636a, 1643b–1644a
Santo Domingo, 676b
Santos-Dumont, Alberto, 769a
Saperstein, Abe, 1771a
Sarah Lawrence College, 1824b
Sarasohn, Kasriel, 1569a
Sargent, John Singer, 1694b
Sargent, Thomas, 1303a
Sarnoff, David, 804b, 806b–807a, 808b,
    1471a,b–1472b, 1475b
    about television, 1475a
    television, 815a
Sartre, Jean-Paul, 701a, 1451b, 1657b
Satellite Business Systems, 821a
Satellites, 753a, 754b, 755b, 756a, 787a,b,
    1032a
    communications, 788b, 821a, 824a, 826a,
    1032b, 1348b–1349a, 1480b
    spy, 781a
Saturday Evening Post, 37b, 264a, 1440b,
    1482b
Saturn rockets, 788a, 790b
Satz, Ludwig, 1570b
Sauvage, Henri, 1681a
Savannah River Reactors, 750b
Save Our State (S.O.S.), 189a
Save-the-Redwoods League, 1366a
Savigny, F. K. von, 918a
Savings, *1177a–b*
    consumption, 1026a
    and investments, 1155a, 1158a, 1159a–b,
    1160b, 1164a,b, 1173a, 1176a, 1264b
Savings and loan institutions (S&Ls), 1029a,
    1236b, 1238b
    credit cards, 1032a
Savo Island, Battle of, 641b
Sawyer, Charles, 1280a, 1281a
Say, Jean Baptiste, 1289a
Säyen, H. Lyman, 1701a
Scale and Scope (Chandler), 838b
Scalia, Antonin, 391a–b tab, 421b
    Employment Division v. Smith (1990),
    opinion in, 418a–b
Scanlan, Patrick, 1519a
Scarlet fever, 960a, 968a,b, 977a
Schamberg, Morton, 1701a
Schapiro, Meyer, 1444a
Schapiro, Miriam, 1719b, 1721a,b
Schappes, Morris, 1586b
Schechner, Mark, 1450b
Schechter, Solomon, 1567a, 1574b, 1589a
Scheiber, Harry N., *as contributor,* 427a–450b
Schelling, Friedrich, 1635a
Schelling, Thomas, 613a, 663b, 1305a
"Schelomo, a Hebrew Rhapsody" (Bloch),
    1581a
Schelting, Alexander von, 926b
Schenck, Joseph, 1752b
Schick, Allen, 358a,b, 360b, 361a
Schiff, Jacob, 1215a, 1216b, 1229b, 1567a,
    1727b

Schindler, Rudolph, 1680a, 1682b
Schlafly, Phyllis, 121a
Schlesinger, Arthur M., Jr., 189b, 1739b
  and Americans for Democratic Action,
    285a
  Vital Center, The, 285a
Schlick, Moritz, 1647a
Schlink, F. J., 1027a
Schlipp, Paul Arthur, 277b
Schlitz distillery, 1132a
Schmeling, Max, 1772b
Schmetz, Joseph, 260b
Schmidt, Walter S., 459a
Schnabel, Julian, 1587a
Schneerson, Menachem Mendel, 1585a
Schneider, Susan Weidman, 1587a
Schneiderman, Rose, 1574a
Schoenberg, Arnold, 1617a, 1621a, 1630a
School and Society, The (Dewey), 201a, 1805a
School desegregation
  busing, 387a, 388b–389a
  integration, 1813a
  resegregation, 1815b
  Supreme Court and, 386b–387b
Schoolman, Albert, 1576a
Schools
  centralization v. decentralization, 1815b
  desegregation. *See* School desegregation
  health programs, 974b, 975a
  one-room, 51a, 56b
  prayer, 306b
Schools of Tomorrow (Dewey and Dewey),
  1808a
Schroeder, John P., 460b
Schulman, Bruce J., 68b
Schulman, Grace, 1587a
Schuman, William, 1622a
Schumpeter, Joseph, 1289a, 1290b, 1295a,
  1299a, 1300b–1301a, 1416b
Schutz, Alfred, 928b
Schuyler, George, 153a
Schuyler, Montgomery, 453b, 1669a, 1675b
Schwartz, Abe, 1571a
Schwartz, Anna, 1162a
Schwartz, Delmore, 1445a, 1581a
Schwartz, I. J., 1569b
Schwartz, Maurice, 1570b
Schwarz, Anna, 1301b
Schwarzenegger, Arnold, 1798b
Schweiker, Richard, 30a
Schwerner, Michael, 153b
Schwimmer, Rosika, 546b
Science, 866b
Science
  industrial processes, 1142b, 1144a
  as justification of racism, 134a–b, 136b
  liberal Protestantism, 1495b–1496b,
    1496b, 1497a, 1502a
  linear model, 846b, 847b, 848b, 851a,
    854b
Science Advisory Committee, 755b, 759a
Science and Creationism, 873b
Science and Health (Eddy), 1544b, 1545a,b
Science and Human Behavior (Skinner), 891b
Science (Bush), 1828b
Science—The Endless Frontier (Bush), 846b,
  847b, 851b
Scientific American, 1475a
Scientific Creationism (Morris), 873a
Scientific equipment industry, 28a
Scientific management

managerial authority, 1103a
and mass production, 1092a–1096a
offices, 1106a
Scientists
  and federal government, 605b
  versus inventors, 832b
Scientists against Time (Baxter), 846b
Scientology, 1557b
SCLC. *See* Southern Christian Leadership
  Conference (SCLC)
Scofield, Cyrus, 1499a–b
Scofield Reference Bible, 1499b, 1500a
  gap creation theory, 861b
Scopes, John Thomas, 866a, *867a–b,* 1415b
Scopes trial, 866a, *867a–b,* 1497b, 1500b,
  1501b, 1503a, 1516b, 1825b
  radio broadcast, 805b
Scorsese, Martin, 1458a
Scott, James, 147a
Scott, James Brown, 545a, 550b
Scott, Kerr, 72b
Scott, Lawrence, 559a
Scott, Nathan A., Jr., 1456a
Scottish American Celodonian clubs, 1748a
Screen (Miss), 1721a
Scripps Foundation, 228a
Sculptors, 1694b, 1729b, 1730a, 1733a
SDS. *See* Students for a Democratic Society
  (SDS)
Seager, Henry, 1292a
Seagram Building (New York), 1685a,
  1685b
Searle, John, 1658a
Searle Company, 946b
Sears, Roebuck, 55b, 452a, 1018a, 1022b,
  1030b, 1051a
  catalog, 48b, 51b, 1019a, 1064a
Sears Tower (Chicago), 464a, 1686a
SEATO. *See* Southeast Asian Treaty
  Organization (SEATO)
Seattle, revitalization, 1346a
Seavey, Jane, 1104a
SEC. *See* Securities and Exchange
  Commission (SEC)
Secondary (trading) markets, 1209a
  formed after assumption of the states'
    debts, 1211b
Second Bank of the United States, 1212b
  investment banking functions, 1213a
  rechartering vetoed by Jackson, Andrew,
    1213a
Second Hague Peace Conference (1907),
  543b, 544b, 599a
Second Industrial Divide (Piore and Sabel),
  855b
Sectionalism, 7a, 8b
Secularism, 1517a
  Catholics, 1520b–1521b, 1526a
Secular Jews, 1573a
Secunda, Brant, 1561a
Securities
  analysis, 1231a
  corporate, 1230a
  government, 731a, 1214b, 1230a, 1244b,
    1245a, 1254a, 1255b
  rating, 1231a
Securities Act (1933), 1226a, 1227a–b tab,
  1420a
Securities Act Amendments (1964),
  1227a–b tab
Securities and Exchange Commission

(SEC), 524b, 1226a, 1227a–b tab,
  1420a
Securities Exchange Act (1934), 1226b,
  1227a–b tab, 1420a
Securities-industry regulatory legislation,
  1227a–b tab
Securities Investor Protection Act (1970),
  1227a–b tab
Securities Investor Protection Corporation
  (SPIC), 1227a–b tab, 1232b
Securities markets
  democratization, 1222b
  investment trusts, 1223a
  mass marketing of commercial banks,
    1222b
  over-the-counter market, 1228a
  public utility holding companies, 1223a
Securities Reform Act (1975), 1227a–b tab,
  1233a
Sedition Act (1918), 171b, 257a, 416a, 626a
Seduction of the Innocent (Wertham), 1483b
Seedbed (Acconci), 1720a
Seeger, Pete, 1627a
Segal, Daniel, 252b, 253b, 255b
Segal, George, 1587a, 1717a
  Gay Liberation, 1718a
Segal, Lore, 1589b
Segmented market, 1059a–1061b
Segré, Emilio, 750a
Segregation, 95a, 97b, 142a, 436b, 437b,
  439b, 440b
  housing, 50b, 58b
  increase at turn of the century, 163a
  Jim Crow system, 255b
  in poor houses, 473a
  residential, 97b, 1086a
  separate-but-equal doctrine, 386b
  South, 65b, 66a–b, 71a–b, 73a, 74a–b
  State government, 428b
Seidel, Emil, 335a–b tab
Seidel, Robert, 746a,b, 751a, 849b
Seismology, 743b
Select Commission on Immigration and
  Refugee Policy (1979), 185b
Selective Draft Law cases (1918), 407b
Selective Service Act (1917), 523a, 549a,
  596b
Selective service lottery, *576a*
Selective Training and Service Act (1940),
  525b, 555b, 601b
  effect on number of marriages, 230a
Self-determination, 679b
Self-realization, 234b
Self-Realization Fellowship, 1550a, 1551a–b
Selig Company, 1465b
Seligman, Edwin R. A., 274b, 920a, 1291a,
  1292a, 1315a
Seligman, Isaac, 1214a, 1218b
Sellars, Roy Wood, 1643a
  in *Contemporary American Philosophy,*
    1643b
  Critical Realism, 1643b
  Evolutionary Naturalism, 1643b
Sellars, Wilfrid, 1653a
Sellers, James, 61b
Selma civil rights march (1965), 74a, 1524b
Sematech, 852b
Semel, Bernard, 1567a, 1573a
Semi-Automatic Ground Environment
  (SAGE), 812b
Semiskilled workers, 166a, 205b, 1107a

Semitics scholars, 1579a–b
Semmel, Joan, 1721a
Senate
    committees, 356b–357b, 360a, 363a *See
        also* Congress: committees
    Democrats by region, 370a–b tab
    religious affiliations, 369a–b tab
    and Republican party, 302b
    See also Congress
Sender, Ramón, 1826a
Senior citizens
    Great Depression, 229b
    monetary grants to indigent, 474b
    national hospital insurance, 1001a
    as special interest group, 1001a
Senior Executive Service, 532b
Seoul, 657a
Separation of church and state, 1516b,
    1521a–1522a, 1584a
Sephardic Jews, 1565b, 1566a
Serology research, 974a
Serra, Richard, 1718b
Serrano, Andres, 1740a
Service economy, 1201a
Service industry, 38b, 58a
    employment in South, 76a–b
    foreign trade, 1244a, 1246b, 1262b,
        1264b
    growth, 1106b, 1118a
    versus manufacturing, 1201a
    Midwest, 59a
    as percentage of economy, *1157a–b*
Servicemen's Readjustment Act (1944). *See*
    GI Bill
Sessions, Roger, 1610a, 1617a, 1618a,
    1622a
Settlement houses, 121b, 174b, 453b–454a,
    477b
    baseball, 1762b–1763a
    Dreier, Katherine, and, 1700a
    emphasis on children, 1804b
    immigrants and sports, 1766a
    Jewish, 1582b
    Progressivism, 275a
    South, 65a
    students in, 1823a
    See also Henry Street Settlement; Hull
        House
Seven Arts, 1439b, 1567b
Seven Storey Mountain, The (Merton), 1523b
Seventh-Day Adventists, 1498a,b, 1501b
    and Deluge Geology Society, 868a
Sewage systems, 975a
Sewall, Arthur, 335a–b tab
Seward, William, 570b
Sewing machines, 1044a, 1136b–1137a
Sex and Personality (Terman and Miles),
    907b
Sex and Temperament in Three Cultures
    (Mead), 908b
Sex education, 227b
    funded by foundations, 228a
Sex surveys, 227b
Sexton, Anne, 1458a
Sexual Behavior of the Human Female, The
    (Kinsey), 103b
Sexual Behavior of the Human Male, The
    (Kinsey), 103b
Sexual Politics (Millett), 288b, 913a
Sexual revolution, 103a, 234b–235a
Seymour, William, 1500b

Shahn, Ben, 175b, 1579a, 1709a, 1710b,
    1714a, 1721b
Shakespeare, 1461b, 1462b, 1463a
Shamanism, 1561a,b
Shame of the Cities, The (Steffens), 256a
Shange, Ntozake, 1604b
Shapiro, Harvey, 1587a
Shapiro, Karl, 1581a
Sharecroppers
    effect of AAA, 68b
    sociological study, 68a
    South, 63b–64a
    See also Farming: tenant
Shareholders
    individual, 1234a tab
    institutional, 1239a
Share Our Wealth movement, 1320a
Sharp, Cecil, 1618b
Shasta Dam, 1373a
Shaw, Howard Van Doren, 1679b
Shaw, Irwin, 1587a
Sheeler, Charles, 1699a, 1700a, 1702a
Sheen, Fulton J., 1519a, 1523b
Sheet music, 1462b, 1463b
Sheffield Scientific School (Yale), 1408a
Shell, 1145b, 1249b
Sheppard-Towner Maternity and Infancy
    Protection Act (1921), 122a–b,
    431b–432a, 477b, 478a,b, 975a,b, 995a,
    996a–b tab
Shepsle, Kenneth, 367a, 370a
Sherman, Cindy, 1720b
Sherman, James S., 335a–b tab
Sherman, Stuart, 1827a
Sherman, William Tecumseh, 652a
Sherman Antitrust Act (1890), 379a, 429a,
    518a, 520a, 1136a, 1145b, 1215b,
    1269a, 1271a, 1278a
    economists' opposition, 1295a
    and Motion Picture Patents Company,
        1469a
    oil industry, 1134b
    oligopolistic market structures, 1280b
    Supreme Court, 379a, 520b
    tobacco industry, 1131a
Sherry, Michael, 607a
Shiite Muslims, 1549a, 1560b
Shils, Edward, 197b
Shinn, Everett, 1696a–b
Shipping Board and Fleet Corporation,
    596b
Ship-to-shore communications, 803b
Shipyards
    South, 70a–b
    West, 85a–b
Sh'ma, 1587a
Shockley, William B., 812a
Shoe industry, 27b, 28a, 1093b, 1130b,
    1789b
Sholem Aleichem Folk Institute, 1574a
Shopping, 1017a
    consumption, 1031b–1032a, 1034b
    malls, 466b, 468a–b, 1017a, 1030a,b,
        1034a
    women and, 1017b
    See also Retailing
Short, William H., 550a, 1484b
"Shortcut to Realism Examined, The"
    (Dewey), 1642a
Short-wave radio, 1473b
Shotwell, James T., 553a

Showalter, Elaine, 1457b
Shriver, E. Sargent, 1080b, 1081a,b
    presidential elections, 336a–b tab
Shryock, Richard H., 942a
Shumaker, Ann, 1808a
Shunryu Suzuki, 1555b
SIC. *See* Standard Industrial Classification
    (SIC)
Siegel, Bugsy, 462b, 1579b
Siegel, Gwathmey, 1689a
Siegel, Martin, 1238b
Siegfried, André, 702b, 1072b
Siemens, 835b, 1137b, 1138a
    furnace, 1133a
Siemens, Werner von, 1101a
Sierra Club, 1359b, 1366a, 1370b, 1378b,
    1560b
    Echo Park, 1373a
    Glen Canyon, 1373b
    growth in the 1980s, 1377b
    and Hetch Hetchy project, 1365a
Sigmund, Jay, 1706a
"Significance of the Frontier in American
    History, The" (Turner), 7a, 83a, 1357b
Sikorsky, Igor, 774a
Silent Spring (Carson), 1375a–b
Silicon, 1139a, 1149b
    computers, 812a
Silk mills, 29b
Silver, 86a, 1387b
Silver, Abba Hillel, 1582b, 1583b, 1584a
Silver, Eliezer, 1575b
Silverware industry, 27b
Simi Valley (Calif.), 97b
Simmel, Georg, 926a
Simon, Kate, 1586b
Simon, Neil, 1578b
Simon, Theodore, 881a
Simon Wiesenthal Center, 1589b
Simplex Automobile Company, 769b
Simpson, Alan, 187b
Simpson, George Gaylord, 869a, 870b
Sinatra, Frank, 1628a
Sinclair, Barbara, 372a, 373a
Sinclair, Upton, 1438b
    Jungle, The, 1359a, 1438b, 1440b
Singal, Daniel J., 1445a
Singapore, 693b
Singer, Edward, 1636a
Singer, I. J., 1569b, 1570b
Singer, Isaac Bashevis, 1588a
Singer Building (New York), 1674a
Singer Sewing Machine Company,
    1044a–1045a, 1136b–1137a
    foreign investments, 1247a
Singing cowboys, 84a
Single parenthood, 105b
Sins of the Fathers, The, 223a
Sioux tribe, 50b
Siqueiros, David, 1707a
Siskind, Aaron, 1714b
Sister Carrie (Dreiser), 33b, 1437b
Sisters of the Immaculate Heart of Mary,
    1530b
Skidmore, Max J., 1001b
Skidmore, Owings and Merrill
    John Hancock Center (Chicago), 1686a
    Lever House (New York), 1685b
    Manufacturers Hanover Trust Building
        (New York), 1686a
    Sears Tower (Chicago), 1686a

Skilled workers, 166a, 205a
  reduction with mass production, 1093b
Skillen, Edward, 1525b
Skinner, B. F., 891a–892a
  Quine, W. V. O., on, 1651a
Sklar, Martin, 208b
Sklar, Robert, 1440b, 1754b
Skocpol, Theda, 477a, 932b
  Protecting Soldiers and Mothers, 215b
Skowronek, Stephen, 295b, 299a, 514a, 1270a
Skulnik, Menashe, 1570b
Skylab space missions, 790b
Skyscrapers, 454a, 464a
  as icon, 1674a–1676b
  Midwest, 47a, 59a
SLAC. *See* Stanford Linear Accelerator
Slave, The (Baraka), 1604a
Slavery
  indentured servants, 132a
  South, 63a
  and states' rights, 402b
  Thirteenth Amendment, 403a
Slawson, John, 1584a
Slichter, Sumner H., 1298b
Sloan, Alfred P., Jr., 1038b, 1058b, 1141a, 1414a
Sloan, John, 1696a, *1696b,* 1703a, 1729b
  art editor for *The Masses,* 1697a
Sloan-Kettering Institute, 941b
Slogans, political, 322b
Slosson, Edwin E., 1822b
Slum Clearance Project, 1734b
Small, Albion, 274b, 920b
Small, Melvin, *as contributor,* 569a–592b
Small-claims courts, 395b
Smallpox, 959b, 977a
Smith, A. O., Corporation, 1112a
Smith, Adam, 274b, 918a, 1017a, 1289a,b, 1311a, 1312b, 1384a
Smith, Alfred E., 172b, 198b, 1516b, 1526a
  presidential elections, 335a–b tab
Smith, Anthony, 182b
Smith, Bessie, 1597b, 1615b
Smith, David, 1712b
Smith, Edgard L., 1230b
Smith, George David, *as contributor,* 1209a–1241b
Smith, Gerald L. K., 175b, 1578b
Smith, Henry Nash, 10a
  on Twain, 1438a
Smith, Hoke, 64b, 66b
Smith, Joseph, 93b, 1540a, 1542a
Smith, Lillian, 71b, 147b
Smith, Mamie, 1597b
Smith, Robert W., *as contributor,* 739a–765b
Smith, Steven S., 360a
Smith, Tommy, 1782a
Smith, W. Eugene, 1710a, 1715a
Smith, Wendell, 1777b
Smith, William Kennedy, 397b
Smith College, 32a, 102a, 1819b
Smith-Connally Act, 603b, 605b
Smith-Hughes Vocational Education Act (1917), 201b, 1811b, 1812a–b tab
Smith Kline, 1148a
Smith-Lever Act (1914), 1160b, 1325b, 1820a–b tab, 1822a
Smith-Mundt Act (1948), 704b
Smithson, Alison, 1689b
Smithson, Peter, 1689b

Smithson, Robert, 1717b
Smithsonian Institution, 493b, 1734a
  airplanes, 767a–b
Smokey the Bear, 1363b
Smoot-Hawley Tariff (1930), 575b, 631b, 723b, 1193b, 1247b, 1250a, 1298b
Smothers, Dick, 1477b
Smothers, Tom, 1477b
Smulyan, Susan, 1755b
Smyth, Henry, 749b
SNCC. *See* Student Nonviolent
  Coordinating Committee (SNCC)
Snedden, David, 1806a, 1807a
Snow, C. P., 1453a
Snow White (Barthelme), 1452b
Snyder, Gary, 1555a–b
Soap operas, 1477a
  on radio, 1473a
Social activism
  Catholic labor priests, 1524a
  Catholics, 1516b, 1524a
  feminism, 121b
  Jewish women, 1567b
Social and athletic clubs, 1748a
Social Aspects of the Business Cycle, The (Thomas), 920a
Social Change (Ogburn), 923b–924a
Social Darwinism, 161a, 274a
  influence on sports development, 1762a
  and managerial authority, 1102b
  in preservationism, 1359b
Social Democratic party (Europe), 308b
Social Forces, 68a
Social Frontier, 282a
Social Gospel, 1494b
  Progressivism, 275a
Social History, 205a
Social History of the State of Indiana, The (Benton), 1705b
Social insurance, 476b, 479b, 480a
  funded by high tariffs, 1312b
Socialism
  Catholics, 1517a
  Jews, 1568a
  labor unions, 86b
  Midwest, 49b
  Protestantism, 1496b, 1497a, 1499a, 1502a, 1506b
Socialism and Social Reform (Ely), 274b
Socialist immigrants, 169a
Socialist Labor Party, 167a
Socialist party, 167a, 549b, 1502a
  Debs, Eugene V., 204a
Socializing
  mixed-sex, 113b, 114a
  single-sex, 113b
Social justice, 1315b
  Catholics, 1525b, 1528a, 1529a–1531a, 1534a
  taxation, 1313b
Social legislation, 1071a–b
Social Origins of Dictatorship and Democracy (Moore), 932b
Social protest art, 1707a, 1714b
Social Rule (Parsons), 904b
Social Science Research Council, 495a,b, 499a,b, 1651b
Social sciences
  early, 919a–b
  and ethnicity, 184a
  foundations and, 495a, 496a–b

international exchange programs, 926b
Laura Spelman Rockefeller Memorial, 495a
melioristic programs, 173b
national morale during World War II, 926b
postmodernism, 936b
and poverty, 1070b
Progressivism, 274b, 278b
rational choice theory, 937a
standard of living, 1070b
Social Security, 30b, 433a, 439b, 442b, 447a, 1075b–1076a, 1167b, 1327b
  amendments in 1939, 482a
  amendments in 1950, 483a
  benefits indexed, 488b
  bipartisan support, 483b
  compared to Townsend plan, 480a–b
  development, 481b–483a
  election-year increases, 483a
  expansion vs. rehabilitation, 485a
  financed by payroll taxes, 1320a
  growth of programs, 484a–b tab
  self-employed, 483a
  tax rates, 1324b
Social Security Act (1935), 230a, 471a, 478b, 480a, 481a, 975b, 996a–b tab, 1074a,b, 1277b, 1750b, 1827a
  upheld by Supreme Court, 411a
Social Security Administration, 524b
  computers, 810a
Social Security Advisory Council, 482a
Social Security Amendments (1983), 488b
Social Security Amendments of 1965 (Medicare and Medicaid), 996a–b tab, 1002a
Social Security Board, 482a
Social System, The (Parsons), 927a–b
Social Transformation of American Medicine, The (Starr), 988a
Social Value (Anderson), 1293a–b
Social welfare, **471a–490b**
  public expenditures, 472a–b tab
  Russel Sage Foundation, 493a
Social work
  evolution of profession, 1414b–1415a
  New Deal and, 1421a
  public support of, 1417b
Société Anonyme, 1700a
Societies for the Prevention of Cruelty to Children, 237b
Society, **917a–939b**
Society for Advancement of American Philosophy, 1658b
Society for Ethical Culture, 1567b
Society for Spaceflight (Germany), 786a
Society for the Propagation of the Faith, 1520b, 1523b
Society for the Study of Experimental Evolution, 864a
Society for Women in Philosophy, 1658b
Society of American Artists, 1696a
Society of Christian Socialists, 275a
Society of Independent Artists, 1699b
Society of Mayflower Descendants, 163a
Sociobiology, 893b–894a
Sociobiology: The New Synthesis (Wilson), 871a, 894a
Sociological Imagination, The (Mills), 930a
Sociology
  Catholic, 1523a

gender theories, 904a
Sociology and Scientism (Bannister), 920b, 923a
Sociology for the South (Fitzhugh), 918b
Socoloff, Miriam, 1719b
Software, 1149a–1150b
Sohn, Louis B., 558b
Soil Conservation Service, 1369b, 1370a, 1380b
  photographs for, 1709a
Soka Gakkai, 1556a
Sokatsu Shaku Roshi, 1555b
Sokoloff, Nikolai, 1730a
Sokolow, Anna, 1579a
Solar-terrestrial relations, 743b, 755a–b
Soldier and the State, The (Huntington), 607a
Soldiers, Statesmen, and Cold War Crisis (Betts), 610b
Soldiers' home, 472a
Soleri, Paolo, 1689a
Solidarity (Guerrero and Weber), 1719b
Solid-state electronics, 799a, 812b, 821b
Sollors, Werner, 161b, 190b, 256b
Solo, Robert, 850b–851a
Solomon, "Rabbi of Swat" Mose, 1766b
Soloveichik, Joseph, 1575a, 1589a
Solow, Herbert, 1581b
Solvay Process Company, 1139a
Sombart, Werner, 203a, 204b
"Some Psychical Consequences of the Anatomical Distinction Between the Sexes" (Freud), 906a
Sometimes a Great Notion (Kesey), 1452b
Sondheim, Stephen, 1625b, 1631a
"Song of Hiawatha, The" (Longfellow), 1437a
"Song of Kentucky" (Schwartz), 1569b
Sons of the American Revolution, 163a, 254a
Sontag, Susan, 1453b
Sony Corporation, 825a, 1474a
  Betamax, 1032b
Sophie Newcomb College, 1824b
Sophisticated Lady (Ellington), 1620b
Soriano, Ralph S., 1682b
Sorokin, Pitirim, 924a
Soto, Gary, 1456b
Soule, George, 1298b
Soul music, 150a
Souls of Black Folk, The (Du Bois), 259a, 276b, 1456a, 1594b
Sound and the Fury, The (Faulkner), 1445a
Sound barrier, 781b, 792b
"Sources of Soviet Conduct, The" (Kennan), 608a
Sousa, John Philip, 1613b
Souter, David, 391a–b tab, 392b, 393a
South, The, **61a–79b**
  agriculture in, 1386a
  beneficiary of federal programs, 300b
  civil rights movement, 95a
  Congress, 365b–366b
  Depression, 70a–b
  desegregation, 440b
  development during World War II, 457a
  map, 62a–b
  migration to, post-World War II, 1345a
  plantations, 1386a
  urbanization, 456a–b
  World War II housing, 1343a
  See also Southerners

South Africa, 1084b
Southam, Chester, 950b
South and Christian Ethics, The (Sellers), 61b
Southdale Center Mall, 1030b
Southeast Asian Treaty Organization (SEATO), 610a, 689a
Southern Baptist Convention, 1503b
Southern Baptists, 1493a
Southern Christian Leadership Conference (SCLC), 288b, 1602b
  Anti-Vietnam War movement, 562a
Southern Democrats, 307b, 309a, 313a, 361b, 366b
  and coalition under New Deal, 300b–301a
Southerners
  class relations and race, 196a
  described, 61a–b
  history, 63a
  identity, 77b
  versus Northerners, 61b
Southerners (Reed), 77b
Southern Pacific Railroad, 91a
Southern Regional Council, 71a
Southern Regions of the United States (Odum), 13b
Southern Sociological Congress, 65a
Southern Tenant Farmers Union, 68b
Southland, 1238a
South Shore Bank (Chicago), 504b
Southwest
  arid lands development, 1360b
  development during World War II, 457a
  employment in Albuquerque, N.M., 113a
  migration to, 1345a
Southwest Scene, The (Botkin), 10a
Soviet Union
  armament, 684a
  Big Science, 757b
  collapse, 733a, 855a
  dissolution, 693a, 1261a
  five industrial countries compared, 1990, 1332a–b tab
  foreign policy, 574b–575a, 576a, 578a–579b, 582b–583a,585a, 589a
  jazz in, 701a
  League of Nations, 684b
  nuclear tests, 610a
  nuclear weapons, 849b
  world economy, 726a
Soyen Shaku, 1553b, 1555a
Soyer, Isaac, 1579a, 1704b, 1721b
Soyer, Moses, 1579a, 1704b, 1721b
Soyer, Raphael, 1579a, 1704b, 1721b
Space
  communication satellites, 710a
  exploration, 1145a
  flight, 784b–792a
  Kennedy and, 341b
Spacelab, 790b
Space Shuttle, 739b, 790b–791a
Space Telescope. *See* Hubble Space Telescope
Spalding, A. G., 1762b–1763a
  A.G. Spalding and Brothers, 1763a
  America's National Game, 1762b
Spanish-American War, 570b, 621a, 720b
  effect on peace movement, 542a
  influence on Army, 593b
  influence on Navy, 593b–594a
  nationalism, 255a–b

Spanish Civil War, 175b, 634a
  Catholics, 1519a
  Loyalist Abraham Lincoln Brigade, 175b
Spanish language televison, 824b
Spargo, John, 1804b
Sparkman, John, 335a–b tab
Sparr, Arnold, 1516b
Special Committee to Investigate the National Defense Program, 606a
Species redefinition, 865a
Specter, Arlen, 30a
Spectroscopes, 743b
Spellman, Francis, 1523b
Spelman College, 1833b
Spelman Fund, 496a
Spencer, Herbert, 901b, 918b, 1102b, 1494a
  social evolution, 862b, 863a
  Study of Sociology, The, 918b
Spencer, Nils, 1702a
Spero, Nancy, 1719b
Spero, Sterling, 929b
Sperry Rand, 462b
Spheres of Justice (Walzer), 291a
Spiegel, Shalom, 1579a
Spiegelman, Art, 1484a
Spielberg, Steven, 1469b, 1477b
Spingarn, Arthur, 1567b
Spiral Jetty (Smithson), 1717b
Spirit of St. Louis, 701a, 772a–b
Spiritualism, 1540a–b, 1542b–1543a
Spock, Benjamin, 232a–b, 895a, 976a
  SANE, 559b
Spoils system, 299b
  politics, 297a
Sports, 1477a, **1761a–1783b**
  amateur code, 1744a
  Eastern region, 38b
  gender in, 114b
  Jews, 1579b
  race in, 114b
  television programs, 1480b
  upper class, 1744a
Sports Illustrated, 1481b, 1779a, 1781a
Sportswriters, 1767a
Springsteen, Bruce, 1631a
Sputnik, 583a, 850b
Sputnik I, 753b, 754a–755b, 757b, 787a
Spy planes, 583a, 584a, 781a
Square Deal, 322b
Squibb, 1147b, 1148a
Squire, Peverill, 328b–329a
Sri Aurobindo Society, 1552b
SSC. *See* Superconducting Super–collider
SST. *See* Supersonic transport
Stadiums, domed, 1775a–b
Stagflation, 347b, 730b, 1084b, *1169a–b,* 1169b, 1257b, 1283a, 1284a, 1303a
  onset, 1959-1975, 1155b
  rise of business influence on universities, 1832b
  social security, 488a
Stagg, Amos Alonzo, 1767b
Stalin, Joseph, 577b, 578a,b, 579a, 581a, 656a
  postwar organization, 556b
  at Yalta, *606a–b,* 687a
Stalingrad, 643b
Stallings, George, 1530a
Stallone, Sylvester, 268b, 1798b
Standard and Poor, 1231a

Standard Forms for Financial Reports of Colleges, Universities and Business Schools, 1409a

Standard Industrial Classification (SIC), 1127b, 1131a, 1132b, 1133a–b, 1136a–b, 1140b, 1147b, 1151b–1152b, 1153b
  U.S. manufacturing industries, 1128a tab
  See also Census Bureau

Standard of living, 198b, 1067a, 1072a, 1077b, 1155a, 1158a
  economic status and mortality, 966b–967a
  health, 976b
  minimum, 1069a–b
  regional variations, 1353a
  residence and mortality, 966a

Standard Oil Company, 86b, 91a, 1134a, 1215b, 1218a, 1219b, 1397b, 1411a

Standard Oil of California, 1145b

Standard Oil of Indiana
  research, 835b

Standard Oil of New Jersey
  foreign investments, 1247a
  pipelines, 1335b

Standard Oil Trust, 1134a–b

Standards (Brownell), 1439b

Standing Again at Sinai (Plaskow), 1589a

Standing Figure (Thomas), 1721b

Standing Liaison Committee, 605a

Stanford, Leland, 1752a

Stanford Linear Accelerator (SLAC), 759a–b, 762b

Stanford Medical School, 949a

Stanford Research Institute, 1030a

Stanford University, 1833a
  government contracts, 1828b

Starhawk, 1557b

Stark, Harold R., 601b, 603b

Starr, Paul, 988a, 998a

"Star-Spangled Banner, The," 254a

START (Strategic Arms Reduction Talks) I (1991), 564b, 566a–b tab

START (Strategic Arms Reduction Talks) II (1993), 564b

Star Wars. *See* Strategic Defense Initiative

Stassen, Harold, 560a

State, County, and Municipal Workers of America, 1108b

"State, The" (Bourne), 257b

State, War, Navy Coordinating Committee, 605a

State action doctrine, 404a

State arts councils, 59b, 1725a, 1736b, 1737b
  and recession, 1740b

State autonomy, 440b, 444b, 446a–448b, 448a–b

State court organization, 395b–396b

State fairs, 48b–49a
  Midwest, 42a, 58b

State Fair (Strong), 55a

State government, 428a, 431b–432a, 434a–b, 437b
  centralization, 431a, 438a, 448b
  fiscal policy, 1313a, 1314b–1315a, 1321b
  growth, 1314b, 1318b
  human services, 1318a, 1325b
  New Deal, 433b
  See also Property taxes

State Hospital, The (Kienholz), 1719a

State law, federal courts and, 383a–b

"Statement on Academic Freedom and Tenure" (1940), 1826a

State of the Union Address (1949), 998a

State policy
  and gender, 121b–124a
  power, 516a

State progressive regulatory commissions, 1270a–b

States' rights, 402a–b, 431b, 436b, 440b, 444a
  See also Segregation

State taxes, 1312b–1313a
  franchise taxes, 1313b
  income taxes, 1313a, 1319a
  inheritance taxes, 1319a
  sales taxes, 1318b
  taxes on banks, 1319a
  taxes on utilities, 1319a
  user charges, 1318b
  utility taxes, 1313a

State universities, 1819a
  Midwest, 49b, 51a, 54b–55a, 58a, 59a

State University of Minnesota, 1821a

State University of New York, 1828a

Statue of Liberty-Ellis Island Centennial Commission, 185a

Staudinger, Hermann, 845a

Stauffer, Donald A., 1447b

Stead, W. T., 695a

Steagall, Henry, 1226b

Stealth aircraft, 784b, *785a–b*

Steamships, 1128a, 1129a, 1141a

Stearns, Harold, 279a

Stearns, Peter, 105a, 114b

Stebbins, G. Ledyard, 869a

Steber, Eleanor, 1621a

Stedman, Edmund Clarence, 1436b, 1437a

Stedman, Seymour, 335a–b tab

Steel, Danielle, 1482b

Steel industry, 29b, 30a, 45b, *46a,* 70b, 1091b, 1155b, 1164a,b, 1262b
  basic oxygen furnace (BOF), 1151b
  eroded market share, 1235b
  foreign competition, 313a
  Great Depression, 1161b
  imports, 1254b
  international competition, 1200a
  Midwest, 45b, 55a, 57a,b, 59a
  South, 69b
  turnover rate, 1098a
  world trade, 1166b

Steenbock, Harry, 944b

Steffens, Lincoln, 33b, 256a

Stegner, Wallace, 10b

Steichen, Edward, 1697b, 1698a, *1710a,* 1721b
  Family of Men, 1714b
  World War I, 1701b

Stein, Clarence S., 12a, 1679a, 1684a

Stein, Gertrude, 1441b, 1442a, 1455b, 1697b, 1728b
  on Pound, 1450a

Stein, Leo, 1697b

Steinbeck, John
  In Dubious Battle, 1443a
  Grapes of Wrath, The, 10a, 262a, 1443a
  Of Mice and Men, 1443a

Steinberg, Saul, 41b

Steinmetz, Charles, 836a–b

Stella, Frank, 1717a

Stella, Joseph, 1701a,b, 1702b

Stephenson, C. L., 1655a

Sterilization laws, 864b

Stern, Bill, 1773b

Stern, David, 1774b

Stern, Robert A. M., 1687a

Sternberg, George Miller, 942a

Stern College for Women (Yeshiva U.), 1585b

Sternlieb, George, 468a

Stettheimer, Florine, 1699a, 1704a

Stevens, John Paul, 390a–b tab

Stevens, May, 1720a

Stevens, Roger L., 1736b

Stevens, Rosemary A., 995a, 1004a

Stevens, Wallace, 1445b, 1448a, 1449b, 1455b
  Collected Poems, 1449b
  Man with the Blue Guitar, The, 1449b
  Notes toward a Supreme Fiction, 1449b

Stevens Institute of Technology, 32b

Stevenson, Adlai E. (1835–1914)
  presidential elections, 335a–b tab

Stevenson, Adlai E. (1900–1965), 578a, 580b, 581b
  presidential elections, 335a–b tab

Stevenson-Wydler Technology Innovation Act (1980), 853a

Stewart, Dugald, 877a

Stewart, James, 84a

Stewart, Potter, 390a–b tab

Stickley, Gustav, 1679a

Stieglitz, Alfred, *1697a,* 1701a
  African art, 1703a,b
  An American Place, 1706b
  on Cézanne, 1697b
  children art show, 1716b
  291 Gallery, 1567b, 1697a, 1698a
  Intimate Gallery, 1702b
  and O'Keeffe, Georgia, 1704a
  photography, 1697b

Stigler, George, 1299a, 1303b

Stigma (Goffman), 929b

Stiles, Charles Wardell, 942b

Still, Clyfford, 1712a,b

Stillman, James, 1229a

Stilwell, Joseph W., 642a, 686b

Stimson, Henry L., *177a,* 576a, *576a,* 578a, 600a, 632b, 633b, 635a, 637a, 638a

Stimson Doctrine, 600a, 632b, 636b

Stinson, Katherine, 770a

Stockdale, James B., 336a–b tab

Stockman, David, 1739b

Stock market, 31a, 1209a
  anticompetitive practices, 1232b
  boom of the 1920s, 1192b
  crash of 1929, 575b, 1024a, 1161a, 1193b, 1250a, 1319a
  crash of 1987, 1238b
  fixed-rate commission structure, 1232b–1233a
  Great Crash of 1929, 31a
  large-block trades, 1232a
  mini crash in 1989, 1238b
  trading volumes, 1232a
  See also New York Stock Exchange

Stocks, 1230a
  early unpopularity of, 1215b–1216a
  preferred, 1216a, 1230a
  worth defined, 1230b

Stockyards, 47a

Stokes, Carl, 58b

Stokowski, Leopold, 1616b
Stone, Edward Durell, 1689a
  Museum of Moden Art, *1684b,* 1684b
Stone, Elisa, 1790b
Stone, Harlan F., 383b, 390a–b tab, 413b,
  419a, 434b, 435b
  Black and White Taxicab Co. v. *Brown and
    Yellow Taxicab Co.* (1928), dissent in,
    383b
  footnote four of *Carolene Products,* 384a
  and individual rights, 384a
Stone, Oliver, 1477b
Stone City, Iowa (Wood), 55a
Stonewall riot (1969), 1531b
Stone & Webster, 846a
Storrs, John, 1702a
Stowe, Harriet Beecher, 150a–b, 1438a,
  1593a
Strand, Paul, 1702a
Strange Brother, 104a
Strange Career of Jim Crow, The (Woodward),
  142b
Strangers in the Land (Higham), 597a
Strassburg, Bernard, 820b
Strasser, Susan, *as contributor,* 1017a–1035b
Strategic Air Command (SAC), 779b–780a
Strategic Arms Limitation Talks. *See* SALT
Strategic Arms Reduction Talks. *See*
  START
Strategic Defense Initiative, 564a, 739b,
  787b
  funding of research, 851b
Strategy of Conflict, The (Schelling), 1305a
Straton, John Roach, 866a
Stravinsky, Igor, 1617a, 1621a, 1630a,
  1728b
Strawberry Bank, 37b
Strawberry Statement, The (1969), 267a
Strawson, Peter
  "In Defense of a Dogma," 1654a
  "On Referring," 1653b
Strayhorn, Billy, 1620b
Streetcars, 89b–90a, 452b–453b, 454b,
  1021b, 1337b
Streetstyle (Polhemus), 1791b, 1793a
Strict constructionism, 402a
Strikes, 29b, 86b, 95a, 311b
  in 1919, 171b
  aircraft controllers, 794a
  East Texas (1930), 1398a
  Flint sit-down strike, 1108b
  Homestead, 254b–255a, 1096a, 1290b
  McCormick, 1290b
  Midwest, 54a*454a–b*
  New York City cloakmakers, 1574a
  pre-World War I, 1097b
  Pullman, 255a, 1290b
  sit-down strikes of 1936-1937, 205b
  South, 68a
  See also Labor unions
Stroke, 969a
Strong, Josiah, 254b, 1497a
Strong, Phil, 55a
Structuralism, 878a–b, 879a
  in Europe, 893a
Structure of Science, The (Nagel), 1649a
Structure of Scientific Revolutions, The (Kuhn),
  267a, 1655b
Structure of Social Action, The (Parsons),
  924b–925a
Stryker, Roy, 1709a

Studebaker, 46b
Studebaker Building (Chicago), 1675b
Student as Nigger, The, 266b, 1830b
Student League for Industrial Democracy,
  924b, 1827a
Student Nonviolent Coordinating
  Committee (SNCC), 180a, 266b,
  288b, 1602b, 1830a
  Anti-Vietnam War movement, 562a
  women in, 119a–b
Student Progressive League, 1830a
Students for a Democratic Society (SDS),
  206b, 266b, 286b–287a, 1830b
  Anti-Vietnam War movement, 562a
  women, 119b
Studies in Logical Theory, 1641a
Studies in Prejudice (Horkheimer and
  Flowerman), 1584b
Studies of Methods of Americanization
  series, 173b
Study of Man, The (Linton), 926a
Study of Sociology, The (Spencer), 918b
Styron, William, 1603a
Submarines, 849b
  allied antisubmarine campaign, 642b
  research on detection, 841b–842a
  during World War I, 573b, 623b–624b
  during World War II, 636a
Subnational diversity, 691a
Substantive due process, 404b–405a
Suburban Trend, The (Douglass), 460a
Suburbs, 231b–232a, 1029a, 1030a–b, 1345b
  city and, 451a–470b
  culture of, 105a
  development, 1338a,b
  downtowns, 468a–b
  Eastern region, 26b–27a, 28b, 30a, 33b
  influence on movie attendance, 1467a
  in late nineteenth century, 454b
  Midwest, 47b, 51b
  migration to, 459a, 466a, 1334a
  Protestant, 34b
  real estate development, 459a, 466b
  refusal to consolidate with cities, 459b
  retail, 59a, 466b
  South, 77a–b
  telephones, 802a–b
  West, 81a, 91a–b
  white migration to, 154b
Subway, The (Tooker), 1714a
Subway systems, 453a, 465b
Suckow, Ruth, 1706a
Suez Crisis, 582a
Suffragists, 117a
  propaganda films, 117a
Sufis, 1549a
Sullivan, Ed, 1476a
Sullivan, Harry Stack, 890a
Sullivan, John L., 143a, 1745b
Sullivan, Louis, 37b, 1665a, 1667a,b,
  1675a,b
Sullivan, Mary Quinn, 1728b
Sullivan, William, 290b
Summer camps, 1576b, 1578b
Summer colonies, 1743b
Sumner, Charles, 1744a
Sumner, William Graham, 195a, 862b,
  919b, 920a, 1494a
Sun Also Rises, The (Hemingway), 1440a
Sunbelt, 75a–77a, 452a
  economy, 76a

Latinos in, 210b
versus Midwest, 57b
suburbs, 461a–467b
term conceived, 456b
Sunday, Billy, 1415b
"Sunday Morning" (Stevens), 1449b
Sundquist, Eric J., 1437b
Sundquist, James
  *Constitutional Reform and Effective
    Government,* 363b, 364a
  Decline and Resurgence of Congress, The,
    355b, 364a
Sunni Muslims, 1549a,b
Sunnyside Gardens (Queens), 1679b, 1684a
Sun Recording Studios, 73b
Sunset, 455a
"Sunset" legislation, 362a, 363a
Superconducting Super-collider (SSC),
  761b–762b
Superfund, 1377b
Supersonic transport (SST), 781b, 792b
Supplemental Security Income (SSI), 487b,
  1082a
Supply Priorities and Allocation Board,
  602b
Supply-side economics, 731a–733a,
  1203a–1204a, 1284b, 1285a
  fiscal policy, 1327a
Supreme Court, 427b, 438b
  appointments, 389a–393a, 418a
  black vote in primaries, 71a
  on blue-sky laws, 1224b
  and busing, 388b–389a
  class bias, 404b
  congressional acts overturned, 403a–b tab
  desegregation, 438a, 439b, 441b–442a
  entertainment, 1467a–1469b
  expansive view of its own authority, 402a
  flag desecration, 417a
  government and religion, 418a
  and income tax, 1314a
  invalidation of Agricultural Adjustment
    Act, 1320b
  Japanese American internment during
    World War II, 96b,605b
  Judaism, 1585b
  Justices, 390a–b tab, 391a–b tab, 1568a
  limitation of Congress, 409a
  limitation of reform legislation,
    377b–379b
  movie censorship, 1468a,b
  National Recovery Administration, 69a,
    311a, 433a
  New Deal, 380a–381b, 524b
  and obscenity, 1483a
  overruled decisions, 403a–b tab
  probusiness bias, 408b, 409a
  protector of property, 404b
  race defined by, 141a
  railroad strike, 429b
  secularist interpretation of First
    Amendment, 1521b
  segregation, 73b
  state action doctrine, 404a
  state and local legislation overturned,
    403a–b tab
  State government, 428b, 429a
  television, 1476b
  unsuccessful nominations, 391a–b tab
  use of negative prohibitions in the
    Constitution, 409a

Supreme Court (*cont.*)
  working hours, 310a
  See also Legal cases
Surface Mining Control Reclamation Act
  (1977), 528a
Surface-to-air-missiles (SAM), 783b–784a
Surgery, 977b
Suro, Robert, 188b
Surrey, Stanley, 1323a, 1326a
Survey, 259b
Susan B. Anthony Coven, 1557b
Sussex, 624a
Sutherland, George, 141a, 382b, 390a–b tab
Svie (Surroundings), 1570a
Swaggart, Jimmy, 1506a
Swami Muktananda Paramahansa, 1552b
Swami Satchidananda, 1552b
Swarthmore College, 32a
  honors program, 1826b
Swartwout, Egerton, 1672b
Swayze, John Cameron, 1477b
Sweatshops, 186b, 1020b
Sweden, 960b
Swedenborg, Immanuel, 1540a
Sweezy, Paul, 1304a
Swidler, Ann, 290b
Swift, Gustavus, 1132a
Swift & Company, 1132a–b
Swing music, 1620b
Switzerland, 960b
Swivel Buggy and Wagon Company, 769b
Sword of the Lord, 1503b
Sylla, Richard, *as contributor,* 1209a–1241b
Symbolic ethnicity, 183a
Symphony Hall (Boston), 1611a
Symphony in Black (Ellington), 1602a, 1620b
Symphony orchestras. *See* Orchestras
Synagogue Council of America, 1576a
Synagogues, 1572a–b, 1574b, 1577a–b
  sisterhoods, 1587b–1588a
Syndicate, 1462b
Synthetic fibers, 1372a
Synthetic Fuels Corporation, 87a
Syracuse University, 32b
Syria, 679b
Syrkin, Marie, 176a, 1582a, 1585b
Syrkin, Nachman, 1568b
Systematics and population genetics, 869a
Systematics and the Origin of Species (Mayr),
  869a
Szasz, Thomas, 896b
Szilard, Leo, 558b, 1584a
Szold, Henrietta, 1567a,b
Szporluk, Roman, 252b

T

Taft, Jessie, 276a, 904a
Taft, Lorado, 1693b, 1695a
Taft, Robert A., 55b, 609a, 662a, 725b
Taft, William Howard, 29b, 297a, 327a,
  390a–b tab, 427b, 435a, 493b, 523a,
  550a, 572a,b
  antitrust, 521a, 1271a
  Chamber of Commerce, 309b
  chief justice, 408b
  conservation, 1364b
  land withdrawal, 1360a, 1397b
  peace movement, 543b, 545a

presidential elections, 335a–b tab, 380a
presidential power, 406b
on Supreme Court activism, 380a
vetoes, 347a tab
Taft-Hartley Act (1947), 178a, 311b, 312a,
  525b, 1110a, 1278b–1279a
Tageblat, 1569a
Taiwan, 693b
Takaki, Ronald, 134b–135a, 190b
Talent Search, 1834a
Talmage, Thomas DeWitt, 1437b
Tamiment Lodge, 1578b
Tandy Corporation, 1149a
Tanguy, Yves, 1710a
Tanner, Henry Ossawa, 1694b
Taoism, 1541b
Tapping Reeve law school, 1819b
Tariff Act (1913), 1246b
Tariff Commission, 1272a, 1275a
Tariff History of the United States (Taussig),
  1290b–1291a
Tariff policy, 29b, 575b, 719b–720a, 723b,
  724a, 726b, 1161b, 1166a,
  1246b–1247a,b, 1248a–b, 1250a–b,
  1254a, 1259b, 1262b, 1271b, 1311b
  after World War I, 631b
  Civil War, 1312a–1313a
  economists and, 1298b
  high tariff policy, 1312b
  movement for reform pre-World War I,
  721b
  protectionism, 1193b
  raise in 1921 and 1922, 722b
  regulatory effects, 1312a
  tariff duties, 1895-1990, *1260a–b*
  taxation, 1314a
Tarkington, Booth, 52a
Tarras, Dave, 1571a
Tarski, Alfred, 1646a
Tarthang Tulku, 1555b
Tate, Allen, 10b, 14a,b, 1444b
Taussig, Frank, 1290b, 1292a, 1295a, 1296a,
  1298b, 1305b
Tawney, R. H., 924b
Taxation, **1309a–1330b**
  budget deficits, 1173b
  power, 358a
  reduction under supply-side economics,
  1204a
  as regulatory devic, 1314a
  taxpayers' revolt, 1203b
  tax structure inequities, 1083b
Taxation (Mellon), 1318a
Tax commissions, 1315a, 1318b
Tax Equity and Fiscal Responsibility Act
  (1982), 996a–b tab
Tax Reconstruction Act (1980), 1326b
Tax reform, 318b, 438a, 446b, 1329b
  California, 445a
  effect on interest groups, 317a–b
  Nixon-era, 442b
  World War I and, 1315a–1317b
Tax Reform Act (1969), 504b, 507a, 1733b
Tax Reform Act (1986), 532a,
  1327b–1328a
Taylor, Charles, 291a
Taylor, Frederick W., 205b, 475a, 885a,
  1093b–1094a,b–1095a, 1409a, 1411a
  and foreman's role, 1096b
  management, 1103a
Taylor, Glen H., 335a–b tab

Taylor, Marshall, 1770a
Taylor, Maxwell, 663a
Taylor Grazing Act (1934), 84b, 87b, 1369a
Taylor Grazing Lands Act, 433b
TCI cable television, 824a–b
Teachers Colleges, 1822a, 1824b
Teachers for a Democratic Culture, 1834a
Teaching profession, 1415a–b
Teaford, Jon C., *as contributor,* 451a–470b
Teamoh, George, 142a
Teamsters, 310b, 1110b
Technical Committee on Medical Care,
  997a
Technical workers, 1107a, 1118b
Technoburbs, 468a
Technocrats, 202a
Technology, 1019a, 1164b
  consumption, 1031b–1034b
  democratization of leisure, 1757a
  economic performance, 1160a–b
  effect on infrastructure, 1331b
  foreign trade, 1247a
  health improvements, 975b
  industries, 1259a
  innovations, 1252b, 1461a
  progress, 1254b, 1264b
  revolution, 1128b, 1146b
  as threat to professionalism, 1427a–b
Technology and the Pursuit of Economic Growth
  (Mowery), 843b
Technology transfer, 853a, 1155b, 1246a,
  1247a, 1249b
  space program, 791b
Tedlow, Richard S., *as contributor,*
  1037a–1066b
Teenagers. *See* Adolescence
Teheran conference, 654b
Tehran hostages, 588b, 589a
Teitelbaum, Joel, 1584b
Telecommunications, 28a, 799a, 1150a,
  1160b
  deregulation, 820b, 1349a–b
  market restoration, 1285a
  Midwest, 58a
  regulated monopoly of AT&T, 1349a
  regulation, 1168a–b
Tele-Communications, Inc., 1480a
Telegraph, 801a, 802a, 833a–b, 1128a,
  1129a, 1130b, 1340a
  marketing, 1048a
  wireless, 1471a,b
Telephones, 799a, 819b, 1020a, 1128a,
  1138b, 1333b, 1339a
  early development, 1336a
  emergence, 801a–803a
  fibre-optics, 38a
  long distance service, 837b
  Midwest, 48a
  party lines, 803a
  rural, 803a
  suburbs, 455b
  telephone-wire infrastructure, 1920-1990,
  1339b tab
  video signals, 1480a
Telescopes, 743b–745b, 752b, 756b, 761a–b
Television, 38a, 1461b, 1470b, 1756a–1757a
  advertising, 1059b
  American programming worldwide, 713a
  anchors, 1477b
  cable, 1033a, 1348b, 1470b, 1757a

color, 816b, 817b, 1475b
consumption, 1029b
courts and, 397a–b
criminal trial coverage, 397b
cultural homogenization, 179b
Eastern region, 38a
effect on sports, 1773b–1774a
Eisenhower's use of, 338b
in Europe, 712b
family on, 106a, 232b
federal regulation, 1475b
film studios and, 1469b
history, 1475a
Hollywood directors and, 1477b
Holocaust portrayal, 1589b
Kennedy's use of, 338b, 341a
networks, 814b–819a, 1029b, 1032b,
   1034b, 1476a
news specials, 1478a
New York City, 31b
overseas syndication, 708a
philanthropy campaigns, 509a
politics, 1477b, 1478b, 1479a
programming, 817b–818a
and racism, 154b
radio, television, and cable television,
   1921–1990, 1349a–b tab
ratings, 1477b
rival to film audiences, 1754b
sets, 1475b
shift to West coast, 1476a
special-interest, 1757a
sponsored shows, 1029b
superstations, 1757a
support by AM radio network, 1474a
syndication, 1476b
transformation of sports, 1774b
urban entertainment medium, 1756b
Westerns, 84a
WGN television, 824a
WTBS television, 824a
Television programs
   All in the Family, 1477b
   American Gladiators, 1761a
   Andy Griffith Show, 1479b
   Ben Casey, 1477a
   Beverly Hillbillies, 1479b
   Catholics, 1523b
   Cheyenne, 1477a
   Cosmos, 871a
   Divorce Court, 397a
   Dr. Kildare, 1477a
   documentaries, 1478a–b
   Dragnet, 1477a
   effect on audiences, 1480b
   Eternal Light, The, 1585b
   family time, 1479a
   Father Knows Best, 154b, 179b, 232b
   Frontier Justice, 1477a
   Frontiers of Faith, 1585b
   Gunsmoke, 1477a
   Have Gun Will Travel, 1477a
   Holocaust, 1589b
   Honeymooners, The, 1477b, 1756b
   I Love Lucy, 1476a, 1477b
   late night, 1477a
   Leave It to Beaver, 232b
   Life Is Worth Living, 1523b
   live, 1478a
   Mary Tyler Moore Show, The, 1477b

   Maverick, 1477a
   miniseries, 1477b, 1482a
   Monday Night Football, 1477a, 1774b
   Nightline, 1478b
   People's Court, The, 397a–b
   Perry Mason, 397a, 1477a
   prime time, 1477a
   public affairs, 1477a
   religious, 1477a
   Rifleman, 1477a
   Roots, 1477b
   series, 1477a
   Sesame Street, 1479b
   Sixty Minutes, 1478b
   sports shows, 1756b
   Texaco Star Theater, 1476a, 1756b
   Today, 1476a, 1477a
   Untouchables, The, 179b, 1477a
   Wagon Train, 1477a
   Wide World of Sports, 1774b
   Wyatt Earp, 1477a
   You Bet Your Life, 1476a
   See It Now, 1478a
Telex, 1149b
Teller, Edward, 559a, 1584a
Telshe Yeshiva, 1585a
Telstar I satellite, 1478a
   See also Satellite communications
Temple, Shirley, 151b
Temple Emanuel, 1567b, 1568b–1569a
Tempo and Mode in Evolution (Simpson),
   869a
Temporary National Economic Committee
   (TNEC), 1229a, 1277b
Tenant farmers, 63b
   effect of AAA, 68b
Tenements, 453b
   See also Settlement houses
Tengle Children, 70a–b
Tennessee Coal, Iron, and Railroad
   Company, 844a
Tennessee Valley Authority (TVA), 15b–16a,
   70a, 432b, 524b, 1026a, 1278a, 1338b,
   1369b, 1380b
Tennis, 1768a
   African Americans, 1778a
   "Battle of Sexes," 1780a
   influence of television, 1775a
   Virginia Slims, 1780a
Tennyson, Albert, 544b
Tennyson, Alfred Lord, 1436a
Tenth Commandment, The (Goldfaden),
   1570b
Terman, Lewis, 228a, 903a, 907b, 1806b,
   1807a
Terrestrial Magnetism, 742b
Terrestrial Magnetism (Carnegie Institution
   of Washington), 742b, 746b, 752a
Texaco, 1737a
Texaco Star Theater, 1029b
Texas
   air conditioning, 72b
   resistance to high-speed passenger trains,
      1353b
Texas Medical Center, 38a
Texas Monthly, 463a
Texas Railroad Commission, 1398a
Textile industry, 27b, 28a, 29b, 67a, 69a,
   76a–b, 452a, 1024a, 1130a,b, 1146a,
   1150b, 1262b
   child labor in, 65a

   foreign competition, 313a
   imports, 1254b
   South, 63b, 66b
   turnover rate, 1098a
   world trade, 1166b
Textiles
   artificial fibers, 1786a
   cotton, 1785b
   elastic yarns, 1797b
   nylon. See Nylon
   as sign of wealth, 1785b–1786a
   silk, 1785b
   wool, 1785b
Textile Workers Union, 108b
Thackeray, William Makepeace, 1436a
Thailand, 693b
Thalberg, Sigismond, 1612a
"Thanatopsis" (Bryant), 1437a
Theater Project, 1730b, 1731a
Theaters, 1463a, 1733a, 1741a
   Eastern region, 31b
   ethnic, 1461b, 1463a
   Ford grants, 1737b
   Midwest, 55a
   nonprofit, 1727b
   playwrights, 1581b, 1733a
   regional, grants to, 1729a–b
   Syndicate, 1462b
   university programs, 1729b
   Yiddish, 1570a–b
Their Eyes Were Watching God (Hurston),
   1599a
Theme parks. See Amusement parks
Theory of Business Enterprise, The (Veblen),
   1294b
Theory of Capitalist Development, The
   (Sweezy), 1304a
Theory of Film (Kracauer), 1484a
Theory of Games and Economic Behavior, The
   (Neumann and Morgenstern), 1304b
Theory of Imperfect Competition, The
   (Robinson), 1297b
Theory of Justice, A (Rawls), 290b–291a,
   1655a
Theory of Monopolistic Competition
   (Chamberlin), 1297b
Theory of the Labor Movement, A (Selig),
   204b–205a
Theory of the Leisure Class, The (Veblen),
   1026b, 1294b, 1795b
"Theory of Valuation" (Dewey), 1651a
Theory of Value (Debreu), 1300a
Theosophical Society, 1540b, 1541a, 1542b,
   1543a,b–1544a
   and Asian religions, 1543b
   Buddhism, 1554a–b
Theravada Buddhism, 1553b–1554a
Thernstrom, Stephan, 206b
"These United States" (Nation), 279a
Thiebaud, Wayne, 1718b–1719a
Think tanks, 499b
Third International, 682a
Third-party politics, 296b, 298b, 306b,
   436b, 447b
Third Reich, 702b
   Catholics, 1519b
Third Time Around, The (Burns), 1766a
Third World, 678a
   new economic order, 692b
   newly industrializing countries, 730a
   and U.S. during Depression, 684b–685a

Third World (*cont.*)
U.S. military and political initiatives, 678b
Third World Press, 1604a
"Thirty Million New Americans" (Adamic), 174a
This Side of Paradise (Fitzgerald), 1440b
Thomas, Albert, 758a
Thomas, C. David, 1721b
Thomas, Clarence, 156b–157a, 302b, 391a–b tab, 392b–393a
Thomas, Dorothy Swaine, 920a
Thomas, John L., *as contributor*, 7a–23b
Thomas, Norman, 281b, 282b, 549b, 1497a
presidential elections, 335a–b tab
SANE, 559b
Thomas, Theodore, 1611b
Thomas, William I., 173b, 904a, 922b–923a
Thomas Aquinas, 1516b
Thomashevsky, Boris, 1570a
Thomist, 1517a
Thompson, E. P., 205a, 932b
Thompson, Helen, 903b
Thompson, J. Walter, agency, 1023a
Thompson, King, 454b, 459a, 460a
Thompson, William R., 874a
Thompson Products, 1141a, 1145a
Thomson, Elihu, 836a
Thomson, J. Edgar, Works, 1135a
Thomson-Houston Company, 835b, 1137b–1138a
Thoreau, Henry David, 204a, 549b, 1436b
Mumford and, 11a–b
Thornburgh, Dick, 987a
Thorndike, Edward L., 879a, 1806a–b
Thought, 1517a
Three Cities (Asch), 1569b
"Three Essays of the Theory of Sexuality" (Freud), 906a
3M. *See* Minnesota Mining and Manufacturing Company
Three Mile Island (Pa.), 1346b
Three Pillars of Zen, The (Kapleau), 1555b
Three Places in New England (Ives), 1613a
Three Rival Versions of Moral Enquiry (MacIntyre), 291a
Threshold Test Ban Treaty (1974), 561a–b
Thünen, J. H. von, 16b–17a
Thurmond, J. Strom, 25a, 391a
presidential elections, 335a–b tab
Thurow, Lester, 1117b, 1259a
Tibetan Buddhism, 1555b–1556a
Tiffany, Paul, 844a
Tigerman, Stanley, 1665b
Tijerina, Reies, 95a
Tikkun, 1587a
Till, Emmet, 153b
Tillich, Paul, 1505a
Tilly, Charles, 325b
Timber, 1384a
conservationism and, 1361a
and early settlers, 1401a–b
relative producer price index for lumber, 1900–1987, *1402a–b*
transportation cost, 1401b
U.S. per capita consumption of timber products, 1900–1987, *1404a–b*
U.S. production and consumption of industrial roundwood, *1403a–b*
See also Logging industry
Time, 31b, 191a, 1481a–b, 1532b, 1706a, 1713a

on New York City, 468a
Time Inc., 824a, 1024b, 1479b
Times (London), 1746b
Time Warner, 1470a, 1482b, 1488a
See also Time Inc.; Warner Brothers; Warner Communications
Tin Pan Alley, 1462b, 1571b, 1580a, 1614a
Tipton, Steven, 290b
Tire factories, 46b, 47a, 57a
Titanic (ship), 1471b, 1473b
Titchener, Edward Bradford, 878a–b
TNEC. *See* Temporary National Economic Committee
Tobacco industry, 1131a–b
effect of AAA, 68b
South, 66b
See also Crops: tobacco
Tobacco taxation, 1314a
Tobey, Mark, 1714b
Tobin, James, 1026a, 1299a, 1300b
Tocqueville, Alexis de, 202b, 295a, 308b, 427a, 569a, 590b, 591b, 1067a
on American associations, 491a, 510b
on American culture, 1611a
Democracy in America, 196b
Todorov, Tzvetan, 133a
Toennies, Ferdinand, 918b
Tog, 1569a
Tojo, Hidekei, 637b
Toklas, Alice B., 1697b
Tolan, Eddie, 1772b
Tolman, Edward A., 887b–888a
Tolstoy, Leon, 549b
Tomas, C. David, 1721b
Tonkin Gulf resolution (1964), 363b
Tooker, George, 1714a
Toomer, Jean (Nathan Eugene), 150b, 1456a
Cane, 1597a
Torero, Mario, 1720b
Tornadoes, 41b
Torrey Canyon, 1376b
Toscanini, Arturo, 1616b
To the Finland Station (Wilson), 1442a–b
Touching Evil (Rosen), 1589b
Toulmin, Stephen, 1655a
Tourism, 38b, 1167a
airlines, 795a
South, 75b
sunbelt, 462b–463a
West, 81a, 91b–92a
"Toward Neutral Principles of Constitutional Law" (Weschler), 388a
Townsend, Francis, 199a, 282a, 480a
Townsend, Luther T., 861a
Toxic Substances Control Act (1976), 1375b
Toxic waste, 76b
Toynbee, Arnold, 63a
Toys "R" Us, 814a
TPO. *See* Traditional party organizations
Tractatus Logico-Philosophicus (Wittgenstein), 1646b
Tractors, 50b, 56a, 57a, 1141a,b
industrial growth, 1160b
Trade
agreements, 1263a
associations, 38b, 310b, 313b
balance, 1167a, 1169b, *1178a–b,* 1244a, 1256b, 1259b
barriers, 723b, 725a, 726a, 731b
decline during Depression, 683b
deficits, 313a, 1202b

ethnic niches, 169a
liberalization, 726b, 727a, 728a, 729b, 1155b, 1262b,1263a
natural resources, 1396a
negotiations, 317a
policy, 1271b
protectionist policies, 1193b
ratios for selected industries, 1976 and 1977, 1200b tab
surplus, 1166b
wars, 724a
Trade cycles
equilibrium theory, 1183a–1188a
overproduction, 1185b
price inflexibility, 1185b–1186a
secular cycles, 1184a
underconsumption, 1185b
See also Business cycles
Trade Expansion Act. *See* Omnibus Trade and Competitiveness Act
Trade-related intellectual property rights (TRIPS), 1262b
Trade-related investment matters (TRIMS), 1262b
Trade Union Congress (Britain), 310b
Trading partners, 1244a, 1245b, 1246b, 1249a,b, 1253b, 1262a
Trading with the Enemy Act, 523a
Tradition, 1587a
Traditional party organizations (TPO), 297a
Traffic
courts, 395b
safety, 1377b
Traffic in Souls, The, 223a
Traffic Safety Act (1966), 527b
"Tragedy of the Commons, The" (Hardin), 1374b, 1375b–1376a
Tragedy of Waste, The (Chase), 1027a
Trains. *See* Railroads
Transamerica Building (San Franciso), 1687b
Transamerica Corporation, 1470a
Transcendentalists, 1541a
Transcendental Meditation, 1551b
Transistors, 812a, 818b, 848b, 1474a
See also Solid-state electronics
Transjordan, 679b
"Trans-National America" (Bourne), 258a
Transportation, 56b, 1130a, 1155a, 1158b, 1281a, 1349b
commercial, 1144b
Congress, 356a–b
cost, 38a
deregulation, 1284a
development, 1340a
domestic intercity passenger traffic, percent of total volume, 1950–1990, 1352a tab
early mergers, 1218a
economic performance, 1160a
farming, 45a
federal outlays and private railroad investment, 1970-1988, 1350a–b tab
importance for natural resources, 1391a
intercity freight traffic by type of transport, percent of tonnage, 1939–1990, 1350a tab
market restoration, 1285a
meat-packing industry, 1132b
regulation, 431b, 433a, 1168a–b
shipping, 85a
systems, 1128a,b, 1130a

West, 83b, 88b
world trade, 1166b
Transportation Act (1920), 519b
Transportation Act (1940), 1341a
Transportation Workers Association, 148b
Trans World Airlines, 1030a
Travel
  democratization, 1750b–1752a
  middle class, 1746a
  upper class, 1744a
Travelers' Aid societies, 223b
Traveling exhibitions, 1465a
Treasury, Department of the, 358a,b, 1254a,
  1316a–1317a, 1323b
  under Mellon, 1318a
  plan for "Modernizing the Financial
    System" (1991), 1238b
  Section on Painting and Sculpture, 1730a
Treasury Relief Art Project, 1705b
Treaty of Brest-Litovsk (1918), 628a
Treaty of Guadalupe Hidalgo (1848), 140a
Treaty of Portsmouth (1905), 678a
Treaty of Rome (1957), 726b, 853b, 1253b
Treaty of Versailles, 551a, 574a, 722b, 1249b
  and stability of world finances, 1193a
Treaty of Washington (1922). *See* Five-
  power Naval Limitation Treaty (1922)
Treaty on conventional arms forces in
  Europe (CFE) (1990), 564b
Treaty on Open Skies, 564b
Treaty on the Elimination of Intermediate-
  Range and Shorter-Range Missiles
  (1978), 566a–b tab
Tree farming, 1403a
Tree Grows in Brooklyn, A (B. Smith), 34a
Treemonisha (Joplin), 1596a, 1615a
Trends in American Economic Growth
  (Denison), 1165b
Trial, The (Reisman), 1714a
Tribune Tower, *1680b*, 1681a
  competition for, 1680a
Trigere, Pauline, 1790b
Trilling, Lionel, 1443b, 1444a, 1448a,
  1581b
  "On the Teaching of Modern Literature,"
    1448b–1449a, 1452b
TRIMS. *See* Trade-related investment
  matters
Trine, Ralph Waldo, 1496a, 1546a
Trinity Church (New York), 36b
Tripartite Agreement (1936), 724a
Tri-Partite Pact, 637b
TRIPS. *See* Trade-related intellectual
  property rights
Trist, Eric, 1119a
Trost and Trost, 1681a
Trotsky, Leon, 1443a
Trotter, Monroe, 145b, 146a
Trow, James, 934b
Trucking industry, 1160b
  cartel-like regulation, 1341a
  deregulation, 1283b
  South, 72a
  World War II, 1344b
"True Americanism" (Brandeis), 258a
Trueblood, Benjamin F., 543a,b
Truly Disadvantaged, The (W. J. Wilson),
  210a
Truman, Harry S., 284b, 321a, 322b, *333a,*
  337b, 577b, *647a,* 1278b, 1279a, 1280a
  arts patronage, 1735a

blue-collar vote, 300a
Campaign of truth, 705a
civil rights, 73a, 436b, 437a
demobilization, 607a
draft violators, 556a
foreign policy, 579a–580b, 725b
Graham, Billy, 1504a
health legislation, 997b
and Hoover Commission report, 526b
industrial research, 847a, 849a
limited war, 662b
national security state, 333b, 334a
nuclear weapons, 750b
presidential elections, 334b, 335a–b tab
public approval, 336b
Special Committee to Investigate the
  National Defense Program, 606a
steel mills seizure, 386a, 412a
Supreme Court appointments, 389b
vetoes, 347a tab
Truman Doctrine, 579b, 608a, 725b, 849b
Trust Indenture Act (1939), 1227a–b tab,
  1228a
Trust Problem, The (Jenks), 1295a
Trusts, 1132b, 1188b, 1215b
  growing influence, 1291a–b
Truth in Lending Act (1968), 527b
TRW, 849b, 1145a, 1150b
  work reform, 1119b
Tschumi, Bernard, 1689b
Tsiolkowsky, Konstantin, 785b
Tsukunft, 1569a
Tuberculosis, 959b, 960b, 977a
  drug-resistant strains, 970a
  government health care, 989b
  leading cause of death in 1900, 968a
  tuberculin skin test, 973b
Tucker, Richard, 1578a
Tucker, Sophie, 1464a, 1579b
Tufts, James Hayden, 1640b
  in *Contemporary American Philosophy,*
    1641a
Tugwell, Rexford G., 281b, 1296a, 1298b,
  1305b, 1369b
  Greenbelt program, 460b
Tulane University, 1824b
Tulis, Jeffrey, 328a
Tullock, Gordon, 1302a
Tunney, Jim, 1768a
Turkey, 608a, 679a, 682b, 689b
Turner, Frederick Jackson, 7a, 8a–9b, 17a,
  42a, 49a, 55a, 83a, 846b, 864b, 1380a
  "Significance of the Frontier in American
    History, The," 1357b
Turner, Ted, 1478a
Turner, Thomas Wyatt, 1517b
Turner Broadcasting Network, 1032b
Turrell, James, 1718b
Tuskegee Institute, 1595a, 1598b, 1809b
Tussman, Malka Heifetz, 1570a
Tuve, Merle, 752a–b, 753a–b, 763a
TVA. *See* Tennessee Valley Authority
TVA: Democracy on the March (Lilienthal),
  10a
TVA (Lilienthal), 748b
TV Guide, 1482b
Twain, Mark, 33b, 274a, 1437a–b, 1438a,
  1746b
  Adventures of Huckleberry Finn, The, 1438a,
    1456a
  on baseball, 1745a

Connecticut Yankee in King Arthur's Court,
  A, 1438a
Innocents Abroad, The, 1746a
  "Mysterious Stranger, The," 1438a
Twatchtman, John H., 1695b
Twentieth Century Fox, 1466b, 1754a
  foreign ownership, 715a
Twentieth Century Fund, 18b, 1735b
Twenty Years at Hull-House (Addams), 275a
Two Cultures, The (Snow), 1453a
"Two Dogmas of Empiricism" (Quine),
  1649b–1650a
Twombly, Robert, *1666a, 1670a, 1674b,*
  1678a–b, 1683a–b, 1690a–b, 1691a–b
  as contributor, 1665a–1692b
Two-party politics, 296b
Tyack, David, 1806b
Tydings-McDuffie Act (1934), 97a
Typhoid, 959b, 960b, 968a
Typhus, 942b
Typographical Union, 1749b
Tyson, Mike, 397b

U

U-boats. *See* Submarines
Udall, Morris, 301a
UFO cults, 1557b
Ugarte, Manuel, 702a
Ukraine, 565b
Ullman, Al, 1326b
Ullman, Edward L., 18a
Ulysses solar polar mission, 790a
Un-American Activities Committee
  (House), 178b, 265a, 1469b
  artists depiction of, 1714a
  Hollywood investigation, 1467a–1468b,
    1754b
  student protest against hearings, 1830a
  television coverage, 1478b
  Writers and Theater Projects
    investigation, 1731a
Unanswered Question, The (Ives), 1613b
Uncle Tom's Children (Wright), 1601a
Underclass, 209a–210b
  family dissolution, 236a–b
Underclass, The (Auletta), 210a
"Underclass" Debate, The (Katz), 210b
Under Fire (North), 589a
Under God (Wills), 1497b
Underwood, Oscar, 599a
Underwood Tariff (1913), 721b, 1271b,
  1314b
Undistributed profits tax, 1320b–1321a
Unemployment, 1169a
  aggregate, (in percent), 1929-1940, *1194a*
  compensation, 433a, 439b, 1075b
  consumption, 1024a
  Great Depression, 1073a, 1161a, *1162a–b,*
    1163a
  insurance cuts under Reagan, 1204a
  Midwest, 57b
  nineteenth century, 1068b
  structural in the 1930s, 1197b
UNESCO. *See* United Nations Economic
  and Social Council (UNESCO)
UNIA. *See* Universal Negro Improvement
  Association (UNIA)
Uniates, 1547b

Uniform Commercial Code (1950), 1411b, 1420b

Unilever (Lever Brothers), 1249b

Union Carbide, 846a, 1138b, 1143b, 1145b, 1146a, 1147a

Union Carbon & Carbide, 1143b

Union Democracy, 934b

Union for Traditional Conservative Judaism, 1589a

Union League Club, 1726b

Union of American Hebrew Congregations, 1566a

Union of Orthodox Jewish Congregations of America, 1575b

Union of Orthodox Rabbis of the United States and Canada, 1575b

Union of Radical Political Economists, 1304a

Union of Soviet Social Republics. *See* Soviet Union

Union Oil of California, 87a

Unions. *See* Labor unions

Union Theological Seminary, 1501b, 1504a, 1505b

Unitarian-Universalist Association, 1493b–1494a, 1541a

United Aircraft, 1145a

United Airlines, 795a, 1238a

United Artists, 1465b, 1469a,b, 1470a, 1754a

United Automobile Workers, 110a, 310b, 314b, 1108b, 1110a,b
  Equal Rights Amendment, 120b

United Booking Office of America, 1463b–1464a

United Cannery, Agricultural, Packing, and Allied Workers of American, 149a

United Church of Christ, 1492b, 1493a

United Cigar Store Chain, 1043b

United Committee of South Slavic Americans, 178b

United Farm Workers, 95a, 115b, 149a,b

United Federal Workers, 1108b

United Fruit Company, 654a, 1471b

United Jewish Appeal, 1583a, 1587b

United Mine Workers of America, 167a, 310b, 1108b, 1110a

United Nations, 264b–265a, 686b, 1252b
  Centre for Transnational Corporations, 1257b
  founding, 556b–557b
  headquarters, 1685b
  Jewish state in Palestine, 1584a
  Korea, 782a

United Nations Association, 556b

United Nations Atomic Energy Commission, 557b

United Nations Economic and Social Council (UNESCO), 710b
  Statement on Race, 869b

United Nations Resolution (678), 364b

United Office and Professional Workers of America, 1108b

United Palestine Appeal, 1583a

United Press (UP), 698b

United Shoe Machinery, 1136b

United States and the Washington Conference, The (Buckley), 599a

United States bicentennial 1976, 58b

United States Bureau of Education, 1408b, 1409a

United States Catholic Conference bishops, 1532a

United States Conference of Mayors, 1081a

United States Geological Survey (USGS), 8a, 1389a

United States Industrial Commission, 107b, 1268a, 1269b, 1271a, 1291b, 1295a
  Jenks, Jeremiah, 1295a

United States Information Agency (USIA), 614a, 705b–706a

United States manufacturing productivity
  compared to Britain, 1202a
  compared to Japan, 1202a
  compared to West Germany, 1202a

United States National Health Interview Survey, 979b

"United States Objectives and Programs for National Security," 610b

United States Public Health Service, 942a
  Veneral Disease Division research, 951a

United States Railroad Administration, 519b

United States Reclamation Service, 1272b

United States Rubber Company, 1109a, 1133b, 1142a

United States trade in manufactured goods, 1965–1980, 1200b tab

United States v. *Carolene Products* (1938), 384a, 435b
  footnote four, 413b–414a, 419a,b

United Steelworkers Union, 999a, 1108b

United Synagogue, 1574b

United Technologies, 1145a

United World Federalists, 558b

Unity, 1540a, 1545b

Unity School of Christianity, 1546a

Universalism. *See* Unitarian-universalist Association
  decline, 267a

Universal Negro Improvement Association (UNIA), 96a, 145b–146a, 259b, 1599a–b

Universal Peace Union, 542a

Universal Product Code (UPC), 1032a

Universal Studio, 1469a, 1754a
  television, 1476b

Universities, **1819a–1839b**
  African American studies, 183b, 1604a–1605a
  Black studies, 183b, 1604a–1605a
  versus colleges, 1824b
  defense contracting as source of revenue, 613b
  Eastern region, 32a–b, 32b
  ethnic studies, 183b
  foundation staffs and, 502a–b
  German model, 1820b
  Jewish studies, 1579a–b
  Jewish universities, 1585b–1586a
  laboratories, 1826b
  liberal Protestants, 1495b
  music departments, 1612b, 1621a
  recruitment programs, 1834a
  research institutes, 1824b
  Semitics departments, 1579b
  South, 72a, 75b
  systematization of knowledge, 198a
  violence on campus, 1835a
  Women's studies, 1831b
  See also Catholic colleges and universities; Colleges; Higher education

Universities Research Association, 760a–b

University Government (Cattell), 1823b

University of Birmingham, 1486b

University of California, 1821a
  Berkeley, 745b
  effect of McCarthyism, 1832a
  mining college, 1389b

University of Chicago, 49b, 1495b, 1820b, 1821a
  philosophers, 1640b
  Rockefellers and, 494b
  Rosenwald, Julius, 494b

University of Colorado, 1825a

University of Iowa
  women's debate club, 51b
  Wood, Grant, at fine arts school, 1827a

University of Judaism, 1585b

University of Kansas, 839a

University of Maryland, 32b

University of Michigan
  business support, 1825a
  foreign students, 55b
  Robert Frost, writer in residence, 1827a
  speech code, 1834a

University of Mississipi, 1828b

University of New Mexico, 91a

University of North Carolina
  Chapel Hill, 68a
  theater studies, 1827a

University of Notre Dame, 1528b
  NBC, 1776b

University of Pennsylvania, 1821b
  law school, 31a

University of Pittsburgh, 839a

University of Rochester, 32b, 944b

University of Southern California, 1828a

University of Virginia, 1819a–b

University of Wisconsin, 55a, 1825a
  Biotron, 758b
  student violence, 1830b

Unsafe at Any Speed (Nader), 1031a

Unskilled workers, 166a, 205a

Unterberg, Israel, 1567a, 1575a

Untermyer, Samuel, 1220a, 1221a

Unwanted Workers (Wilcock and Franke), 112b

UP. *See* United Press (UP)

Updike, John, 34b

Up from Slavery (Washington), 1595b

Upjohn, 1148a

Upper class
  country clubs, 1763a–b
  leisure, 1743b–1744b

Upward Bound, 1081a

Uranium, 85b–86a

Urbanization, 1019a–b
  and consumption, 1019a–b
  Eastern region, 26a
  effect on family, 222a
  employment for artists, 1693b
  taxation, 1314b
  West, 88b–92a
  women and, 902a
  See also Cities

Urban League, 178a

Urban renewal, 451a, 458a–b, 465a,b–466a, 1734b
  Catholics, 1524a
  federal programs, 1325a
  Lincoln Center, 1734b

Urban villages, 468a

Uris, Leon, 1587b

"U.S. Catholicism: A Church Divided," 1532b
U.S. English, 188a
U.S. News & World Report, 1481b
U.S. Steel Company, 742a, 1096b, 1142b, 1254b
  creation, 1135b, 1218a–1219b
  foreign investments, 1246b
  Gary Works, 45b, 46a
  and research, 843b–844b
  unions, 1108b
USA Today, 1481b
USDA. *See* Agriculture, Department of
Uses of the University, The (Kerr), 1829b
USGS. *See* United States Geological Survey (USGS)
Usselman, Steven W., *as contributor,* 799a–829b
Utilities, 1019b
  foreign investments, 1248b
  investment expenditures for new private construction of public utilities, millions of dollars, 1915–1990, 1339a–b tab
  public utility holding companies, 1223a
  regulation, 1275a
  regulation of municipal services, 1335a–b
Utopian communities, 460a–b
Utopian socialists, 918b

V

Va'ad Hatzolah, 1583b
Vacuum tube technology, 803b–804a
Vail, Theodore N., 801b–802a,b, 837b, 1414a
Vajrayana Buddhism, 1554a
Valentino, Rudolph, 173a
Valéry, Paul, 1442a
Value added by manufacture, 1129a–b tab
Value added manufacturing, 1139b, 1144a, 1146a
Value-added taxes, 1326b, 1328b
Value of Money, The (Anderson), 1293b
Van Alen, William, 1682a
Van Allen radiation belts, 755b, 787a
van Amerongen, 1236a
Vance, Cyrus, 561a
Vance, Rupert, 10b, 13b, 14b
Vandenberg, Arthur S., 55b, 334b, 481b, 482a, 554a, 557a, 579b, 615b, 725b
Vanderbilt, Cornelius, 769a
Vanderbilt, George Washington, 1669a
Vanderbilt, William K., 1669a
Vanderbilt University, 68a, 75b
Van Dusen, Henry, 1504a
Van Gogh, Vincent, 1698a, 1699a, 1705a
Vanguard rocket, 754b, 755b, 787a
Van Helden, Albert, 744a
Van Hise, Charles R., 1822a
Van Sweringen brothers, 454b, 459a, 460a
Van Waters, Miriam, 236b
Vanzetti, Bartolomeo, 172b
Vaquero (Jiménez), 1720b
Vardaman, James K., 66b
Varèse, Edgard, 1617a
Variation and Evolution in Plants (Stebbins), 869a
Variety, 31a
  on nickelodeons, 1465a

Variety shows, 1025a
Vassar College, 32a, 102a, 1819b
  coeducation, 1834b
  field hockey team, *1765a–b*
Vatican Councils
  First, 1511a
  Second, 1512a, 1522a–b, 1526b, 1527a–b, 1533a–1534b
Vatter, Harold, 1077b
Vaudeville, 1021b, 1461b, 1462b, 1463b–1464b, 1473a, 1748b
  Jews, 1579b
  Midwest, 48a
  national entertainment network, 1464a
Vaughan, Sarah, 1623b, *1624b*
VCRs. *See* Videocassette recorders
Veblen, Thorstein, 921a–b, 1026b–1027a, 1290b, 1294a–1295a, 1296a, 1303b, 1657a, 1763b
  Theory of the Leisure Class, The, 1795b
Vechten, Carl Van, 1593a, *1616, 1624a, 1697a, 1704a, 1713b*
Vecoli, Rudolph J., *as contributor,* 161a–193b
Vedanta Society, 1541a, 1550a, 1551a
Veeck, Bill, 1778a
Veiller, Lawrence, 453b
Velde, Harold, 338b
Velikovsky, Immanuel, 871a
Venereal disease, 223a
Venturi, Robert, 1453b, 1665a, 1689b
  Learning From Las Vegas, 1665a
  Tucker House, 1665b
Vernacular architecture, 1665a
  modern, 1688b
Verne, Jules, 785a
Vertical integration, 1040b–1046a
Vertinsky, Patricia, 901b
"Very Idea of a Conceptual Scheme, The" (Davidson), 1660a
Veterans
  hospitals. *See* Veterans hospitals
  programs, 482b
Veterans Administration, 1421a
  mortgages, 1029a
Veterans hospitals, 995b
  desegregation, 1002b
  federal funding, 1001a
Vetoes, presidential, 347a tab
Vezin, Charles, 1703a
VHS. *See* JVC: Video Home System
Victorianism, 1436a–1437b, 1438a
Victor recording company, 807a
Victory, 703b
Victory Program, 603a
Videocassette recorders (VCRs), 823b, 825a–b, 1032b, 1033a, 1470b, 1480a
Video games, 1470b
Vienna Circle, 1645b, 1647a–1648b
Vienna Summit, 584b
Vietnamese refugees, 186a
Vietnam Moratorium Committee, 562b
Vietnam Scene (Hanson), 1719b
Vietnam syndrome, 672a
Vietnam Veterans Against the War, 562a
Vietnam Veterans Memorial, 268a, 269a
Vietnam War, 267a–b, 440b, 615b, 664a–671a, *665a–b,* 690b, 1282a
  aircraft, 782b–784b
  antiwar movement. *See* Anti Vietnam War movement
  and colleges, 1830b

Congress, 363b–364a
  effect on economy, 1084a,b
  foreign policy, 585a–587b, 671b
  foreign trade, 1256b
  immigration, 97a
  imperial presidency, 362a
  Johnson, 343b, 344a
  limited war, 651a, 671b–672a
  national budget, 1345a
  Nixon, 344b, 345b
  political art, 1719b
  protests, 1529b
  religious liberals, 1505b, 1506b
  secret peace talks in Paris, 671a
  social and economic cost, 1235a
  taxation, 1324b
  television, 1478b, 1479a
  Tet Offensive, 585b, 669a
  Vietnamization, 669b–670a
Vietor, Richard H. K., *as contributor,* 1155a–1181b
Vigilancia, 625a
Viking Portable Conrad, The, 1447b
Viking space program, 756b, 788b
Villa, Francisco, 548a
"Village Blacksmith, The" (Longfellow), 1437a
Village Voice, 31a
Villanova University, 32b
Villard, Fanny Garrison, 546b
Villard, Henry, 1669b
Villard, Oswald Garrison, 547b
Villarreal, José Antonio, 1456b
Villiers de l'Isle-Adam, Auguste de, 1448b
Vindication of the Rights of Woman, A (Wollstonecraft), 918a
Viner, Jacob, 1300a
Vinson, Carl, 72a, 600a
Vinson, Fred M., 387a, 390a–b tab
Vinson-Trammell Act (1934), 600a
Violence
  comic books, 1483b
  movies, 1468b
Viollet-le-Duc, Eugène-Emmanuel, 1668b
Visible Hand, The (Chandler), 197b, 1042a, 1158b, 1302b
Visual arts, **1693a–1723b**
  Federal Arts Project, 1730b
  Ford Foundation, 1733a
  visual culture, 1481b
Vital Center, The (Schlesinger), 285a
Vitamins, 977b
Vivekananda, Swami, 1550a,b–1551a
Vocabulary
  identity politics, 156a
  name-calling in ethnicization, 164a–b
  and race as a social reality, 133a
  racist, 138a
Vocational Education Act (1963), 1812a–b tab
Vocational rehabilitation
  expansion under Johnson, 485b
  federal support, 477b
Vogel, David, 209a
Vogel, Ezra, 1259a
Vogue, 31a
Voice of America, 614a, 703b, 705a, 706b
Volcano under the City, The, 255a
Volcker, Paul, 731a, 732a, 1172b, 1174a–b, 1327b
Volkswagen Beetle, 1064a

Volunteers in Service to America (VISTA), 1080b
von Neumann, John, 811b
Vostok satellite, 787b
Voting
   gender patterns, 121a
   ideological choice, 307b
   registration drives, 507b
Voting rights, 427b
   Fifteenth Amendment, 403a
   South, 65b, 71a–b
Voting Rights Act (1965), 74a–b, 288b, 295a, 342a, 365a, 366b, 447b, 1602b
   litigation under, 394b
Voyager space program, 788b, *790a*
V (Pynchon), 1452b

W

Wade, John Donald, 14b
Wages, 1170a, 1172b, *1178a–b*
   doctrine of high wages, 1193a
   Midwest, 46b, 50a, 51a, 57b
   minimum, 434a
   raised by Ford, Henry, 1099b
   real average weeekly wages, 1955-1991, *1171a–b*
   South, 68b, 69a,b, 70b, 71a
Wagner, Robert F., 997a
Wagner Act (1935), 69a, 310a, 381a, 432b, 524a, 999a, 1108a, 1109a, 1277b, 1750b
   upheld by Supreme Court, 382a, 410a
Wagner-Dingell bills, 997b
Wainwright, Jonathan, 640b
Waiting for the Signal (Morris), 382a
Walcott, C. D., 744a
Wald, Abraham, 1299b
Wald, Lillian D., 277b, 477b, 546b, 547b, *548a,* 549b, 1567a,b
Walden Two (Skinner), 891b
Wales, Julia Grace, 546b
Walker, Alice, 1456a, 1604b
Walker, C. J. (Madame), 1792a
Walker, Charles, 1112b
Walker, Francis, 7b, 1291a
Walker, George, 1596a,b
Walker, Moses Fleetwood, 1770a
Walker in the City, A (Kazin), 34a, 1586b
Walkowitz, Abraham, 1579a, 1698a, 1704b, 1721b
Wallace, David, 21a
Wallace, George, 58b, 155b, 181b, 344b, 388b, 389a,b, 422b
   presidential elections, 336a–b tab
   third-party politics, 296b
Wallace, Henry, 1321b
Wallace, Henry A., 50b, 178a, 281b, 283b, 284b, 556b, 1369b
   presidential elections, 335a–b tab
Wallace, Henry C., 51a
Wallace, Lila, 1737b
Wallace Foundation, 1737b
Wallace's Farmer, 51a,b
Wallant, Edward, 1589b
Wallin, Paul, 103a
Wall Street, 1211a
   concentration of investment banks, 1220b
   investigation by Pujo Committe, 1220a

Wall Street Journal, 31a, 1481b
   on banking fragmentation, 1220b
   on development of PertPlus shampoo, 1063a–b
Wall Street (Strand), 1702a
Wal-Mart, 1032a
Walras, Leon, 1289b–1290a, 1299b
Walt Disney Studios. *See* Disney Studios
Walter Baker's Chocolate, 1050a
Walters, Barbara, 1477b
Walters, Ronald G., *as contributor,* 1461a–1490b
Walters Art Gallery, 33a
Walton, Izaak, 58b
Walton, Richard, 1119a
Walton League. *See* Izaak Walton League
Walzer, Michael, 291a
Wanderer, The Catholics, 1533b
Wang, An, 821b, 823a
Wang Industries, 821b–822a
War
   industries, 71a
   outlawry of, 553b
   prevention, 553a–b
   readiness, 748b–749a
War, declaration of, 570b, 573b
   Congress, 356b, 363b–364b, 372b
   executive branch, 363b
War against the Jews, The (Dawidowicz), 1589b
War and Society (Polenberg), 603a
Warburg, Edward, 1727b
Warburg, Felix, 1567a
Ward, Edward, 1807a
Ward, Harry F., 1497a
Ward, Lester Frank, 860a, 918a, 919b
War Department, 598b
Ware, Caroline, 161b, 175b
War Finance Board, 1416a
War Food Administration. *See* Food Administration
Warhol, Andy, *1716a,* 1716a,b
War Industries Board, 257a, 407a, 597a, 748b, 1273b, 1416a
War Industries Board, The (Cuff), 597a
War Labor Board, 999a
War Labor Disputes Act, 525b
War Labor Relations Board, 1077a
War Manpower Commission, 603a
Warner, Charles, 274a
Warner, Jack, 1467b
Warner, W. Lloyd, 199b, 925b, 1112b
Warner Brothers, 1030a, 1467b, 1469a, 1470a, 1580a, 1752b, 1754a
   Looney Tunes, 703b
   television, 1476b
   See also Time Warner; Warner Communications
Warner Communications, 1470a
Warnke, Paul, 560b
War on drugs, 419a
War on Poverty, 441a, 466a
   national budget, 1345a
War Powers Acts (1941, 1942), 525b
"War Powers" (Katzmann), 363b
War Powers Resolution (1973), 364a–b, 413a, 587b, 616a
War Production Board, 262b, 1027b, 1278a
War Prohibition Act (1918), 407b
War Refugee Board, 1583b

Warren, Earl, 387a, 388a, 390a–b tab, 415b, 417b, 440a, 605b, 1813a
   on case backlog, 394a
   presidential elections, 335a–b tab
Warren, Kenneth W., *as contributor,* 1593a–1607b
Warren, Leonard, 1621b
Warren, Robert Penn, 10a,b, 14a,b, 1444b
   All the King's Men, 1445b, 1446a–b
Warren, William, 1323a
Warren and Wetmore, 1671b
Warren Court, 386b–389a, 416b
   antimajoritarian, 422b
   Eisenhower and, 438b
   equal protection, 419b
   political attack on, 422b
War Resisters League, 555b
War Resources Board, 602a
War Risk Insurance Act (1917), 995b, 996a–b tab
Wars
   estimates of total costs and number of battle deaths, 648a–b tab
   of national liberation, 616b
   presidential power, 326a
Warshow, Robert, 1581b
Wartime science projects, 848b
War Trade Board, 1273b
Wasdworth Atheneum, 33a
Washburn, Margaret, 879a
Washburn-Crosby, 1131a
Washing machines, automatic, 1028a
Washington, Booker T., 142b, 145a–b, 212b, 1595a, 1598b
   counsel to McKinley, 145a
   counsel to T. Roosevelt, 145a
   education, 1809b
   Up from Slavery, 1595b
Washington, George, 37a
Washington, Harold, 58b
Washington, D.C.
   growth, 330b
   suburbs, 460b
Washington Heights
   Judaism, 1585a
Washington Naval Conference (1921–1922), 551b, 575b, 599a, 632a, 682a
Washington Naval Treaty (1922), 566a–b tab, 599b
Washington Post, 393b, 397b, 468a
Washington University, 1821b
Wasp and Pear (Murphy), 1704b
WASPs in elite professions, 1413a–b
Water
   agriculture and, 1386b
   conservationism and, 1361a
   health, 975a
   impact of testing on health, 973b
   reclamation, 1362b
   See also water supply
Watergate affair, 312b–313a, 346a, 530a, 616b
   Nixon, 443a, 587b
   Republican party, 313a
Waterman, Alan, 757b
Waters, Ethel, 1464a
Waters, Mary, 155a, 190a
Waters, Vincent, 1524b
Waters and Hainlin, *1767a–b*
Water supply, 90b, 1165a
   allocation, 83a

for irrigation, 88a
management, 84b
resources, 98b
rights, 89a, 92b
West, 81a,b
See also Aqueducts; Aquifers
Water Tower (Chicago), 1673a
Water transportation, 1340a–b
freight hauling, 1351a
internal waterborne tonnage and federal
expenditures for rivers and harbors,
1900–1988, 1340a–b tab
Watkins, Arthur, 92a
Watson, James, 763a,b
Watson, John Broadus, 279a, 879a,b–880a,
886a, 887b, 888a,b–889a
Watson, Thomas, Jr., 1148b
Watson, Thomas J., Sr., 847a
Watts
race riots, 96a, 180b
theater project, 1738b
Watts, Alan, 1555a
Watts Tower (Rodia), *1719a,* 1719a
Wave mechanics, 845a
Wayne, John, 84a, 1488b
Ways, Max, 441a
Wayside Inn, 37a
Wealth
inequality, 1071a, 1085b
percentage held by top 1 percent of
Americans, *203a*
redistribution, 514b, 1313b
signaled by clothing, 1785b, 1786b, 1787a
taxation, 1315b, 1320a
taxes, 1311a
Wealth and poverty, **1067a–1090b**
Wealth of Nations, The (Smith), 274b, 1017a,
1311a
Weapons
development, 841a, 849b
systems, 1144a
We Are Not a Minority (Torero), 1720b
Weavers, 1627a
Webb, Walter Prescott, 10a,b
Webb-Pomerene Act (1918), 1248b
Weber, Adna, 454b, 460a
Weber, Alfred, 17a
Weber, Eugen, 252a
Weber, John Pitman, 1719b
Weber, Max, 199b, 513b, 924b, 926a,b,
932a, 1697b, 1698a, 1703a, 1721b
Brooklyn Bridge, 1701b
Wedemeyer, Albert C., 603a
Weegee, 1709b
Weekend, 1750b
We Hold These Truths (Murray), 1522a
Weicker, Lowell, 30a
Weiland, Steven, 936a
Weill, Kurt, 1584a
Weinberg, Alvin, 753b–754a, 761b
Weinreich, Max, 1584b
Weinstein, James, 207b
Weintraub, Sidney, 1304b
Weir, J. Alden, 1695b
Weisberg, Harold, 1588a
Weismann, August, 860a, 862a
Weiss, Cythnia, 1719b
Weiss, Paul, 1652b
Weiss, Richard, 211b
Weiss-Rosmarin, Trude, 1582a
Weitzman, Leonore, 123a

Weizman, Ezer, 1587b
Welfare, 433a–b, 437a, 445b, 1325a
categorical assistance, 1074a, 1075a,
1082a
class discrimination, 123a
dependency, 484a, 1074a–b, 1088a
eligibility requirements, 1082b
gender discrimination, 121b, 123a,b
grant-in-aid structure, 478a
growth, 1309a–b
homeless men, 123a
impact on the family, 122b, 238b–239a
indexed benefits, 1076a
inhibited growth in predepression, 1071b
medicine program, 1000b
New Deal, 300b
race discrimination, 123a,b
rehabilitation, 485a,b
work requirements, 487a
Welfare capitalism, 475a
Welfare Conference, 1515a
Welfare rights movement, 1082b
Welfare state, 1072b
effect on ethnic communities, 211b
Ely and, 274b
gender analysis, 121b
traditional family and, 122a
Welles, Orson, 1755a
Welles, Sumner, 556b, 685b
Wellesley College, 32a, 102a, 1819b
coeducation, 1834b
Well of Loneliness, The, 104a
Wells, David A., 1291a
Wells, Herman, 59b
Wells, Ida B.. *See* Wells–Barnett, Ida B.
Wells-Barnett, Ida B., 145a,b, 398a, 697a
Niagara movement, 146a
Wells College, 32a, 102a
Welty, Eudora, 68a
Wendell, Barrett, 1439b
Wertham, Frederic, 1483b
Wertheimer, Max, 888a
Weschler, Herbert, 388a
Wesleyan University, 1822b
West, **81a–99b,** *82a–b*
Congress, 365b–366b
migration to, post-World War II, 1345a
urbanization, 455b–456a
West, Cornel, 156a, 291b, 1505b
West, Mae, 1466a
and Production Code Administration,
1467b
West, Nathaniel, 1581b
Westbrook, Robert, 263b
Westermann, H. C., 1714b
Western Electric, 837b, 885b, 1138b, 1143a
foreign investments, 1247a
radio transmitters, 1472a
Western Federation of Miners, 86b
Western Hemisphere
after World War I, 682b
American investment and trade, 682b
economic growth, 693b
good neighbor policy, 685a
joint defense during World War II, 686a
Wilson and, 679b–679b
See also Canada; Caribbean; Central
America; Latin America
Western-style clothing, 1792b
Western Union, 833b
Westfall, Catherine, 760b

Westinghouse, 846a, 849b, 1137b, 1138a,
1142b, 1143a,b, 1145a, 1152b, 1472a,
1475a
Air Brake, 1136b
foreign investments, 1247a
radio broadcasting, 804a–b, 805b, 806b,
807a
research programs, 842a
television, 815a–b
Westinghouse, George, 833a
Westinghouse Electric, 1411a
Westmoreland, William, 666b, 668b, 669a
Weston, Edward, 262a, 1709b
West Point, 1820a
*We the People: An Atlas of America's Ethnic
Diversity,* 167b
Weyerhaeuser Corporation, 88b, 1364a,
1402b
Weyl, Walter, 276b, 1568a, 1581b
Wharton, Clifton, Jr., 1835b
Wharton, Edith, 33b, 1438b, 1457b,
1458a
Wharton School, 1409a
What Social Classes Owe to Each Other
(Sumner), 195a
Whatsoever a Man Soweth, 223a
What the Negro Wants (Logan), 71a–b
Wheat
embargo to the Soviet Union, 589b
farmers, 311b
"Wheat Farmers and the Battle for
Democracy" (Wickard), 384b
Wheaton College, 1503b, 1504a
Wheeler, Burton K., 335a–b tab
Wheeler, William Morton, 863a
Wheeler & Wilson, 1044a,b, 1045a
Where It's At, 930a,b
Whiffen, Marcus, 1669a, 1672b
Whiskey Trust, 1132a
Whitby, Kenny J., 366b
Whitcomb, John C., Jr., 871b
White, Alma, 1501a
White, Andrew D., 544a
White, Byron R., 390a–b tab
White, Edward D., 390a–b tab
White, Ellen, 866b, 1498a
White, Harry Dexter, 334a, 724b
White, John E., 64b
White, Minor, 1712a
White, Richard, 132b, 133a
White, Stanford, 1669a
White, Walter, 152a
White, William Allen, 55b, 279a, 635a
"White Christmas" (Berlin), 1581a
White Collar (Mills), 200a, 1111b
White-collar workers, 1099b–1103b, 1107a,
1117a
increase, 198a
increased proportion in labor force, 1197a
middle class, 198a, 200b
White Committee. *See* Committee to
Defend America by Aiding the Allies
White ethnicity, 181a–b
Whitehead, Alfred North, 833b, 842b,
1647a, 1652b
White House
Brownlow Committee, 525a
private funding of restoration, 503b
staff under Nixon, 345a–b
White House Conference on Conservation
(1908), 1272a

White House Domestic Policy Council, 532b
Whiteman, Paul, 1615b, 1616a, 1619a
White Motor, 1140b
White privilege, 97b
White Sands, N.M., 786b
Whites as minority, 156b
White Slave Traffic Act. *See* Mann Act
White supremacy, 64a, 65b, 67b, 68b, 71b, 74a–b
  replaced by consensus politics, 72b
  Republican party and, 77a
  use of educational reform, 64b
  See also Racism
Whitford, Albert, 745a
Whitman, Charles Otis, 863a
Whitman, Ruth, 1587a
Whitman, Walt, 204a, 427b, 1436b, 1449a
  Mumford and, 11a–b
Whitney, Dudley Joseph, 867b, 868a
Whitney, Gertrude Vanderbilt, 1706b, 1728b
Whitney, Richard, 1419b
  and Gray-Pecora investigation, 1225b
Whitney, William C., 1669b
Whitney, Willis R., 836a–b, 838b, 840b, 841b, 842a, 843b, 1138a
Whittaker, Charles E., 390a–b tab
Whittaker and Baxter, 998a
Whittier, John Greenleaf, 1436b
Whittle, Frank, 781a
Whole Earth Catalog, 1031b
Whole Life Expo, 1562a
Wholesalers, 1130b, 1131b, 1137a
Whooping cough, 960a, 968a,b
Who Rules America? (Domhoff), 208a,b
Whose Justice? Which Rationality? (MacIntyre), 291a
Why Americans Hate Politics (Dionne), 292a
"Why Is Economics Not an Evolutionary Science?" (Veblen), 1290b
"Why Is There No Socialism in the United States?" (Sombart), 203a
"Why Modernism Still Matters" (Berman), 1455a
Whyte, William H., 21a, 198b, 265b, 340a
  Organization Man, The, 1111a–b
Why We Fought (Grattan), 633a
Wickard, Claude P., 384b
Wicksell, Knut, 1290b
Wicksteed, Philip, 1290b
Wiener, Norbert, 751b
Wiesel, Elie, 1589a,b
Wife-Dressing (Fogarty), 1790b
Wilberforce University, 1819b
Wilcock, Richard, 112b
Wild and Scenic Rivers Act (1968), 1373b
Wilde, Oscar, 1448b, 1746b
Wilder, Laura Ingalls, 55a
Wilderness Act (1964), 1373b
Wilderness Society, 1370a,b, 1371a
  Echo Park, 1373a
Wildlife, 1384a
  conservationism and, 1361a
Wildman, Donald, 1740b
Wild West shows, 83b, *697a–b,* 697b, 698a, 1461b, 1462a, 1463a
Wiley, Harvey, 943a
Wiley, Maude, 155b
Wilhelmsen, Frederick, 1525a
Wilkes, Charles, 740a

Wilkes Expedition, 740a–b
Wilkins, Mira, *as contributor,* 1243a–1266b
Wilkins, Roy, 152a
Will, George, 189b
Willard, Jess, 1772a
William and Mary College, 1819a
Williams, Bert, 1464a, 1596a,b
Williams, Francis, 709b
Williams, Hank, 1626b
Williams, Joan, 289a, 291b
Williams, John, 487b
Williams, Marion, 1624b
Williams, Martin, 1625b
Williams, Raymond, 917a, 932a
Williams, William Carlos, 1448a, 1449b, 1701b
  Paterson, 1449b
Williams Act (1968), 1227a–b tab, 1238a
Williams College, 32a
Williamson, Joel, 142b
  New People, 212b
Williamson, Oliver, 1296b
William Styron's Nat Turner: Ten Black Writers Respond, 1603a
Willis, Henry Parker, 1293a
  banking reform, 1295b
Willkie, Wendell, 264b, 577a, 635a
  One World, 556b
  presidential elections, 335a–b tab
Willowbrook State School, 950b
Wills, Garry, 1497b
Wilson, Charles E., 1280a
Wilson, Edmund, 33b, 262a, 1442a–b, 1446a, 1448b
  Axel's Castle, 1442a, 1446a, 1448b
  To the Finland Station, 1442a–b
Wilson, Edmund Beecher, 860a–b
Wilson, Edward O., 871a, 894a
Wilson, Graham K, *as contributor,* 295a–320b
Wilson, James Q., 361a
Wilson, Pete, 189a
Wilson, Robert, 760b, 762b
Wilson, Samuel, 257b
Wilson, Sloan, 179b
Wilson, William Julius, 239b, 488a, 930b
  Declining Significance of Race, The, 214b
  Truly Disadvantaged, The, 210a
Wilson, Woodrow, 322a–b, 326a, 327a, 327b, 328a, 332b, 380a, 430a–b, 521a, 523a, *598a–b,* 623b–624a, 721b, 722b, 1271a,b
  on *Birth of a Nation,* 1593a
  Congressional Government, 355b, 360b–361a
  Constitutional Government in the United States, 428a
  Dewey, John, on, 278a
  fiscal policy, 1315b, 1316a–1317b
  foreign policy, 572a–574b
  Fourteen Points, 550b, 551b, 627b, 679a
  Lippmann, Walter, and, 279b
  neutrality, 621a
  peace, 543b, 547b, 630a
  preparedness, 596a
  presidential elections, 335a–b tab
  presidential power, 406b, 407a, 522a
  Progressivism, 1314b
  radio broadcasts, 807a
  segregation, 255b
  and separation of powers, 522a–b
  and Southern politicians, 67b

  tariff policy, 1246b, 1314a
  U.S. Railroad Administration, 519b
  in Versailles, 597a–b
  vetoes, 347a tab
  World War I, 494a, 596a, 678b
  Wilson-Gorman Tariff (1894), 1313b
    overruled by Supreme Court, 1314a
Wilson the Diplomatist (Link), 596b, 597b
Wind tunnels, 772b, 841b
Winesburg, Ohio (Anderson), 1440a, 1702a
Wings of the Dove (H. James), 1439b
Winkler, Allan M., 605a
Winston, Ellen, 484b
Winters decision (1908), 92b
Winterthur, 33a
Wireless. *See* Telegraph
Wireless communications, 803a–b
Wireless hook-ups, 799a
Wirsum, Karl, 1719a
Wirt, William, 1807b
Wisconsin
  bureaucracy, 1270b
  income tax, 1315a
Wisconsin Alumni Research Foundation, 945a
Wisconsin Cutover District, *1361a–b*
Wisconsin Idea, 49a
Wise, George, 840b
Wise, Isaac Mayer, 1566b
Wise, Stephen, 1567a, 1576b, 1579a, 1583a, 1584a
Wister, Owen, 83b
Witmer, Lightner, 880b
Wittgenstein, Ludwig, 1646a, 1647b, 1653b
  Tractatus Logico-Philosophicus, 1646b
Wobblies. *See* Industrial Workers of the World
Wofford, Harris, 987a
Wohlstetter, Albert, 613a
Wohlstetter, Roberta, 602b
Wolf, Eric, 917b, 937b
Wolf, Naomi, 1797a
Wolfe, Catherine Lorillard, 1728a
Wolfe, Thomas, 68a
Wolfe, Tom, 34a, 1238b
Wolfson, Harry, 1579a
Wolfson, Louis, 1233b
Wolven, E. L., 1765a–b
Woman Movement from the Point of View of Social Consciousness, The (Taft), 276a
Woman's Dress for Success Book, The (Molloy), 1785b, 1796a
Woman's Peace Party, 546b, 548b
Woman Warrior, The (Kingston), 1456b
Women
  access to health care, 1005b
  arts patronage, 1728a,b
  aviation, 770a, 779b
  career vs. domesticity, 102a
  clerical work, 1104b
  clothing, 1789a, 1794a–1795b
  Congress, 365a–b, 367a–b tab
  consciousness-raising, 120a
  Conservative Judaism, 1575a
  as consumers, 115a
  economic contribution to family, 107b
  education, 102a, 1021a, 1809a
  employment, 1173a
  at end of nineteenth century, 223a
  ethnicity and work, 107b

female labor force by marital status,
111a–b
fertility of white women in 1900, 222b
foreign mission movement, 1495a–b
in higher education, 32a, 1104b, 1828a,
1832a
homemaking skills, 1025a
Judaism, 1573a, 1574b,
1587b–1588a,b–1589a
in labor force, 65b, 902b, 1029b, 1033a,
1164a
large-scale science, 741b
leisure activities, 1746b–1747a, 1748a–b
lobbying for medical research, 947a
married in work force by race, 113a–b
tab
in medical science, 947b
Midwest, 50a, 51b
minimum wages for, 381b
ministers, 1501a, 1506a
Muller v. Oregon (1908), 378b
new role defined in 1950s, 233a
ordination, 1531a, 1534a
in peace movement, 546b
physical educators, 1763a, 1764b
political participation, 117b
protective legislation, 117b
race and work, 107b
reformers, 922a
regulation of work, 378b
religious, 1527a,b, 1528b
seminaries, 1819b
in service sector, 1201a
shopping, 1017b
South, 63a
Southern reformers, 65a–b
space programs, 790b
sports, 1763b, 1779a–1781b
suffrage. *See* Women's suffrage
Supreme Court and discrimination
against, 420a–b
1950s work force increase, 215b
teachers, 1809b
telephone systems, 802a
in unions, 107a, 109b, 112a
weapons, 810b
in white-collar professions, 112a
in work force, 105a, 113b tab, 124a, 223b
in work force by family status, 111a–b tab
in work force by marital status, *111a–b*
in work force during World War II, 71a
World War II, 264a
writers, 34a, 1604b–1605a
Zionism, 1582a
See also Feminism; Women artists
Women Airforce Service Pilots, 779b
Women and Economics (Gilman), 275b, 905a
Women and Madness (Chesler), 912a
Women artists, 1703b–1704a, 1720b–1721a,
1732a, 1738a,b–1739b
WPA programs, 1730b–1731a
"Women as a Minority Group" (Hacker),
910a
Women Employed (Chicago), 120b
Women in the Modern World (Komarovsky),
929a
Women's American ORT, 1587b
Women's Army Corps, 104a
Women's Bureau, 110a–b, 122a
Women's Equal Pay Act, 110b

Women's International League for Peace and
Freedom, 554b, 697a
nuclear pacifism, 558b
reformist approach to war prevention,
553a
Women's liberation. *See* Feminism; Women's
movement
Women's movement, 266b, 267a, 319b
athletic programs, 1814a
Catholicism, 1530b–1531a
education, 1814a
Women's Peace Union, 553a
Women's Political Council of Montgomery,
118b
Women's Political Union, 117a
Women's Sports Foundation, 1781a
Women's suffrage, 65b, 278b, 295a, 309a
Dreier, Katherine, and, 1700a
Women's Temperance Crusade, 117a
Women's Trade Union League, 110b, 115a,
117a, 1574a
Women Strike for Peace, 585a
Women's Wear Daily, 31a
Wong, Jade Snow, 176a
Fifth Chinese Daughter, 1456b
Wood, Grant, 10b, 55a,b, 1705b, 1706a,
1706a
American Gothic, 1706a
Midnight Ride of Paul Revere, The, 1706a
at University of Iowa, 1827a
Wood, Leonard, 595b, *595b,* 623b, 942a
Wood, Robert E., 55b
Wood, Stuart, 1290b
Woodbridge, Frederick J. E., 1644b
in *Contemporary American Philosophy,*
1644b
Woodbridge, George, 919a
Woodbury, George E., 1437a
Wood products, 1130b
See also Forest industries; Furniture
industry; Logging industry; Timber
industry; Wood pulp industry
Wood pulp industry, 70b, 1132b–1133a
Woodruff, Robert W., 1833b
Woodward, C. Vann, 142b
Woodward, Ellen, 122a
Woodward, Robert S., 742b
Woolf, Virginia, 1447b
Wool industry
vertical integration, 1041a–b, *1041b*
World War I, 1191a
Woolridge, Dean, 849b
Woolstonecraft, Mary, 918a
Woolworth, 700b
Woolworth Building (New York), *35a–b,*
1674a, 1675a, 1700b, *1700b*
Woonsocket, R.I., working class evolution
in, 205b, 206a
Worcester Foundation for Experimental
Biology, 946b
Worcester Polytechnic Institute, 32b
"Word of Wisdom" (Smith), 93b
Word Peace through World Law (Clark and
Sohn), 558b
Work, 1091a–1126b
*Work, Culture, and Society in Industrializing
America* (Gutman), 205a
Workers' compensation, 49a, 122a,
475b–476b, 482b
Workers' Control in America (Montgomery),
205b

*Work Ethic in Industrial America, 1850–1920,
The* (Rodgers), 207a
Work in America, 1118b
Working class, 202b–206b
consumption, 1018b
leisure activities, 1747a–1749a
Republican vote, 301b
women leisure activities, 1748a–b
Working-class Americanism (Gerstle), 206a
Working hours decrease, 1749a–b
Ford and, 1099b
Working Woman, 114b
Workmen's Circle, 1574a–b
"Work of Art in the Age of Mechanical
Reproduction, The" (Benjamin),
1486b
Work of Nations, The (Reich), 854a
Work reform efforts, 1119a–1120a
Works Progress Administration (WPA), 70a,
261b, 433a, 524b, 1074a, 1321b,
1421a, 1730a–1731b, 1732a, 1738b
school construction, 1809a
traditional family, 122b
Works Projects Administration. *See* Works
Progress
Administration (WPA)
World, 31a
World Bank. *See* International Bank for
Reconstruction and Development
World Baptist Fellowship, 1503b
World Community of al-Islam in the West,
1548a
World Council of Masajid, 1548b
World Court. *See* Permanent Court of
International Justice (World Court)
World Disarmament Conference in Geneva
(1932), 552b
World Echo, 1600a
World economy, 1252b–1253a, 1254a–b,
1263b–1265b
America and, 719a–734b
bilateral negotiations under F. Roosevelt,
684a
cooperation, 1204b
dollar devaluation, 1257b
foreign investments, 1261b
World federation, 733a
World Federation of Trade Unions, 705a
"World is a Wedding, The" (Schwartz),
1581a
World manufacturing exports, *1166b*
World Peace Foundation, 545a, 575b
World regions, **675a–694b**
World's Christian Fundamentals Association,
866a
World's Fairs, 1030a
Century of Progress World's Fair, 1731a
Chicago 1933 (Century of Progress), 55a
Columbian Exposition (Chicago), 255b,
1726b
New York 1939, 1025b
New York (1939), 1475b
New York (1964), 1734b
St. Louis 1904, 47a
Seattle 1962, 91b
Worlds in Collision (Velikovsky), 871a
World's Parliament of Religions, 1541a
Buddhism, 1553b, 1555a
Hinduism, 1550a
World Trade Center (New York), 464a,
1686a

World Trade Organization, 1262b
World War I
  agencies as model, 1191b
  Alien Enemies Act (1798), 597a
  Allied and Associated Powers, 625b
  American contributions to victory, 629b
  Americanization crusade, 170b
  American neutrality, 573a, 623a–625a
  armistice (1918), 628b
  artists in, 1701b
  bureaucracy, 522b–523a
  cooperation between federal government
    and professionalgroups, 1416a
  demobilization, 598a
  economy, 171b, 573a, 1273a–1276b
  effect on home front, 596b
  employment opportunities for African
    Americans, 108b
  employment opportunities for
    immigrants, 171b
  ethnic nationalism, 170a–172a
  exports to belligerents, 623a–b tab
  foreign elements in United States, 625a–b
    tab
  foreign trade, 1248a
  full-scale participation, 652a
  German militarism and neo-Darwinism,
    861b–862a
  industrial research, 840a–842b
  infrastructure development, 1337a, 1341a
  Liberty Loans, 1026a
  loans to Allies, 722a, 723a
  mental testing during, 881a
  Meuse-Argonne offensive, 628b, 652b
  movement for neutral mediation,
    546b–547b
  nationalism, 256b–257a
  and national security state, 595a–597b
  noncombatant service during, 549a
  onset, 573a
  pattern for private philanthropy and
    public policy, 494a
  peace movement, 545b–551b, 678b
  100 percent Americanism, 170b, 597a
  preparedness, 170b, 596a
  and presidential power, 523a
  Progressivism, 278b
  propaganda, 597a
  Registration Day, 626b
  Revenue Acts, 1315b
  Saint Mihiel, 652b
  Saint-Mihiel, 628b
  South and, 67b
  and tax reform, 1315a–1317b
  U.S. as belligerent, 625a–630a
  U.S. as creditor state, 1190b, 1193a
  U.S. leadership role in military terms,
    1190a–1191b
  U.S. leadership role in political terms,
    1190a–1191b
  war-loan issue, 631b
  western front, 629a–b
  world economy, 721b, 722a–b,
    1190a–1191b, 1245a–b, 1247b–1248a
World War II, 685b–687a
  acceptance of federal regulations of
    economy, 1342b
  advertising, 1028a
  American Jews, 1583a–1585a
  artists, 1712a
  Big Science, 751a

bureaucratic centralization, 525b
  Catholics, 1520a
  computers, 810b
  concept of race, 152a–b
  conscientious objectors, 555b
  Consumers Union, 1027b
  and cultural preeminence, 703a
  defense industries, 457a
  demobilization, 607a
  economic recovery, 1197b, 1278a–b
  effect on economy, 1077a
  effect on South, 70a–71b, 457a
  ethnic groups and, 176b
  Europe and North Africa, 645a–b
  and existing infrastructure, 1343a
  expansion of bureaucracy, 262b
  extensive cultural offensives, 704a
  family, 230a–231a
  fashion design and federal regulations,
    1790a
  Federalism, 436b
  foreign trade, 1252b–1256a
  full-scale participation, 652b
  higher education, 1827b
  and homosexuals, 104a
  income tax propaganda, 1323b
  industrial research, 846a–849a
  inland waterways, 1344b
  Italian campaign, 646a
  Japan, 96a
  Japanese Americans' internment, 231a
  Japanese surrender, 647b
  labor shortage and immigration, 94a
  manpower, 603a
  Midwest, 55b
  nationalism, 262b
  national security state, 601a–607a
  ORANGE plan, 638b
  Pacific, 640a–b
  photographers, 1710a
  postwar planning, 686b
  presidential role, 330b
  professions and, 1421b
  propaganda films, 1467b
  radio, 1473b, 1475b
  Supreme Court and expansion of federal
    power, 385a
  taxation, 1322b–1324a
  total mobilization, 603a
  total wartime expenditures, 643a
  unions, 1109a
  urban growth in West, 457a, 1343a
  and U.S. role in world economy, 1245b
  war plants in South, 70a
  women in work force after, 110a
  women in work force during, 110a, 230b
World Wars, The, 621a–649b
"World Well Lost, A" (Rorty), 1660b
Worthington Pump, 1136b
Wouk, Herman, 1587b
Wounded Knee, 93a, 134b, 139b
Wozniak, Stephen, 823a
WPA. See Works Progress Administration;
  Works Progress Administration (WPA)
WPA State Guide Series, 15b
Wretched of the Earth, The (Fanon), 287b,
  1603b
Wright, Carroll D., 215a
Wright, Charles Alan, 383b
Wright, Elizabeth Washburn, 697a
Wright, Fielding L., 335a–b tab

Wright, Frank Lloyd, 20b, 47b, 1667a,b,
    1676b, 1677a–1678b, 1680a, 1684a
  Fallingwater, 1683a
  Herbert Jacobs residence, 1683b
  Johnson Wax Administration Building,
    1683a
  prairie house, 1677a,b, 1678a–b
  Taliesin West school, 1683b
  Wingspread, 1683b
Wright, Gavin, 1159a, 1264a, 1388b
  as contributor, 1383a–1406b
Wright, George Frederick, 861a
Wright, Henry, 1679b, 1684a
Wright, James, 123a
Wright, Jim, 303a
Wright, Orville, 767a–769b, 768a–b
Wright, Richard, 68a, 154a, 176a, 213b,
    1456a, 1600b
  "Blueprint for Negro Writing," 1600b
  Communist Party, 1601a
  Native Son, 1450b, 1601a,b
  Uncle Tom's Children, 1601a
Wright, Sewall, 868b, 869a
Wright, Stanton Macdonald, 1704b
Wright, Wilbur, 767a–768b, 768a–b
Wright, Willard Huntington, 1699a
Wright Exhibition Company, 769b
Wright-Martin Company, 769b
Wrigley, E. A., 1384a
Wrigley, Philip, 1779b
Writers, 34a–b, 1733a
  consumption, 1034b
  Midwest, 52a–b, 55a
  playwrights, 1733a
  public tours, 1746b
  See also Literature
Writers Project, 1730b, 1731a
WTO. See World Trade Organization
  (WTO)
Wundt, Wilhelm, 1639a
Wurzweiler School of Social Work (Yeshiva
  University), 1585b
Wyeth, Andrew, 1714b
Wylie, Paul, 1781a
Wylies, Philip, 910a
Wynn, Ed, 1755a

X

Xerox Corporation, 28a, 822a, 850b
XYZ buildings (New York), 1686a, 1686b

Y

Yakima, 1378a
Yale Institute of Human Relations, 888a
Yale University, 506b, 1819a, 1820b, 1824a
  art courses, 1729a
  divestment of stock in corporations doing
    business in South Africa, 1835a
  drama department, 1827a
  law school, 31a
  Report of 1828, 1819b
  secularization, 1825b
  staff strike, 1836a
Yalta Conference (1945), 557a, 577b, 578a,
  580a, 646b–647a
Yalta system, 687a

Yamamoto, Isoruku, 639b, 640b–641a
Yamasaki, Minoru, 1689a
  Pruitt-Igoe Houses (Saint Louis), 1689a
  World Trade Center (New York), 1686a
Yankee City studies (Warner), 199b
Yankee ethnicity, 162b
Yankee Stadium, 1775b
Yannacone, Victor, 1373b–1374a
Yardley, Herbert O., 599b
Yates, JoAnne, 1104b
Yates, Peter, 1622b
Yeager, Chuck, 781b
Yeats, William Butler, 1442a, 1448b
Yehoash. *See* Bloomgarden, Solomon
Yehoshua, A. B., 1588a
Yellow fever, 942b, 959b
  Yellow Fever Board, 942a
Yellow peril, 96b
Yellowstone National Park, 84b
Yellow Wall-Paper, The (Gilman), 1438b,
  1458a
Yen bonds, 1262a
Yerkes, Robert M., 879a, 881a, 885b,
  1806b
Yerkes, T. C., 743b
Yeshiva College, 1575a,b
  See also Yeshiva University
Yeshiva Metivta Tiffereth Jerusalem, 1585a
Yeshivas, 1572a, 1575b, 1585a
Yeshiva University, 32a, 1576a, 1585b,
  1586a
  See also Yeshiva College
Yezierska, Anzia, 397a, 1578a
Yiddish Art Theater, 1570b
Yiddish culture, 1568a–b, 1569a,
  1570a–1571b, 1573a, 1580a
  films, 1570b
  literature translated into English, 1588a
  music, 1571a,b
  newspapers, 1569a
  radio, 1571a
  theater, 1570a–b, 1574a
  Yiddish press, 1569a–b
YIVO Institute for Jewish Research, 1584b
YMCA. *See* Young Men's Christian
  Association
YMHA. *See* Young Men's Hebrew
  Association

Yntema, Theodore, 1298a
Yoga, 1550a, 1551a
  Integral Yoga, 1552b
  Siddha Yoga, 1552b
Yogananda, Paramahansa, 1550a, 1551a–b
"Yom Kippur 1984" (Rich), 1587a
Yom Kippur War (1973), 587b, 1199a
Yosemite and The Range of Light (Adams),
  1373b
Yoshe Kalb, 1570b
Yoshida, Ray, 1714b
Yost, Fielding "Hurry-Up," 1767b
Young, Allyn, 1305b
Young, Andrew, 75a
Young, Brigham, 1542a
Young, Coleman, 58b
Young, Ella Flagg, 1810a
Young, Owen D., 700a, 843a
Young, Robert, 232b
Young, Shirley, 1052b
Young, Stark, 14a,b
Young Israel, 1575b
Young Lonigan (Farrell), 1443a
Young Manhood of Studs Lonigan, The
  (Farrell), 1443a
Young Men's Christian Association
  immigrants and sports, 1766a
  Student Volunteer Movement, 696a
Young Men's Hebrew Association (YMHA),
  1566a, 1576a, 1579a, 1582a
Young Plan (1929), 632a, 723a,
  1249b–1250a
Young Socialist Alliance, 1827a
Young Women's Christian Association
  (YMCA), 65b
Young Women's Christian Association
  (YWCA)
  Equal Rights Amendment, 120b
Young Women's Hebrew Assocation
  (YWHA), 1572b, 1576a
Your Money's Worth (Chase and Schlink),
  1027a
Youth
  automobiles and, 1751b
  concerts, 1586b
  new identity in 1950s, 233a
  as separate culture, 1793a
Yugoslavia, 679a

YWCA. *See* Young Women's Christian
  Association
YWHA. *See* Young Women's Hebrew
  Assocation

Z

Zabel, Morton Dauwen, 1447b, 1448a
Zahm, John, 859b
Zahniser, Howard, 1369b, 1373a
Zanesville, Ohio, 1019a, 1020a, 1024b
Zangwill, Israel, 163b, 1568b
Zaretsky, Eli, 923a
Zayas, Marius de, 1698a
Z Budapest, 1557b
Zemach, Benjamin, 1579a
Zen Buddhism, 1553b, 1555a–b
Zevin, Robert, 464b
Zhitlowsky, Hayim, 1567a, 1568b
Zhongshan Hot Springs Golf Club, 712a
Ziegler, Karl, 1146a
Zimmerman, Carle, 924a
Zimmermann, Arthur
Zimmermann telegram, 624b
Zinc, 1387b, 1392b
Zionism, 578b, 1568a–1569a, 1569a,
  1573a–1574a, 1577a, 1578b, 1582a–b,
  1583a, 1586a
  division, 1573b
  revisionists, 1583b
Zionist Organization of America, 1573b
Znaniecki, Florian, 922b
Zola, Émile, 1437b
Zoot suit, 1792a–b
  riots during World War II, 1792b
Zorach, Marguerite, 1704a
Zoroastrianism, 1550a
Zuboff, Shoshana, *as contributor,*
  1091a–1126b
Zukofsky, Louis, 1580b
Zukor, Adolph, 1580a, 1752b
Zunz, Olivier, 107b, 1101b
  Changing Face of Inequality, The, 206a
  as contributor, 195a–220b
Zweig, Paul, 1587a
Zworykin, Vladimir, 815a
Zygon: Journal of Religion and Science, 871a